Contraband Corridor

Contraband Corridor

Making a Living at the Mexico–Guatemala Border

Rebecca Berke Galemba

Stanford University Press
Stanford, California

Stanford University Press
Stanford, California

Printed in the United States of America on acid-free, archival-quality paper

Library of Congress Cataloging-in-Publication Data

Names: Galemba, Rebecca B., 1981– author.
Title: Contraband corridor : making a living at the Mexico–Guatemala border /
    Rebecca Berke Galemba.
Description: Stanford, California : Stanford University Press, 2018. | Includes
    bibliographical references and index.
Identifiers: LCCN 2017006525 | ISBN 9780804799133 (cloth : alk. paper) |
    ISBN 9781503603981 (pbk. : alk. paper) | ISBN 9781503603998 (epub)
Subjects: LCSH: Smuggling—Mexican-Guatemalan Border Region. | Mexican-Guatemalan
    Border Region—Commerce. | Border security—Mexican-Guatemalan Border Region. |
    Borderlands—Economic aspects—Mexico. | Borderlands—Economic aspects—
    Guatemala.
Classification: LCC HJ6767 .G35 2018 | DDC 364.1/33609727—dc23 LC record available at
    https://lccn.loc.gov/2017006525

Typeset by Thompson Type in 9.75/15 Sabon

For my daughters:
Elena Rose and Alexandra Elizabeth

Contents

Acknowledgments   ix

Introduction: A Paradise for Contraband?   1

Chapter 1   Border Entries and Reentries   27

Chapter 2   Documenting National Life   49

Chapter 3   Corn Is Food, Not Contraband   74

Chapter 4   Taxing the Border   104

Chapter 5   Phantom Commerce   130

Chapter 6   Inheriting the Border   160

Chapter 7   Strike Oil   188

            Conclusion:
            The Illicit Trio: Drugs, Arms, and Migrants 209

            Notes   233

            References   261

            Index   293

Acknowledgments

THIS BOOK HAS CHANGED SHAPE over the past decade, as the border region has changed over time, my own thoughts have shifted, and generous colleagues have shared their insights and pointed me toward new lines of inquiry. First, I thank the many people at the Mexico–Guatemala border who shared their lives with me, opened their homes to me, and trusted me with their stories. I hope that I have done justice to their choices and portrayed them in an honest and holistic way that will impel others to question stereotypes about border-lands, ethical economic choices, and smuggling.

The idea of studying Mexico's southern border came out of my MA research at the U.S.–Mexico border, at a time when few U.S. scholars were ethnographically examining the Mexico–Guatemala border. My first trip to Chiapas in 2005 showed me the rich scholarship that local scholars were pursuing and the work of activists on the ground. I am particularly indebted to Juan Carlos Velasco, who took me on various site visits to the border region, introduced me to the border communities, and continues to send me new information and photos. José Luis Escalona Victoria has been an invaluable mentor in Chiapas. As my supervisor while I was a guest researcher at CIESAS-Sureste, he has continued to advise my work and help me disseminate it in Mexico. While in Chiapas, I benefited from conversations and feedback from Edith Kauffer-Michel, Miguel Pickard, Jan Rus, Daniel Villafuerte Solís, and Alain Basail Rodríguez. Rosalva Aída Hernández Castillo also provided invaluable support. She met with me in Mexico City and Washington, D.C., and even visited me at the border. Fellow students conducting research in Chiapas,

Sarah Osten and Rebecca Englert, also helped me formulate my thoughts in the field and shared insights.

At Brown University, I want to thank my mentors, Kay Warren, Catherine Lutz, Matthew Gutmann, and Nicholas Townsend, who helped guide my thoughts at various junctures of the research and writing process. Kay Warren was the backbone to this project. I was at first nervous about my field plans at the southern border, but her confidence in my abilities consistently propelled me forward. Whether it was a short email of support in the field, offering field tips for potentially risky situations, going line-by-line through chapters over the phone late in the evening once I returned, or giving me advice on making sure my contributions stood out in the final edits for this book, she was always there. She had faith in my work even when I wavered. Kay also always supported me on my not-so-straightforward academic journey as I negotiated family with work, chose to move closer to family, and pursued a teaching intensive lecturer track before acquiring a tenure-track job more than six years after completing my long-term field research for this book. Carolyn Nordstrom also provided invaluable feedback. She was a true inspiration not only for my analysis but for the kind of fieldworker and ethnographer I strive to be. While at Brown, I benefited from extraordinary Latin Americanist graduate student colleagues, with whom I continue to collaborate and exchange drafts: Kathleen Millar, Jennifer Ashley, Kristin Skrabut, and Susan Ellison. My cohort-mate, Katie Rhine, has always been a Google-chat away, offering unwavering advice in the book process, support, and answers to any and all of my technical questions. After Brown, I was lucky to reconnect with Susi Keefe, who has been a helpful sounding board for my work. Writing preliminary versions of the manuscript at Dartmouth College while teaching, away from my colleagues and advisors at Brown, I benefited from the mentorship of John Watanabe, who first sparked my interest in Mexico and Guatemala when I was his undergraduate advisee. At Dartmouth, I was lucky to meet Lourdes Gutiérrez-Najera, who has provided invaluable support over the years. Navigating the transition from graduate school to teaching with new motherhood with Jennifer Darrah Okike at Harvard University helped me prioritize, persevere, and take the next steps.

In the past few years, my work has evolved to engage critical conversations around illegality, borders, and social legitimacy, and the more complex relationship between the states and illegal practices. The development of my work and this book benefited immensely from conversations and collaborations with Peter Andreas, Josiah McC. Heyman, Madeleine Reeves, Kedron Thomas, Ieva Jusionyte, and Noelle Bridgden. I would like to thank Peter Andreas, José Luis Escalona Victoria, Alain Basail Rodríguez, Kay Warren, Daniel Goldstein, Kathleen Millar, Ieva Jusionyte, Jan Rus, Henio Hoyo, Beatriz Reyes-Foster, Noelle Brigden, and Wendy Vogt for generously commenting on chapters or earlier versions of this work, as well as the two anonymous reviewers for Stanford University Press. Michelle Lipinski at Stanford University Press has been incredibly supportive in this process. She has helped ensure that my ethnographic voice stood out. I would like to thank Margaret Pinette at Thompson Type for her careful copyedits and suggestions and Gaby Driessen for providing an insightful editorial eye for the manuscript. For assistance with editing and general flow of earlier versions of the manuscript, I appreciated the comments of John Elder, Susi Keefe, my father Michael Meyers, and my husband Dan Galemba. With a father and husband who were both English majors, I was constantly under scrutiny. Because of them, I can hope that nonacademics will also enjoy this book! At the University of Denver, I have been lucky to be surrounded by strong Latin Americanist scholars who have helped me broaden my work beyond anthropology. For this, I am especially grateful to Aaron Schneider for his mentorship and support.

I would like to acknowledge the Wenner-Gren Foundation for Anthropological Research for funding the long-term fieldwork on which the majority of the book is based, in addition to the Anthropology Department at Brown University, the Population Studies and Training Center at Brown University, and the Craig M. Cogut Award from the Center for Latin American Studies at Brown University. The Dartmouth College Ethics Institute also provided me with a support structure for writing away from my home institution.

Portions of Chapter 3 were previously published in Rebecca B. Galemba. 2012. "'Corn Is Food, Not Contraband': The Right to Free Trade at the Mexico–Guatemala Border." *American Ethnologist* 39(4): 716–734, November 2012. Reprinted by permission of the American Anthropological Association. Parts of Chapter 4 appear in Rebecca B. Galemba, "Remapping the Border: Taxation, Territory, and (Trans)National Identity at the Mexico–Guatemala Border." *Environment and Planning D: Society and Space*, 30(5): 822–841, October 2012. (c)2012 by Pion and its Licensors. Reprinted by permission of SAGE Publications, Ltd. Small portions of Chapter 6 appear in Rebecca B. Galemba, 2012. "Taking Contraband Seriously: Practicing 'Legitimate Work' at the Mexico–Guatemala Border." *The Anthropology of Work Review* 33(1):

3–14, July 2012. Reprinted by permission of the American Anthropological Association.

I would also like to thank my family for supporting me over the years, including the time it took to step back from the original research to frame the material into this book. My parents Barbara and Michael Meyers always supported my choices even when they would not be their own; they visited me in the field, helped watch my daughters on a follow-up site visit, and always offered support. My mother, Barbara Meyers, who returned to school for her psychology doctorate when I was in middle school, motivated my path and taught me about work–life balance. My grandmother, Rose Berke, also inspired the kind of teacher, mentor, and mother I hope to be. Her parents would not allow her to attend Cornell University despite a partial scholarship just because she was a woman; she persevered nevertheless to become a teacher, assistant principal, gym teacher, and Title IX advocate. Most of all, my husband Dan Galemba encouraged me to continue this project and finish the book. I would especially like to thank him for accompanying me for the majority of the fieldwork, which meant taking a break from his own career to help teach English, learn about the border, confront his fear of spiders, and relearn a language he had not spoken since high school. Clearly not in his comfort zone, he continuously validated and supported my passion for anthropology and fieldwork, reminding me how unusual it is to find your passion. Thank you for always being by my side.

My two daughters, Elena and Alexandra were born in 2010 and 2013. This book is dedicated to them and my hope that they will pursue their passions even when they may encounter a longer, winding path rather than a straight road. With a heavy teaching load and two young daughters, the completion of this book would not have been possible without a strong support network. I would like to thank my husband, Dan Galemba, my parents Barbara and Michael Meyers, my in-laws Anita and Ed Galemba, as well as the child care providers, sitters, schools, and day care facilities that helped give me the time to write. I would also like to acknowledge all the other academic moms I met along the way who gave me advice on the diverse ways to balance an academic career with family. I appreciate how truly lucky I have been.

Finally, while they are not their real names, I am especially grateful to "Tito's" family for being my surrogate family at the border and inviting me into their home, "Paco" for his immediate friendship, "Héctor" for sharing his knowledge, "Fani" and "Francisca" for constant friendship over the years, and "Ramón" and "Alonso" for trusting and teaching me. I hope that readers will understand how people make a living at the border through their eyes and come to question their prior assumptions regarding borders, legitimate economic activities, and legality. This book demonstrates the necessity of not only examining others paths and why they are chosen but also challenging the exclusions, privileges, and value judgments embedded in the legitimate or desired order.

Contraband Corridor

Introduction

A Paradise for Contraband?

IN 2006, AN ARTICLE in *El Financiero* described the Mexico–Guatemala border as "a paradise for contraband . . . the problem, which is little spoken about, is that illegality dominates everything at the border."[1] Each day, ten-ton trucks, upwards of twenty years old, rumble through an unmonitored road crossing the Mexico–Guatemala border in the dry lowlands of Frontera Comalapa, Chiapas, Mexico, and La Democracia, Huehuetenango, Guatemala (Figures I.1 and I.2) as they churn up a mixture of dirt and cracked pavement. Local newspapers report that at least 100 trucks transit the route each day, smuggling anything from corn to sugar, coffee, clothing, vegetables, sodas, and gasoline.[2] The route is also increasingly important to the drug trade. An official border crossing, replete with the modern manifestations of the Mexican and Guatemalan states, straddles the Pan-American Highway a few miles away at Ciudad Cuauhtémoc on the Mexican side and La Mesilla on the Guatemalan side. Hundreds of unmonitored passages traverse the over 540-mile-long Mexico–Guatemala border, including paths crossing through mountains, jungles, and rivers. With just ten official entry points between Mexico and Guatemala, only eight of which are visible, the majority of crossings are informal.[3] Of the forty-five informal vehicular crossings along the Chiapas–Guatemala border, this one hosts the most commercial activity.[4] A recent Mexican government report detailing the security implications of the "blind spots" along the border identified this one with a giant bull's-eye.[5]

Only white monuments extending up into the hillsides mark the border between Mexico and Guatemala. In daily life, these demarcations seem to

1

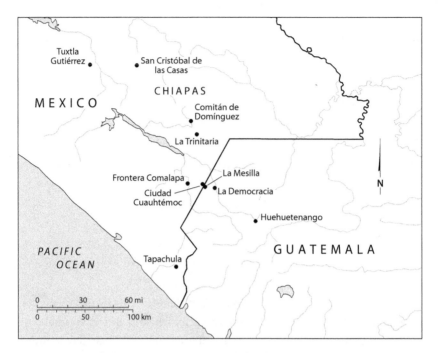

Figure I.1. Map of Chiapas, Mexico–Guatemala border region with key cities.
SOURCE: Map Data@ 2016 Google, INEGI.

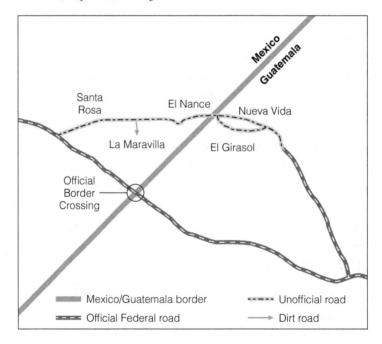

Figure I.2. Map of border communities.
SOURCE: Map made by author.

Figure I.3. Sign demarcating Mexico and Guatemala, erected in summer of 2007.
SOURCE: Author photo.

matter little. Trucks drive across, children play in the small stream that forms at the border in the rainy season, and laborers and families walk across. There are no fences, officials, or other indicators that one is entering another country. A sign delineating the border was erected only in the summer of 2007 (Figure I.3).

Although generally devoid of state officials, the Mexican military was periodically stationed within this route in the spring of 2007. I was told that this was in response to then recently elected President Felipe Calderón's promise to take a hard-line approach to border security and drug violence. At first, smugglers and residents waited for the military Humvees to retreat before crossing the border, but after a few weeks they began conducting business as usual, driving right by the soldiers. Therefore, I was caught by surprise when a Mexican soldier stopped me for questioning in May 2007 when I was driving from my house on the Mexican side to visit friends on the Guatemalan side. As I got out of my car, I grew nervous. After living at the border for eight months, I was unaccustomed to encountering agents of the state, and I was not carrying my passport. "What are you doing in this illegal pathway?" the soldier inquired, implying that because the route lacked official recognition it, along with the people and activities present within it, were illegal. As we were talking, I glanced over my shoulder to see people smuggling gasoline canisters clanging in the back of pickup trucks over the rocky hills to Guatemala. I soon learned that the soldier viewed me more as a curiosity than as a suspect. As I fumbled to explain my research, I realized he was more concerned with what residents thought about the military conducting surveillance in a border route where residents resent official interference. He asked incredulously, "You live here? What do the people think of us?"[6] This encounter led me to question my presumptions about security and illegality. Were security and border control a mirage? Were security and illegality more intimately intertwined rather than opposed? How do designations of illegality become mapped onto border regions and populations and to what effect?

The ease of commerce transiting this unmonitored road contrasted with the official rhetoric to prioritize border security emanating from Washington, D.C.; Mexico City; and Guatemala City. When I arrived at the border in September 2006, I introduced my research by stating that I was studying the paradoxes of a border that was increasingly open to trade through regional trade agreements but that restricted the movement of people through enhanced security measures. The most common response was incredulous laughter. Residents were perplexed at the assumption that there was more security. Each time I have returned to the border since 2006, there has been an increased presence of border policing and military units *and* more visible contraband. Security forces were present, but to residents they did not conjure a sense of security in terms of protection or the curtailment of illicit flows. In the context of regional official trade integration and enhanced border policing, why would residents perceive this security presence as laughable? Why would they be smuggling more goods across the border? Generally, with trade liberalization, smuggling of goods to evade tariffs decreases, concentrating on more prohibited items.[7] Residents were also increasingly justifying the smuggling of basic goods as legitimate and gaining official tolerance for these activities.

Why do official policies lead to contradictory, puzzling, or even counterproductive results? This question can be answered by bringing to the fore the voices of people impacted by policies, who tend to be omitted not only from policy design but also from implementation and evaluation. In contrast to macroeconomic analyses that debate how trade integration and militarized border security affect illicit flows or that posit illicit trade as an inherent threat to state security and stability, everyday interactions among regional inhabitants, officials, and smugglers provide insight into how policies are experienced in particular places and may generate unintended consequences.

Contraband Corridor challenges simplistic assumptions regarding security, trade, and illegality by detailing how residents along the Mexico–Guatemala border engage in, and justify, extralegal practices in the context of heightened border security, restricted economic opportunities, and trade integration policies that exclude local inhabitants. Rather than assuming that extralegal activities necessarily undermine the state and formal economy, this book extracts this question as a topic for ethnographic investigation. At the border, informality, illegality, the formal economy, and security logics intertwine and blur in the context of what I call securitized neoliberalism, or the wedding of security policies to neoliberal economic policies and logics.[8] Securitized neoliberalism works to value certain economic activities and actors and exclude and criminalize others in a context where the informal and illicit economy is increasingly one of the poor's remaining options and informality also permeates the formal sector.[9] The distinction between contraband and business privileges particular economic activities as it criminalizes the livelihood strategies of marginalized inhabitants. Although security, neoliberalism, and illegality are interdependent in complex ways, how they unfold depends on contingent negotiations among diverse border actors.

Extralegal economic activities, like smuggling commodities across the border, provide a means for borderland peasants to make a living in the context of neoliberal economic policies that decimated agricultural livelihoods. Yet smuggling also exacerbates prevailing inequalities, obstructs the possibility of more substantive political and economic change, and provides low-risk benefits to select formal businesses, state agents, and illicit actors, often at the expense of border residents. Moreover, the threat of the extralegal economy bolsters a border security agenda[10] that conflates different illicit and informal activities and fosters a politics of criminalization that makes locals less secure.

Much of the scholarly literature on this region depicts northward migration as a survival outlet in the wake of economic crisis in the 1980s and 1990s.[11] Borderlanders continue to migrate to the United States, but the 2008 economic recession combined with punitive immigration policies, especially in the states where border residents have migrant networks (Florida, North

Carolina, and Georgia), are making this strategy less attractive. After 2008, many border residents began returning home. Fewer studies pay attention to the strategies that peasants pursue at home to earn a living in the face of the deterioration of traditional livelihoods. Many of their options straddle legal/illegal and formal/informal lines. In the borderlands, because the border has been historically porous, commerce—legal and illegal—has long been integral to daily life.[12]

As the Mexico–Guatemala border has emerged in recent years as a geopolitical hot spot to contain illicit flows, *Contraband Corridor* seeks to understand the border from the perspective of its inhabitants. An ethnographic perspective entails not only listening to local viewpoints, but also experiencing border life with residents over time to reveal the larger landscape in which the informal and illicit economy is situated, understood, and debated. People are not only influenced by the inequities of the border but also actively shape and bend it to suit their own goals. Local inhabitants have long depended on the border, before, in the midst of, and when security is repeatedly interrupted.[13] Ethnographic research involved interviews with border residents, local officials, and regional producers, as well as participant observation and engaging in daily border life for one year between September 2006 and September 2007 and follow-up visits in the summers of 2008, 2011, and 2014.

Smuggling as Business

For residents, transporting goods across the border has long been a legitimate form of making a living and accessing goods in a relatively neglected region. Chiapas is Mexico's poorest state, and Huehuetenango is one of Guatemala's poorest departments.[14] Border populations have often historically shared stronger ties across the border than with their fellow nationals.[15] In contrast, states label these cross-border trading practices as contraband, referring to selling goods across the border that may be prohibited, stolen, evade taxes, or avoid official inspections and procedures. As Jean Clot observes, the label of contraband obscures not only historical border interconnections but also how it is the very formalization of the border and its regulations that create the problems of informal and extralegal commerce.[16] Often called *comercio hormiga*, border populations historically smuggled small amounts of goods, often of little monetary value, through repetitive small trips across the border.[17] Yet now this is also occurring using multiple ten-ton trucks and trailers carrying more substantial amounts of goods. Although many people transport goods for personal consumption and subsistence, smuggling has also become a business relied on by border inhabitants, formal businesses, and more illicit actors.

One evening, I sat outside Tito's[18] house on the Mexican side of the border, where I had been living for the past few months. At dusk, the front room of their home became a bustling store where kids bought chips and his daughter sold beers. I met Javier, Tito's nephew, who was home for the summer from university in northern Mexico. He explained how people began growing smuggling businesses even though they had always relied on border exchanges: "People with land or an inheritance had the resources to engage in business. Some people migrated to the U.S. and returned to build larger houses. They bought cars, trucks, and with the money began to conduct business."

Although as old as the border itself, smuggling intensified in the 1990s due to economic crisis on both sides of the border, the collapse of traditional livelihood options, and improvements in infrastructure and technology. Although intended to serve megadevelopment or extractive projects and facilitate regional trade integration, highway expansion in Chiapas in the 1990s also expedited extralegal commerce and communication in the region.[19] Residents began to acquire both the trucks and the capital to invest in smuggling businesses as a result of rising migration to the United States in the 1990s. In this same period, the border communities gained access to telephone service soon after receiving electricity. In the early 2000s, people began purchasing cell phones; in 2013 smartphones were making inroads.

From the 1950s through the 1990s, Mexican and Guatemalan officials, including immigration agents; customs officials; state, municipal, and road police; and the military, intermittently patrolled this route to varying degrees. In the mid- to late 1990s, border residents organized to expel state agents from this route. Residents asserted their authority to control the border; monopolized positions as smugglers, truckers, and cargo loaders in various contraband trades; and erected community tollbooths to tax smugglers using the road to fund local projects. To inhabitants, these practices are not illegal but represent legitimate advancement strategies amid declining opportunities. Yet residents are also ambivalent about smuggling. It provides job opportunities where few legitimate alternatives exist but also exposes residents to risks.

Neoliberalism and Informality

The intersection of neoliberal economic policies with the intensification of security initiatives at the Mexico–Guatemala border did not create contraband, but it provides the context for understanding why residents increasingly relied on smuggling and how and why this historical livelihood strategy has become increasingly criminalized. The advent of neoliberal[20] free market economic policies in Mexico and Guatemala in the 1980s, which accelerated in the 1990s and 2000s, exacerbated prevailing inequities and contributed to rural dispossession, an increasing dependence on the informal economy, and rising internal and international migration.[21] The effects were particularly acute for Mexico's poorer southern states like Chiapas and in Guatemala's western highlands.

International financial institutions, such as the World Bank and the International Monetary Fund (IMF), prioritized shifts from the public sector to the private and a focus on the free market to ameliorate the debt crisis of the 1980s. When oil prices were high in the 1970s, oil-producing nations invested money in multinational banks, which recycled funds into loans to Latin American countries, which were encouraged to borrow large sums of money on the path to industrialization. Given high oil prices, banks and wealthy nations had little reason to fear that loans would not be repaid. In the early 1980s rising interest rates, declining oil prices, a precipitous fall in credit availability, and a drop in commodity prices precipitated a global economic and debt crisis.[22] In 1982, Mexico announced it would default on its debt. To restructure debts, Mexico accepted strict structural adjustment terms from the IMF and World Bank to open markets, liberalize trade, privatize state-owned businesses, deregulate prices and wages, reduce government spending and social supports, and focus on export potential.[23]

Privatization and deregulation in Mexico sped up in the 1980s when Mexico entered the General Agreement on Tariffs and Trade (GATT) in 1986,[24] but deregulation, privatization, and liberalization were intensified during the Carlos Salinas de Gortari administration from 1988 through 1994. The North American Free Trade Agreement (NAFTA), signed in 1992 by Mexico, the United States, and Canada, went into effect on January 1, 1994. NAFTA aimed to reduce tariff barriers among the three countries to facilitate the flow of capital, goods, and services. Yet NAFTA worked to enhance prior advantages in the northern and central regions of Mexico, where agribusinesses and large estates were best able to take advantage of opportunities for agroexport due to access to credit, irrigation inputs, and technology.[25] The southern states came to constitute an "agrisubsistence region" where production is largely geared toward subsistence.[26] In Mexico, structural adjustment also meant abandoning its model of state-directed development, which resulted in decreased public spending and investment, a decline in the minimum wage, and rising unemployment. In particular, agricultural liberalization dealt a drastic blow to small peasants, especially in Mexico's southern states.[27] In 1992, in preparation for NAFTA, Mexico abrogated Article 27 of its Constitution, allowing for the private sale of *ejido* (communal lands) and enacting a moratorium on new *ejido* land petitions to the state. This created an uproar in states like Chiapas where land reform had been late, slow, and incomplete.[28] The collapse of the International Coffee Agreements, a sharp drop in coffee prices, and the dismantling of Mexico's National Coffee Institute (INMECAFE) in 1989, a sector on which many Chiapas farmers depend, compounded difficulties and further spiked northward migration.[29]

The 1980s and early 1990s are often referred to as the "lost decade" in Latin America, characterized by increasing unemployment, inequality, and poverty.[30] Mexico's gross domestic product (GDP) has increased since structural adjustment policies were implemented, but poverty and wealth redistribution have remained stagnant.[31] Mexico has the world's fifteenth-largest GDP but is highly unequal with over half of the population living in poverty.[32] An Organization for Economic Co-Operation and Development (OECD) report in 2011 identified Mexico as the OECD country with the second highest rate of inequality.[33] Chiapas is the Mexican state with the highest percentage of the population living in poverty at 76.2 percent in 2014, an increase from 74.7 percent in 2012.[34] Despite abundant natural resources, it consistently ranks toward the bottom of Mexican states in receipt of foreign direct investment.[35] In Chiapas, the embrace of neoliberalism served to lower the prices of peasants' products, reduce their earning power, and devalue their labor, rendering migration to the United States the most viable option for much of the peasantry.[36]

In Guatemala, neoliberal polices began to be implemented in the 1980s in the midst of the most brutal years of its thirty-six-year civil war, further disenfranchising the rural indigenous population that was targeted for genocidal violence during the war.[37] A focus on export-led development and privatization favored transnational and domestic elite, although few rural Guatemalans had the training or capital to take advantage of export opportunities.[38] Meanwhile, cutbacks in state spending and social services mandated by international lending institutions aggravated poverty and vulnerability while eroding networks of support already rendered fragile by the war.[39] The aftermath of genocidal war, continued repression, and political and economic co-optation left a weak and fragmented popular sector.[40] Guatemala remains marked by stark inequality; according to USAID, "The largest 2.5 percent of farms occupy two-thirds of agricultural land while 90% of the farms are only on one-sixth of the agricultural land."[41]

Neoliberal policies not only strained the lives of the rural poor, who could no longer earn a living growing corn and coffee, but also precipitated a rise in informal sector employment.[42] Along with migration, informal work has cushioned the effects of unemployment,[43] but at the border the extralegal smuggling economy was no longer just a fallback option. It was becoming a preferable and legitimate option.[44]

Security and Trade in the Borderlands

The Mexico–Guatemala border received heightened interest from the United States and Mexico in the 1990s and early 2000s as the security and trade nexus between North and Central America. Mexico is critical to U.S. economic interests as its third-largest trading partner—second in terms of exports and third in imports.[45] Mexico has periodically viewed the southern border as a potential threat to its national identity and sovereignty, but border security really began to emerge as imperative only with the Guatemalan refugee crisis of the 1980s, when thousands of refugees sought to enter Mexico.[46] Prior to the 1990s, transmigration at the Mexico–Guatemala border posed few problems for Mexico. Mexico began building up its border security apparatus with the creation of the National Institute of Migration (Instituto Nacional de Migración, INM) in the early 1990s to deal with the repercussions of the increasing U.S. deportations of Central Americans, which directly affected Mexico.[47]

Mexico also had an interest in aligning with the U.S. hemispheric security agenda. The Vicente Fox administration (2000–2006) hoped collaboration would lead to improved access to the U.S. market and a path to regularize millions of Mexican migrants living in the United States.[48] Mexico inaugurated Plan Sur (Southern Plan) in the summer of 2001, a few months prior to the terrorist attacks of September 11, 2001, to strengthen its southern border. Plan Sur began a shifting of the border-policing sphere from the United States–Mexico to the Mexico–Guatemala border with U.S support.[49] Guatemala followed with a similar border enhancement program, Venceremos 2001

(We Shall Overcome).[50] Because migration became a heightened U.S. security concern after the 9/11 terrorist attacks, which occurred just a few months later, the U.S. security agenda failed to incorporate Mexico's migration concerns.[51] As the more powerful nation, the United States has dominated which security threats take precedence on the hemispheric agenda.[52] Asymmetry in the trade relationship between the United States and Mexico gives the United States considerably more policy influence.[53] In 2002, the Mexico–Guatemala High-Level Border Security Group was created in coordination with Mexico and Guatemala's secretaries of the Interior to facilitate cooperation on migration, human rights, public security, organized crime, terrorism, and judicial issues.[54] In 2005, Mexico's INM was incorporated into the National Security System of Mexico, paralleling the U.S. securitization of migration, which similarly shifted the Immigration and Naturalization Services (INS) from the Department of Justice to the Department of Homeland Security in 2003.[55]

As the Mexico–Guatemala border converts into a security arena, it has also become integral to regional trade integration, which positions the region as the new frontier between the northern trading block and Central America.[56] The United States, Mexico, and Canada entered into NAFTA in 1994, Guatemala signed onto the Central American Free Trade Agreement (DR-CAFTA, or CAFTA) with the United States in 2006, and Guatemala, Mexico, and other Central American countries entered into the Mexico–Northern Triangle Free Trade Agreement in 2001. Through regional integration, trade and security are increasingly interconnected.[57] In 2001, then Mexican President Vicente Fox unveiled plans for Plan Puebla-Panamá (PPP) to create a regional development corridor encompassing Mexico's southern states and Central American countries. The plan officially receded due to protests from civil society, indigenous, and environmental groups, but many of its projects nonetheless proceeded and have been revived (see Conclusion).[58]

In 2012, Alan Bersin, then U.S. Assistant Secretary of Homeland Security, stated, "The Guatemalan border with Chiapas is now our southern border" in the fight to curtail the northward flow of undocumented migrants, criminal networks, drugs, and other illicit flows.[59] In July 2014, Mexican President Enrique Peña Nieto implemented Programa Frontera Sur, the Southern Border Program, in coordination with the United States to curtail rising numbers of Central American minors crossing the U.S.–Mexico border in the summer of 2014. In the cartography of U.S. hemispheric security, the Mexico–Guatemala border, deemed comparatively less important economically than the U.S.–Mexico border, began to take on "the function of the 'last border,' where the geneses of problems occur, which can contaminate the northern border."[60] Symbolically, politically, and economically, the Mexico–Guatemala border is at once depicted as a region of potential opportunity and threat, mostly in line with U.S. economic and security interests.[61] Recent media and policy outcries directed to Mexico's southern border reflect an intensification of the situation but often misconstrue it as something new. The shift of U.S. border enforcement and moral panics about unruly borders to Mexico's southern border has been underway since the 1990s and early 2000s.

Some scholars have questioned whether the mandate to secure the border would imperil NAFTA and impede trade relations.[62] Yet trade liberalization and demands for border security do not represent a paradox; rather, "Bilateral and North American security was an inevitable result of NAFTA, and the evolution of this agreement . . . link[s] commerce with trade and security."[63] Border security can slow down commerce and pose additional costs, but prior phases of border militarization, such as the 1990s intensification of the U.S.–Mexico border to contain drugs and undocumented immigrants, balanced security with the needs of businesses that depended on trade.[64] Although past and current border buildups often failed to contain illicit flows, they did succeed in demonstrating a visible image of a border that is "under control" by concentrating enforcement in select visible locations as smuggling was diverted to more remote areas.[65] Security directives did not impede cross-border transactions; trade between the United States and Mexico has grown 600 percent since 1990.[66] Rather than a contradiction, Joseph Nevins points to how trade and security integration complement one another because border enforcement is critical to creating an atmosphere conducive to capital accumulation.[67] Further securing the U.S.–Mexico border in the 1990s alongside NAFTA served the goal of containing the "anticipated increase in authorized migration" from Mexico that accompanied the liberalization of the Mexican economy and regional trade integration.[68] Rather than deter unauthorized migrants, securitization rendered them illegal and therefore more exploitable for employers demanding cheap labor.[69]

At the Mexico–Guatemala border, local inhabitants and migrants encounter border enforcement most palpably in terms of the expansion of mobile checkpoints along Chiapas's highways. In accordance with the Southern Border Program, Mexico modernized existing points of entry but also instituted over 100 mobile highway inspection points.[70] Officials interviewed by a Washington Office on Latin America (WOLA) team at Mexico's southern border pointed to how bolstered security also contributed to providing "security for development" and "development for security," in line with President Peña Nieto's larger plans for regional development, including resource extraction and Special Economic Zones.[71] A few rumors were circulating when I arrived at the border in September 2006. One was that the municipality of Frontera Comalapa, Chiapas, would be bulldozed to construct a hydroelectric dam. Another was that then U.S. President George W. Bush wanted to purchase Chiapas for its oil. As one border resident told me, "Mexico is already sold. The U.S. wants the resources without the people. But we will not sell it." Although neither of these rumors was true, residents grasped the climate of dispossession. As of 2015, there are ninety-nine mining concessions in Chiapas, which were awarded by the Mexican government to primarily Canadian and Chinese companies and constitute over 14 percent of Chiapas's territory.[72] Licenses will last until 2050 and 2060; activists argue more concessions are underway in addition to plans for five hydroelectric dams along Chiapas's Usumacinta River.[73] According to Mexico's National Institute of Statistics and Geography (INEGI), Chiapas provides 44.5 percent of Mexico's hydroelectric power, 7.5 percent of its electrical production, 1.8 percent of its crude oil, and 3.1 percent of its natural gas.[74] Although coverage has improved, Chiapas ranks toward the bottom of Mexican states with regards to the percentage of households possessing electricity.[75] In the context of securitized neoliberalism, a heightened security and military presence in Chiapas creates a climate conducive to securing investment, resource extraction, and road construction that serves megadevelopment projects while silencing and criminalizing opposition and controlling mobility.[76] In 2015 Mexico passed the Federal Law to Prevent and Punish Crimes in the Field of Hydrocarbons, which criminalized social protest and limited transparency around resource extraction projects further facilitated by the 2013 Energy Reform.[77]

Mexico and Guatemala are also integrated into the U.S. security agenda to address the drug trade and criminal violence. In 2006, then Mexican President Felipe Calderón declared a war on drug cartels and drug-related violence. Mexico entered into the Mérida Initiative in 2008, a security agreement with the United States to combat drug trafficking and transnational crime and to secure Mexico's borders. From 2008 through 2016, the U.S. Congress appropriated over $2.5 billion to Mexico under the Mérida Initiative and disbursed over $1.6 billion in "training, equipment, and technical assistance" as of 2016.[78] The northern border originally took priority, but in the past few years the southern border began to attract more attention. In addition to Mérida support, since 2011 the Department of Defense has provided assistance under the Mexico–Guatemala–Belize Border Region Program.[79] Although it was previously a more marginal component of the Mérida Initiative, in 2014 more attention and resources were directed to Pillar 3, or "creating a twenty-first-century border" and securing Mexico's borders, including the southern border.[80] Military and police aid, including the militarization of policing, dominate funding despite the second phase of the initiative's focus on building institutions and the poor human rights records and corruption of the Mexican police and military.[81] As a result of Mexico's militarized approach to the drug war, since 2006 over 150,000 have died, more than 42,000 have disappeared, and systemic corruption and rising human rights abuses remain unaddressed with fewer than 5 percent of crimes investigated.[82]

The Central American Regional Security Initiative (CARSI), which split off from the Mérida Initiative in 2010 and has received $979 million in civilian security assistance from the Bureau of International Narcotics and Law Enforcement Affairs (INL) from 2008 to 2017, articulates a similar militarized strategy to combating drug trafficking and insecurity in Guatemala and other Central American nations.[83] Rather than improving security, critics like the Mesoamerican Working Group (MAWG) argue that "a militarized approach to security has not led to a decrease in criminal activity or violence. Instead, it has led to increased repression, human rights violations, and debilitated Guatemala's transitional justice process" in a postwar context where close connections between criminal organizations and the military are well documented.[84] The Guatemalan state's paramilitary units and death squads were not rehabilitated and reintegrated after its thirty-six-year civil war from 1960 to 1996 but now form the ranks of drug cartels, criminal gangs, and private security forces.[85] Criminal elements infuse almost every level of governance, creating a postwar blurring between extralegal actors and the state.[86] A reintroduction of the military into public security through CARSI imperils postwar reforms in Guatemala that sought to limit the power of the military.[87]

Nearly every Mexican security brief, transborder initiative, and even WikiLeaks cables target unmonitored border routes as hotbeds for drug trafficking and criminality with little additional context. Official accounts assume that informal activities, and official tolerance of them, generate a larger climate of insecurity and lawlessness conducive to organized crime without parsing out the differences between different actors, practices, and underlying conditions. Local newspapers and state officials depict border residents as criminals or stubborn peasants ready to blockade the road with machetes. Official sources posit the remedy to be the regularization of informal crossings. According to recent estimates, only 125 immigration agents patrol the entire Mexico–Guatemala border.[88] Unregulated commerce also occurs though, and within plain view of, official crossings, such as across the Suchiate River in Ciudad Hidalgo, Mexico, and Tecún Umán, Guatemala. Moral panics over informal and illicit commerce fail to grasp how informal commerce has provided a livelihood for generations and how it is integrated into the wider economy. Furthermore, placing the responsibility for security in the hands of official units often linked to corruption and the very criminal groups they are charged with combating only serves to augment the climate of violence and insecurity.

Informality, Illegality, and Illicitness at Borders

As I witnessed truckers smuggle goods across the border in broad daylight, I struggled with my expectations regarding informality, illegality, and illicitness. This commerce did not look very different from what occurs at official points of entry or even from commerce within a country's borders. Most of these goods were considered illegal only because they used the unmonitored route to enter and exit either country; otherwise they were mundane items such as corn, coffee, and clothing. Many residents could distinguish legal commerce from contraband, but others could not. If this commerce were illegal, they reasoned, it would not be allowed to occur so openly. One woman explained, "For us, this is free trade because it [commerce] passes through every day. If it were contraband, this would not be allowed. It is purely business."

In the 1970s, the term *informal economy*, drawing from the work of Keith Hart, came into fashion to describe the self-employed and small-scale capitalist work practices that exist outside of formal protections and regulations.[89] Yet this route also hosts the smuggling of what states determine to be more illicit activities, such as the trafficking of narcotics, weapons, and undocumented migrants. Miguel Angel Centeno and Alejandro Portes differentiate informal from illegal by arguing that illegal enterprises involve producing and commercializing goods that societies consider to be illicit, whereas informal enterprises tend to center on producing and commercializing licit commodities outside of state regulation.[90] They contend that the difference between formality and informality has to do with the process by which goods are transferred and not the product itself.[91] Yet these distinctions do not fully capture how and why border residents' informal smuggling practices of licit goods, which evade official regulations, inspections, and taxes, become increasingly viewed as illicit commerce in a securitized border climate. Instead of accepting illegality as static and from a state-centered standpoint, it is necessary to interrogate how and under what conditions certain activities or people are deemed informal, illegal, or illicit. Rather than distinct realms, informal, formal, legal, and illegal commerce merge together, and are mutually constituted, in the flow of global commerce across borders.[92]

Smuggling goods across the border appears to interrupt both the Mexican and Guatemalan states' abilities to control their borders. Although contraband economies may threaten to undermine this authority, "Paradoxically, these activities reaffirm the very borders which they seek to subvert, for without borders these activities would simply cease to exist."[93] As residents reminded me, without the border, the sale of corn, coffee, and clothing across the border would be regular commerce. At the same time, the intermittently policed border and different prices, regulations, and taxes in each country are what make this commerce lucrative. It is why Guatemalan border residents, like Francisca, purchase goods in Mexico to sell in their Guatemalan stores. The relation between the state and illegal practices is rarely marked by strict opposition but instead vacillates along a continuum encompassing cooperation, antagonism, and interdependency.[94] It is the state's regulations, and the gap between these regulations and the state's willingness and ability to enforce them, that shape informality and illegality in the first place.[95]

Local inhabitants largely view smuggling commodities as legitimate business, whereas state officials deride this as illegal contraband.[96] Residents define themselves as *negociantes* (businessmen), *fleteros* (truckers who provide rides), or *comisionistas* (people who work on commission) rather than as smugglers. I use the terms *businessmen* and *middlemen* (those who act as intermediaries in border exchanges) because business tends to be dominated by, and associated with, men. Yet women also play important roles in these enterprises. Itty Abraham and Willem Van Schendel distinguish between illegality and illicitness by drawing attention to how illegality, a political determination of acceptability determined by states, and licitness, a social distinction of legitimacy, may clash; ideas about what is considered to be legitimate or illegitimate by states may not be shared by those engaging in these activities.[97] They emphasize how borderlands complicate the assessment of activities that cross between different social and political spheres of regulation.[98] Border inhabitants may carry legacies of exclusion by the state, experience state violence directed at asserting sovereignty at the margins, encounter different legal systems in close proximity, and continue cross-border social, kinship, ethnic, and economic ties.[99] The imposition and enforcement, or lack thereof, of national borders may create or interrupt cross-border ties, whereas border enforcement facilitates some interactions as it criminalizes others that could otherwise be viewed as petty commerce.[100] Differentiating between licitness and legality, however, also fails to account for the complexity of contingent views of legality and licitness.[101] Social perceptions often shift situationally and in relation to one's particular position in relation to the smuggling economy.

Taking local ethical evaluations seriously challenges dominant state-determined assumptions of illegality by drawing attention to illegalization as the social and political process by which people, places, or objects become designated as illegal and therefore the target of sanction, moral outrage, and violent containment, prohibition, and enforcement.[102] By illuminating illegalization as a social and political process rather than as a natural and normative state of affairs, I call attention to illegality fetishism, drawing loosely from Marx's notion of commodity fetishism.[103] Illegality surfaces as a thing in and of itself with an associated inherent negative value. It functions to validate, and leave unquestioned, a host of disciplinary measures, which become divorced from the political, economic, and social processes that produce, designate, and naturalize illegality.[104] Illegality as process highlights how these perceptions and their salience shift over time and space. Illegalization, as immigration scholars have argued, is often invoked as a rationale to justify differential treatment while denying the ways the extralegal economy may subsidize the formal economy and preserve prevailing arrangements of economic, racial, and political privilege.[105] At the border, viewing the route and its inhabitants as illegal at once justifies state neglect as well as surveillance and discipline. In practice, however, everyday dealings between state agents and border residents vary, ranging among neglect, opposition, suppression, collusion, and even mutual benefit.[106] It is through such daily maneuvers that the relationship among security, illegality, and trade takes shape in the borderlands.

Illegality, Security, and Neoliberalism

Illegalization works in tandem with securitization, meaning the designation of specific people, topics, and places as a threat, whereby the use of force becomes a justifiable means to uphold security.[107] Security functions as a tautology—more security is needed in the name of preserving security.[108] Illegalization and criminalization, as social and political processes that serve to identify potentially threatening populations, places, and activities, exemplify security's roving target, detracting attention from underlying causes of insecurity, including persistent inequality, erosion of economic alternatives, and weak and corrupt state institutions.[109] Meanwhile, aggressive policing to combat illegality may aggravate violence in contexts where enforcement agents are viewed as corrupt or illegitimate. In Mexico, despite reforms, local and state police forces continue to be plagued by corruption, abuse, low salaries, and low public trust.[110]

Drawing from the Copenhagen school, scholars draw attention to security as socially, politically, and performatively constructed; the ability to label a threat, and to suspend normal protections, laws, and rights to combat that threat, indexes power.[111] Expanding notions of security from the national security of the state, since the 1990s Latin American states have been increasingly concerned with "citizen security" to take into account mounting concerns with crime and insecurity.[112] Yet, in practice, this approach has led to a dampening of citizen security's potential to consider citizens' rights to, instead, prioritizing preserving public order by any means necessary.[113] The state maintains the power to determine a threat as it also encourages citizens to take individual responsibility, leading to what Daniel Goldstein calls the "privatization" or "neoliberalization" of violence, as people take security into their own hands when the state fails to meet their needs.[114] In this framing, the insecurities generated by neoliberalism are displaced onto the figure of the criminal, as security becomes an overarching framework to animate violent responses to address crime and the fear of crime.[115] Rather than providing a sense of safety, these approaches often exacerbate insecurity and further the criminalization of marginalized populations. Elana Zilberg argues that the simultaneous advance of security policies (like "tough on crime" approaches) and neoliberalism produce a "neoliberal securityscape," which generates insecurity and violence.[116] She further contends that "security policies and neoliberal trade agreements both rest upon and provoke flows across borders . . . licit and illicit."[117]

At the border, residents have taken border control into their own hands in a context where both states neglected to protect and provide for them. Residents largely enact this authority peacefully but will hold uncooperative officials hostage, put people who threaten local safety into community jails, and use road blockades when necessary. Even as residents lack faith in the state, many support heavy-handed state approaches to tackle insecurity. They welcome officials to enter the route if it is to perform their jobs of protection—not to interfere in border business. As Chapter 4 illustrates, however, local control does not necessarily ensure safety.

In Guatemala, violence currently takes the form of everyday criminal, gang, community, narco, and domestic and interpersonal violence.[118] This new violence now means that "for many Guatemalans, it is more likely they will be killed than it was during the war."[119] The United Nations and World Bank reported in 2007 that Guatemala had the third-highest homicide rate in the world and one of the highest impunity rates at 97 percent.[120] In Guatemala, high crime rates and insecurity in the postwar era are often attributed to gangs, drug cartels, and *delincuentes*, or delinquent youth, as discourses of blame justify an increasingly repressive state response, as well as violent extralegal reactions from communities and other actors.[121] However, reducing Guatemala's current violence to gangs and organized crime draws attention away from "a legacy of state violence; deep socioeconomic inequality; the penetration of extractive industries; the erosion of political and social infrastructures; and disparate access to healthcare, education, and life chances" that create the conditions for everyday forms of violence to thrive.[122] As during the war, indigenous communities and the urban poor are blamed for criminality as the means of violence privatize into the hands of everyday actors, evidenced by the rise in public security firms (who often employ former parastate military actors), local vigilante groups and security committees, and urban gangs.[123] In response to fears of crime and either a lack of state response or its direct collusion with criminal agents, compounded by poverty and socioeconomic exclusion, some communities have taken on their own crime control by engaging in security committees and patrols, as well as by perpetrating community lynchings of criminals.[124] Lynchings were most prominent in Huehuetenango in 2009, which was also the department that suffered some of the most severe wartime violence.[125] Through the search for security, these communities end up further criminalized as momentum for *mano dura*, or tough on crime, policies grow despite the fact that these approaches contribute to the erosion of human rights and remilitarization of a postwar society.[126]

As neoliberal states rolled back their provision of services and supports for their populations, they have increasingly played the function of "security providers for global capital," which I have earlier depicted as "security for development and development for security" or securitized neoliberalism.[127] This role often conflicts with the needs and security of citizens, who may be constructed as impediments or threats to development and legitimate business.[128] In Chiapas, some communities and activists express concern that security forces are positioned more to mitigate conflicts surrounding resource extraction than to fulfill their stated purpose of interdicting drugs and unauthorized migrants.[129] Under securitized neoliberalism, security policies ensure a friendly environment for capital alongside neoliberal commitments to deregulation, privatization, and liberalization, which translates to minimal taxation and regulation, low wages, lax labor conditions, and restricted opposition.[130] In Latin American economies already plagued by high levels of inequality, these measures perpetuate inequality, reliance on the informal sector, and distrust of the state and its institutions.[131] The criminalization of contraband moralizes the limited options of the poor by blaming them for their own plight while allowing more powerful entities to claim and protect legitimate profits and determine who can sell and have access to goods.[132] As Alexander Dent notes in his work on piracy, "The presence of the pirated in informal economies . . . [is] used to *keep* the informal informal."[133]

Critical anthropological studies of security and neoliberalism point to how people marginalized by state-driven security policies experience, contest, and construct security.[134] Yet, as Heyman and Campbell note, the lens of social construction can fall short in explaining "what, how, and why particular constructions [of crime, threat] emerge" in particular places and times.[135] It is therefore necessary to unpack how and why clandestine border commerce and borderlands become constituted as threats to, as they are fundamentally integrated into, the regional political economy.

The Border Economy

To the casual observer, it seems that no one knows about this unmonitored road. Border residents use the term *extravío* to describe the route, which comes from the verb *extraviar*, which can be translated in various ways, all of which have negative connotations: to become lost, to veer from the [desired] pathway, to err, to deviate in an irregular fashion, to mislead, or lead astray. Rather than a deviation in the social and political geography, the *extravío* is central to understanding cross-border flows of goods, people, capital, information, and evolving patterns of governance in the region. Such gaps are not evidence of state failure or necessarily state absence; rather they are as integral to defining the state and formal economy as exceptions are to revealing the rule.[136] *Extravíos* are where nothing and everything cross. The majority of cross-border commodity flows in this region occur through such routes. Residents, merchants, and officials all related that everyone knows about this crossing, although it officially does not exist. It is both hidden, yet known.[137] This selective (in)visibility maintains the image of border security and the importance of official flows, while allowing various stakeholders to reap the benefits of extralegal commerce.

One afternoon, I was hanging out in a dusty abandoned field, which border residents call a depot, on the Mexican side of the border. These spaces are barren fields in times of low commerce, but most have been converted into parking lots where trucks meet to transfer cargo. Merchants meet in this unmonitored corridor to transfer cargo and evade the official border crossing, taxes, and inspections. A truck can enter the route from the Mexican highway and proceed to the Guatemalan highway without encountering any official surveillance (and vice versa). Covertly exchanging cargo between trucks within the unmonitored route has a Superman's phone booth effect—Mexican goods brought into the route are transferred into Guatemalan trucks, and then exit to the Guatemalan highway in Guatemalan trucks transformed into Guatemalan goods (and vice versa from Guatemala to Mexico). A Mexican truck in Guatemalan territory (and vice versa) otherwise invites official scrutiny for inspections and permits.

Groups of men wait at depots along the border route gossiping, searching for shade, and waiting for trucks so they can unload and reload cargo. These seemingly marginal, dusty lots are, in fact, critical hubs in legal and extralegal commercial chains. Trucking reveals how legal and illegal flows intertwine in the daily business of international trade.[138] On this particular day when I was at the depot, I met a man I call Eduardo from Puebla, Mexico. He arrived at the Mexican border depot to deliver onions to a Guatemalan merchant. A marketplace in Mexico City contacted him, because he was a member of a union of truck drivers, to meet a Guatemalan buyer at this depot. As we were talking, two Mexican military Humvees from a nearby military base drove by. They did not stop and soon turned around to exit to the Mexican highway. No one appeared nervous, stating that officials occasionally entered the route but "did not bother business." If officials enter to disturb their business, one cargo loader told me, "We would all be advised. There are people here who are spies.

Or the officials that work with the businessmen [who live] here call to alert them. We would all stop working. There would be no movement." I realized that the implementation and experience of security did not depend on official policies or policing mandates to stem illicit flows but on intimate knowledge and personal networks.

Eduardo had limited knowledge of the border; it was only his second time there. He acknowledged the Guatemalan buyer would be illegally transporting onions to Guatemala, evading inspections, taxes, and documentation and traversing an unmonitored, rather than official, border crossing. However, he felt secure because he had permits to sell onions in Mexico and was technically not breaking any laws. Eduardo grew impatient as he waited. He worried, "I still have to pick up papayas in Comitán [a nearby Mexican city] to bring to Mexico City." Especially in light of rising fuel prices in the spring of 2007, it was worth the trip only if he could transport cargo in both directions. Such is the necessity for truckers, which highlights how disparate commercial activities, both legal and illegal, become interconnected.[139] Local cargo loaders had also been waiting most of the day for work to transfer the Mexican onions to Guatemalan trucks. They risked time they could otherwise spend tending their harvests or working as field hands. For most, the wait was worth it. A cargo loader earns 50 to 60 pesos (roughly US$5 to US$6 in 2007) for each truck loaded, which is equivalent to wages for a full day of work as a field hand (Figure I.4).

The Guatemalan merchant, Mauricio, finally arrived with two ten-ton Guatemalan trucks. He makes weekly trips from Guatemala City to the border to purchase beans, onions, and sometimes corn to sell in his market stall in Guatemala City. He had been coming to the border for ten years and had established local friendships. Previously, he bought products only in Guatemala. He learned about the border crossing from a friend. Before, Mexican border resident contacts would bring corn to the Guatemalan side, where he would purchase it. Then, he said, border residents "told me I could purchase onions more easily on the Mexican side. It wasn't a problem" to cross the border.

Cross-border connections informed Mauricio about, and facilitated new, market exchange opportunities. Local contacts taught him about regional patterns of state surveillance as he realized the route was relatively unpatrolled. He learned he could gain access to goods on the Mexican side without encountering state agents (who were present on Mexican highways) or using Guatemalan border intermediaries. Over time, as he cultivated friendships, he could avoid using local border intermediaries for his exchanges, which border residents usually require of long-distance merchants to preserve work

Figure I.4. Loading onions between trucks in the border depot.
SOURCE: Author photo.

for themselves. Although the onions were from Mexico City, he maintained local relationships by purchasing their corn and beans.

I asked Mauricio how he would transport his onions to Guatemala. Where did the onions go next? Following the chain of exchanges placed onions in a transnational chain where the legal and illegal blur. Mauricio explained:

I called the marketplace in Mexico yesterday. That is how I knew when to arrive [at the border]. I call to check the prices of onions, to see if they are worth buying. If they are, I arrange to have them transported to the border. To get the onions to Guatemala I have to pay a lot of authorities. There are always people to be paid. Then everything is in agreement. I need to get a pass in La Mesilla in case the authorities detain me. I also have an agreement with SAT [Superintendencia de Adminstración Tributaria, Guatemala's tax administration body].[140] Whenever I come to purchase onions, I talk to SAT first. They give me receipts for my onions in Huehuetenango. I pay for a receipt that certifies that the onions are from Huehuetenango so the police do not bother me at inspection posts. It is a little bit of corruption. Since the receipts say [the onions are from] Huehuetenango, I don't get inspected, and I don't pay any more. I just show the authorities the receipts, and they let me pass.

Because he transfers the Mexican onions to his Guatemalan truck within the unmonitored route, the onions appear to be, and to always have been, Guatemalan replete with certification. I asked what happens when he gets to Guatemala.

"In Guatemala, I sell the onions to Honduran merchants," he said.

"How do the Hondurans purchase them?" I asked.

He replied matter-of-factly, "The sale to Hondurans is legal. They cross the official border and have the product inspected." Mauricio transports onions from Mexico to Guatemala illegally, but legally to Honduras. He continued, "I give the Hondurans the same receipts I get from SAT. The receipts make a big difference. If I transported the onions legally at La Mesilla, I would pay 6,000 quetzales per truck. Instead, I pay 200 per truck to some customs agents."

This route is not a "black hole" or irregular deviation in the economy where "the norms that regulate social order do not exist."[141] Instead, it is integral to the regional economy. At first, I was surprised by Mauricio's candor. Eduardo and Mauricio render simplistic distinctions between merchants and smugglers problematic. Both men conduct business exchanges across legal and illegal designations and borders. Particular places like this route are critical to facilitating transnational flows across legal and illegal lines whereas extralegal trade also shapes the border route and its residents. Tensions among security, trade, and livelihood do not play out through official dictates but instead through social, economic, and historical ties and contingent negotiations.

The Border Ethnography

Contraband Corridor delves into the everyday lives of people residing along an unmonitored border crossing. It explores how people cope with, and reinterpret, regional security and trade directives not of their own making that nonetheless have an impact on their lives as they strive to provide for their families amid limited choices. I aim to temper sensationalized, dehistoricized, and decontextualized media and policy discourses about crises of criminality and illicit flows. Ethnography demonstrates the tensions between policy and practice, intentions and realities, and how seemingly neutral trade and security policies reflect particular economic interests and cultural logics that may clash with local experiences.

Chapter 1 situates the ethnographic approach of conducting research on extralegal flows and presents the border context and communities. It examines the contested and unfinished process by which the borderlands and Mexican and Guatemalan nations took shape to contextualize how residents became marginalized from, yet also integrated into, two nation-states. Chapter 2 picks up on the indeterminate border to detail how border residents use extralegal strategies and local resources to live across multiple nation-states. The chapter follows residents like Fani, Rosa, Daniela, and Ramón, who achieve dual nationality through extralegal means by certifying they were born in both Mexico and Guatemala. As residents rely on extralegal practices to bend the border to their advantage, they undermine state attempts to manage border populations as they simultaneously participate in practices that bring the state into being at the margins.[142]

Chapter 3 explores the context of agricultural liberalization policies that have undermined traditional forms of livelihood and informed an increasing reliance on smuggling at the border. Examining corn, the basic subsistence crop in the region, as well as the good most frequently smuggled across this border, helps reveal the local ethics that underpin the legitimacy of contraband. Residents reinterpreted corn smuggling as "free trade" in a context where official free trade provisions excluded them and decimated their livelihoods. To smuggle Mexican corn to Guatemala, border residents capitalized on a wider climate of political and economic crisis in the 1990s to prevent state agents from monitoring the route. Chapter 4 traces how this border became relatively free of officials as residents negotiated a degree of autonomy from state officials and other regional players. However, the border also vacillates between local control and official tolerance, reflecting wider tensions among security, trade, poverty, and political (in)stability. Chapter 5 shifts to front-line customs agents as they describe how they balance maintaining border security with the realities of trade, scarce resources, and regional demands. Through the lens of "phantom commerce," or clandestine commerce, which is technically invisible but nonetheless produces tangible effects, the chapter demonstrates the complex interdependence, rather than necessary antagonism, among illicit flows, security, and formal trade.

Chapter 6 examines how border merchants, truckers, and smugglers understand their work and navigate the intersections between the legal and illegal economy. As middleman intermediary smugglers, truckers, and cargo loaders, residents enable "phantom commerce" to distribute low-risk rewards to select state agents and formal businesses. Even when residents benefit, they also bear the risks. Chapter 7 focuses on a conflict over gasoline smuggling to illustrate how border residents depend on the state to evade it. It also shows how border residents are increasingly situated in an unpredictable context, as conflicts between and within criminal groups and state forces permeate the wider region.

When I conducted the majority of my fieldwork in 2006 and 2007, Mexico's crackdown on drug cartels, and the ensuing escalation of violence, was just beginning. Mexico's launch of the Southern Border Program in 2014, which intensified efforts to contain Central American migrant flows, had not yet occurred, but its precursors were operating. This is not a book about the drug war or a perceived "migrant crisis."[143] Yet it points to the political, social, and economic backdrop that is often omitted when criminality, drugs, and clandestine migration are isolated from the contexts in which they are produced and reproduced.[144] This backdrop has not only enabled the drug war and "migrant crisis" to thrive while prolonging criminal violence, corruption, and insecurity; it has also sustained their unresolved and undergirding sources—the structural and symbolic violences of poverty, criminalization, and social and economic exclusion. The Conclusion brings the implications of the unsettled interdependences among security, trade, and illegality up to the present to explore how the securitization of migration and drugs have combined to make people less secure while generating increased clandestine flows across borders.

Border Entries and Reentries

*As the peripheries of nations, borderlands are subject to
frontier forces and international influences that mold the
unique life of borderlanders, prompting them to confront
myriad challenges stemming from the paradoxical nature of
the setting in which they live.*

—Oscar J. Martínez, "Border People," 25

Entry

"*Comalapa, Comalapa, Comalapa,*"[1] the van driver's assistant yelled from
a cement building off the Pan-American highway in Comitán, Chiapas. He
played with the tone of his voice, alternately stressing different syllables of
CO-ma-lap-a. He beckoned travelers to board the minivans, or *combis*, destined for the municipality of Frontera Comalapa. With seats for seven to eight
passengers, vans generally pack in at least fifteen people with their goods. Inhabitants from the border region travel to Comitán to shop for cheaper used
clothing and furniture. They shop in fruit and vegetable markets, flea markets,
and recent installations of Walmart and Sam's Club. I boarded the *combi*, my
backpack and I crammed into a window corner. I held my breath as the driver
crossed himself and touched the Jesus ornament hanging from his rearview
mirror each time we rounded a curve. We hurtled down the Pan-American
Highway from the cool highlands of Comitán into the hot, dry Frontera Comalapa lowlands. I convinced myself that the faster the *combi* traveled the
curves, the better it could cling to the hillside due to pure friction and momentum . . . or perhaps it was the driver's prayer.

It was the summer of 2005 and my first trip to the border to choose a
field site to conduct research. Juan Carlos Velasco,[2] a research assistant from
ECOSUR (*El Colegio de la Frontera Sur*) in San Cristóbal de las Casas, was
taking me on excursions throughout the border region where he had been
part of a research team conducting a multisited study on the integration of
former Guatemalan refugees into Mexico.[3] I did not know what to expect

27

when we got to Frontera Comalapa, a small town with a colonial square, municipal building, open-air market, stores, a few restaurants and motels, and the recent arrival of cyber cafes and *agencias de viaje*, or tourist agencies, advertising trips to Tijuana, Altar Sonora, and Tecate.[4] Anyone who has been to Altar Sonora knows it is not a tourist destination. These buses occupy a lucrative niche providing transport through Mexico for those wishing to journey into the United States, dropping them in Mexico's northern desert, where they can contact smugglers or attempt to traverse the desert on their own. The proliferation of tourist agencies reflects the role that the Mexico–Guatemala border plays as a migrant sending and transit zone. In the past decade, Frontera Comalapa has transformed into a hub for migration, petty commerce, prostitution, and the drug trade.

Juan Carlos knew that *combis* destined for communities residing along the particular unmonitored border route where I ended up conducting fieldwork left from the corner across from the market stalls in Frontera Comalapa. As we boarded the *combi*, Juan Carlos began chatting with a man I call Federico. From their friendly interchange, I assumed they must have met before, but Juan Carlos had a knack for ethnographic serendipity. Federico not only spoke with us for the entire ride but also proceeded to take us on a tour of his Mexican community of Santa Rosa[5] and introduce us to his Guatemalan neighbors across the border. We hopped into the back of his friend's pickup truck to traverse the unmonitored road through the three Mexican border communities of Santa Rosa, La Maravilla, and El Nance and directly uphill into the two Guatemalan border communities of El Girasol and Nueva Vida. Because we were not transporting any commerce, we were waved through each community's *cadena*, or chain. Each border community erects a chain across a section of the road to demarcate its territory and establish a tollbooth to levy tolls on smugglers using the road. Federico laughed off our need for a passport as we traveled up a rocky hill, past some white monuments that were the only indication that we were crossing the international border into Guatemala. The first house we saw in Guatemala had a Guatemalan flag on one side of its fence and a Mexican flag on the other. The house's owner laughed when we commented that his goat was technically grazing in Mexico. Were we in Mexico or Guatemala? This chapter details my initial and multiple entries into the border and fieldwork in an unmonitored crossing. Moving from my own entry, it details the making of the borderlands and the border communities in relation to the regional and national contexts. Local inhabitants have

Figure 1.1. Border monuments delineating the division between Mexico and Guatemala.
SOURCE: Author photo.

historically been marginalized by both nation-states as they also helped shape them from their margins[6] (see Figure 1.1).

Reentry

In September 2006 when I returned to live at the border for a year, Juan Carlos arranged for my husband and me to rent a home in Santa Rosa, Mexico. We were then on our own. I learned the limitations of Juan Carlos's connections due to time constraints on the larger project on refugee integration. His research team had not crossed into Guatemala because it was outside their scope. After hearing rumors that journalists had been run out of the Mexican border community of El Nance in the past, I grew nervous.

Paco, a lanky seventeen-year-old from El Nance, luckily became my local guide. Jokingly called "El Gringo" due to his interest in the United States, Paco knew everyone and sought out a friendship with my husband and me. He explained how nearly all of his community's 100 households belonged to four families, introduced me to local merchant smugglers, took me to meet friends in Guatemala, and extended invitations to parties, soccer games, and meals. *"Puro Hernández,"*[7] he laughed, referring to how people on both sides of the border shared surnames and kinship ties. His family included local smugglers, cousins in North Carolina factories, and his father, who worked as a cargo loader for coffee smugglers and as a field hand.

Paco wanted to become an immigration agent like his cousin, Rigo. He showed me Rigo's two-story house near the international borderline. At first, when I heard a man who worked for immigration lived there, I assumed it was an outpost of state surveillance. I learned, though, that Rigo had lived there his entire life and worked most of his career in other parts of Mexico. Recently, his post changed to rotating between various Chiapas immigration offices, meaning that border residents could call on him, or mention his name, for favors. Paco's desire to become an immigration agent was the first blow to my preconceived notions of security and illegality at the border. A young man whose life was intimately shaped by smuggling also wanted to work for a state agency supposedly committed to policing unauthorized flows.

When I first arrived at the border, I explained my research in the assembly meetings of each community and met key local authorities; most people were receptive. Looking back, I think people appreciated that I wanted to hear their points of view in contrast to how officials and journalists often associated the border with criminality. When I went to the immigration office in Ciudad Cuauhtémoc to register my fieldwork residence according to Mexican regulations for foreign researchers, the agent derisively commented, "That is a place without law. The people there [think] they are above the law. It is no good. The communities make the law." When interviewing officials, I subsequently did not mention where I resided. The longer I lived at the border, the more suspicions subsided as people witnessed my daily activities, got to know me, and saw nothing was changing. Some residents laughed off the notion that I could threaten their enterprises. They knew where the threats originated and were compensating these individuals accordingly. Their livelihoods depended on it.

This crossing is also not as hidden as it appears. This is the myth of illegality—that is it hidden and unknown. In fact, clandestinity may be key to the maintenance of state sovereignty and the justification of border policing. In her work on undocumented migrants in the United States, Susan Coutin defines clandestinity as the "hidden, but known," drawing from Gupta and Ferguson (1997) to show how disruptions and exclusions are critical to defining territorial integrity.[8] This route is legally prohibited from existing even though officials, regional inhabitants, and merchants admit it provides a central corridor for the movement of goods and people. Vacillations between depicting the crossing as selectively invisible or hypervisible reinforce the myth of an orderly border while enabling extra flows on which regional inhabitants depend to proceed.[9] At the same time, periodically drawing attention to these gaps justifies dramatic displays of state violence to recover authority.[10] The route is well known to anyone involved in transnational commerce, as well as to officials and the Mexican, Guatemalan, and U.S. governments. I have been following policy briefs from Mexico, Guatemala, and the United States that mention this crossing since 2004, and I have yet to see any changes. Still, because the situation is uncertain, I disguise the names of the communities, some of their characteristics, and individual identities. I acknowledge that the responsibility for information taken out of context to support further criminalization is my own. I balance this fear of misrepresentation with the importance of giving voice to those rendered illegal by official designations, who illustrate firsthand the spirals of violence and insecurity that may ensue from militarized approaches to combating illegality.

A *Gringa* Amid Male Smugglers

How does a young, white, North American female anthropologist gain access to the world of border smuggling? Mexican researchers who knew about my fieldwork, and had visited me, worried about my safety. My family thought I was crazy. However, I rarely felt unsafe at the border. Ethnography situates extralegal practices within the everyday, which in the rural borderlands is also filled with family meals, harvesting corn, making tortillas and *tamales*, and sipping coffee on patios. The extralegal does not belong to a separate shadowy underworld. Smuggling goods and facilitating the passage of truckers are a part of daily life. Being embedded in border life, and developing relationships with local families, also helped me develop border smarts, knowing where I should not go, whom I should talk to, and what I should not talk or write about. I started my ethnography not as one about smuggling or migration, but one about what it meant to people to live at the border. I initially asked what people liked and did not like about the border, and the common theme that emerged was the benefit of the business opportunities offered by the border. Yet business could not be separated from border relationships, histories, and the course of social life. I grew to understand why journalists were unwelcome and why communities were suspicious of parachute research, as one resident told me about a previous researcher she had met who "took pictures of us, but I don't know what happened to them." Only paying attention to, and reporting on, the extraordinary or the criminal divorces extralegal activity from its social context, making illegality seem like the defining characteristic of the border and its inhabitants. With time, people began to share their lives with me and look out for me. Midway through my fieldwork, my parents came to visit, and we traveled for a week in Guatemala. During the trip, I received phone calls from border residents who were worried about me because they had heard on the radio that criminals assaulted a *gringa* in the nearby border crossing of La Mesilla, Guatemala.

The border communities had never hosted a foreign academic researcher for an extended period of time. They were familiar with the mandates of a thesis because some youth now attend university, write theses, and conduct a social service in rural communities. They wondered, however, why I was working there and not in an indigenous community, which is a legacy of academic research, especially anthropology, in Mexico (and in U.S. anthropology to an extent). Some people struggled to place me despite my insistence that I was a researcher who was writing a thesis. Was I sure I wasn't with a church? A friend or relative of a migrant's friends or relatives in the United States? A member of AFI, the equivalent of the Mexican FBI? These were the only avenues through which many could imagine a *gringa* residing in their community. Even after I established substantial rapport, a resident confided that one man was suspicious and was following me on his motorcycle for a week to see what "I was really doing." There were always some people who preferred not to speak with me. I therefore began and continued research slowly, having to constantly maintain rapport.

Being a young married female with my husband from the United States, and in subsequent visits, a mother of two young daughters, opened some doors and closed others. It took time to establish rapport with smugglers. Smuggling is a male-dominated enterprise where men tease one another about having girlfriends across borders to enhance their masculine and business prowess. Sometimes the banter grew uncomfortable as men repeatedly asked me if North American women were more promiscuous.

Yet men were often willing to share information with me that they were less willing to divulge with other men. When my husband started a fair trade business with indigenous artisans in San Cristóbal, Chiapas, some men

Figure 1.2. Children hang out and play on a truck.
SOURCE: Author photo.

criticized his strategies. They told him he could make more money by smuggling artisan goods from Guatemala to sell in Chiapas, as many of them did. Some offered advice, whereas others sensed competition. In the male-dominated arenas of both policing and smuggling, I was not suspected as a threat or competitor. Women also play important roles in sustaining businesses behind the scenes, whether by doing accounting, forging certifications, selling food and beverages to smugglers, or entertaining business partners. Perhaps being a woman led some people to see me as someone who understood how smuggling was critical to sustaining their families and communities (Figure 1.2). However, there is also information I was not privy to as not only a female but also an outsider.

My methodological approach balanced following smuggling trades with intensive research with residents in the unmonitored route, whose lives are intimately affected by extralegal flows. I sought the perspectives of locals with different levels of involvement from smugglers to cargo loaders, widows, and teachers who worry about the influence this economy may have on youth. Smugglers wield more power to shape the decisions and culture of their communities, but other viewpoints provide insight into how these players acquire and maintain such power, as well as into how their influence is contested and mitigated in daily life. The repercussions of living in an unofficial crossing are usually felt most acutely by more immobile residents[11] rather than by mobile smugglers.

It was necessary to establish rapport in the border communities with multiple actors before interviewing state agents, politicians, merchants, or corn producers outside of the border route. This taught me what I could say and what I needed to omit to protect those with whom I was residing as well as myself. Living in one of the Mexican border communities, I began by attending community meetings on both sides of the border, going house-to-house to meet neighbors, and arranging interviews with current and past community authorities. As a service to the communities, I taught English one day a week in each community. After class, I ate dinner with a student's family, which broadened my networks. By following their connections across the border, I learned how social, kin, and economic relations tied the cross-border communities together.

By hanging out in depots where merchant smugglers exchange cargo, I was able to interview and conduct participant observation with local merchants and smugglers, truckers, and cargo loaders who depend on the unmonitored road for their livelihoods, as well as meet long-distance truckers. I conducted participant observation at the community tollbooths, where residents levy taxes on passing smugglers. Spending time at the tollbooths, and serving a twelve-hour shift, showed me how the taxes benefit the community, as well as how residents gain familiarity with truckers and their wares.

Halfway through my research, my landlord decided to sell the house we were renting. Chatting with residents at a local fiesta, Paco introduced me to his Uncle Tito, a coffee smuggler, or businessman. Perhaps it was the festivities or *Coronitas* (mini *Corona* beers) talking, but Tito suggested I move in with his family. He lamented how he built an extension on his home, but it remained empty because his children had moved to other cities or built their own homes. I put off the request until a more sober afternoon and was surprised when he re-extended the offer. By getting to know their family, I learned how they combined diverse income strategies and relied on an unpredictable landscape and patronage ties to politicians and officials to remain in business. Getting to know smugglers and their families complicated black-and-white mediagenic dichotomies of criminals and victims, revealing the gray areas in which all struggled to *superarse*, or get ahead. Many of these individuals were actually commissioned by legitimate companies to supplement their inventories (Chapter 6).

I also interviewed local police, immigration officials, politicians, and customs agents to understand official rules and regulations. I learned that the rules were inconsistently understood and applied; instead they were contingent on local social, economic, and political dynamics and interactions. Largely, I spent time with families, attended social events, and conversed with people who suspected smugglers' all-of-a-sudden earnings. By embedding myself in the border communities, I examined transborder flows while I came to understand how residents simultaneously support smugglers due to some community economic benefits, as they also desire a more legitimate state presence to protect and provide for them.

Residing with border residents and listening to their justifications for extralegal practices, however, could blind me to the negative aspects. Could it also make me complicit? I attempted to listen openly, but I also asked provocative questions. Engaging in debates with residents, and exposing some of my own biases in the process, revealed how people balanced acknowledged discrepancies among the justifications for their actions, the reality of their lives, and their diverse motivations and anxieties.

To protect myself and border residents, I did not directly inquire about activities considered risky or illicit in the local context, including the drug trade, arms smuggling, and trafficking undocumented migrants. Although these topics arose in conversations, they were often rumors, which also illustrated local understandings of the evolving landscape. I followed residents' strategies: close your eyes, ears—and mouth. I also, however, analytically probed the silences and discursive shifting of risk as certain kinds of activities, like migrant smuggling, have become increasingly criminalized.

Making the Borderlands

It was through initially traversing the road with Juan Carlos and Federico that I began to understand how the communities that straddled the border became mutually interdependent seemingly regardless of, but also because of, the international border. Each community has its own dynamics and interests, but they are linked by their mutual dependence on maintaining a route conducive to commerce. If one community raises its tolls too high or fails to maintain its portion of the road, commerce for all is threatened. A historically indeterminate and porous border, alongside marginalization from larger economic and political centers, has often led border residents to depend more on relationships across the border than on their own nationals and states.[12]

Rather than taking the marginality of the borderlands at face value, processes of nation building and economic development have rendered the borders and their inhabitants marginal from, yet also integral to, the modern nation-state.[13] Residing at the margins of the territorial state, border populations are often represented in ways that suggest their unruliness, which serves to justify state attempts to "manage" them and render them legible to the state.[14] The margins, and their potential threat to the territorial state, are critical to state efforts to assert sovereignty where it is often most contested. The borderlands, and especially the official disruptions in the border landscape, are often associated with the potential for illegality as borderlanders are pulled, attracted, and repulsed in conflicting directions.[15] Rather than an inherent state, this reflects historical processes of exclusion combined with forms of forcible inclusion in the name of asserting the boundaries of the state, enhancing security, or extracting capital, resources, and labor for the needs of the modern state. Border residents' livelihood strategies, often stigmatized as illegal, reflect how those at the margins of nation-building processes have adapted to resist state incorporation and surveillance,[16] while also seeking out inclusion on their own terms. Both sides of the border are characterized by their peripheral relationship to their nation-states, marked by high levels of poverty and lack of services and infrastructure.[17] Yet it is also in the interstices among the law, state, and nation that alternative modes of subject making, legibility, and survival emerge even as borderlanders may continue to be subject to exclusion and criminalization.[18]

Demarcating the Border, Making Mexico

When I explained my research to border residents, I identified myself as an anthropologist. However, residents had trouble understanding what studying border life had to do with anthropology, which they equated with the study of indigenous peoples. They thought I should be studying in the Chiapas or Guatemalan highlands where there were more indigenous people, as they drew on a history of nationalist anthropology in Mexico.[19] One Mexican border resident was perplexed as he noted, "But there are no indigenous people here. The indigenous people here, it is because they are really from Guatemala." Despite the fluid history between Chiapas and Guatemala and a strong indigenous underpinning of the region, Mexican border residents erased indigenous peoples from the border or relocated them to Guatemala.

Mexican border residents in El Nance call seventy-four-year-old Héctor the community historian due to his penchant for collecting history books. One day as we sat at a small wooden table on his patio drinking *atole*,[20] he retrieved a book on the history of Chiapas. He flipped to a page he had earmarked to show me how Chiapas was part of Guatemala during the colonial period. "It was not always like this . . ." He read from the book, "Iturbide signed on the 16th of January, 1822, that Chiapas was to be declared part of Mexico." In the colonial period, Chiapas was part of the *capitanía* of Guatemala; after independence from Spain in 1821, Mexico and Guatemala both wanted to influence Chiapas.[21] Chiapas formally joined Mexico in 1824, but Guatemala continued to assert territorial claims, and some regions of Chiapas initially favored joining Guatemala.[22] The Soconusco region of Chiapas held out incorporating into Mexico even longer, maintaining autonomy until 1842.[23] The border between Chiapas and Guatemala was only agreed on in a boundary treaty of 1882 and finalized in 1895.[24] For residents, the border remained porous and imprecise for generations, leading to close connections between border Chiapans and Guatemalans.[25] Héctor continued, "Until the 1960s there was a lot of confusion at the border. Many people were unaware where the actual line was." Because colonial boundaries were obscure and data lacking, the countries "drew straight cartographic lines" where there was uncertainty.[26] Within this border crossing, many people were unsure where the border was located because the monuments demarcating the border were spread apart at great distances. In the 1960s the International Commission of Limits and Water installed additional monuments to clarify the borderline. Some landowners had to exchange land accordingly; they did not realize that their territory was in the other nation.

Most inhabitants on both sides of the border trace their roots to Guatemala and have family on both sides. Alonso, who lives in Santa Rosa, Mexico, added, "Ask almost anyone [referring to adult border residents] here on either side of the border where their grandparents are from. Almost everyone will tell you Guatemala." Héctor reminded me that flows did not always go one way. His wife's family fled to Guatemala from Mexico during the violence of Mexico's revolutionary years around 1915. According to Héctor, "They didn't know exactly where the border was. It wasn't well marked. They accidentally went into Guatemala."

Ethnic groups historically crossed the Mexico–Guatemala borderlands due to the relatively recent historical imposition of the international border, as well as a pattern of seasonal migration of Guatemalan laborers to work in the coffee plantations in southern Chiapas. In the late 1800s, because the border region and coffee growing areas of southern Chiapas were sparsely inhabited, Mexico encouraged importation of Guatemalan labor as well as colonization by Guatemalans (who were often indigenous), who subsequently were naturalized as Mexicans.[27] Although Guatemalans were recruited for labor, the Porfirio Díaz administration of late nineteenth-century Mexico had a strong racial component underlying its goals to modernize and develop the coffee economy and agriculture in the Soconusco region.[28] Modernization did not intend to include peasants but was instead oriented to attract foreign investment and recruit European and U.S. immigrants; Germans were the largest contingent that came to Chiapas.[29] Porfirio Díaz and his successors believed that "indigenous peoples depressed economic development" and immigrants would "improve the quality of the people of Mexico."[30]

In the early twentieth-century post-Revolution period, Mexico changed course from viewing its indigenous population as a blight on the nation to embracing its indigenous heritage. However, it did so through the logic of the mestizo nation, which referred to a mixed population between the Spanish colonizers and its indigenous peoples. Mexico created national institutions such as the Ministry of Education and the Office of Anthropology and Regional Populations of the Republic, which would later become the National Indigenous Institute (INI) to integrate the indigenous population and prepare the nation for "racial fusion."[31] As this strategy aimed to incorporate diverse populations into the nation-state, it also exuded a strong assimilationist tone that erased not only an elite white population of Spanish descent from the national narrative but also a large and marginalized indigenous population.[32]

Because Guatemala continued to harbor resentment about the loss of territory and periodically attempted to reclaim it, Mexico targeted border regions for nationalization efforts to assert the border.[33] In the 1930s, Mexico's assimilationist policies manifested in Chiapas in the form of a campaign of forced acculturation, including forbidding the use of indigenous languages, the burning of indigenous clothing, and installing Hispanicization centers and frontier schools.[34] To secure the Mexican identity of the borderlands, Mexico offered to grant citizenship and land to Guatemalan workers in Chiapas frontier areas.[35] The campaign was most dramatic in border regions where indigenous groups shared ethnic identities and languages with Guatemalans, including Mam, Chuj, Kaqchikel, and K'anjobal.[36] Even though indigenous communities in the highlands of Chiapas were also targeted for integration policies, highland indigenous groups were considered distinctly Mexican. In contrast, indigenous groups at the border were more intensely targeted for assimilation because they shared ethnic affinities with Guatemalan indigenous groups.[37] According to Rosalva Aída Hernández Castillo, "Mexicanization policy fulfilled the political functions of establishing the nation's limits . . . while border inhabitants . . . [came to] represent not only cultural backwardness but also antinationalism."[38] Becoming Mexican at the border necessarily relied on an anti-Guatemalan rhetoric.[39] As of 2010, Chiapas had the second largest number of indigenous language speakers in Mexico,[40] but the border region is one of the least indigenous parts of the state.

As a result of this history, most inhabitants in the Frontera Comalapa region no longer identify with an indigenous group, although they recall that their ancestors were likely indigenous. However, this region was transformed by the arrival of 150,000 to 200,000 indigenous refugees fleeing to Mexico during the height of Guatemala's civil war in the early 1980s.[41] As Guatemalan refugees crossed the border, Mexico feared the conflict would spill into Chiapas and exacerbate mounting land tensions. Mexico adopted the view of the Guatemalan military that the indigenous peoples were *guerilleros*, or members of the guerilla insurgency. Due to their precarious situation, refugees worked for less than minimum wage, attended Mexican schools, and rented land from Mexicans—some were sympathetic and others exploited their vulnerability.[42]

Despite a history of offering asylum to aggrieved populations, Mexico was not a signatory to the 1951 United Nations Refugee Convention and had no legal mechanisms to deal with the prolonged refugee situation.[43] As international pressure mounted and the Guatemalan conflict continued, Mexico changed course and provided the refugees with identity cards in 1983, rather than treating them as illegal migrants. Mexico established refugee camps, but restricted the movements of the refugees, who could not travel outside the camps or purchase land.[44] Identity documents governed the refugees as marginal, temporary inhabitants while guaranteeing their exploitation as local field hands. They were only recognized if they remained in the camps; otherwise they were illegal migrants and vulnerable to deportation.[45] Faustino, a former Guatemalan refugee who now lives on the Mexican side of the border in La Maravilla, related:

> We went to the [refugee camp] since we did not have any other choice. We
> needed to acquire documents as refugees, and we could only get them if we
> were in a camp. Previously, immigration deported many people to Guatemala.
> If we lived in the camp, Mexico would accept us. If not, they would not help
> us. We had to accept how things were because of Mexican law.

Refugees hid their indigenous identity and were afraid to travel out of fear
that Mexican immigration officials would send them home where they feared
for their lives.[46] One woman recalled, "We had to remove our indigenous
clothing [traje] so immigration would not deport us . . . so we would not be
recognized as Guatemalans."

Due to social, ethnic, and land tensions in Chiapas, and close affinities
between Chiapas and Guatemala from historical, kinship, and wage labor
relations, the Mexican government preferred for refugees to be located in
Campeche and Quintana Roo in the Yucatán instead of in Chiapas.[47] In 1984,
Mexico adopted a policy to move the refugees to Campeche and Quintana
Roo and discouraged service providers from aiding those who decided to
remain in Chiapas.[48] Due to geographic, cultural, and physical proximity to
their homes in Guatemala, 18,000 relocated and 25,000 refused.[49] Simeon, a
former refugee who lives in Nueva Vida, Guatemala, lived in Campeche for
six years. He stated, "The Mexican government did not want us in Chiapas.
They would run after us and send us back [to Guatemala], where we could
be killed." After he fell ill, however, he returned to Chiapas to be closer to
family. The Guatemalan military also made several incursions into Mexican
territory, including attacks where refugees resided.[50] The Chiapas governor
also resented the presence of the refugees.[51] Mexican residents remembered
hearing gunshots in the night. Héctor recalled when Guatemalan soldiers accidentally entered his cornfields. He convinced them to leave by informing
them that they were mistakenly in Mexico.

When Mexico offered a path to naturalization in the mid-1990s for refugees who wanted to become Mexican through the Migrant Stabilization Program, this policy was extended in the Yucatán two years prior to Chiapas in
1998.[52] Mexico preferred refugee return; 43,000 refugees returned to their
origin or newly established communities in Guatemala in the 1990s.[53] In
1999, however, it was estimated that 22,000 Guatemalan refugees, with more
than half being born in refugee camps on Mexican soil, would remain.[54] By
2000, 25,000 Central Americans regularized their status in Mexico under

permanent resident or visitor status options for those who would eventually want to return, and 4,700 had naturalized.[55]

Despite integration into Mexico, former refugees remain materially and symbolically excluded from Mexico as they are more likely to lack water, latrines, electricity, land, and respect from their Mexican neighbors.[56] Many remain outsiders, excluded as indigenous populations, which is synonymous with Guatemala in this region. Due to scarce land and resources, many Mexicans viewed the refugees as competition and resented the aid they received. To border Mexicans, indigenous identity, Guatemalan nationality, and "otherness" merge. Some Mexican residents still call them "refugees" and "Guatemalans" despite their naturalization.[57] Since the 1990s, although political, economic, and social reasons for migration blur, Guatemalans are the largest demographic of deportations from Mexico.[58]

The presence of the indigenous refugees was especially contentious in Chiapas after the Zapatista rebellion in 1994, as indigenous identity became equated with subversion. On January 1, 1994, coinciding with the implementation of NAFTA, a guerilla army of a few thousand organized and armed masked indigenous peasants descended from the Lacandón jungle to seize multiple towns and municipalities throughout Chiapas as they demanded a more substantive commitment to democracy, land, identity, and rights. Drawing from the legacy of Emiliano Zapata, a hero of the Mexican Revolution whom peasants remember for his commitment to land reform, they appropriated his name to establish the Zapatista Army of National Liberation, henceforth referred to as the Zapatistas or the EZLN. The confrontation between the Zapatistas and the Mexican army lasted less than a week, but Mexico militarized Chiapas; one-third of the military was stationed in Chiapas in 2001.[59] Mexican President Ernesto Zedillo (1994–2000) postured to negotiate with the Zapatistas and signed the San Andrés Accords in 1996 respecting claims for indigenous rights and autonomy. However, he reneged on the promises shortly thereafter. In 2001, Mexico passed the Law on Indigenous Rights instead. This legislation watered down commitments to indigenous rights and further wedded Mexico to neoliberal multiculturalism, which constituted a limited and regulated form of recognition with no mention of autonomy.[60] Although the legislation passed, nine states were in opposition, including Guerrero, Hidalgo, Oaxaca, and Chiapas—the Mexican states with the largest indigenous populations.[61]

Militarization in Chiapas in response to the Zapatistas manifested in the form of the escalation of temporary and ad hoc military bases and road-blocks, as well as surprise raids throughout the state.[62] The main targets were indigenous communities as militarization played off national narratives and prejudices against indigenous peoples as inferior and threats to the unity of the mestizo nation to render them suspects, subject them to human rights abuses, limit their movement, and inculcate fear.[63] Chiapas has experienced low-intensity warfare since the 1990s, as the government exercised a mix of selective concessions to supporters, harassment, and targeted repression often meted out by allied paramilitary units. A military base by this border route on the Mexican highway was installed in the 1990s.

Chiapas historically served as Mexico's bridge to, and distinction from, Guatemala. From the historical ties that inhabitants shared with Guatema-lans to the specter of indigenous subversion threatening the nation-state sup-posedly emanating from both Guatemalan refugees and Zapatista supporters, Chiapas's inhabitants have embodied the anxieties, fears, and disciplinary impulses of the state to control its borders.

Nation and Ethnicity in Guatemala

In contrast, a more explicit hierarchy between indigenous Maya and *ladinos*, or those of mixed descent who have been Hispanicized and are often coded as nonindigenous, has informed Guatemala's racial division. The *ladino*–indigenous dichotomy was critical to the process of the making of the modern Guatemalan nation-state as the state manipulated the distinction to uphold *ladino* superiority, denigrate the indigenous population while appropriating its labor, and cement Creole elite privileges.[64]

By the mid-1930s, a history of land expropriation, labor conscription, and displacement combined with population increases to aggravate the land and economic pressures faced by indigenous Maya communities.[65] Fed up with elite privilege and influenced by labor and agrarian reforms in Mexico, Gua-temala's swelling middle class overthrew then President Jorge Ubico in 1944, which inaugurated "ten years of spring" of democratic political opening and social reforms from 1944 until the CIA-orchestrated, covert overthrow of former President Jacobo Arbenz in 1954 and the installation of the mili-tary leader, Carlos Casillo Armas.[66] One of the most contentious reforms of the "ten years of spring" included an agrarian reform. This reform posed a threat not only to local landowning elites but also to the interests of foreign capital—most notably the United States–based United Fruit Company. United Fruit had close ties to the U.S. State Department and the CIA, whose director sat on the company's board and was invested in the company.[67] U.S. President Eisenhower came into power promising a tough stance against communism, and Guatemala provided a place to enact a precedent for the U.S.'s developing Cold War covert operations strategy to contain communism.[68]

After the coup, Guatemalan society and governing institutions were increasingly militarized as Maya and *ladino* leftists and peasants organized to contest the state's brutal crackdown on reform.[69] Guerilla groups formed among the leftist opposition in the 1970s as the growing leftist insurgency movements contested state and army repression.[70] The conflict escalated into a thirty-six-year civil war from 1960 to 1996, with the Guatemalan army receiving funds and training from the United States in the name of combating communism.[71] Targeted violence early in the conflict transformed into the widespread militarization and the "scorched earth" policies inaugurated by then President Efraín Ríos Montt in the early 1980s to contain the "internal enemy," which was deliberately tied to eliminating the Maya.[72] Maya men, women, and children were tortured, killed, and terrorized as everyday forms of community were attacked and the army reorganized and resettled communities along military models of control.[73] The military mandated cooperation or designation as the enemy, instituting a system of civil defense patrols (PACs) in 1983 as part of a form of psychological warfare to divide communities and mandate community members to inform the military of suspicious activities that could be linked to the guerillas.[74] Contrary to the military's claims that the guerillas committed a substantial portion of the atrocities, according to the Truth Commission for Historical Clarification Report issued between 1997 and 1999, genocide was committed against the indigenous population. Of the 200,000 deaths, 83 percent were borne by the Maya while the state and allied paramilitary units were responsible for 93 percent of atrocities.[75]

The end of the war and signing of the Peace Accords in 1996 represented a victor's peace for the elite.[76] Many Guatemalan border residents who collaborated with the military assert that "the army won the war." The social, ethnic, and economic grievances underlying the conflict, including land concentration, economic inequality, poverty, elite privilege, and racism, remain. Poverty is concentrated in rural areas, where over half of the population resides, and especially in indigenous communities.[77]

The Border Communities

The Mexican border communities are located in the municipality of Frontera Comalapa in the Fronteriza region of Chiapas. As of 2010, 80.3 percent of the population of Frontera Comalapa lived in poverty and nearly 66 percent over the age of fifteen had not completed primary school.[78] Although inhabitants of Frontera Comalapa do not identify with an indigenous group, they recognize an indigenous heritage. There were nearly 100 camps hosting Guatemalan indigenous refugees by the mid-1980s in Chiapas. Most camps were clustered near the border, with Frontera Comalapa being one of the main settlement areas.[79] Indigenous refugees who were naturalized in the late 1990s and early 2000s also established communities and homes in this region.

The Guatemalan border communities are located in the municipality of La Democracia in the department (Guatemala's equivalent of a state) of Huehuetenango, which is one of the most linguistically and ethnically diverse departments of Guatemala. Although in 2012 57.5 percent of Huehuetenango identified as indigenous, La Democracia has a smaller population that identifies with an indigenous group (especially compared to the highlands) at about 44 percent.[80] Along with other western departments, Huehuetenango has 25 percent of the worst poverty and development indicators.[81] As of 2011, over 60 percent of the population in Huehuetenango (down from over 70 percent in 2006) lived in poverty and 9.6 percent (down from over 20 percent in 2006) experienced extreme poverty.[82] Similar to Frontera Comalapa, Guatemalan border regions have generated new forms of employment around undocumented migration, drugs, and the sex trade. The vigor of the border has led Huehuetenango and La Democracia to transform into important points for informal and extra-legal trade.[83] Telling of the rapid regional changes, La Democracia registered the most homicides in the department of Huehuetenango in 2012; Huehuetenango is the department that experienced the largest relative increase in homicides from 1996 to 2010.[84]

Three Mexican communities reside along this unmonitored route. To protect the location of the route and its inhabitants, I call them Santa Rosa, El Nance, and La Maravilla. The majority of Mexican residents in this border route do not identify as indigenous, but there is a small community of naturalized former Guatemalan refugees in La Maravilla who identify with the Mam ethnic group. Most children in La Maravilla were born in Mexico and do not speak Mam.

Entering the route from the Mexican side of the Pan-American Highway, one first encounters Santa Rosa. Santa Rosa is an *ejido*, or a community based on collective land tenure with about 400 families. Currently, most properties are privately held and farmed. Due to land pressures, in 2007, Santa Rosa halted new *ejido* entries. Up a steep, half-paved hill from the main border road and between Santa Rosa and El Nance lies La Maravilla. La Maravilla is home to about thirty families of former indigenous Guatemalan refugees and their mostly Mexican-born children. A group of indigenous Mam living in diverse refugee camps in Chiapas united to establish La Maravilla in 2000 after deciding to naturalize as Mexicans. They chose to stay in Mexico rather than return to Guatemala mostly *"por los hijos"* (for the children), residents say, believing Mexico offered better economic, educational, and peaceful prospects for their children. Adult residents received Mexican citizenship documents with the aid of the Mexican government agency COMAR (Mexican Commission for Refugee Assistance) in the early 2000s.[85] Because inhabitants of La Maravilla do not own farmland, most rent land from, or work for, their Mexican neighbors. In this role, they occupy similar niches to, while competing with, Guatemalan day laborers who have historically crossed the border to work on Mexican farms and continue to do so.

El Nance is composed of about 100 families of small private property owners. Some residents have over thirty hectares of land whereas others are landless. The main form of livelihood in Santa Rosa, El Nance, and La Maravilla is subsistence corn farming, but there are small store owners and a small rising class of professionals including teachers, nurses, politicians, accountants, and engineers. To find employment, however, most commute or move to larger regional cities. Some residents cultivate coffee, beans, and peanuts for consumption and small sales, but the majority of time and land is devoted to corn. In El Nance, some residents have developed a more lucrative niche in cattle raising; some sell cattle across the border to Guatemala.

The rural appearance of the border belies the extent to which residents are, and have long been, integrated into regional and transnational commercial networks. More youth are completing technical high school, and a few are pursuing university degrees. Still, between 43 and 48 percent of Santa Rosa's and El Nance's residents over the age of fifteen have not completed primary school.[86] Many families have lived at the border for generations, but nearly all Mexican border residents recognize their recent kinship connections to Guatemala. Others trace their residence along the border to the extension of the Pan-American

Highway in the 1940s and early 1950s, when their relatives were recruited from other Mexican municipalities and states as construction laborers.

Two Guatemalan border communities reside a few miles up the road from their Mexican counterparts, located in the municipality of La Democracia in the department of Huehuetenango. One community, which I call El Girasol, is inhabited by about 120 families, who are largely *ladino*, or nonindigenous, peasants. About eighty families of resettled former Guatemalan refugees who identify with the Mam ethnic group inhabit the neighboring community, which I call Nueva Vida.

Most inhabitants of Nueva Vida were originally from the highlands of Huehuetenango near San Ildefonso Ixtahuacán; they fled the scorched earth tactics of the counterinsurgency war in 1980–1981. After residing in refugee camps for over a decade, they began searching for land to return to Guatemala. A group of refugees found this plot near the border, which they thought offered better access to commerce, land, and safety than their origin communities. Settling in 1993 prior to the Peace Accords, they were among the first refugees to return to Guatemala. Simeon called Nueva Vida a test case: "We were one of the first ones to go back. Everyone was watching, so it was important to Guatemala that we had no problems." There was still a small military outpost in El Girasol, and some residents did not want the former refugees. Simeon related, "They called us refugees *guerilleros* . . . they wanted us to go back where we came from."

The border location provided various benefits. It enabled former refugees to maintain connections they had made in Mexico while it also made return to Mexico relatively simple if violence resumed. They heard stories of others who had participated in government-organized collective returns to distant, marginal lands or who had returned to their origin communities to encounter hostility from those who had remained and, in many cases, had taken their land.[87] Simeon was wary of the government-organized returns because, as he related, "The government . . . and the organizations bought the land, but you had to go where they said." He knew people who had been sent to places where the land was less arable and they felt unsafe. The Guatemalan government would not have permitted them to settle at the border through the official return process because, as Simeon said, they were "afraid of subversive influence. So we organized ourselves and presented ourselves not as *guerilleros* . . . even though some of us were . . . not as organized in this way with the leftists, but as people who wanted to live here peacefully." Nueva

Vida received assistance from CEAR (Special Commission for Attention to the Displaced, Returnees, and Refugees), FONAPAZ (The National Fund for Peace), FORELAP (The Fund for Labor and Productive Reinsertion of the Returnee Population), and UNHCR. They purchased the land parcel through FORELAP under a loan with payments over ten years.[88]

Residents of Nueva Viva, like their counterparts who remained in Mexico, also cited rights, land, and more freedom and opportunities as reasons for their postwar settlement decision but, in their case, for returning to Guatemala. As one resident asserted, "[In Guatemala] we have rights. In Mexico we can only rent land, or people have to purchase land in the name of their children because they have no rights. Here [in Guatemala] we know we can buy land, and no one can take it from us." He was referring to the long process of naturalization. Despite Mexico's promise to provide a path to naturalization in Chiapas in 1998, most residents in La Maravilla received documents between 2003 and 2005. Lack of documents left people in economic and political limbo for years. Without documents, they could not purchase land. Instead, parents bought land in the names of their Mexican-born children. Some were still struggling to transfer these rights. Many feared that Mexicans could take away their land. There was a basis for this fear; residents of La Gloria (another community of naturalized former refugees in Chiapas) reportedly had to purchase their land three times. The land in Nueva Vida is a *finca*, which operates similarly to an *ejido* in the sense that everyone has a right to the land, which is then passed down to children.

El Girasol, in contrast, is composed of individually owned housing plots. A few individuals identify as Mam, but the majority identify as *ladino*. The land previously belonged to one man who passed it down to his three sons who began selling off parcels in the 1980s during the war, the last of which was purchased by Nueva Vida in 1993. During the war, residents of El Girasol complied with military mandates to engage in civil patrols. Because they never directly witnessed violence or encountered guerillas, many inhabitants of El Girasol believed that the military protected them. Their views contrast with their neighbors in Nueva Vida, who witnessed the army's brutality in the highlands. At first both communities were suspicious of one another. Residents of Nueva Vida recall young men hiding in the bushes in El Girasol with masks to scare them. When civil society groups provided workshops in Nueva Vida in the mid-1990s on the Peace Accords, Maya culture, women's rights, and indigenous rights, people in El Girasol believed that the guerillas were brainwashing them. With time, in addition to the imperatives to collaborate not only to establish a joint primary school but also to ensure a stable climate for cross-border commerce, the communities began to coexist relatively peacefully. However, differences reemerge around political issues and elections, especially prominent during the first 2007 campaign of former President Otto Pérez Molina (2012–2015), a former military officer during the counterinsurgency war and an advocate of *mano dura* approaches. Pedro, an elderly resident of Nueva Vida, feared they would have to start patrolling their community, which reminded him of the wartime civil patrols. Residents in Nueva Vida pointed to El Girasol as a support base for Pérez Molina. There is also little intermarriage between the communities; youth in Girasol are more likely to have Mexican spouses than spouses from Nueva Vida.

Compared with their Mexican neighbors, Guatemalan border residents have less land that is also less conducive to farming due to rockier soil. Many either work on coffee plantations near the municipal seat of La Democracia and in nearby Camojá or rent or work the lands of their Mexican neighbors as inhabitants of Huehuetenango have done for generations.[89] Some residents in Nueva Vida are involved in corn smuggling, but most remain in marginal roles like cargo loading. Class differences are becoming starker in El Girasol as many are involved as intermediaries in the corn smuggling business, and a few men have recently earned more substantial profits smuggling coffee and sugar.

Fraught Ethnonationalist Spaces

The nation-state's anxieties about the fit among culture, economy, and geography often play out at borders.[90] Frontiers and borders are integral to the definition of the state, although they always threaten to undermine its control. The majority of the protagonists in this book no longer identify with an indigenous identity, but they occupy fraught ethnonational spaces where the Mexican and Guatemalan states have sought to assimilate, pacify, marginalize, or extinguish indigenous peoples and border populations. At the same time, border populations have creatively found ways to bend the border and its unequal relationships to their benefit.[91] However, as this region becomes a geopolitical hotspot to contain illicit flows and encourage transnational investment, narratives of threat and illegality that reflect political, economic, and racial prejudices in the region reemerge with renewed vigor.

2 Documenting National Life

You know that Chiapas is only [part of Mexico] because it was bought. You see [the word] Chiapaneco (Chiapan) is very close to the word chapín [slang for Guatemalan].

—Guatemalan customs agent

ROSA AND FANI ARE BEST FRIENDS. Both are nineteen and preparing to take exams to become teachers. They live in neighboring communities on the Guatemalan side of the border. Rosa lives in Nueva Vida, the community formed in 1993 of Mam indigenous families that returned to Guatemala after living in refuge in Mexico. Fani and her family have lived in adjacent El Girasol for generations. The girls stand out from their peers for their desire to pursue a university education. Both laugh at the prospect of getting married, preferring to play basketball and continue their studies. Rosa's mother wears her traditional *corte* (indigenous skirt characteristic of her village of origin in San Ildefonso Ixtahuacán), weaves, and is the president of Nueva Vida's women's committee. Rosa has *traje* (indigenous skirt, *corte*, and blouse, *huipil*) but does not wear it. She and her mother speak Mam together, and her father is a migrant in Florida. Fani is tall and slim, and her eyes have a tint of green. Her father works as an intermediary in the corn smuggling business. Her father was born in Mexico but raised in Guatemala by his aunts. Rosa's uncle was murdered in La Democracia in the early 1980s by the Guatemalan army during the war, which prompted her mother to flee to Mexico. In contrast, Fani's father served in the Guatemalan army-mandated civil patrols during the war,[1] believing he was maintaining his community's safety against insurgents. Both girls know their tense family histories but view the war as part of a past they did not directly experience. It does not influence their friendship.

Rosa was born in a refugee camp in Chiapas and Fani in El Girasol, Guatemala. Rosa's mother brought her back to Guatemala as a small child. Both

49

girls possess Mexican and Guatemalan birth certificates; each documents that they were born in that country. They tell me that they identify as "a bit Mexican and a bit Guatemalan." They vote only in Guatemala, but debate obtaining citizenship documents in Mexico as well. Rosa's and Fani's brothers used their Mexican birth certificates, despite living in Guatemala, to more easily pass through Mexico to migrate to the United States. Although Mexico and Guatemala now permit dual nationality, it was not allowed when any of them were born. Nor, obviously, can someone be born in two countries simultaneously. A child born in Guatemala to Mexican parents is entitled to Mexican nationality due to the nationality of his or her parents. When the child receives a Mexican birth certificate, however, it should state the location of his or her birth and the nationality of the parents. It should not say they were born where they were not.

One May evening as I attended the Mother's Day school dances in El Nance, Mexico, I saw children running around in costumes as clowns and cowboys on the basketball court. I was surprised to see twelve-year-old Daniela posing with the fifth grade clowns for my pictures. I knew Daniela lived on the Guatemalan side of the border. "What are you doing here?" I asked her after the photos. "I go to school here." She elaborated, "I am also Mexican. I have papers so I can attend school here." "So you were born here in Mexico?" I asked. She giggled, "Well, actually, no. I was born in the United States. But my parents brought me back here as a baby. So I am all three." She explained how her parents acquired birth certificates for her from all three countries even though they live in Guatemala. At one point, her parents had also lived in Santa Rosa, Mexico. Her parents lived straddling three countries, illustrating the complexities of defining nationality. At first, Daniela's story confused me—three nationalities? Born in one country, living in another, and attending school in yet another? Trying to sort out her family's migration history was messy to say the least. And she was also not the only one. There were a handful of children who lived on the Guatemalan side who walked a mile downhill each day past the white border monuments to attend school in Mexico.

I realized the extent of multiple nationalities—individuals like Fani, Rosa, and Daniela—when I conducted a survey with fifth and sixth graders on both sides of the border on national and ethnic identities.[2] When I asked from where students had birth certificates, I was surprised that many children circled Mexico and Guatemala. At first I thought that perhaps only children in Nueva Vida might have two birth certificates because, like Rosa, many were born in Mexico to Guatemalan parents when their parents were refugees. As a child of Guatemalans, their parents can take the child's birth certificate, along with their own and another form of identification such as a voting card or passport, to a RENAP (National Registry of Persons) office to register their child as Guatemalan. The child then receives a Guatemalan birth certificate that identifies the child as being born in Mexico to Guatemalan parents. It is required to bring both parents' documents if both are listed on the child's birth certificate, meaning that, given a history of war and flight, this could present a barrier.[3]

Many parents lacked these documents or access to information on this process. It was easier to petition the municipality in Democracia for new birth certificates that certify the children were born in Guatemala. It was simpler to claim that the original documents had burned with the municipal building during the war than to attempt to acquire nationality on the basis of having Guatemalan parents. Or maybe, I thought, this condition of multiple nationalities also applied to the naturalized Mexicans in La Maravilla who may have retained their Guatemalan documents even after naturalizing as Mexicans. I was surprised to encounter multiple nationalities not only among families with histories of exile, refuge, return, and naturalization but also among people whose families had lived at the border for generations, like Fani and Daniela. Their birth certificates did not certify they were born in Mexico to Guatemalan parents or vice versa; each claimed they were born in that country.

Border residents have intermarried and informally pursued dual nationality for themselves and their children for generations, but the refugee situation heightened the issue of dual nationality, introduced new processes, and revealed fissures in border residents' associations among nationality, legality, and ethnicity. In Guatemala programs were established to redocument former refugees who had left and lost their documents. However, many former refugees like Rosa's mother distrusted the government and chose to register their Mexican-born children on return as if they had been born in Guatemala. In Mexico, government agencies like COMAR helped naturalize former Guatemalans, which introduced an official element into a historically informal process. Due to the difficulty that foreigners often face when seeking to naturalize in Mexico, assistance to the refugees provoked resentment among many border residents who have long sought to naturalize their spouses.

At the border, dual national documents help people fulfill daily social, economic, and familial obligations that cross borders. Border residents desire

Figure 2.1. Dual-national children (a) in their Mexican home with the flag and (b) at their grandparents' home in El Girasol, Guatemala, in front of the Guatemalan flag. These children have birth certificates from both Mexico and Guatemala.

SOURCE: Author photos.

multiple national documents for their children to, in the words of one resident, "give them the most opportunities," referring to the ability to work, live, marry, and travel in either country (Figures 2.1a and 2.1b). Mexican nationality gives people more options if they want to migrate to the United States, enabling them to pass through Mexico's increasing surveillance posts. Without documents in Mexico, individuals cannot legally marry despite the fact that cross-border romantic relationships are common. However, for border residents, laws regarding dual nationality and national registration are ambiguous in both countries and not well monitored in practice. Additional confusion arose at the border when Mexico revised its Nationality Law to lift restrictions prohibiting dual nationality in 1997 (which went into effect in 1998), especially because this occurred in the midst of the refugee integration and naturalization processes. However, Mexico made this revision in the interests of courting its large population in the United States.[4] Rather than allowing for the active pursuit of dual nationality, which some diplomats and officials

b

feared could lead to an influx of Central Americans,[5] the reform just guarantees the non-loss, or permanence, of Mexican nationality for Mexicans by
birth.[6] Mexicans by birth who naturalize abroad always retain their Mexican
nationality and can recover it if they previously lost it upon naturalizing in
another country.[7] In contrast, for those who become Mexican through naturalization, exclusive citizenship still applies.[8] In 1996, Guatemala also began to

recognize dual nationality, provided that both nationalities are not exercised simultaneously and the other country permits it.[9] Due to the recent changes, and lack of clarity in how they are applied, many border residents did not know whether and how they and their children could be dual nationals. What occurs in practice, therefore, has little relation to the law. When I spoke with a representative at the Guatemalan consulate in the United States, she also referenced the lack of clarity; at first, she too, was uncertain if she could keep her Guatemalan nationality. Border residents capitalize on the illegibility of official procedures to obtain multiple national documents through informal or illegal means that enable them to live their lives across borders. The actual documents are real, not fakes, even though people obtain them through extralegal avenues.

By focusing on how residents navigate the border and evaluate acquiring multiple national documents,[10] I go beyond reductionist assumptions of law-breaking to examine how the law is not neutral but is instead influenced by personal discretion and judgments, class differences, nationalist ideologies, racism, and personal experiences. As I tried to decipher whether it was legal for border residents to have dual nationality and how to legally acquire it, I realized that focusing on the law was beside the point. Instead, the necessities of daily life, as well as the individual discretion, power, and politics of state officials and local inhabitants, shaped how the law was applied and dual nationality was practiced.[11] As Madeleine Reeves documents in Moscow, uncertainties around the "authenticity" of documents illuminate the racial politics animating who is considered a target for scrutiny and suspicion.[12] As border residents struggle to document themselves across two countries, they ironically produce a "state effect."[13] Their documentary practices work to bring the state into being, meaning that the nation-state comes to appear as an abstract, powerful, and unitary, if often illegible, entity even as they technically evade the state's legal requirements and reveal the tenuous negotiations underlying states' claims to territorial integrity and rationality.[14]

Feeling Crossed

National identity is complicated at the border where individuals encounter and renegotiate colliding national discourses in their daily lives. As Rosalva Aída Hernández Castillo explains, "Border identities confront not only cultural traditions but also the way 'the tradition' itself is defined."[15] The tensions between belonging and exclusion that characterize the borderlands, in addition to vacillating border enforcement, contextualize the strategies that border residents pursue to enact livelihoods that depend on, resist, and reshape the border.

Geographically removed from the centers of both nation-states and their dominant cultural and linguistic norms, Mexicans often believe that border residents share more in common with Guatemala, whereas Guatemalans in the interior assert that Guatemalans at the border are Mexicanized. This positions border residents as "neither here nor there"[16] even as they use their ability to cross borders to their advantage. Rosa, who was born in a Mexican refugee camp to Guatemalan parents and now lives on the Guatemalan side of the border, told me that Guatemalans "say we are Mexicans. At school [in La Democracia] we ask for a *refresco* [soft drink] since we live near Mexico, and that is what they say in Mexico. But people in La Democracia laugh at us and say we are Mexican because in Guatemala they call a *refresco* an *agua*." *Regionalismos* (words used in the region) at times cross the border, and often do not, differentiating even people who speak the same language. The necessities of everyday life at the border depend on fluidity, crossing, and the manipulation of social and ethnic identities.[17]

Many border residents espouse strong nationalist sentiments while others portray a fluid notion of belonging. When I asked seventy-four-year-old Mexican border resident Héctor if he felt Mexican or Guatemala, he interlinked his fingers together to argue that he felt as if the border crossed his very body. He responded, "I feel both." Héctor's parents were from Guatemala, and all of his siblings were born there. After his father died, his pregnant mother crossed the border for work opportunities and gave birth to Héctor in Mexico. He related, "People from all over the border [region] have always been coming from Guatemala." One border resident told me he felt "crossed," which exemplified overlapping sentiments of belonging to both Mexico and Guatemala. The notion of feeling crossed lends itself to multiple interpretations, especially regarding the intersecting identities experienced at the border, including national, ethic, religious, social, and class borders.[18] Border residents are not referring to the multiple postmodern interpretations raised by the border metaphor.[19] Being crossed referred to the exigencies of living daily lives that span borders. Residents may feel that they belong to two countries while they simultaneously experience exclusion from both nations. Others strongly identify with one nationality even as this identification is in constant tension and relation with another across the border. Residents realize their identities and border lives cannot be conceptualized or actualized without considering the mutual imbrication of both nationalities on their histories, genealogies, and the practicalities of daily life. Another resident added, "I have a Guatemalan flag on the right side of my forehead and a Mexican one on the other side." His friend laughed, "And a United States one," referring to the amount of time he had spent there.

Even as some border residents identify with both nations, others strongly espouse the state-centric view that associates exclusive national identity with one territory. Mexican border resident Tito asked me: "How can someone be from two places?" Yet even people who believe that their ethnic and national identities are rooted in one national territory cross legal, national, socioeconomic, and ethnic borders nearly every day.

In daily life the border often appears to be nonexistent due to the lack of an official state presence, but it nevertheless politicizes mundane actions. Depending on their own relations with state officials, resources, and knowledge of policing patterns, residents are aware of how simply visiting friends in a neighboring community, marrying someone from across the border, and bringing goods across to sell may be viewed through the criminalized lenses of smuggling and unauthorized border crossing.[20] I regularly provided rides to border residents within this route to visit friends or attend parties, often forgetting how we were crossing the geopolitical, yet unmonitored, border.[21] When my friend in El Girasol, Guatemala, Francisca, hosted a birthday party for her son, I was the chauffer for her Mexican friends who did not have a car. After a few months in the field, I did not think much about taking them to Francisca's house in El Girasol, Guatemala, and then back to their homes in Santa Rosa, Mexico. I had naturalized the nonexistence of the border even as it inevitably conditioned a wide range of extralegal commerce. Driving them in this manner would have been risky when officials monitored this route prior to the mid-1990s, thereby illustrating the contingency and political construction of illegality, as well as of the border itself. Although the borderline may seem inconsequential on a daily basis, in an increasingly securitized climate that elevates the risk-based premiums associated with illegal activities, it is also a potential resource that has led savvy residents to convert the small-scale smuggling of goods into larger businesses. It is what makes their cross-border businesses possible, profitable, and risky.

As the Mexico–Guatemala border becomes increasingly treacherous for Central Americans to cross due to more official checkpoints, official corruption, and the presence of gangs and drug cartels, border residents' networks continue to provide them with a degree of mobility. Some residents like Fani and Rosa have multiple national documents that enable freedom of movement, but others rely on border knowledge and relationships with particular authorities.

A Car Can't Have Two Nationalities, but a Person Can

As one resident told me, "We feel at home on both sides [of the border]"; daily social, economic, and kinship relations span the border. For example, currency usage transcends and complicates the border. Guatemalan border intermediaries sell Mexican corn to Guatemalan merchants for Mexican pesos, and stores on both sides accept pesos and quetzales. Because only Guatemalan cell phones work on both sides of the border route (Mexican cell phones do not get reception even on the Mexican side), women sell Guatemalan phone cards in Guatemalan quetzales on both sides. Television, cable, and radio stations cross the border in complex fashion. Tito's family has a Mexican landline phone, but they all have Guatemalan cell phones. The costs to call me in the United States from their Guatemalan cell phones are actually lower than to call their own Mexican landline. Residents receive broadcast television service from Mexico, cable from Guatemala, and radio stations from both nations.

Although the immigration office at the nearby official border crossing at Ciudad Cuauhtémoc, Mexico, and La Mesilla, Guatemala, issues free temporary local passes to border residents living between Huehuetenango, Guatemala, and Comitán, Chiapas, to travel as far as Comitán or Huehuetenango respectively, most border residents do not acquire passes because the official post is out of the way and they know people and the region. I soon learned when I needed to go through the official border versus when it was a similar nuisance to what residents encountered. Beyond Comitán in Mexico, residents knew they needed a passport and that Mexico was stricter, but one resident told me Guatemalan local passes were seldom enforced, arguing you could get as far as El Salvador. Although I crossed the border almost every day, I have only a few Guatemalan stamps in my passport, from before I learned how to cross the border and from when I went on more extended excursions to the capital.

Beyond Comitán in Chiapas, Mexico, and Huehuetenango in Guatemala was when officials usually began checking documents.[22] Accusations of corruption levied against immigration agents are common. Residents argue that immigration agents charge for border passes even though they should not. I also experienced sporadic enforcement. Sometimes I was charged to officially enter Guatemala, and other times I was not. There is also a fumigation charge for the wheels of a vehicle when crossing the border. Some residents surmise this may just be water or air. Border inspectors charge a fee to cross the border in a personal vehicle, which with the fumigation charges usually amounts to about US$10. Yet the rates varied. Fani's brother is a taxi driver. Although he occasionally provides rides to people to the Mexican side of the border, he drives primarily in Guatemala because he has only a Guatemalan license plate and license. Because he also has Mexican nationality, he told me he could acquire a Mexican license, but he would need to use the license plate on a different car. "So a car can't have two nationalities, but a person can?" I asked. "I guess you could say that," he laughed, explaining that otherwise it is difficult for the country to keep track of the vehicle and to register where it is entering and exiting. Guatemalan border residents generally seek a ride in a Mexican vehicle beyond the border route to avoid detection by authorities because vehicles with foreign license plates stand out more than individuals.

It is relatively simple to cross even at the nearby official border in Ciudad Cuauhtémoc, Mexico, and La Mesilla, Guatemala. At the time, no one systematically verified that people passed through immigration and received the appropriate stamps. I once encountered a bus of confused U.S. tourists who did not know that when their Guatemalan van dropped them at the border that they were supposed to check out with Guatemalan immigration and check in with Mexican immigration before boarding a Mexican minivan to their next destination. One could easily get on the next van without checking in at either office. However, Mexico has implemented more checkpoints in the interior, including customs and immigration inspection posts throughout Chiapas, as well as mobile military, customs, and immigration checkpoints that seem to disappear and reappear with little notice. Mexico's official border crossings with Guatemala may still be relatively porous, but Mexico has tightened security at "belts of control" along strategic highway routes to curtail unauthorized flows.[23]

In this context, Guatemalan border residents use personal connections to traverse the border. During the Easter holidays Francisca (from El Girasol, Guatemala) invited me to go with her family to the Lagos de Colón (lakes) near Chamic, Mexico. We would need to travel the Mexican portion of the Pan-American Highway to get there. Once Guatemalan residents exited the border road to the Mexican highway they were often wary about travel. Francisca usually asked for a ride from a Mexican border resident when she needed to travel the Mexican highway to shop in nearby Las Champas or Frontera Comalapa. As I got into her son's Guatemalan pickup, I began to worry. I offered to take them because my car had a Mexican license plate. Francisca, the same woman who told me how Mexican officials, who were intermittently stationed in the border route from the 1960s through the 1990s, used to confiscate even a package of cookies if you crossed the border with them, brushed off my concerns. She explained that officials were lenient around the holidays. They knew people were just going to *pasear* (for a brief outing). If not, she knew she could talk to whoever was patrolling the checkpoint at Chamic. Francisca knew Rigo, the man from El Nance who works for immigration. She reasoned that he is often stationed in Chamic. "Everyone knows him. [If he's not there], we mention his name, and [the officials] understand. We explain we are from [the border] and just going to the lake." Our car was never stopped during the outing.

In contrast to Francisca's knowledge, when I visited an immigration office in Comitán, I met three women being detained from further in the Guatemalan interior. They complained about their detention; they were awaiting deportation on suspicion of the attempt to migrate to the United States, but they had just wanted to go shopping. One woman related, "It was stupid, [we] wish we knew to get a [border] pass. But [the agents] didn't let us return on our own and took us here [to detention]. [We explained it was an] innocent mistake, but they did not understand and locked us up like this." Lacking border networks like Francisca, these women were unaware that interior inspections had become stricter.

I also learned how to navigate the border, while acknowledging how my race and citizenship provided a layer of protection my informants lacked. Even so, I was routinely checked at the Mexican military base near the border crossing, where soldiers frequently erected temporary inspections for cars coming from Guatemala and the market in La Mesilla. In contrast, I saw residents who I knew were smuggling coffee breeze through without being stopped. Foreign tourists are often suspected of transporting drugs; La Mesilla is a popular tourist crossing.

In the gap between the geopolitical and the enforced border (for example, in Comitán), possessing multiple national documents and the social, political, and economic resources of border residence are critical. Those without border capital who cannot convincingly perform belonging,[24] however, like distant migrants, or those who appear to be indigenous and, hence, out of place, are more vulnerable to inconsistent or corrupt authorities, unpredictable checkpoints, and criminals and gangs.

The Life of Documents

One woman in El Nance, Mexico asserted, "If you do not have *papeles* [papers or documents], you have no guarantee to life." The document itself comes to stand in for, and become detached from, what it purportedly represents, having a power unto itself whose very instability begets the possibility of the forgery.[25] The falsified document, or the real document obtained via extralegal means, is used to signal national belonging. Yet it also reveals what Veena Das calls the "illegibility" of state power at the margins as it is the very "unreadability of [the state's] rules and regulations" that enable the forgery and make the state feel hauntingly present even as it is either absent or being undermined.[26] The state and the law feel absent to border residents who lack access to official processes to obtain nationality documents, whereas residing at the margins makes these documents even more vital. For rural borderlanders, distanced from the centers of government power, engaging bureaucracy is not only arduous but also uncertain and often stigmatizing.[27] Daniel Goldstein refers to this simultaneous "absent presence" of the state as the "phantom state," whereby the state's rules and laws exist but seldom materialize.[28] The power of the state is also felt, and brought into being, through its more magical or haunting manifestations generated by this very absent presence and everyday practices of rumor, mockery, and mimicry.[29] The uncertain search for documents reproduces the engagement between the margins and the state and may extend insecurity and suspicion; however, it also provides space for people to devise alternatives and to "adopt the appearances of legality while lacking the law's true approbation."[30]

Obtaining national documents from both Mexico and Guatemala is ideal to engage in cross-border life. Yet the document's power routinely fails to hold due to the unstable foundations and relations of power undergirding even the legal document. The document, real or false, is always subject to those who read and interpret it.[31] On the Mexican side of the border, documents and their claims to what they represent are mediated through ethnicity, class, and politics to locate people and determine belonging. For documents to function, borderlanders and migrants struggle to perform the national and racial scripts they represent to officials and to one another, whereas immigration officials retain the discretion to interrupt their claims.[32]

Official Mexican and Guatemalan attitudes toward national identity embody anything but the fluidity characterizing border life. In Mexico, the change to permit dual nationality was intended to enable Mexicans living abroad in the United States to invest and buy property at home and to make Mexican nationality by birth permanent.[33] It did not have in mind those living on the Mexico–Guatemala border who live their daily lives between two nations. Even though Guatemala permits dual nationality, most border residents are either unaware of or lack the resources and information to acquire it for their children. Immigration officials informed me that one first needs to acquire a passport, a complex bureaucratic process involving fees most border residents cannot afford and documents they may not have, in addition to trips to Guatemala City, a seven- to eight-hour bus ride from the border. The Guatemalan consulate, in contrast, told me that Guatemalan parents can register a Mexico-born child in any RENAP office, including one in Huehuetenango, and that a voting card can be used instead of a passport. Removed politically, economically, and geographically from the national and regional centers, Mexican and Guatemalan border residents lack access to, and knowledge about, official dual nationality and national registration procedures for children whose parents are of mixed nationalities.

Belonging is further complicated at the border due to an understanding I call *border citizenship*, which describes how those living along this border route assert that the right to work in the local contraband economy and levy tolls on smugglers is based on border residence. At times, national identity overlaps or competes with sentiments of border belonging. The individuals who are most capable of capitalizing on, and effectively performing, multiple forms of belonging—national and border—have the most economic, social, and political capital. In effect, long-term border residence and narratives that fuse nationality, politics, and ethnicity, independent of the actual documents, determine who can assert certain rights, claims, and resources.

The treatment of former indigenous refugees in the border region exemplifies regional politics of nationality, race, and ethnicity. Mexicans in the borderlands, who historically embodied elastic identities, began to more strongly assert their Mexican identities after the massive flows of Guatemalan refugees in the 1980s began to shift the border region into a security arena.[34] In spite of their legal documents, many long-term Mexican border residents exclude the residents of La Maravilla, who are former refugees from Guatemala, from belonging to the border. The other two Mexican border communities prohibit La Maravilla from levying tolls on cross-border contraband. They justify this exclusion by arguing that, because the residents of La Maravilla arrived in 2000, they did not contribute to building the border road in the 1980s and therefore have no right to its proceeds. Some Mexican neighbors, based on political sentiments stemming from the Guatemalan war in the 1980s, doubt the moral integrity of former refugees. Mexican border resident Lorenzo claimed the former refugees did not deserve rights. He asserted, "Those people are *guerilleros*. They are from Guatemala. The subversives came here. Now their children are Mexican, but [their parents] are refugees." I questioned, "But didn't they naturalize and now have documents?" "I don't think so," he continued, "and if they do [have documents], they are not like ours. It is different. Have any of them shown you [their documents]? It is not so easy to naturalize." War politics and land scarcity, coupled with recent settlement, render residents of La Maravilla local second-class citizens and infuse the reading of their documents. Mexico also places many limitations on the rights of naturalized citizens. Most liberal democracies guarantee the same political rights to those born in the country as to those who naturalize, except that many do reserve certain rights for select high-level government and intelligence positions.[35] However, in Mexico, Mexicans via naturalization cannot occupy a wide variety of posts spanning the branches of government and cannot have another nationality, in contrast to Mexicans by birth.

At the border, though, there are many Guatemalans who have lived in Mexico with their Mexican partners and families for decades. Lorenzo's son has been partnered with a Guatemalan woman who has been unable to naturalize for eight years. He asked, "If it were so easy, then why doesn't she have papers? She didn't enter as a subversive hiding in the mountains . . . but married." Many of these individuals lack the Mexican citizenship documents that the former refugees possess. Their long-term residence and socioeconomic and political connections, however, enable them not only to have access to resources but to assert that they have more of a right to be Mexican than former refugees, whom some Mexican border residents continue to refer to as Guatemalans or refugees.[36] National and border systems of belonging often clash, fostering a dynamic where official documents enable individuals to claim national identity and citizenship rights, but local hierarchies of politics, ethnicity, and class determine how rights can be realized and their material effects.

Mexico offered a path to naturalization in Chiapas in 1998 for former refugees who wished to remain. Because Mexico does not allow those who naturalize to retain their nationality of origin, and Guatemala permits dual nationality except when the country into which Guatemalans naturalize prohibits it, refugees who naturalized legally cannot retain Guatemalan nationality.[37] Yet many retained their documents if they had not lost them during the war and refugee period. Documents were useful because many people still owned land and had family in Guatemala. As one resident of La Maravilla related, "No one told us to give them back or came collecting the [documents]." Currently, nearly all[38] of the inhabitants of La Maravilla possess official Mexican documents, but they realized they had few guarantees of economic, cultural, and social rights in Mexico. Once receiving documents, naturalized Mexicans were largely left to themselves as COMAR withdrew. They continue to lack adequate access to water, drainage, and farmable land. Their children attend schools that teach only Mexican culture and history.[39] There are few opportunities to teach the younger generations about Guatemala, the war and hardships endured, and their Mam culture and language; until recently, Mexico did not officially recognize the Mam as a Mexican ethnic group.[40]

As the community of La Maravilla grows, many worry that there will not be enough land for their children to build homes. As Mariana, from La Maravilla, said, "We don't have land. That is our biggest problem. Now we are looking for a place to bury our dead. We used to bury them in Santa Rosa, but now they tell us there is no more room." I asked, "So now what will happen when people die?" "We throw them away," she snickered with a half-smile.

Access to the Mexican government aid program, Oportunidades (now Prospera), is another government service that those in La Maravilla lacked until a few years ago. The program provides conditional cash transfers to families to help pay for their children's schooling and aims to implement public health programs; in return mothers must attend health talks, participate in workshops, and ensure that their children regularly attend school and doctor's visits.[41] When one woman in La Maravilla finally figured out where to go to talk to the director of the corresponding government institution in Tuxtla to bring Oportunidades to the community (maneuvering a complex bureaucratic landscape), she lamented the official's response as to why they were not included in the program, "[Our community was] not even on their map!" In terms of access to services, they did not exist.

Despite their marginal position, the inhabitants of La Maravilla possess official Mexican documents, which they proudly display. When I asked residents if they identified as Mexican or Guatemalan, they would rush to show me their Mexican voting credentials. Documents enable them to attempt to assert some superiority over neighboring Mexicans, who questioned their claims to nationality and documents. As one man in La Maravilla said, "They [neighboring Mexicans] now respect us as Mexican as well." Referring to the difficulty of acquiring documents and the mixed nationality of many long-term border residents, both "new Mexicans" and some of their neighbors agree that many "new Mexicans are more Mexican than the Mexicans." "We have papers, whereas many of their [border Mexican's] wives don't!" exclaimed one new Mexican. Papers, in this sense, come to represent and legitimize claims to national belonging even as former refugees remain materially and symbolically excluded.

Because the naturalization process for former refugees occurred between 1998 and 2005 in the midst of Mexico's acceptance of dual nationality, many people (including government employees and consular authorities I spoke with) were uncertain if the former refugees could retain both nationalities once they naturalized in Mexico. One former COMAR staff member thought the former refugees should have renounced their Guatemalan citizenship, but no one compelled them to return their former documents. Mexico requires those who become Mexican via naturalization to have only one nationality.[42] But Guatemala maintains a system of dormant citizenship, which enables Guatemalans by birth who lost their nationality upon naturalization (this was required by Mexico), to return and recover it.[43] Therefore, there was confusion due to prior restrictions on dual nationality, conflicting national rules, the prevalence of misinformation, and the inability to effectively monitor actions across borders. For most residents in La Maravilla, this was not an issue because they had lost their Guatemalan documents during the war and refugee periods. Many former refugees, like Carlos, rejected Guatemala. He told me:

> Ya no Guatemala (no more Guatemala). I left Guatemala for Mexico because of the fear and the violence. Later I decided I did not want to return. I was afraid the war would happen again.

Yet even though Carlos rejected Guatemala, he retained his Guatemalan documents. He still owned land in Guatemala and wanted to be able to sell it.[44] With Guatemalan documents, he can also more easily visit family in Guatemala. Although many reject Guatemala in theory, they value retaining their documents.

The ambiguities of dual nationality, however, do not apply only to former refugees but also to many lifelong border residents. Close family, social, and economic ties have historically made cross-border romantic relationships common, further reproducing the fluid concept of cross-border belonging. Individuals adept at negotiating the ambiguities can reap benefits from both nations. Some can avoid the surveillance of both nations and their attempts to manage populations through practices of documentation and enumeration.[45] Others, however, are left in the gaps.

When I met seventy-five-year old Pedro, I learned that he was born in La Democracia, Guatemala, but had lived most of his life in Santa Rosa, Mexico. I asked him a question I asked many border residents, "Do you feel Mexican or Guatemalan?" His answer surprised me:

> Neither. I do not feel like I belong to either country. My papers died. I don't have a birth certificate from either country. But I identify more as Mexican than Guatemalan since I live here, and when my papers come, I will be recognized as Mexican by the government.

After meeting many individuals with two and three birth certificates, I was surprised to hear that Pedro had been living in Mexico for fifty-nine years with no birth certificate, which left him feeling as if he did not belong anywhere. He identified as a Mexican with Guatemalan roots and family, but his lack of documents shaped his feelings of exclusion. Although many individuals capitalize on border residence and networks to acquire multiple documents to strategically assert multiple identities, I learned that, in the fluctuating interstices of the border, it was just as possible to have no documents as it was to have multiple ones. Pedro explained:

> I was born in 1934 in La Democracia [Guatemala]. But my mother brought me to Santa Rosa [Mexico] as a child. We came to live here because my stepfather was from here and wanted us to live with him. My mother naturalized in Mexico because my stepfather helped her. But he didn't get papers for me, although he could have. He never helped me. My siblings all have papers since they were born in Mexico. My mother and stepfather are now dead, so they can no longer help me get my Mexican papers. In those days, it was easier to get documents, but not now. I don't have a birth certificate from Guatemala

either. After we left La Democracia, the municipality burned down during the war, and many documents were destroyed. I have not renounced Guatemala, though. I have a Guatemalan voting card, but I do not use it since I am hoping to get Mexican papers. I could probably use it if I wanted to in Guatemala and apply for a new birth certificate, but I don't want to be [in Guatemala] anymore. I was able to get a voting card in Mexico since before this was easier. Now you need a birth certificate [or proof of naturalization] to get a voting card. I can vote and buy land, but you really need a birth certificate for many things, like if I want to travel further in Mexico. I am applying for Mexican documents in Tapachula. I have been two or three times. It takes a long time ... no one helps. Before local authorities would give out credentials in the municipality; now you need a lot more papers.

The papers take on a life of their own for Pedro and shape his understanding of his own belonging, whereas the search for papers in itself brings the state and its power over his daily (im)mobilities into being even through its absence at the border.[46]

Pedro distinguishes between a voting credential (*cédula*, and now a Documento Personal de Identificación, or DPI[47]) in Guatemala and *credencial para votar*, elector's credential, or INE[48] in Mexico) and a birth certificate (an *acta de nacimiento*). An *acta* symbolizes claims to nationality, but having an elector's credential or *cédula*/DPI is necessary for individuals to actualize their citizenship at eighteen by enabling them to vote, gain formal-sector employment, engage in military service, and have access to state benefits. A birth certificate is useful for people seeking to travel further north than Comitán. Frontera Comalapa has developed a thriving business in forging birth certificates for Central American migrants. In Frontera Comalapa, Héctor told me, "You can buy any document you want." In Mexico, proof of nationality in the form of a birth certificate or naturalization document (in addition to proof of address and a form of photo identification) is required to apply for a voting card at age eighteen. Yet Pedro has a voting card with no evidence of nationality.

As some residents capitalize on the border to enact multiple nationalities, others, like Pedro, struggle for a place to call home. One day I met twenty-eight-year-old Miguel, a Guatemalan border resident, on his way to a party in Santa Rosa, Mexico. He told me that forty years ago much of his family had moved to Mexico; he has a lot of family and friends in the Mexican border region. His mother fled violence in Guatemala in the early 1980s to the United States, when his brother was a young child and Miguel was a toddler. He lived in the United States for fifteen years and considers it to be his home. He was an excellent soccer player who was being scouted by Duke University but lamented that he lacked possibilities due to his lack of citizenship. He was deported in 2004. When I asked if he was indigenous, he responded, "I'm not sure. Probably not, since none of my relatives speak Mam. But some probably did at some point." He added, "I don't know what I am."

In contrast, Ramón, a resident of Santa Rosa, Mexico, acquired multiple nationalities for himself and his children through extralegal means. Ramón was born and grew up in the Guatemalan border community of El Girasol. He has family on the Mexican side and frequently went there for work, soccer tournaments, and parties. At one party, he met Laura from Santa Rosa, Mexico, and they fell in love. Recognizing greater economic opportunities in Mexico, he decided to move there with her. At first, he could not purchase land due to lack of citizenship. Luckily a friend of his was the community vice president in Santa Rosa. His friend authorized and witnessed that Ramón was born in Mexico so he could acquire a birth certificate in the municipality of Frontera Comalapa, taking advantage of a Mexican procedure that grants extemporaneous citizenship to people born in Mexico who never acquired birth certificates. Under-registration of births is common in many poor areas of the country.[49] Over 7 million Mexicans do not have birth certificates; Chiapas is the state with the lowest level of birth registrations with less than half the population registered as of 2009.[50] Community authorities broker connections between individuals and the state by providing documents of land and livestock sales, births, deaths, and marriages to the municipality. Informally acquiring documents for fabricated births depends on small bribes, friendship, and the disposition of the community authority. In contrast, the current community vice president claims that such actions constitute "illegal corruption." In recent years, these practices have become less common.

Despite acquiring his Mexican birth certificate through dishonest means, Ramón's document is real (not fake), he is listed in the municipal register, and he can vote in Mexico. When he and his wife had their three children, they registered them as being born in Guatemala *and* in Mexico in case they decided to live on either side. Ramón also has documents certifying that he was born in both countries. Some Mexican residents complain when people like

Ramón vote in elections on both sides of the border, but he appears legally in both registers with supporting documentation.

Ramón identifies as Mexican, but how his Mexican and Guatemalan peers judge him reflects how he is able to enact his dual identity. One afternoon as I sat talking to a group of men in El Nance, Mexico, we saw Ramón drive by. I waved, yelling out, "*Hola* Ramón." One of the men laughed, "You mean Panchito [a nickname or diminutive for Francisco]? He prefers that name. It is his real name. But he changed his name when he moved to Mexico. He is Guatemalan and is from Guatemala. He lives here [in Mexico] now, but he is from *there* [*es de allá*]." A corn merchant from Ramón's natal town of El Girasol, where his parents still reside, later commented, "Panchito and I grew up together. That was his nickname in Guatemala. Now he rejects this name when he is in Mexico and gets angry when people call him that." Some residents dispute the method by which Ramón obtained documents, which leads them to delegitimize his claims to Mexico. Others, however, support his dual nationality based on the fact that his father was born in Mexico, although he was taken to Guatemala as a child and his mother was born in Guatemala. He has a right to Mexican nationality, albeit not in the manner he acquired it.

Cross-border marriages, like that between Ramón and his wife, became more common as official surveillance within the route declined and road improvements and the spread of vehicle ownership facilitated cross-border interactions. Mexican boys often joked about searching for a Guatemalan girlfriend as a teenage rite of passage. According to both nations' laws, a person has a right to Mexican or Guatemalan nationality if one is born in the country, if at least one parent was born in that country, or through naturalization. Most people in Ramón's position, though, prefer to certify that they were actually born in the country, which is a simpler and cheaper process, although in their cases untrue, than to acquire nationality as a child of a Mexican or Guatemalan parent. Residents also attach more authenticity to being born in the country. Individuals therefore capitalize on official procedures in Mexico that periodically offer registration drives to enable individuals who have lost, or who have never acquired, birth certificates (relatively common in many rural communities) but who were born in Mexico to acquire such documents. To do this, they need a *constancia*, or documentation of one's origin, authorized by a community authority and municipal authorities in Frontera Comalapa.

Changing his name when he moved from Guatemala to Mexico symbolized Ramón's attempt to assert his Mexicanness and separation from Guatemala. Ramón, however, needed more than documents to assert his dual nationality in the eyes of his peers, who often suspect how foreigners acquire documents. He invoked his family connections and blood ties to assert belonging in both nations. The ability to convince others of his nationality, his long-term border residence, and how others judged his enactments, mattered more than the "real status of the document[s]."[51]

Local attitudes toward those who become Mexican are harsher than the other way around, because Mexicans believe that becoming Mexican is more desirable and difficult due to perceived better economic and educational opportunities in Mexico. In Guatemala, most border residents think that it is easier to register in the municipality because many records were destroyed during the violence of the 1980s. There were historical junctures, however, when it has been more desirable to become Guatemalan. For example, when residents saw that more official work visas to the United States were available for Guatemalans than for Mexicans in the 1990s, many Mexican border residents acquired Guatemalan documents to *legally* enter the United States and acquire respectable work. Border residents' strategies for acquiring national documents reveal the complex intertwining of the legal and the illegal in navigating limited opportunities and confusing, and often inaccessible, official processes.

Nationality and the Law

As I heard about border residents' efforts to acquire dual nationality through extralegal means, I continued to wonder if a person could legally have dual nationality in Mexico and Guatemala and what this process entailed. I spent months asking people and receiving different answers, which indicated how concerns with the law have little relevance to what actually transpires. It made clear why people acquired these documents through informal and extralegal means. Even though both nations revised their nationality laws in the late 1990s, they were largely concerned with their diaspora populations in the United States retaining their birth nationalities. The processes around dual nationality at the southern border become easily convoluted. Even officials gave conflicting information. An immigration delegate in Chiapas demonstrated how racial prejudices infused perceptions of the right to belonging:

No. Mexico does not allow dual nationality with Guatemala. With some countries we accept dual, but not with Guatemala. The refugees who came here from Guatemala naturalized, but they should renounce their Guatemalan citizenship. Some kept their old documents; they [the refugees] were hard to keep track of since there were thousands of them. Those who still use them are participating in corruption. It is illegal to have both; there is no legal document that says you can legally have both like this. The moment you renounce one nation, you swear allegiance to Mexico. Often they are still in the registers of their country. In reality they belong there. They go around quiet, and when they are in Guatemala, they say "I am Guatemalan," and when in Mexico say, "I am Mexican," and many register their kids as being born in both places. It is convenient to have both citizenships, but they shouldn't. People who returned to Guatemala but were born Mexico can decide where they want to live, but they need to choose. They can't have both. They need to declare their intentions with the government.

The agent informed me that the process for any foreigner to marry a Mexican was complex, requiring an individual to go through a host of migratory processes to complete the required paperwork. Yet, as she derided, "Many don't do this. For a small fee they buy false documents. But since we work for immigration we know these things and how to detect false papers."

I asked, "But what about people who acquire legal papers through extralegal means?" She responded:

You can sometimes catch them later. They will eventually encounter problems with immigration if they have documents they shouldn't . . . like when they want to get married or register a child. We can tell from experience, how they talk, dress. They still have their own characteristics even when they live close to Mexico. We can often detect by the smell.

The delegate supported her argument with legalistic terms as she read from documents off her computer. Her interpretation of the law, however, was inflected with a racist, nationalistic, and classist undertone as when she asserted that one could detect by smell or by dress those who do not belong. Officials often come from northern Mexico and perpetuate historically derogatory depictions of southern Mexico associated with its indigeneity, often coded as backwards, uneducated, and inferior.[52] Similar to the bureaucrats described in Goldstein's analysis in Bolivia, border populations not only find it difficult to gain physical access to the centers of power but are also excluded in spatial terms that reflect racial prejudices so that "race, gender, and language . . . [are used to] delegitimize the client."[53]

When I called the Mexican consulate a few weeks later, they told me Mexico permits dual nationality with Guatemala, albeit under certain conditions. People are not supposed to use both nationalities simultaneously and strategically as border residents attempt to do and the immigration agent detected. Mexico also does not permit those who become Mexican via naturalization to retain their birth citizenship even though it makes nationality irrevocable for Mexicans by birth when they adopt another nationality. For example, Mexico considers a Mexican by birth who naturalizes in Guatemala to be a dual national because Mexican nationality is permanent regardless of the requirements of the other nation.[54] Guatemala, however, does honor these requirements; it considers Guatemalan nationality by birth permanent except when the naturalizing country obligates renunciation. Yet, Guatemalans who naturalize in Mexico can recover their Guatemalan nationality on return to Guatemala.[55] In 2013, a bill was proposed in Mexico to allow people who become Mexican via naturalization to retain their original citizenships; as of spring 2015, it had "not been discussed or voted upon."[56] Although Guatemala recognizes dual nationality, it leaves many of the details and possible conflicts open to interpretation.[57] Inconsistencies between countries and scant international monitoring between them created murkiness, as well as room for strategic maneuvering.

In a setting where rules toward nationality are ambiguous and often illegible, it becomes evident how seemingly clear-cut notions of the legal and illegal are influenced by relations of class, race, politics, particular experiences, and historically constructed ideas of the nation's identity. Hegemonic and restrictive ideals of nationalism inflected by race intersect with daily fluidity. These contradictions are omnipresent at the border. For example, because the Mexican and Guatemalan Independence Days are one day apart, each side hosts festivities. Residents cross back and forth to sell food, watch the parades, and participate in soccer games and dances.

Due to the inaccessibility and opacity of the legal process, individuals evaluate others' claims to nationality using their own subjective judgments. These assessments often mimic the state's own class, race, and gendered assumptions undergirding the objective semblance of law. In turn, a focus on the law naturalizes the acceptance of territorial boundaries, cloaking how power relations of gender, class, and race have constituted nations and their boundaries.[58] Yet personal experiences also complicate residents' perceptions. Lorenzo from El Nance, Mexico, drew on patriarchal logics of national belonging to argue, "It is illegal to have two nationalities. It would be like having two fathers or two bosses. You can't respect two fathers or bosses; how can you respect two nations?" Yet when he refers to the fact that his son's partner has not yet been able to obtain Mexican nationality and has been waiting for documents for many years, he argued, "Love knows no borders."

Attempts by local community authorities, border residents, and individual bureaucrats to properly locate border residents reinforce forms of governmentality that rely on documents to determine who has specific rights and who the state recognizes as persons who can be born, marry, work, and die.[59] By circumventing the law and generating alternative discourses around dual nationality, border residents' strategies enable some to selectively assert transnational citizenship across borders as others hide from the gaze of a single state.[60] The changing and cryptic nature of navigating nationality laws across two or more countries and the borderlands' economic, racial, and geographic exclusion from bureaucratic center motivate residents to acquire documents outside the law. At the same time, the creative yet uncertain search for, and insistence on, documents invokes the ordering presence of the state by chasing and mimetically reproducing its phantoms.[61]

Documents Unhinged

Living at the margins of both nation-states, many border residents acquire national documents through extralegal means and use personal connections to negotiate the border. As residents maintain the importance of and often desperately seek national documents, they simultaneously support and undermine the importance of these documents and the states they are stitched to. In doing so, they reinforce the power, or magic, of the state over national lives at the margins[62] while also showing that the actual law and documents may be beside the point. The link between the documents and what they are supposed to guarantee becomes unhinged. The documents take on a life of their own while the real documents also fail to fulfill their function of guaranteeing national inclusion. Deciphering the real from the forgery distracts from recognizing how the document's original referent may also be a phantom. Residents' daily practices reveal the state's own legal procedures to be as discretionary and politicized as their own; both rely on nationalist ideologies, class, gender, and race to authorize judgments about proper belonging. Madeleine Reeves argues that in contexts where documents are uncertain and fakes abound, "the physical person becomes scrutinized all the more intensely as the locus of truth."[63] In its recent commitment to enhance immigration enforcement to curtail Central American migrants, Mexico's immigration authorities have been accused of using racially infused evaluations.[64] As a result, increasing numbers of indigenous Mexicans have been detained in the quest to "detain Central Americans at any cost."[65] When I rode a bus from Frontera Comalapa to the northern border in March 2007, immigration agents detained three passengers at a checkpoint near Tuxtla. They claimed they were Mexican but were kicked off the bus without the chance to retrieve additional documents they had stored under the bus. The agents attempted to judge the authenticity behind what their papers documented regardless of whether they were Mexican nationals.

The borderlands are characterized by tensions between fluidity and restriction, governance and evasion, and marginalization and opportunity. The following chapters illustrate how residents navigate these tensions to earn a living in the context of official regional trade integration and border securitization policies, which define local inhabitants as marginal, or even direct, threats to these agendas. Border residents' justifications for engaging in smuggling as a response to economic exclusion are intimately related to how they conceive of who they are and their embeddedness in the border. Residents carry the border and its ethnonational and class tensions with them as their daily interactions reshape the border. Yet the border also crossed them, and it continues to shape their lives at increasingly unpredictable junctures.

3 Corn Is Food, Not Contraband

Sown to be eaten it is the sacred sustenance of the men who were made of maize. Sown to make money it means famine for the men who were made of maize."

—Miguel Ángel Asturias, "Men of Maize", 1993: 11

IN 2006, AT LEAST 24,000 TONS of Mexican corn entered Guatemala through this unmonitored road (Figure 3.1).[1] Officially, this was contraband because merchants were selling corn across an unmonitored international border and evading official inspections, documentation, and tariffs. Border residents had a different idea. When I asked why truckloads of corn traveled unencumbered across the border, residents asserted it was "free," meaning state officials would not interfere. They were "free" to do this and insisted, "Corn is food, not contraband." Some said the trade was permitted because "Mexico signed a free trade agreement."

Agricultural liberalization in Mexico in the 1980s and 1990s, and especially Mexico's entrance into the North American Free Trade Agreement (NAFTA) in 1994, generated a corn crisis in rural Mexico. Agricultural liberalization meant that farmers lost previous state agricultural subsidies and price guarantees and were forced to compete with cheaper imported U.S. corn, which retained U.S. government subsidies. Mexico imports over one-third of its corn.[2] In the 1990s, Mexico dismantled its state-run CONASUPO (National Company of Popular Subsistence) warehouses, which previously guaranteed the purchase of peasants' harvests and regulated the distribution chain to provide consumers with affordable corn. Without a buyer for their harvests, border residents and regional producers capitalized on a larger climate of social discontent with neoliberal reforms in the 1990s to organize to demand the right to sell corn from Mexico to Guatemala without official interference. They established informal agreements with regional officials

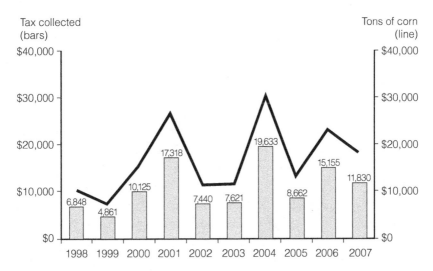

Figure 3.1. Taxes levied by the municipality of La Democracia, Guatemala, on the cross-border corn trade and tons of corn entering Guatemala from Mexico through the clandestine crossing: 1998–2007.

Declines in 2007 may be due to the rumored corn shortages, even though border residents asserted that the corn flow resumed to high levels in the fall of 2007. The decline could also be the result of a lack of reporting and/or mis-accounting on the part of residents and/or the municipality. It is possible that many truckers do not pay their "tax" and prefer to evade this documentation, especially because municipal officials believe that the levels of commerce are relatively low and that commerce is only local. *Note*: I converted the taxes of 50 quetzales per 50-ton truck into U.S. dollars. These data are converted according to 2007 exchange rates when I conducted fieldwork, whereby 10 quetzales equaled 14 pesos, which was roughly US$1.30, depending on monthly fluctuations.

SOURCE: Municipal Archives, La Democracia, Huehuetenango, Guatemala; compiled by the author, who would like to thank Dan Galemba for assistance with the graph.

to permit this corn trade. Because there is no nationally mandated policy in either country, though, this commerce is officially illegal and subject to the discretion of particular state agents. Corn farmers in this region were detrimentally affected by the liberalization tenets of free trade agreements, which forced them to compete with U.S. imports and removed previous guarantees and protections. They were simultaneously excluded from free trade's potential opportunities for international trade, which privileged multinational corporations. The local, informal agreements that enable this corn flow are what residents experience as free trade.

I was baffled to observe so much corn being transported through this route and to hear residents justify it as free. Residents acknowledged that, if not legal, this corn trade was "more permitted" by officials. In contrast to other smuggling enterprises, officials did not demand bribes from corn smugglers. Corn became a sacrosanct good in the context of an agricultural crisis in a region where it is the main daily staple. Even though residents smuggle various goods across the border that they defend as socially legitimate, they uniquely justify corn as a free commodity. I therefore refer to people who sell corn across the border as merchants, rather than smugglers, although acknowledging that they evade legal requisites for cross-border trade.

Corn was not always free from official intervention. Prior to the mid-1990s, residents reported that this corn trade was "more illegal." Mexican policing units previously demanded bribes or confiscated corn from merchants. Some merchants were even arrested. In Guatemala at the height of the counterinsurgency war in the 1980s, the military was periodically stationed near the border and made commerce difficult. When the war ended in 1996, the Guatemalan civil police (PNC) took on the task of monitoring contraband but seldom intervened as Guatemalan border residents and merchants began to organize to facilitate the corn trade. Now, according to Mexican border resident Manuel, "We put [the officials] in our jail if they interfere." People outside the region, in contrast, either were unaware of this commerce or asserted it must be contraband because the corn was being sold across the border via an unmonitored route.

Border residents largely monopolize roles as intermediary merchants, truckers, and cargo loaders in the corn trade. Mexican corn merchants, and their counterparts of Guatemalan brokers, each organized associations to ensure fair work practices. Cargo loaders on both sides of the border formed rotating associations to take turns working different days of the week. Mexican truckers created an association to include all local truckers while insisting that long-distance truckers deliver goods to them to transport over the border.[3] They no longer allow long-distance truckers to proceed directly to Guatemala. "Whoever is hungry that day goes to [the depot to] work," a trucker explained. The association records members' names in a notebook; when a long-distance truck arrives to deliver corn to merchants to transport to Guatemala, the first name on the list takes the transport. These practices provide more work opportunities for residents but exclude outsiders.

Corn's critical subsistence role extends to ethics governing its cross-border sale. Opening up the corn merchant association to more members diminishes the profits of individuals because there are more buyers. Yet residents believe that all locals with sufficient capital and connections should have the opportunity to enter the association because there is no alternative. Norms designating rights to engage in commerce based on residence are similar to traditions governing access to community resources and land, but residents also apply these rules to the contraband economy. In the past decade, more individuals began amassing start-up capital and purchasing trucks from earnings as migrants in the United States. As more residents want to participate, group members are beginning to reassess the rules and charge fees for new entrants.

This chapter follows the corn trade from the irrigation canal region in Trinitaria, Chiapas, to the Mexican border communities and across the border to Guatemala to illustrate how corn became free to sell across the border. Border residents evaluate what is economically fair in a context where smuggling corn is socially legitimate and necessary to survival, but is officially illegal.[4] Residents' critical views of free trade policies, coupled with their articulation of their own informal "free trading" practices, question the ethical underpinnings of official trade policies. The corn trade reflects how border residents experienced and reinterpreted the implications of free trade agreements as the ability to sell corn to the best buyer, which was Guatemala. They justified smuggling corn as a more legitimate variant of free trade to official policies that excluded them. As residents organized to smuggle corn across the border, they developed the know-how and networks to engage in a variety of border smuggling businesses and to assert their control over the border route. The critical significance of corn, the exclusions of official trade policies, and the devastation that agricultural liberalization wrought on the Mexican countryside generated the climate in which corn smuggling became justifiable and free. It also stimulated a larger regional acceptance, and reliance on, the smuggling of a variety of commodities. Peasants were not merely pushed into informal and illegal activities; instead they actively pursued and reframed them as more just alternatives. However, contraband as a form of resistance to economic marginalization is limited, as it may reinforce, or simply leave unquestioned, patron–client relations with corrupt state authorities and underdevelopment in the countryside.

Trucking Corn

Ramón, described in Chapter 2, resides in Santa Rosa, Mexico, but was born across the border in El Girasol, Guatemala. He owns a small plot of land to grow beans and corn, but it is insufficient to meet subsistence needs. Ramón has been a small-scale corn merchant for almost fifteen years. He uses his family connections in Guatemala to work; his uncle Nelson in El Girasol is his business partner. Nelson belongs to a group of thirty Guatemalan *comisionistas*, or brokers. Brokers are Guatemalan border residents who collaborate with Mexican merchants to connect Mexican corn producers to Guatemalan long-distance buyers. Social networks and kinship relations that span the border connect Mexican merchants and Guatemalan brokers. Some Mexican merchants and Guatemalan brokers combine funds to purchase corn, but the Mexicans usually supply the majority of the funds. In Ramón's case, he is often short on capital so he depends on his uncle to help him. Long-distance Guatemalan merchants arrive in El Girasol and Nueva Vida, Guatemala, to purchase corn to distribute throughout Guatemala. Guatemalan brokers mediate the exchange.

Ramón agreed to let me accompany him to the canal region to purchase corn. One February day in 2007, he called my cell phone to ensure I was on my way. The ten-ton truck he rented from his friend had arrived, and Ramón was eager to teach me how to search for good corn in the irrigation canal region near Trinitaria (Figure 3.2). This region supplies the majority of corn that border merchants sell to Guatemala. Irrigation canals enable farmers to reap two harvests per year versus one in other regions. Ramón belongs to the association of twenty-two Mexican border-resident corn merchants, whom residents sometimes call coyotes. To residents, this term usually lacks the pejorative connotation it carries in Mesoamerica in reference to migrant smugglers or abusive middlemen.[5] However, farmers and other residents will apply the term *coyote* in a negative fashion when merchants violate the redistributive norms of the trade or when producers feel that coyotes exert undue influence. Each season, association members agree to purchase corn at a set price from regional producers to ensure that no one manipulates the market and all can work. Mexican merchants purchase corn throughout Chiapas in Frontera Comalapa, Tierra Blanca, Guadalupe Grijalva, Chicomuselo, and near Trinitaria. They deliver corn to the Guatemalan brokers in El Girasol and Nueva Vida where Guatemalan long-distance merchants arrive to purchase it. Some Mexican merchants have connections to long-distance Mexican producers

Figure 3.2. A merchant inspects his corn.
SOURCE: Author photo.

and warehouses, who deliver corn to the Mexican merchants at the border, who then transport it for sale to Guatemala. Due to their monopoly over access to the border route, and connections to the Guatemalan market, border corn merchants insist that long-distance truckers deliver corn to them to arrange the sale to Guatemalans. Border residents do not permit long-distance merchants and truckers to cross the border to gain direct access to the Guatemalan market. Otherwise, as merchants explain, "They will screw up our business. It would take away our work. If they start to work here, where would we work?" Long-distance merchants rely on border intermediaries because they do not have the connections to evade official border inspections and gain access to the Guatemalan market.

In practice, some corn merchants circumvent the ethical rules governing the association as new business opportunities arise. Merchants who own ten-ton trucks earn more money not only because they save the expense of renting trucks, but also because long-distance merchants seek them out to transport a variety of goods across the border to evade official regulations. Ramón was able to purchase a pickup truck after working in Florida, but it is insufficient for a business that depends on multiple ten-ton trucks. Ramón longs for a ten-ton truck and is debating a second trip to the United States to acquire the funds. "People with [ten-ton] trucks can make money. I make barely enough to feed my family," he lamented. In the January through March corn season, when sales are good, Ramón can make twenty to twenty-five trips to the canal region to purchase corn and earns about US$2,000.[6] Merchants with ten-ton trucks, he told me, can earn about US$10,000.

Leandro is a larger corn merchant in Santa Rosa. He and his two sons each have a ten-ton truck that they park in a sheet-metal covered garage next to their home. Larger merchants can transport thirty tons of corn per day whereas smaller ones do as much in one week. Leandro and his sons supplement corn earnings by transporting others' commerce and renting trucks to other merchants. His sons now rely on renting their trucks for income; they earn about US$60 to US$70 for each truck trip to the canal region and back to the border. Leandro also has clients in northern Mexico who deliver corn to him to transport to Guatemala in the summer months when there is little regional corn. Yet even larger merchants like Leandro depend on loans from other residents or banks and face risks when prices fluctuate.

In the spring of 2007, merchants grew apprehensive about the corn business. Global demands for ethanol, speculation and hoarding by large agribusiness, and anticipation of the complete liberalization of the Mexican corn sector in 2008 led to corn shortages, price hikes, and a tortilla crisis, generating protest throughout Mexico.[7] Border residents expressed anxiety about selling corn to Guatemala because they believed that "Mexico lacked corn," even though Mexico's corn supply was actually at a record high.[8] Border merchants

Figure 3.3. Cornfields in the irrigation canal region.
SOURCE: Author photo.

delayed their purchases in the spring of 2007 as they hoped prices would fall. They waited for prices to rise in Guatemala to make the exchange worthwhile. Due to uncertainty in February of 2007, Ramón was nervous about his next purchase. He visited his uncle's depot in El Girasol each morning to check if his previous load of corn had sold so he could purchase more. Ramón made frequent trips to the canal region just to verify prices. When prices were too high, he returned home to wait. Larger merchants, like Leandro, have sufficient capital to continue purchasing and selling corn.

A second truck transporting cargo loaders from Santa Rosa, Mexico followed us to the canal region. The trucks parked in the field of a farmer who belongs to an association of 4,000 canal corn producers (Figure 3.3). The farmer hired local field hands to fill and sew up the satchels, which originated from the now defunct CONASUPO warehouses. Cargo loaders from Santa Rosa carried the satchels into the trucks using a makeshift wooden ramp (Figure 3.4). Four men load a truck and earn the equivalent of US$5 each per truck, which takes about one hour. This wage is equivalent to an entire day working as a

Figure 3.4. Loading corn onto trucks for sale to Guatemala.
SOURCE: Author photo.

field hand, but the work can be grueling. Each satchel weighs over 175 pounds and temperatures hover around 90 degrees year-round. The only respite in the dry, hot Frontera Comalapa plains is the summer torrential downpours. Some Mexican merchants work with particular cargo loaders and phone them when a truck arrives, which enables cargo loaders to otherwise pursue alternative employment options. Other cargo loaders take shifts on different days waiting at the border depots for, as one related, "whatever comes."

Rogelio is the leader of the association of canal corn producers. The association is organized to ensure fair prices and to negotiate with state officials, border merchants, and regional peasant organizations. Border merchants like Ramón must register with the producers' association and negotiate prices each year. In the past few years, the canal producers periodically blockaded the highway to demand higher prices and protest the influence border merchants hold over the corn trade, but they have rarely achieved substantial price increases. With a limited available market, they recognize the value of border merchants' access to cross-border networks, trucks, and Guatemalan buyers.

As we returned to the border in the trucks full of corn, Ramón pointed to places along the highway where police previously monitored contraband. He told me not to worry: "Now no one bothers us because corn is free." As we re-entered the border route, Ramón paid about US$5 at each of the two Mexican communities' tollbooths. Although tolls cut into his meager profits, Ramón appreciates the benefits they provide to his community—a new park, school repairs, and extension of electric and water services.

The truck churned uphill onto an unpaved, rocky portion of the road. The white monuments to our right and left were the only indicators we were entering Guatemala. The Guatemalan border communities of El Girasol and Nueva Vida each have plazas where Guatemalan corn brokers rent space from the community or from individual landowners to construct depots. Depots, little more that small sheet metal lean-tos, store corn until buyers are available.

We stopped at Ramón's uncle Nelson's depot in El Girasol. In 2011, there were about thirty members of the Guatemalan brokers association, and in August of 2014 they formed a civil association. Brokers receive a fixed commission of roughly US$20 from the Mexican merchant per ten-ton truckload of corn in exchange for arranging the Guatemalan buyer. Brokers also retrieve corn satchels at the end of the commodity chain to return to Mexican corn producers. Corn is sold in Guatemala by the *quintal* whereas in Mexico it is packaged by the *costal/bulto*, which carries different amounts of corn. Further down the commodity chain, Mexican *bultos* are repackaged into *quintales* to be sold to Guatemalan consumers, who otherwise, according to one broker, "would not know how much was in there." Retrieving the Mexican satchels is imperative because many are from the old CONASUPO warehouses. One broker commented, "Sometimes the [satchels] last, but look at how old they are . . . in really bad shape. I'm not sure what we will do when [the bags] run out or break. We often sew them back together." Government officials in La Democracia, Guatemala believed the corn trade was only regional, but brokers have tracked down satchels as far as Guatemala City. Other merchants related selling corn that went to El Salvador.

Because trucking is most viable if truckers transport goods in both directions, Guatemalan brokers arrange for the sale of cement blocks from Guatemalan merchants in the interior to corn farmers in the Mexican canal region. Previously, Guatemalan brokers negotiated independently with Guatemalan merchants and profited from the exchange. Some brokers complain about the loss of control implied by the fixed commission, whereas the Mexican merchants profit from the price differential between Mexican and Guatemalan corn. However, Guatemalan brokers with minimal resources appreciate the fixed rate because they avoid the financial risks of a volatile business where prices, currency differentials, and official tolerance fluctuate.

Four Guatemalan cargo loaders, who belong to a rotating association of about eighty Guatemalan border residents who take shifts during the week, waited to unload the truck. Guatemalan brokers prefer to have buyers available so they can directly transfer cargo. Otherwise they need to pay cargo loaders multiple times to unload and reload. In an atmosphere of fluctuating prices, though, they often unload, store the corn, and wait for buyers.

Ramón introduced me to his uncle and brokers who shared the depot in El Girasol. He assured a broker, "We are friends; she has eaten in my home [and] knows my children." The men asked where in the United States I lived, where I was living here, what I was doing, and if the government was paying me. Ramón joked as he pointed to another man, "Just be careful of him, he's a narco."[9] The man teased back, "Be careful. Ramón has a large secret house here." Ramón brushed this off, "She already knows I am *gente pobre* [poor folk]. She has spent time in my house." I began to spend more time hanging out at depots to understand the pace of business because it involved a lot of waiting, joking, and gossiping. Largely a male sphere where merchants exchange money for work, wait for commerce, tease, boast, and play cards, at first it was helpful to be introduced by individuals like Ramón, with whom I had rapport. Yet because most depots are located in central community locations, women and children also occupy these spaces and sell food and drinks to truckers, cargo loaders, and merchants.

The trucking trip with Ramón demonstrated how the corn trade reflects ethical values held at the border. The number of players, including Mexican producers, Mexican merchants, Mexican truckers, Mexican cargo loaders, Guatemalan brokers, Guatemalan cargo loaders, and long-distance Guatemalan buyers, does not lend itself to economic efficiency. Because the corn trade is relatively unpoliced by either state, multiple levels of intermediation cannot be solely explained by the need to disperse risk and avoid detection, which is common in other illegal commodity chains.[10] Instead, it points to the ethical primacy on securing livelihoods for residents in a region dependent on corn with few remaining options. It would be more advantageous for merchants to negotiate prices independent of community, group, and regional agreements. Yet border residents and merchants established price protections based on local ethics that link the right to sell corn across the border with land owner-ship and local residence. To avoid price competition with outside corn, and enforced when necessary through road blockades, border residents first sell their own harvests to Guatemala, then they allow regional corn, and lastly, permit corn from other regions and states to be transported across the border. To understand why residents defend the right to sell corn, the next section focuses on the regional importance of corn and the effects of the NAFTA on corn farming.

Corn as Culture, Crop, and Commodity

Mesoamerica is the center of maize's origin and genetic diversity. In addi-tion to its significance as a grain necessary for survival, corn is a powerful cultural symbol and marker of national and regional identity, past and pres-ent. Notably, the *Popol Vuh* refers to Mesoamericans as "people of maize."[11] However, depicting corn as an essentialist symbol of Mesoamerican culture risks romanticizing peasants and maize agriculture and neglects how peas-ants are integrated into larger political-economic contexts.[12] Various actors deploy corn's cultural and material importance to different ends.[13] In Mexico, the state historically invoked corn as a national symbol even as "state policy continued to associate maize agriculture with economic backwardness and inefficiency."[14] Elizabeth Fitting highlights the Mexican state's central role in agriculture, in which "maize provisioning and food policy were central to state corporatism and political campaigns."[15] From the 1930s until the 1990s, the Mexican state was directly involved in agriculture.[16] The establishment of CONASUPO in 1965 integrated the agricultural production and distribution chain to regulate relations between producers and consumers so low-income consumers could have access to basic foodstuffs and small producers could earn a living.[17] Mexico's path to agricultural liberalization meant departing from state support of agriculture. Nevertheless, even as the state's capacity to influence corn prices declined, many peasant movements continued to target the state to demand the renewal of supports, credit, and higher corn prices, leading to selective instances of co-optation, limited concessions, and repres-sion.[18] Border residents are no exception; as one producer argued, "When the state offers us a fair price, we will sell to them." Diego, a former secretary of Santa Rosa, Mexico and a corn farmer, reasoned, "The Mexican government needs to improve its prices and purchase our products at a just price so we can have an internal market. Then we would not sell to Guatemala." Due to its cultural, economic, and national importance, corn has been central to many peasant protests against neoliberal policies in Mexico since the 1980s.[19] The decline of the corn sector threatened not only the livelihoods of peasants but also the essence of who they are.[20]

Guatemalan corn cargo loader Emilio taught me how to distinguish between U.S. corn, which he called "corn for animals," and regional, "good-quality corn."[21] As a novice, I could not recognize the difference. He showed me the bottom of the corn kernel. "Look, [the United States] removes part of the kernel . . . what we call the heart, to use for fuel . . . Then they send us back the garbage. U.S. corn is cheaper, but it is not the same. It arrives without the same nutrients, or as we say, without a heart." Emilio's comment illustrated how free-trade agreements and their accompanying policies toward corn endangered residents' economic livelihoods as they also enhanced inequalities between Mexico and Guatemala and the United States. Corn's deep cultural ties in the region led these threats to peasant livelihoods to manifest as corporeal experiences.

Border residents draw on the symbolic and material significance of corn to serve various goals: defend their right to subsistence, protest agricultural liberalization, and assert their right to sell corn across the border. On both sides of the border, corn is the central agricultural crop and source of livelihood. The dry soil in this region inhibits the growth of the larger variety of crops grown in the Chiapas and Guatemalan highlands. Despite obstacles to subsistence maize cultivation and the rising role of commerce, border residents still primarily identify as farmers. One resident wondered, "If we did not have corn, how would we survive?"

Corn smuggling has a long regional history that both nations previously policed to varying degrees. Throughout the twentieth century, farmers traded small quantities of corn across the border on donkeys. Chiapans long found better corn prices in Guatemala, and Mexican corn mitigated price hikes amid frequent shortages in Guatemala, especially in Huehuetenango.[22] The Guatemalan border departments of Huehuetenango and San Marcos are net consumers of corn.[23] Although Huehuetenango produces corn, beans, and fruits and has diversified to produce other crops such as potatoes, French beans, and broccoli for the Central American and U.S. markets, it is one of the most food insecure departments.[24] Inhabitants of Huehuetenango have long recognized they cannot solely depend on subsistence maize agriculture.[25] Contraband often supplemented shortages; "In many cases the border regions are closer to the markets or zones of production in [Mexico] than [in Guatemala]."[26] Guatemalan border residents are accustomed to purchasing corn from, or planting in, Mexico.

The majority of Mexican corn in the region, however, was produced for consumption or sold to local state-run CONASUPO warehouses, which provided price guarantees and supports until CONASUPO was gradually dismantled and closed in the late 1990s. Corn smuggling to Guatemala became vital for Mexican border residents and regional farmers after agricultural reforms left them without a buyer for their harvests. Producer Rogelio related, "We always sold some corn to Guatemala, but now nearly 100 percent." In 2006, Mexican merchants told me the price for a ton of corn was about US$300, which they could sell for 25 percent more in Guatemala. Yet the main problem was a lack of Mexican buyers. Diego clarified, "Well, that is [the price] if Mexico purchased our corn. The warehouses are still here, but they are empty. The [companies] buy from the U.S." After CONASUPO closed, transnational milling companies became producers' only options, even though they were also the leading importers and exporters of U.S. corn.[27] Rogelio added that multinational corn flour and tortilla companies like Maseca, a global brand of Grupo Gruma, and Minsa did not purchase from their association but from larger growers in northern Mexico. The dearth of options for farmers and the local effects of NAFTA on the corn sector contextualize local reinterpretations of free trade.

Free Trade in the Borderlands

For months I wondered why corn could be sold so seamlessly through this border road. Leandro stressed, "We work in the light of day, as you can see . . . we do not hide." At first, I thought, maybe the trade was legal. Perhaps corn was inspected elsewhere with permission granted to be transported here for convenience? But I knew cross-border trade needed to be inspected and documented through official points of entry. I did not understand what residents meant when they repeated that this corn trade was "free." As I probed the meaning of this term, I learned that many residents believed it was free because of NAFTA. Héctor, the Mexican farmer in Chapters 1 and 2, even quoted former Mexican President Salinas de Gortari (1988–1994) to legitimize the trade. The connection seems ironic because many Mexicans chastise Salinas as the architect of the neoliberal economic and agrarian policies that contributed to devastating peasant agriculture. Héctor began, "People began to hear that [the sale of corn] was free. Salinas told us on the radio. He announced he signed a free-trade agreement with the U.S. This caused corn prices to fall. So Salinas told farmers we were free to sell to the best buyer."

Although Héctor's recounting of NAFTA did not correspond to the official policy, his explanation illustrates how border peasants experienced and vernaculurized,[28] or translated, the agreement within their cultural context. In many ways, Héctor truly understood the political and economic dynamics. He demonstrated his savvy as he explained the repercussions of the end of land reform, large-scale privatization, and the end of subsidies and price guarantees for corn. Another Mexican border resident pointed to the vacant worn-down building that once housed the CONASUPO warehouse where he sold his harvests. He reminisced, "Look, [the warehouses] are still there. They could reopen them and bring them back!" From the late 1980s through the 1990s, CONASUPO consistently lowered its prices and reduced purchases. According to June Nash:

> CONASUPO once provided an essential service to producers who had little access to alternative markets and who lacked storage facilities . . . By the year 2000, the weakened CONASUPO had ceased to function, and the estimated 450,000 cultivators of subsistence crops experienced the worst crisis of their history.[29]

In Mexico, agricultural liberalization, declining prices, and the withdrawal of state support from agriculture had been occurring since the 1980s in line with structural adjustment policies mandated by the IMF in the wake of the debt crisis. For farmers, though, NAFTA "institutionalized and rendered irreversible [these agricultural reforms], signifying the destruction of the protection of agriculture and the system of state-run commercialization of basic foodstuffs that had been in effect since 1936."[30] Although farmers protested the inclusion of basic grains into NAFTA, they entered the agreement.[31] As Mexico began to allow the influx of cheaper subsidized U.S. corn, it became increasingly difficult for farmers to earn a living. Since the early 1990s, U.S. corn exports to Mexico have increased over 400 percent.[32] Corn was assigned a special status under NAFTA as a subsistence necessity, but despite the fifteen-year period allotted to phase out the tariff rate quota, Mexico did not enforce the protections and compressed the adjustment period to less than three years to reduce prices and combat inflation.[33] The U.S. exported corn at prices "below what it cost to produce" in violation of World Trade Organization anti-dumping rules, which depressed Mexican producer prices as corn prices fell 66 percent.[34] Timothy Wise estimates the cost of U.S. dumping prices and Mexico's failure to enforce the tariff rate quota to Mexican corn producers to be $700 million per year from the early 1990s through 2007.[35] Amid the peso devaluation in 1994 (which made agricultural inputs more expensive), state divestment from agriculture, inflation, rising fertilizer costs, and the elimination of credit subsidies and price supports, small farmers had few supports to transition to the liberalization process.[36] Neil Harvey pointed to the dire effects on small and medium-scale producers that depended on corn sales for income:

> 67% percent of maize production within the social sector of Chiapas is sold on the market, while 33% goes to household consumption[37] . . . Lower maize prices will therefore have a direct effect on thousands of producers that until 1994 depended on the guaranteed price.[38]

Since NAFTA, 2.3 million people abandoned the agricultural sector, but Timothy Wise argues that this actually understates the effects; "Since 1991, some 5 million family farm members stopped depending on farm income, according to the 2007 agricultural census."[39] According to the World Bank, employment in agricultural dropped from 26.8 percent of total employment in 1991 to just over 13 percent by 2011.[40] Increases in jobs in the *maquila* sector, formal services, and the export and seasonal agricultural sectors did not compensate for this decline in agriculture, which particularly affected small farmers.[41]

Despite the fact that agricultural liberalization was supposed to phase out small-holder farming, corn production actually increased by 50 percent, illustrating the dearth of alternatives as many peasants intensified subsistence farming, migrated north, or entered the informal economy in the 1990s.[42] Without an outlet to sell their harvests, border residents took the neoliberal logics implied in free trade literally—"to sell their products to the best buyer." Although Salinas de Gortari never mentioned Guatemala, it was the obvious best buyer in the region. Diego also attributed permission to the former president: "Because we all grow and consume corn, [the government] made it possible for us to sell it where we could. It was an order of Salinas." Amanda King's study of NAFTA's influence on Veracruz farmers uncovered similar reapplications of neoliberal economic logics, which exposed their inconsistencies.[43] As Roberto Russ from the Unión de Maiceros (Union of Corn

Producers) asked in King's study, "If we in Mexico do not have a comparative advantage in the production of maize, then what exactly do we have a comparative advantage in?"[44]

Some border residents like Héctor assert the corn trade is free because of the official free trade agreement, seamlessly merging the official agreement with their local practices, but other residents offer more critical interpretations. They know that this corn trade was not legislated in accordance with official trade agreements. Diego explained, "Free trade [commerce] should be transported through official inspections posts," but:

> Peasants lack the orientation to participate. We need technical training. We wanted the government to teach us and provide us with the opportunities to benefit from free trade. They do not train peasants or small producers about quality [controls] for export. We can't compete . . . just the larger companies.

Like Diego, many residents recognize the difference between the two interpretations of free trade but assert their version is more equitable and free despite its official illegal status. Leandro's son labeled the trade "illegal, but permitted." After hearing another corn merchant explain, "Corn is free because Mexico signed a free-trade agreement," I asked, "Wasn't that [agreement] among the United States, Mexico, and Canada?" "Yes," he half-smiled, "But with us [border residents], too." His experience of free trade referred to informal accords reached among border residents, producers, merchants, and local authorities in the mid-1990s to enable this cross-border corn trade. Excluded from official variants, this extralegal, yet informally sanctioned, commerce is the relevant free trade at the border. For peasants, the regulations and bureaucratic processes to register in official free trade make it increasingly exclusive—not free at all.

Agustín, Santa Rosa's community's president in the late 1990s, reflected on the dismantling of CONASUPO as he learned inconsistent information about free trade:

> [After CONASUPO closed] people were looking for a place to sell their corn. We had meetings with the municipal president. He informed us about free trade. We made an agreement [to sell corn to Guatemala] since there was nowhere to sell it. Now corn comes from all over the municipality and sometimes further. There are agreements that no one should bother this. This is called free trade.

I probed Agustín as to why he thought this corn trade was free: "For us, it is free trade because it passes through here daily. If it were contraband, [the government] would not let it pass. It does not harm anyone. It is a primary necessity."

Border residents had little access to information about official trade agreements and were socially and geographically removed from protests against them in Chiapas cities like San Cristóbal and Tapachula. Most people heard about free trade from the radio and municipal authorities. Producer Rogelio qualified the information sources:

> Many people misunderstood free trade. We are not involved in commerce, so we do not know the requirements. The municipal president often knows less than people like me about what free trade is. Many gave bad information. Free trade does not mean that there is no tax. There are still requirements.

Diego concurred, "People don't understand what [free trade] is. They think all the illicit commerce that passes through here is free trade, but no. 'Free trade' refers to what crosses through the official line legally." Few people had detailed knowledge of free trade agreements and how they could participate. Residents often lumped together NAFTA, CAFTA, and free trade agreements established between Mexico and Guatemala as "free trade" without understanding the distinctions or processes.

Yet even when producers and residents knew the requirements, they encountered bureaucratic obstacles. A disagreement between two Guatemalan fiscal agents in La Mesilla, Guatemala revealed the dearth of information surrounding free trade and the obstacles to commercialization. When I inquired about tariffs on corn from Mexico to Guatemala, the agents in La Mesilla argued back and forth about what the tariff was and how free trade provisions affected the rate. I soon realized the confusion did not simply stem from lack of knowledge about the agreement or tariff rate. It was because they had never levied the tariff! Because of bureaucratic obstacles that restrict commerce at the official customs post at Ciudad Cuauhtémoc, Mexico, they had never seen more than an individual harvest pass through their office in La Mesilla. Corn commerce, they admitted, occurred through unmonitored routes. According to documents from Guatemala's tax administration body, SAT, imported white corn is subject to a 20 percent tariff and was excluded from the free trade agreement between Mexico and Guatemala.[45]

Because many border inhabitants learned about free trade from the media, it is noteworthy that many Guatemalan border residents receive radio and television service from Mexico. Guatemalan border residents, many of whom have family in Mexico and have worked on Mexican land or rented land from Mexicans for generations, often had more knowledge about developments in Mexico than about CAFTA's implications for Guatemala. Because CAFTA did not go into effect until July 2006, in 2006–2007 residents were just beginning to surmise its impact. They used the Mexican countryside's experience with NAFTA as a dismal forecast. Guatemalan border residents thought CAFTA would have a limited impact on this corn trade because their remoteness from national distribution circuits long made getting access to corn cheaper and easier from Mexico than from other parts of Guatemala. Even so, the existence of an official agreement lent credence to local explanations that the corn trade was legitimate due to free trade.

Juan Carlos Velasco, a research assistant at El Colegio de la Frontera Sur explained that border populations have long participated in their own types of free trade.[46] He told me, "The agreements did not change anything since they did not apply to them." As alternative discourses of free trade spread, municipal and community authorities circulated misinformed definitions. As peasants persuaded state officials to comply with their demands to sell corn across the border, the informal variants of free trade moved from the realm of misinformation to reality. The cross-border corn trade was not only free because residents believed it should be or were misinformed about official agreements. It was free because officials no longer interfered, demanded bribes, or confiscated corn. It was free and open.

How Corn Became Free

Corn producers had begun mobilizing for higher corn prices throughout Mexico since liberalization in the 1980s, but efforts came to a head in 1983–1987 and then resurfaced with vigor after the passage of NAFTA.[47] A sharp drop in prices and CONASUPO's failure to pay expected prices led to protests in Chiapas in 1996–1997.[48] The state countered with a mixture of repression, selective concessions, and co-optation of some of the peasant leadership into the political establishment.[49] Although these mobilizations inspired some people in this region, border residents and regional producers assert their independence. Their struggles to sell corn to Guatemala were one response to the failure of wider mobilizations to achieve a solution for the majority of farmers.

In the mid 1990s, the border communities repeatedly blockaded the border route to expel corrupt agents who previously exacted bribes or confiscated commerce. These mobilizations are detailed in Chapter 4, but the desire to find an outlet for their corn harvests was the major spark that led residents to organize. Residents maintain that moral appeals to "the right to corn" as a form of subsistence amid economic crisis, in addition to their strong organizational abilities, were responsible for opening the border to the corn trade. In contrast, Rogelio and the canal producers claim their association's efforts facilitated the corn trade. Rogelio challenged border residents' appeals to free trade, recalling that, at first, many border residents resisted the removal of the state authorities because they wanted sole control of the trade, even if it meant paying bribes.

Rogelio told the story from his perspective. The corn crisis became dire in 1995, when the local CONASUPO closed and failed to pay farmers for their harvests. He recounted:

> There were protests all over the region. Producers blockaded the roads so no one could pass. Then some of us went to Tuxtla and took the CONASUPO representative hostage until he paid the money he owed us. We went to see the governor in Tuxtla. We asked him to remove the officers from the border and to not interfere in our corn sales. He agreed to remove them. But of course did not sign anything. That would not work for the government. But the accord stands.

More than 1,000 producers from the canal zone went to the state capital to convince Governor Julio César Ruiz Ferro to allow them to sell corn to Guatemala, or, as Rogelio argued, to "open other doors, remove the police . . . There were many meetings. Maybe 100 in this region."

Many border residents claim credit for expelling state agents from patrolling the border or do not recall why authorities stopped intervening. Border merchants with more experience, like Leandro, remember that the canal producers met with the governor in Tuxtla, whereas merchants and border residents were more involved in organizing within the route and with struggles with state policing units. According to Leandro, "Before we did not have much communication with [the canal producers], but they wanted to sell their product through [the border route]." Many border residents became aware of the informal agreement with the governor only when the canal producers arrived to attempt to use the border route to transport corn to Guatemala. Residents complained that the producers were trying to circumvent locals and "be free and not pay the tolls or a commission [to our merchants]" to use the road.

A secretary from the governor's office and producers from the canal region came to the Mexican border communities to resolve these disputes and to establish that no taxes would be levied for corn. Yet because border residents' controlled access to the border route and claimed that the tolls help maintain the road, border merchants kept levying tolls on merchants using their road and established their role as intermediary merchants. Because they owned the land on which the commerce depends, residents interpreted control of the corn trade as a subsistence right as other means of livelihood dissipated. Leandro explained:

> We came to an agreement that we would transport the product to Guatemala. Guatemalans cannot enter here. Only the producers from the canal region can come here, but [we usually transport the corn to Guatemala]. It has to be us. Since we are at the border, [people began to] dedicate themselves to transport. [Others] need to talk with us so they do not ruin the business and take away our work. They need to abide by the rules.

Agreements established that Mexican border merchants would transport all corn. Any truck transporting corn to the border had to unload it and deliver it to border merchants to sell to Guatemala.

Producer Rogelio derided the manipulations of border intermediaries but admitted their necessity: "I don't know much about commerce, but it's what [border merchants] live from." What was most important to Rogelio was "to receive a good price [for our corn]." Because the larger milling companies do not buy from his association and some small private warehouses in Mexico will pay the producers only about US$270 per ton of corn, they prefer to sell to border merchants who pay US$320. Yet they know Guatemalans will purchase the corn at US$360 per ton. Rogelio blamed Guatemalan brokers for impeding direct access to buyers because he believed, "They take advantage the most since they don't do anything." But, as he mentioned, "Many of us [producers] don't know Guatemalans. We don't know the payments, the weights [in Guatemala]. We prefer to go through the Mexican coyotes since they know and work with [Guatemalan brokers and merchants]."

When Rogelio's association attempted to bypass border merchants to sell corn directly to Guatemala, it failed due to lack of connections to state officials, Guatemalan buyers, and access to transport. They attempted to clear a segment of border terrain to create a new road to transport their corn across the border. Rogelio articulated the problem, "I can try [to sell corn] directly [to Guatemalans], but it doesn't work because they are like a mafia . . . the coyote and the broker . . . They know each other a long time . . . We can't avoid them since they work together." After negotiations in the late 1990s, border merchants made an exception to permit canal producers to transport their own corn directly (without using border intermediaries) to Guatemala, as long as they paid the community tolls. As commerce grew from requiring pickups to ten-ton trucks, however, few producers could afford this invest-ment, leading border merchants to monopolize trade and transport.

Border residents with less involvement in commerce are aware of an un-written accord that allows corn to freely cross the border, but few understand its legality or how it emerged. Guatemalan brokers and Mexican merchants collaborated and discussed the situation on their respective sides of the bor-der, but they negotiated separately with their own state officials to enable the trade. Mexican farmer Héctor adamantly stressed that agreements to allow Mexican corn farmers to sell their harvests to Guatemala were intended to apply only to an individual's harvest, and not to those conducting business: "This is what is free . . . for me to sell my harvest to Guatemala. It's my harvest; not business." But the lines between a farmer's harvest and business, and be-tween a legitimate informal trade and an illegal business, blur as people who used to sell their own corn to Guatemala began selling others' harvests. Diego explained, "Here the business is corn . . . Business grew as producers searched for a place to sell." Diego continued that some people began to say, "If you don't want to transport [your harvest], I will. That is how this commerce grew. It is still a harvest. It is someone from Mexico's product."

Border residents, merchants, brokers, and corn producers mutually ben-efit from the commerce and agree officials should not interfere because "corn is free." However, divergent ideas about subsistence rights and the practices and implications of free trade are emerging as the corn trade grew from a sub-sistence necessity to a transborder business in a region with few economic al-ternatives. Despite their differences, border merchants, border residents, and producers concur that official free trade provisions exclude them, challenge their right to subsistence, and are not free on any terms.

The Authorities Blind Themselves

Mexican border residents stressed that officials respected informal agree-ments to sell corn across the border. But what kept officials in line with an unwritten agreement? Jaime, a politician from Frontera Comalapa, could not recall the specifics of why corn could be transported across this border, but he acknowledged that "the authorities blind themselves." When I asked producer Rogelio how producers and border merchants were able to convince the police to abide by the accord, he responded, "[The police] were still bothering us, so we organized. If they bother producers, we ask them, is this your job to bother us? If you have an order, then show it to us. If you do not, then . . . there is no reason to bother us." "But do they accept this?" I asked with incredulity that state agents would respect these statements from peasant farmers. "They have to understand this," Rogelio argued. "If not the people will set them on fire, burn their cars. This happened in various parts of Chiapas. It is a game that is played. If [authorities didn't understand], the whole state of Chiapas would destabilize."

From discussions with Rogelio and border residents, it became clear that informal pacts undergirding the corn commerce did not arise because peasants fought back against or subverted the state through illegal practices. Instead, official toleration of this corn trade falls in line with Mexico's patterned response to social unrest in Chiapas, whereby the state employs a mix of selective coercion, harassment, appeasement, and concessions to co-opt dissent and maintain the political and economic status quo.[50] Mexico has long relied on clientelism, or the exchange of material or limited social and political benefits in exchange for political loyalty and support.[51] Clientelism has mediated the interdependence between informal actors and the state as the state strives to balance its commitment to the law with the reality of needing to tolerate a degree of informality among a large disempowered and marginalized population.[52] In the context of social uprisings (such as, but not limited to, the Zapatistas), economic crisis, and revelations of pervasive corruption in Mexico in the 1990s, permitting the corn trade was a low-stakes means for the state to mitigate rural discontent, detract attention from ongoing political corruption and state divestment from the countryside, and direct policing resources to more visible, pressing arenas. Governor Ruiz Ferro, whom residents cited as sanctioning the informal agreement, resigned in 1998 amid accusations of "ignoring many warning signs of tension in the region" after the paramilitary massacre of indigenous villagers in Acteal, Chiapas (see Chapter 4).[53] When he became governor in 1995, he was Chiapas's fifth governor since 1993. In light of popular discontent and the rising prominence of social protest, it becomes understandable why he may have placated corn producers and border merchants.

The Mexican state also periodically reminds border residents and producers of its authority to suspend or bend the rules. Rather than appearing as a "frustrated" state, a term that Centeno and Portes[54] use to describe states characterized by a proliferation of regulations combined with limited capacity to enforce them, this is an example of the fleeting appearances of the "phantom state."[55] Specifically, the state's presence and authority becomes felt in the lives of border residents amid its usual absence or neglect, reminding border residents that the phantom always lurks in the shadows.[56] One Mexican corn merchant complained in March 2007 that the nearby military base was "starting to charge us again [demand bribes for the corn trade]. The military is screwing us. They want their present." I asked, "What about the agreement?" "Yes, there is an agreement, but now there is a corn shortage, so Mexico [does not want] corn to leave." He elaborated, "They are saying everyone in the association will need to pay . . . *mil* pesos [about US$100] to the military. I don't know why, but I think it is because they want a transformer for their lights. It's a gift, they are calling it. But without it they will not let us work. It's a threat." In this region, officials were beginning to blame corn smuggling as one source of Mexico's corn shortage and rising prices, which detracted attention from the global demands for ethanol and transnational speculation and hoarding that were driving the crisis. Rogelio's producers were also targeted. Rogelio told me:

> The military detained one of my trucks today. I sent one of my people to talk to them to let them be. There is no reason to detain us. This is not their job. They have no warrant or order to detain us. We are not transporting any drugs. They don't want us selling our corn to Guatemala, but this isn't their job.[57]

Residents and producers point to the fact that Mexicans should be free to transport goods within Mexico, so there is no reason for the military to detain them on Mexican highways. Rogelio stood firm, "There is no reason to pay. People organize to confront these problems when they occur."

Through local organizing and negotiations with officials, producers and merchants returned to the status quo with official tolerance for the corn trade. However, such periodic, yet unpredictable manifestations of official disproval remind merchants that their trade is contingent on and therefore actually reinforces, rather than contests, the power and aura of the state. Whether manifested through raids or demands for bribes, state presence is palpable in fleeting encounters, dramatic displays, or through rumors. Merchant Leandro discussed the necessity of talking with state officials so "they understand . . . They know there is no other source of employment." However, he also recognized that "whether they let us work depends on the will of the authorities." Border residents and merchants worked the tense social climate of Chiapas to their advantage even though their benefits constitute minor concessions in the context of continued insecurity in the countryside. A Guatemalan broker related, "Corn is not worth much; you can't earn a lot. Sometimes merchants have no earnings. If the price rises in Mexico and is the same in Guatemala, there is a risk when you do not know." After paying for truck rentals, cargo loaders, tolls, and gasoline and accounting for volatile prices and small earnings, the corn business can sometimes be more risk than reward.

Rogelio describes the corn trade aptly: "A little bit legal; a little bit illegal. Not *legal* legal, but not really illegal either." With regards to the cross-border corn trade, there is not necessarily a clash between what Abraham and Van Schendel call the illegal (politically unacceptable) and the licit (socially acceptable).[58] The extralegal social definitions governing the corn trade are accepted among producers, merchants, residents, and state officials in a region where official laws and policies hold little salience. The legal and illegal are not necessarily opposed, but rather coexist within the domain of state power.[59] As Comaroff and Comaroff write in *Law and Disorder in the Postcolony*, "Vastly lucrative returns . . . inhere in actively sustaining zones of ambiguity between the presence and absence of the law."[60] The ability of the state to declare an exception for the extralegal flow of corn enhances its power to establish the rules, withhold them at will, and to manipulate the uncertainty of its decisions.[61]

Legalizing Corn

Merchants stated that regardless of informal agreements in Mexico, the main impediments were in Guatemala, where corn's unregulated entrance makes it contraband. Mexican residents positioned the corn trade as somewhat illegal but permitted, but many Guatemalan residents asserted it was legal. Guatemalan cargo loader Emilio assured me that "corn in Guatemala is not prohibited. It is food. If we did not have corn, Guatemalans would die of hunger. People are united to ensure that corn from Mexico is free. If not, we will organize and go on strike against the government."

Huehuetenango, Guatemala, suffers from historical corn shortages, which it has often supplemented with Mexican corn. In the late 1990s and early

2000s, Guatemala registered critical corn shortages due to hurricane damage. Strikes throughout Huehuetenango in 1998, in addition to the devastating effects of Hurricane Mitch on local harvests, convinced the mayor, who claims direct authority over the municipality (on the basis of postwar democratic reforms supporting enhanced municipal autonomy),[62] to meet with Guatemalan border residents, the governor of Huehuetenango, and Guatemalan customs officials (SAT).

Border residents, the governor, the mayor, and corn merchants signed a document to authorize the entrance of Mexican corn. The document was in La Democracia's municipal building.[63] The municipality declared the agreement valid only at this border crossing and only for corn. In return for a tax of about US$7 per ten-ton truckload of corn to the municipality of La Democracia, managed by a woman in El Girasol, truckers receive receipts to protect them from police encroachment.[64] Merchants consider the fees minimal. Although customs officials disagreed over the appropriate tariff for corn, a Guatemalan broker believed the rate in La Mesilla would be nearly US$650 in tariffs for each ten-ton truckload of white corn. Obstacles to legal commercialization, in addition to recognizing how corn shortages increased prices for Guatemalan consumers, motivated the municipality to permit and document the corn flow, thereby giving it the semblance of legality. Customs officials decried the accord as illegal and refused to sign, but the mayor's assertions held sway. One corn broker reiterated the mayor's indignation: "Am I not a representative of the government? Until another accord is signed, this one is valid. If not, then am I not valid as a government authority?" The corn trade is considered more legal on the Guatemalan side, recognized by the mayor and bolstered by receipts and municipal documentation. The lack of a national-level policy, however, makes border residents vulnerable to the proclivities of particular officials. When officials change, police have detained brokers, but Guatemalan brokers will unite with long-distance merchants and community members to blockade highways, and even hold police hostage, until the accord is respected and brokers are released.

Guatemala has periodically removed corn tariffs or increased imports to mitigate shortages and control price hikes, but regional corn shortages, obstacles to commercialization and distribution in Guatemala, and the influence of organized merchants enable the trade to continue despite civil society's growing protests against contraband and corruption.[65] Guatemala temporarily allowed corn to enter duty free to offset shortages in 2011, but contraband increased because few producers were prepared to participate.[66] Guatemalan officials, as in Mexico, manipulate support of the corn trade to their advantage, as they also understand that powerful merchant opposition can threaten their positions and regional stability. When former Guatemalan President Otto Pérez Molina (2012–2015) first campaigned for president in 2006 in La Democracia, residents said he offered to regularize this corn trade. This never transpired; in 2011 police began a renewed campaign of detaining corn merchants despite the agreement. Once again, brokers and merchants mobilized to defend the right to transport corn.

Trucking U.S. Corn

Efforts focused on smuggling corn not only reinforce peasants' dependence on the proclivity of state officials, but also obscure the roots of peasants' hardships: the dominance of agribusiness, the lack of reform of the agricultural sector, and the absence of economic alternatives.[67] Daniel Villafuerte Solís emphasizes the persistence of structural problems plaguing Chiapas's development: dependence on an inefficient primary sector, lack of investment and industrialization, deforestation, the devastation of the agricultural sector, land conflict, a tenuous sociopolitical situation, poverty, the inability to attract foreign investment, and rapid population increase.[68] Border residents have not joined coalitions throughout Mexico mobilizing to demand the renegotiation of free trade agreements and investment in the countryside or to fight for food sovereignty.[69] They remain politically, socially, and geographically removed from these efforts. In Guatemala, temporary agreements to satisfy corn shortages fail to address structural problems plaguing the agricultural sector: poverty, lack of state investment, risks to food security, fragmentation of the maize sector and lack of formal credit for commercialization, and the high costs and inefficiencies of internal commercialization.[70]

More savvy residents and merchants critiqued the exclusions of official free trade policies and the liberalization of agriculture. They understood how these policies diminished their ability to make a living as farmers, put them into competition with cheaper U.S. corn, and excluded them from opportunities to engage in legal forms of cross-border trade. Yet corn smuggling does not provide an alternative grassroots form of free trade.[71] This corn trade is embedded within the very neoliberal corn commodity chain that displaced border farmers to begin with. Each summer when regional corn is scarce, trailers arrive to depots in Santa Rosa, Mexico, full of corn from northern

Mexico and the United States. This corn is easy to identify. It does not come in satchels with labels of defunct CONASUPO warehouses; it comes spilling loose from trailers. Cargo loaders use machines to funnel corn into satchels and earn more than double what they earn loading prepackaged regional corn. Merchants with business connections like Leandro work with these long-distance merchants. Leandro will receive a call about a shipment that will arrive in Santa Rosa. He then transfers the corn to his trucks to sell to Guatemala. Border residents prohibit the entry of this corn until after local and regional corn is sold to protect their prices. However, this does not always occur, resulting in lower prices with which regional producers cannot compete. Facilitating sale of long-distance corn widens inequalities between wealthier merchants and poorer ones, like Ramón, who lack such connections and are out of work this time of year. Furthermore, this corn flow fuels the very economic dynamics that put border peasants out of work in the first place—the influx of cheap U.S. corn.

The Coyote Benefits Most

Just as this corn trade does not necessarily provide an alternative to the neoliberal corn commodity chain, it is also misleading to assume it provides a more viable and equitable economic alternative. The corn trade generates ripple effects through the border by employing merchants, brokers, truckers, and cargo loaders while providing producers with an outlet for their harvests. One merchant explained, "Everyone eats from this commerce—the truckers, the cargo loaders." Small stores and mobile vendors pop up around depots to cater to merchants and cargo loaders. Commerce brings wider benefits because truckers pay tolls to the communities and residents can sell their harvests to Guatemala. Relative to other smuggling ventures, entry costs into the corn market are low. Purchasing corn is less expensive than buying sugar and coffee, and corn merchants do not pay bribes to officials. Yet Mexican politician Jaime qualified that the coyotes (merchants) benefit the most—"the people conducting business. They continue paying the producers a low price, and they profit selling to Guatemala." Jaime stepped back to note, though, that it is not simply a story of exploitation. He noted, "It is not bad since they are working their lands. No one has an interest in stopping the corn flow. They understand [producers'] need to sell their harvests."

Although providing work, the corn trade offers few opportunities for economic mobility. Yolanda, who lives in Nueva Vida, Guatemala, is married to a corn broker, Máximo, who works on commission for Mexican merchant Leandro. "Leandro is his *patrón* [boss]," she stated. "He delivers corn to Máximo, who then looks for someone [to] buy it. It is [Leandro's] corn. He sets the price since he knows where to purchase it."

Some former refugees in Nueva Vida, like Máximo, are well positioned to enter business. After living over a decade in Mexico as refugees, they maintained Mexican contacts as they reestablished themselves in Guatemala in the 1990s. Some retained connections in the Guatemalan interior. But former refugees often lack the economic resources and business experience to become brokers because they have lived largely agricultural lives. In 2007, there were only three brokers in Nueva Vida (but many cargo loaders); the majority of brokers live in El Girasol. Similarly, in the new community of La Maravilla, Mexico, due to exclusion as indigenous former Guatemalans and a lack of economic resources, only one resident is a corn merchant. Successful merchants tend to be long-term residents with deeper cross-border connections and more economic resources.

Few cargo loaders earn enough to become brokers. Máximo used to be a cargo loader; he was able to become a broker only due to a loan of 30 million quetzales from his wife's siblings in the United States. He got to know clients in Guatemala from loading trucks. "To begin, you need money," Yolanda stressed. "In El Girasol there are many merchants, but few here. [Nueva Vida] is a new community, and some people don't think [to enter business]. You need the capacity. You are also responsible. If you lose something you need to pay. It always costs." Many merchants, due to fluctuating prices and corn's relatively low value, struggle to make ends meet. Yolanda supplements her family's income by selling food to merchants and cargo loaders.

Some producers resent the influence of intermediaries, and some Guatemalan brokers desire more active roles over Mexican merchants. Yet instead of developing differing class positions, the trade's dynamics often reflect what Liliana Goldín refers to as a "seesaw" effect: Who is "up" or "down" varies according to circumstances.[72] Accumulation in the corn trade is small because of price fluctuations, corn's relatively low price, and transport costs. Merchants remind others who believe they earn large profits that the corn trade is seasonal from January until March. Many became merchants in the first place because they lacked sufficient land to grow enough corn for subsistence. Poorer merchants like Ramón believe canal producers may have an advantage because they reap two harvests per year, whereas he obtains just one. Most border merchants continue to primarily identify as corn farmers even if they barely farm. In the context of a rural corn crisis, Mexican producers, Mexican merchants, and Guatemalan brokers mutually depend on the trade and agree that if officials were to intervene, they would not survive.

Alternative Free Trade?

At first glance, this corn trade appears to be a form of resistance to the liberalization of the Mexican and Guatemalan countryside and the exclusion of peasants. However, residents' practices do not necessarily contest neoliberal free trade policies; rather, they reconfigure relations with the neoliberal economy and the state in complex, and often contradictory, ways. Local mobilizations surrounding the right to sell corn over the border motivated, as they were enabled by, larger regional and national political, social, and economic shifts that created opportunities for contraband and demands for local border control. The free trade discourses that residents heard through radio, municipal authorities, and rumor, as well as through rising U.S. migration in the 1990s, coincided with the withdrawal of state officials who previously policed this route. In this context, the confusion-convergence over free trade becomes understandable. The next chapter details how residents expelled state agents from the crossing in the context of political and economic crisis.

4 Taxing the Border

ON A HOT AND DUSTY APRIL AFTERNOON in 2007, I sat with Alonso, a primary school teacher, outside Santa Rosa's tollbooth. The tollbooth was a small wooden shack on the edge of the community's territory. More important was the metal-linked chain looped around a metal pole that draped across the road. The chain marks where each truck transporting commerce across the border must stop to pay a toll to Santa Rosa. Residents call the tollbooths *cadenas* (chains) after the chains that each community uses to demarcate its territory and regulate entry. At the *cadenas*, residents levy what they call "taxes" on truckers who use their route to smuggle goods across the border. Considered contraband due to the evasion of official border inspections, taxation, and documentation, their toll system converts this smuggling into a locally regularized commerce.[1] The border communities use the proceeds for road maintenance and local development projects, including a park, a roofed-in basketball court, and extension of water and electrical services. Santa Rosa's park and basketball court are the envy of other rural communities. El Nance began work on theirs in 2007 and Nueva Vida in 2014.

Prices are labeled with marker on a poster-board on the shack: 50 pesos (about US$5[2]) for a ten-ton truck, 30 pesos (about US$3) for a three-ton truck, and 15 pesos (about US$1.50) for a pickup truck. Two community members are always present to maintain accountability and minimize theft. Each pair serves a twelve-hour shift, and the *cadena* is patrolled twenty-four hours a day. At each monthly assembly meeting, the community president announces how much money each pair collected, which publicizes the community's proceeds and each collection team's efforts. When theft is suspected, Santa Rosa will double-check its ledger with El Nance. Patrolling can be monotonous and even grueling when temperatures reach 100 degrees in April and torrential rains hit late every afternoon between June and September. When I expressed my interest in serving a shift, residents were somewhat dumbfounded: "Why would you want to do that?" "Is [your landlord] making you serve his shift? He shouldn't do that." Similar to the *ejido*'s other communal obligations (current and past), each household head is responsible for one shift per month, which is referred to as serving the *cadena*. Residents view the *cadena* as a benefactor of the community. As one woman put it, "We live from the *cadena* [tolls]." In practice, however, I rarely saw wealthier residents or local smugglers patrolling the *cadena*. They usually pay poorer residents to conduct their service. For some residents, this income is a form of livelihood. I once patrolled a twelve-hour shift with Julia, a widow in Santa Rosa who serves the *cadena* a few days a week to support herself. She is one of the only women who patrols because it is generally viewed as a male household responsibility. Julia reflected the intimate knowledge of border flows that residents gain from serving the *cadena*. Not only did she know most of the truckers because, as she said, many came through weekly, but she also knew what each truck was transporting. She knew not by looking inside, but by eyeing how low the truck appeared to be riding. She told me which ones carried corn, cement blocks, or mangos.

There are four community-run tollbooths in this border route that follow similar operations. Alonso was in charge of Santa Rosa's *cadena* record keeping in 2006 and 2007 during my fieldwork. Based on his ledgers, Santa Rosa collected roughly the equivalent of US$60,000 in 2006. Multiplied by four border communities receiving similar tolls, these sums are substantial in rural communities where the average wage for a day in the fields is US$6. Taking Alonso's advice, Santa Rosa set up a bank account in the municipality of Frontera Comalapa and began to raise its prices for trucks from Guatemala (which are often larger and were believed to cause more wear on the road).

Ten-ton trucks sped by, churning up dust and exhaust as they navigated the road alternately composed of dirt and pavement. Each trucker knew to come to a screeching halt at the tollbooth (Figure 4.1). Residents may raise the chain to block officials or smugglers who do not respect the tollbooth, but

Figure 4.1. Woman collecting money from a trucker at the cadena.
SOURCE: Author photo.

this is rare. Truckers know to stop and pay. Perplexed as to why smugglers, who were usually wealthier and more powerful than rural residents, acquiesced to the tolls, I asked Alonso, "Why do they pay? Are there truckers who refuse to stop?" He responded, "[They pay] because they know this is the law [in the route]."[3]

Residents argue that because the international border crosses through their land on a road they largely constructed, they have the right to levy tolls and engage in business that depends on their road. In this view, land ownership, along with road construction and maintenance, gives them the right to, as many people repeated, "make the law" within the route.[4] As one resident put it:

> The police need our permission to enter since this land is ours. The government has no right to enter since they haven't done anything for us. There have been no programs to maintain the road ... it was us who opened the path over the mountains [over the border] ... So what right does the government have to interfere here?

The *cadena* system institutionalizes local control over this route. The *cadenas* provide community funds, enact local authority over the route, and provide an alternative view of the border and the role of the state. However, in practice, local control is partial and negotiated with more powerful regional actors, including long-distance smugglers and state agents. The *cadenas* exemplify the ambivalence that residents exhibit toward the contraband economy, which disproportionately concentrates resources in the hands of smugglers, corrupt government officials, and formal businesses that benefit from smuggled goods. Inhabitants recognize the economic benefits that contraband provides to their communities, even as they also experience increasing inequality and insecurity.

The border route was not always under local control. According to Diego, the former secretary of Santa Rosa, Mexico, "Around 1978 there were more problems . . . The state controlled [this area] more since they were interested in bribes. Before [the officials] bothered business, but no longer after about 1994 [referring to the year of the Zapatista rebellion]." It was difficult to collect reliable information on the history of border policing. There were no official records of the inconsistencies of state regulation, and the communities kept only paper records in their assembly buildings, most often detailing things like land and livestock sales. I relied on triangulating interviews and talking with residents in groups to discern when changes in border surveillance occurred. I asked questions focusing on major family events including marriages, births, baptisms, and land purchases to narrow down dates and jog memories. I spoke with older residents and tracked down former community presidents to gather their reflections. Rather than finding firm dates, there was a general consensus that the border began to change in the mid-1990s. However, how the story was told was inflected by the experience of each individual, as well as that person's past and current position in the community and his or her relation to the contraband economy. Locating information was often, as in much ethnographic fieldwork, the result of serendipity, patience, and perseverance.

Alonso shared the *cadena* records in his notebook from the past two years with me, but he could not remember when the community began levying tolls. Some residents said it was a decade ago, others said fifteen years ago, and others thought it was closer to twenty years. Diego said the community began recording in 1998 but began collecting, albeit in a less organized fashion, a few years prior. Searching for the records to see how flows had changed over time

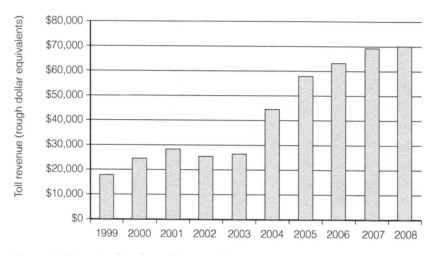

Figure 4.2. Santa Rosa's *cadena* toll proceeds from 1998 to 2006. The amounts are displayed in rough U.S. dollar equivalents using the 2007 exchange rate (about 10.7 pesos to US$1, depending on monthly fluctuations).

SOURCE: Community archives, Santa Rosa, Mexico. Compiled by the author with projections by Dan Galemba.

seemed to be a dead end. No one knew who had the records. Juan, the community vice president of Santa Rosa, took me to the community archive to search. Juan was unsure how to open the locked file cabinet, for which the key seemed to have vanished. At first, I was unsure if the key was truly nowhere to be found or if I were being led in circles. As I persisted, Juan suggested finding someone to break it open. I do not know if it was eventually pried open or if the key magically appeared, but Juan invited me to sift through the contents a few days later. Piled waist-deep in records of land sales, births, assembly attendance records, and cattle sales, I could barely decipher the information written in faint pencil markings. Then one day a student from the English classes I taught to local youth invited me to her grandparents' home for lunch. As we were talking, I learned that her grandfather, Esaúl, was the first person in charge of Santa Rosa's *cadena*.

Like many older Mexican border residents, Esaúl was born in Guatemala, but crossed the border with his mother as a young child. He told me that he became president of the *cadena* in 1996, but the community began levying tolls in 1993. When I mentioned that I was looking for the records, Esaúl stopped talking, got up from his chair on the patio, and went into his house.

I looked around perplexed. When he returned, he handed me a pile of dusty notebooks. Inside were all the penciled-in *cadena* records from the middle of 1998 until when Alonso's notebook left off. The notebooks had been under his bed for years. I saw that toll prices per truck had remained relatively constant, but the number of trucks and amount of commerce had grown dramatically in the past few years (Figure 4.2).

Establishing the *Cadena*

Santa Rosa and El Nance began levying tolls around the same time but residents from both communities admit it was the idea of one man in El Nance, Mexico: Manuel. According to Manuel, in the mid-1980s, a tax collector, or *fiscal*, was assigned to patrol the border route, characteristic of the historical vacillation of border vigilance. The collector rented a room in Manuel's house because he was the community president at the time and there was no official office. Manuel saw the *fiscal* levying tolls on passing vehicles and thought, "If he can charge and put money in his pocket, why shouldn't [the community] also charge? We are the ones who live here, own the land, and maintain the road." Soon after, Manuel erected a post outside his home and began levying taxes alongside the *fiscal*. The neighboring border communities soon followed and began organizing to expel officials from the route. In a setting where state vigilance has been historically haphazard and corrupt, it was the tax collector's, and not Manuel's actions, that seemed arbitrary.[5]

Border residents argue that they can patrol the border and levy taxes because the commerce transits through their territory. Not only did residents on both sides of the border collaborate to construct the road in the 1980s; they also maintain it. Road maintenance is a difficult task when 100 ten-ton trucks may transit the road each day. They argue that their road is not a federal highway; they see no contradiction with state officials patrolling federal highways and official inspection posts. El Nance points to the fact that it is a community of private property owners, where each owner ceded a portion of land to construct the road. Santa Rosa's identification as an *ejido* reveals multiple interpretations of autonomy and landownership rights. Residents assert they pay *ejido* taxes to the government and acknowledge that *ejido* lands were granted by the state. However, Mexico's history of corporatist control gave *ejidos* a large degree of de facto autonomy as this system simultaneously vertically linked local elites and their communities to the Institutional Revolutionary Party (PRI) patronage system.[6] When defending their right to the *cadena*, residents in Santa Rosa assert that "the *ejido* is autonomous to make its own rules." They critically reassess this interpretation of Mexican *ejido* laws to state that their communities are autonomous to enact their laws within their territory.[7] Such local autonomy, of course, was never meant to apply to international commerce. Claims to autonomy also draw on a long history in Chiapas, where the presence of the federal government was thinly felt. After independence from Spain in 1821, Chiapas's elite sought annexation to Mexico in 1824, believing that the distance to Mexico City would allow for greater autonomy and that joining Mexico would provide more stability and prosperity than joining Central America; in fact, Chiapas is the state where the oligarchy most intensely resisted the reforms of the Mexican revolution.[8] Locals have feared that if the state paved the entire border road, officials would have the justification to exert greater surveillance. The desire for a paved road, combined with distrust of the state, led the road to resemble a literal patchwork of state–community authority. Segments of the road are composed of new pavement, which adjoin portions of shoddier pavement and dirt and rocks.

Inhabitants constructed the border road in a fashion that reflects their conceptualization of the border, which predates more explicit official definition. Héctor explained that until the International Commission of Limits and Water "clarified the border with additional monuments, many people thought the border went in the other direction." He drew one line in my notebook and penciled in the official borderline perpendicular to the first line. According to local understandings, in the 1980s the communities constructed the border road perpendicular to, and crossing through, the white monuments delineating the official division between Mexico and Guatemala. Most residents and smugglers do not experience the border at the official line, especially because officials rarely enter the route. Instead, the *cadenas* are the sites of everyday border encounters, where each community marks its territory and levies tolls. Consequently, residents perceive social and economic relations according to the direction of their border road across which they erected the chains. In contrast to the north–south geography implied by the official international border, commerce is depicted as going up (due to the hill) to Guatemala and down to Mexico.

Residents morally assert that they are not only the rightful border authorities, but also more benevolent than state officials whom they deride as engaging in extortion. They reason that "officials belong in their offices" where they have salaries and their appropriate jurisdictions. They believe that if officials come to monitor their border road, they are acting outside of their mandates, which constitutes corruption. Diego highlighted the ethics of local taxation, "We only charge people who are . . . conducting business. If you earn money you have to cooperate. If it is just an individual's harvest, we understand. We appreciate if they contribute, but we don't force them." In fact, residents of El Girasol, Guatemala, stress that paying their tolls, even for smugglers, is voluntary. Residents credit their own efforts for establishing local control over the border. Yet their mobilizations occurred within a wider context of social movements, economic and political crisis, peasant uprisings, and protests against official corruption, which came to a head on both sides of the border in the mid- to late 1990s.

Crises of Governance and Social Movements

From the 1960s into the 1990s, immigration and customs officials, soldiers, and other state officials were intermittently stationed on both sides of this border route. Older residents mention there was even a small Mexican customs house in the route from 1955 to 1972, but that it was subsequently removed. Some people hinted that it was El Nance who ran them out because the officials were renting land from local landowners. During the Guatemalan war in the 1980s, Guatemalan soldiers patrolled the international line. Their presence usually lasted a few days or weeks, and then the border would revert to being unpatrolled. There was a small customs post in El Girasol until the National Civil Police (PNC) was created in 1997. The governor of Huehuetenango said it was removed due to "a lot of problems and corruption"; now the police are in charge of dealing with contraband. A customs house was previously located on the Mexican highway immediately outside of the border route, but this was removed around 1991 during a period of Mexican fiscal reform. The rationale was that having tax inspectors stationed throughout the vast border region with a large degree of autonomy was not only a waste of resources but also would breed corruption and abuse. The only visible state presence near the crossing is a Mexican military base a few miles from the route on the Mexican highway. Throughout the late 1980s and 1990s, periodic mobile inspections by the state police, the federal police, the military, the road police, customs, and immigration became more prevalent on the Mexican side of the route.

In the mid 1990s and early 2000s, border residents took advantage of a regional climate of social movements, economic crisis, and crises in governance in Mexico to expel state agents and assert their control over the border route.[9] Diego refers to this as the period when "people woke up and began to fight for their rights." Similarly, Jan Rus and his coauthors refer to the 1990s as a period of awakening in Chiapas, as rural peasants discovered a newfound "political self-consciousness" to respond to economic and political crisis.[10]

Throughout most of the twentieth century, Mexico relied on a political system of corporatism, mastered by the PRI, which held power for seventy-one years until the year 2000. Corporatist politics was a system by which the Mexican state cultivated the support of peasants, workers, and popular organizations and contained discontent through state patronage. State-sponsored institutions provided access to land, credit, and state resources in exchange for party loyalty and votes.[11] Criticism of government corruption and a crisis in governance were building in Mexico since the late 1960s. This came to a head when soldiers brutally massacred student protestors in the Tlateloco housing complex in Mexico City in 1968. The government failed to investigate, and in the context of the Cold War deflected blame onto "extremists and Communist agitators."[12] The administration of Luis Echeverría Alvarez (1970–1976) attempted to mitigate protests through clientelistic politics using land distribution and an ambitious public spending program backed by foreign loans emboldened by expectations surrounding high oil prices.[13] Yet the debt crisis of the early 1980s exposed the contradictions and shortcomings of the Mexican corporatist system.[14] Problems mounted as the state had fewer resources to placate and co-opt dissent following the 1982 debt crisis, default, and economic crisis. Problems were compounded by the state's poor handling of the 1985 earthquake. Into the 1990s, the 1995 peso collapse, when the peso lost half of its value; and increasing revelations of government corruption, further diminished confidence in the Mexican state. In a context of economic and political crisis, independent, rather than state-affiliated, peasant, indigenous, and worker organizations began to attract greater support as people saw decreasing utility of affiliating with a declining state apparatus in economic crisis.[15] The system of state corporatism practiced by the PRI in Mexico began to unravel in the 1980s and 1990s to reveal wider crises in governance. The Carlos Salinas de Gortari administration (1988–1994) became widely renowned not only for institutionalizing the neoliberal model in Mexico and its devastating effects on peasants and the poor but also for its revelation of extensive corruption with the PRI. The Zapatista rebellion, which began on January 1, 1994 in coordination with the day that NAFTA went into effect, not only revealed the inability of the Mexican state to respond to the needs of its citizens but further demonstrated how the state countered dissent with repression.

The Zapatistas emerged from the jungles of Chiapas on January 1, 1994 to demand the right to land and livelihood, respect for indigenous rights and autonomy, an end to government corruption and abuses, and a revision of the neoliberal policies embodied through NAFTA that threatened peasants' livelihoods. To contain the conflict, the Mexican government strategically employed a mix of co-optation (including the provision of benefits and social programs to organizations and communities friendly to the state), selective repression, and militarization.[16] Rosalva Aída Hérnandez Castillo has termed this strategy the government's "two-faced policy: economic aid and paramilitarization," which intended to "divide the indigenous and peasant movement."[17]

The state mixed militarization and selective repression with strategic concessions to bring peasants back into the state fold. As Mexico militarized the state of Chiapas in the late 1990s, fears that individuals would join the Zapatistas also made some officials more willing to negotiate with local demands and to cultivate clientelist ties. However, despite the fact that the Zapatista rebellion showed the government it could no longer ignore the demands of the marginalized, it also highlighted how protest would have its militarized limits.[18] The 1997 Acteal Massacre in Chiapas, when a PRI-supported and armed vigilante groups murdered forty-five residents, mostly women and children, in the indigenous highland village of Acteal, revealed the complicity and violence of the state in repressing potential dissent.[19] Instability and crises in governance led Chiapas to have five governors in five years in the late 1990s, with communities divided over whether to accept government aid, fall back into clientelistic politics, or join those in rebellion.[20]

Jan Rus and his coauthors describe how economic crisis compounded by a crisis in governance led peasants in Chiapas to organize:

> In the face of deepening economic distress, with a government that had only made things worse by eliminating aid programs and ending agrarian reform, and then had met Indians' demands to solve their own problem through independent organizations and cooperatives by repressing those organizations, indigenous people throughout Chiapas were by the early 1990s increasingly angry with the government and willing to defy it.[21]

It is within this context that border residents, although in a region marginal to the Zapatista struggle, united to expel officials from patrolling the border route. The Zapatista conflict had multiple indirect effects in this region with fewer Zapatista supporters. As Jan Rus and his colleagues assert, "Even for the communities that did not participate directly in the rebellion, life after January 1, 1994, changed dramatically."[22] The Zapatistas provided peasants with a discourse to fuel their struggles against official corruption, distracted official attention from the border due to greater concerns in the highlands and jungle where there were more Zapatista supporters, and made some officials more willing to negotiate with local demands due to increasing fears of a rebellious peasantry. As Mexican border resident Héctor noted, "After the Zapatistas, [peasants] began to lose their fear. They became more aware they could fight for their rights and that authorities could not take advantage [of them]." Diego situated local mobilization within this context of the rise of strong peasant organizations in Chiapas in the 1990s and the Zapatista rebellion in 1994:

> [In the 1970s] there weren't any organizations here. Now there are many that were born out of the Zapatista movement and their influence in the 1990s. [These] influences started in 1978 and came to a head in San Cristóbal in 1994 when the problem became stronger. The roots were problems with government authorities. People were angry about the attitudes of officials. Here not much happened, but there was war in San Cristóbal. Organizations began spreading here at that time . . . businesses, taxi drivers, all joined organizations like OCEZ [Organización Campesino Emiliano Zapata].[23] *Zapatismo* spread all over the state. Some people went to the highlands, to the jungle. Messages also spread by radio. Now if at a moment the fiscal or federal police prevent us from selling [our goods] to Guatemala, there will be a conflict between peasants and the officials. But [the officials] already know, from fear, that there will be conflicts if they bother us.

Most border residents did not have direct contact with the Zapatistas but heard their messages through radio and local affiliations with independent peasant organizations. Yet the border region did change after 1994. The government began selectively offering programs and aid to peasant communities to draw their support. For example, the government began giving out fertilizer to border farmers, but according to Diego this was "very little . . . maybe four or five bags per farmer, and now not everyone receives them." Diego reflected that after 1994 state officials:

> Stopped interfering and began to understand producers more. The people pressured [the authorities] to let them work [in contraband]. The community was tired and fed up with the authorities taking advantage of, and bothering them—acting like they were all powerful. So then when police would come [to the border] the people would trap them, tie them up, and they would turn around in their cars in fear. The people woke up, and now we are fighting.

The Zapatista movement resonated with border residents on some topics more than others; they took to heart its demands for land, livelihood, and respect for the peasantry. Borderlanders did not need the Zapatistas to alert them to official corruption, but the Zapatistas did provide a precedent that marginalized people could contest the corrupt abuses of authorities. This message was effective because often officials heeded it as they became wary of an organized peasantry. For example, Jan Rus and Diego Vigil note the state response to indigenous land invasions in San Cristóbal de las Casas, Chiapas, after 1994, writing, "The state, after an initial, failed attempt by police to retake the invaded land, apparently feared that a more violent response would drive the invaders into the arms of the Zapatistas . . . The state essentially stood aside."[24] This dynamic resonated at the border. Two customs officials recounted how angry locals once set an immigration post, with its agents inside, on fire.

Residents capitalized on a climate revealing the extensive corruption of officials. They realized that when officials detained them in the border route for smuggling and asked them for payment that the officials were collecting not taxes but bribes that they placed in their own pockets. According to a Guatemalan border resident, "These are not fixed payments. When [police] detain you in the road, those are bribes [they are demanding]." Others elaborated, "Officials only come here to extort the people . . . to get bribes. If they see a bag you are selling, they confiscate it and take the money. That's a bribe for them. They are the most corrupt." Virgilio, a small-scale peanut smuggler, related how local consciousness grew and residents began to reject official demands:

> We stopped paying. [We realized] it was never really a tax since customs [authorities] were entering only in their vehicles. This wasn't their office, and they

weren't reporting [what they were collecting]. They were putting it in their pockets. If I were to pass through Comitán or Ciudad Cuauhtémoc [official checkpoints] I would pay a tax that went directly to the government. But these were purely bribes. These were illicit payments . . . not taxes, but bribes.

Virgilio elaborated on the consequences of local resentment, "Now customs [officials] is afraid to enter here. They know if they enter here they will be treated as thieves." I probed Diego, "But what happens if officials do enter?" He smiled:

If the officials come to abuse us, we will run after them. We call all the people over the microphone, and then everyone will gather with sticks and machetes. We have done this before, so now [the officials] know better and don't bother us. We are friends now, and they have respect for us.

Residents proudly narrate stories of the community uniting to expel corrupt authorities as they often label officials—rats, which is the same term they use for criminals. Carlos, a university student, recalled a formative encounter when he was twelve years old:

One time the government entered here and caught someone . . . who was just bringing one bag of sugar from Guatemala. It wasn't even business . . . just for his consumption, but they caught him. So we called all the people together, and they came with stones and sticks that they put in the road so [officials] could not get out. Now the government is afraid of us. The people here captured one of the police officers, and he got scared. We put him in our [community] jail . . . it was many hours we kept him. People stripped him of his weapons, and some talked about setting him on fire, but really they just wanted to scare him. The other police came for him, and the commander came, and we reached an agreement.

After the people released the officer, the police agreed to no longer enter the community. They would no longer interfere in what residents argued was "business."

In another incident, a resident of Santa Rosa recalled how El Nance encircled authorities at their *cadena* who attempted to arrest a community member for smuggling. The officers were so scared to turn around to exit the route lest they encounter Santa Rosa after being surrounded by El Nance. Instead, they left by crossing over the unmonitored border to Guatemala and circling back around to the official highway in Mexico. They went miles out of their way and into Guatemala to avoid encountering Santa Rosa with their sticks. I wondered how the officers explained their reentry into Mexico at the official post. Guatemalan border inhabitants pursued similar tactics. As they stress their strong organization, they also underscore their benevolence to differentiate themselves from officials: "When we trapped the officials here [who attempted to arrest corn smugglers] until their boss came [to negotiate], we did not hurt them. We treated them well. We gave them food and drinks."

Some Guatemalan border residents learned about the Zapatistas from their Mexican neighbors, but others came to similar realizations that organized communities could contest official corruption as an aftereffect of the Guatemalan counterinsurgency conflict. With the end of the war and the signing of the Peace Accords in 1996, Guatemalan residents had high hopes for democratization. They were disillusioned as impunity, inequality, and violence sharpened in the postwar period. In particular, former refugees in Nueva Vida learned critical organizing skills during the war and postwar years, whether they fought directly with the guerillas, organized their peers in Mexican refugee camps and in the return movement, or participated in human rights workshops when they resettled in Guatemala. They had long been contesting official corruption and violence and forging their own alternatives even as they experienced the risks of organizing. Some members of Nueva Vida were directly threatened by the military as suspected guerilla fighters in the Guatemalan highlands during the war. In El Girasol, serving with the military-mandated civil patrols also taught some residents critical lessons about the government, even though many supported the military during the war. As the former community president of El Girasol, Roberto, related:

> It did not have much to do with the Peace Accords, but people did begin to lose their fear when the war was over. People began to respect themselves more, and the community began to rise up. The influence [of the war] was largely that many of us had been in the military. We realized we had rights as a community and people since the army did not place any value on our rights. [It was] a reaction to what we saw in the army. There were bad times when the army killed many people. We saw that the only people in the army who were trained were the officers. Most of the soldiers had no education. We learned [and saw] crazy things. We saw how those soldiers [without education] acted like they had value and the influence they had over things. They felt like they

had worth and respect, but at base it was ignorance. I [did not agree] with the army and saw no reason to follow their orders. People respected them even though they had no reason to. They had no basis from which to issue orders.

Even though they were on opposite sides of the conflict, inhabitants in El Girasol and Nueva Vida both came to realize how peasants had become pawns in a conflict that served the military elite and devastated communities. They lamented the impact that the war, and especially the army-mandated civil patrols, had on community solidarity. Neither community was willing to tolerate the abuse of officials or simply follow orders. As the communities organized, police began to acquiesce. According to Roberto:

If the police come in to conduct vigilance, that is fine, but we do not let them enter to bother us. If they bother us and take our money, we will set them on fire. The people began to realize [the police] should not do this. [The police] were abusive, and we are a humble village. We went to the military base in La Democracia and asked for a meeting with the commanders of the PNC to let them know if the police . . . act like thieves and do not listen . . . we will set them on fire.

Roberto told me that the mayor in La Democracia supported El Girasol's rationale to maintain the *cadena* because the municipality lacked the funds to provide projects like the ones the tolls supported. Roberto now calls the police his friends and adds, "They are afraid of the people. So if [the police] need to conduct vigilance or someone calls them to resolve a personal dispute, the [police] will call me before they come to escort them. They are afraid to come in here alone." However, Roberto admits that each time officials change or rotate, they have to renegotiate their arrangements, which can lead to unpredictability for border residents. Similarly in Chiapas, border residents renegotiate when officials rotate, although the commanders, or heads of each policing unit, often pass down information to subsequent officers on how the region works. Diego explained:

Sometimes there are problems with [officials] who do not know [how things work]. About two weeks ago the military caught someone transporting corn on the highway. [The merchant] called people here on the phone . . . A group of corn merchants went to see the commander [at the military base] to make sure he was in agreement. It was resolved, and he was released. The soldiers who caught him were new and did not know.

Problems are usually quickly resolved; as another resident told me, "It is not convenient for [officials] to denounce anything." Local unit heads will also advise smugglers if more distant police are coming. Then all movement suddenly screeches to a halt.

Limits to Control

Throughout the year from 2006 through 2007, I saw official vehicles traverse the unmonitored route, including military Humvees, local and state police, customs authorities, immigration authorities, and representatives from agricultural and health and sanitary inspections. Few of the vehicles ever stopped. As residents told me, "They are just coming to have a look." Others told me that officials were welcome if they "did their jobs," which according to residents, was to ensure safety and track more illicit or violent traffickers transporting weapons, narcotics, and undocumented migrants. Officials were not welcome if they interfered in what residents considered business, or the smuggling of basic goods such as corn, coffee, sugar, clothing, fruits and vegetables, canned goods and sodas, plants, and gasoline. I also witnessed trucks speed by the *cadena* without paying. Community narratives about the power of local organization belied the fact that local control was at best partial, contested, and contingent.

First, just because officials no longer enter the route to capture smugglers and demand bribes does not mean that no bribes are involved to smuggle goods across the border. To community members not involved in contraband, commerce appears legal and, as many say, "free," because they do not directly witness officials intervening as they did in the past. One woman reasoned if the commerce were illegal, it would occur at night and in secrecy, rather than during the day in the open. However, all smugglers (with the exception of corn) pay bimonthly payments to multiple units to permit them to work. The total count is now eleven for some enterprises like gasoline smuggling. Smugglers prefer this arrangement to impromptu detentions because they are not taken to jail, they can negotiate the amount, and arrangements are relatively predictable. Smugglers either pay the head of each unit in his office, or I learned that sometimes the reason police vehicles entered the route was to come have sodas with smugglers and collect payments in their homes. Once when I asked Diego why I saw more police when I thought they did not enter the route, he responded nonchalantly, "They are just coming to get their bribes. They are not bothering anyone." Even though smugglers still pay bribes, they prefer the prearranged method. According to Alonso, "The person who matters most is the federal highway police officer. He sees all the cars and commerce. If you can [get in] with him, the rest [policing units] are okay. He tells you who else to pay." The regular payments were usually lower amounts (than those demanded if they were caught in the act of smuggling) and more predictable because, according to Alonso:

> Before [the authorities] didn't come in every day, but when they did, it was a large fine. They would just say, give me this, or they would take you in and you had no choice but to pay. Now we talk and arrange payments so they don't bother us. You can negotiate a fair price. You can say, well, if I pay this much I can't work . . . to make him understand. Before we had to do what they demanded.

The border route is left unpatrolled only to the extent that authorities receive bribes and smugglers and officials continue friendly relations. In contrast to past relations of abuse, relationships are now characterized by respect and camaraderie. State agents and border smugglers eat at one another's homes, play soccer together, and share drinks. However, officials retain the power to renege on, or unpredictably alter, agreements, which means border smugglers continue to depend on the state and its agents even as they subvert the law.

Most truckers respect the tolls. They appreciate that the border communities maintain the road and ensure safe passage, but paying is also practical. Truckers would otherwise pay more at official posts or risk traversing more dangerous paths. This border route is renowned for low levels of violence, whereas residents related stories of robberies and assaults in other clandestine corridors. In 2007, drug traffickers murdered workers on a ranch in a sparsely inhabited unmonitored border crossing near Chamic. In contrast, residents and smugglers believe that the organized communities make their route safer. The fact that the communities levy tolls according to the size of the truck, rather than as a percentage of the value of the merchandise (as customs would assess), makes commerce quicker and more efficient for smugglers and residents. This way, residents can also maintain a semblance of not knowing what trucks are transporting, even though most have become experts. Because most truckers use the road regularly, they would ensure the wrath of residents on return if they did not pay.

Despite threats to block the road, borderlanders' control is limited by the realities of living in a highly trafficked unmonitored route. One day when I was at El Nance's *cadena* talking with a few men, a pickup transporting canisters of Mexican gasoline to Guatemala sped by the *cadena* without stopping. Six-year-old Ronaldo yelled after the truck, "I am going to get my gun!" The men laughed as one elaborated:

> Many people have pistols in their homes. We have a loudspeaker by the *cadena* to call people if there is a problem. But there aren't any problems. Ronaldo is just a child. He doesn't know. We live at a border, so we realize bad things and people can come from far away. The trucker should pay, but we don't usually do anything. Generally, the same people travel here and know the rules.

Another man added his unfortunate story, "My car was stolen in [Frontera] Comalapa after a concert one night. And then, can you believe it, we saw it speed by our *cadena*! It happened so fast that by the time we realized we could not do anything." To ensure their safety and moral high ground, the communities levy tolls only on vehicles transporting goods that are not considered illicit in and of themselves (for example, food, gasoline, clothing) but are illegal only because they evade official cross-border taxes, inspection, and documentation.[25] They do not levy tolls on what they deem illicit—smuggling drugs, weapons, and undocumented migrants. In addition to the inherent danger locals ascribe to drugs and weapons, they know the government now highly criminalizes drug, weapons, and migrant trafficking. More criminalization does not necessarily entail better policing, but it does mean higher risks, competition with criminal actors, and larger bribes.[26] One man explained, "If someone offers you money at the *cadena* and he is transporting drugs or migrants, you put that money in your pocket. We don't enter illicit things in the *cadena*." By closing their eyes to activities they consider illicit, residents enable these flows while they can continue to morally claim that tolls provide what they call a "legitimate and clean fund for the community." Meanwhile the communities minimize risky encounters with potentially armed actors. Although recognizing the potential for danger, some residents told me they liked when drug traffickers traversed the route because they bought them sodas or gave them money, saying "fix the road up nice."

Local distinctions between legitimate and illicit commerce maintain community safety and enable border residents to take advantage of border profits even as these flows merge. However, the *cadenas* do not benefit all residents equally, and some people question the value of the toll system as they witness growing inequality and insecurity. In debating the trade-offs between the security provided by better state surveillance versus the economic benefits of contraband, most residents prefer the latter in a context where government presence has been associated more with corruption than safety. As one Guatemalan resident told me, "Here the police are often the dirty ones."

Security or Business?

On the Mexican side of the border, state agents have long acquiesced to the *cadenas*, but one resident reminded me, "When the authorities agreed to allow us to have the *cadena*, they said not to expect them to help us anymore." In the late 1990s, Mexican resident Héctor told me the state government offered to pave the border road in exchange for removing the *cadenas*. The majority of residents approved and desired more state assistance, but the influence of more powerful smugglers, who feared state support would enable officials and police to intervene in smuggling and other border affairs, held sway. The offer was rejected. Residents are ambivalent about tensions between security and the benefits of contraband. One man related:

> It depends who you ask. If you ask ten people like me who aren't business-people, they will tell you it is better to have vigilance . . . for security. But if you ask someone in business, he will of course tell you it would be bad. Business benefits others [in the community] like cargo loaders, chauffers, but at a minimum.

Yet the choice was a false one because there was often no other option. The business opportunities provided by the border offered more possibilities than were available to nearby towns without this resource.

Gregorio, a Mexican businessman and trucker, argued that the smuggling economy might prevent drug addiction and delinquency. He reasoned:

> Business always helps here. Not just the businessmen. It also generates employment for those who load cargo. The *cadena* benefits . . . all the people here. Since there is a source of employment, there is no delinquency, so people don't get involved in dirty businesses. You can work correctly. Since we don't get involved in dirty business, the authorities help us so we can work well. If the [authorities] want to inspect my cargo to see that there is nothing dirty, fine with me. [The authorities] know we are living in a [precarious] economic situation, but we are working well.

Residents who are either uninvolved with, or more tangentially connected to, the contraband economy related that, although it provided job opportunities, the businesspeople benefited most. Diana, a widow in Santa Rosa, worried about potential risks to youth:

> It would be good to have vigilance [to avoid] drug addiction and those sorts of problems. To me, this would be good . . . if the authorities came to control for drugs, combat delinquency . . . especially for the sake of my children.

I asked if she thought the authorities would interfere in local smuggling businesses:

> It depends on what kind of business. If it's dirty business, like drugs or arms that they should be combating, that is good . . . for the authorities to come and control this so we and our children are not victims. But they should not intervene in the good businesses we work in. What are really contraband are drugs. That is what the authorities should be tackling.

Diana stepped back to remind me that the community is tranquil. Residents fear the influence of drugs and delinquency, but these problems were minor in their communities in 2006–2007 even though some youth did use drugs and dress in a style that residents associated with gang youth, despite any proof of affiliation. When asked whether they would prefer vigilance or the *cadena*, even the residents most apprehensive about the risks posed by an unmonitored border chose the *cadena*. Diana asserted, "It is good for the authorities to conduct vigilance as long as they do not interfere with the *cadena*."

As I was talking with Diana, her neighbor Sara stopped by. Sara began to relate a story of a girl who was murdered in La Mesilla, Guatemala. Although she described their border community as calm, she was full of stories she heard on the radio and television about other border regions where people are robbed and killed. She graphically described an incident in the border city of Tecún Umán, Guatemala: "I heard they ate her eyes and threw her in the trash. Because it is a border, many things come through, many people, also marijuana, stolen cars. There are big gangs, *maras* . . . Some kill just for the pleasure. Good thing they are not here." She admitted she was sometimes fearful because anything can pass through this border "because there is no vigilance or immigration authorities." She continued, "Some people wanted to put in an immigration post here, and I thought this was a good thing, but the people did not want it. I heard in Cuauhtémoc that [the government] is talking about putting an inspection post in here." Diana was unaware of this and worried this might interfere with the *cadena*. "No," Sara specified. "It would just be [to inspect for] drugs . . . stolen cars," but both women were uncertain if people would like this. Sara added, "Some people like that [these] things pass [through here]. They make money . . . those involved. Others do not like it. But they won't get involved in the commerce," to which Diana nodded approvingly, "They will still allow the *cadenas*."

In addition to community-funded projects, until recently, ill or poor community members could borrow funds from the *cadena*. In 2007 Santa Rosa began placing more restrictions on borrowing due to unpaid debts and an expanding community. In El Nance, each family receives a portion of proceeds each year after the community pays for community works and road maintenance. In the absence of state support and a dearth of livelihood options, the community, through the *cadena*, provides for itself and its families. Therefore, even if they risk state neglect, lack official security provision, and see the increasing inequality engendered by the contraband economy, the *cadena* continues to be the more reliable community benefactor. As many told me, "The *cadena* always helps us. It is a fund for the community" where there is little else. Due to distrust of the police, economic marginalization, and official corruption, like other communities in Mexico and Guatemala who experience the police and legal system as absent, violent, or corrupt, they have taken security, justice, and lawmaking into their own hands to an extent.[27] Although in other locations this has taken the form of community lynchings of suspected criminals or security communities that justify violence to preserve community safety, local border control has been relatively nonviolent even though authorities may portray local residents as prone to violent responses.[28] The road may appear abandoned by the state and residents seem to actively avoid state incorporation and attempts to render them legible,[29] but it is misleading to view this border route as outside of state control and to characterize residents' strategies as a form of resistance. Local control is not necessarily a rejection of the state; it is a commentary and performance of how border residents relate to, and often seek out a relationship with, the state.[30]

To some municipal authorities, the *cadenas* serves as a pretext to ignore the needs of the border communities. However, the influence of local smugglers may sometimes attract the attention of the municipality due to the campaign contributions and bribes that local smugglers provide to local politicians and authorities. Sometimes the cash flow proves influential in and of itself. When the municipality of Frontera Comalapa began construction on a portion of pavement it promised El Nance, construction came to a freeze halfway through the process. Work halted midstream when the municipality ran out of money to pay the contractors. When construction suddenly resumed a few months later, I learned that El Nance had loaned the municipality US$30,000 from its *cadena* account to pay the contractors.

Most residents applaud when state authorities fulfill their mandate to provide security against the trafficking of drugs, arms, and migrants. Residents assert that for these illicit activities, the army cannot be bribed. Yet they also admitted that traffickers know when the army leaves. When they receive notification from officials on their payroll, smugglers proceed to traffic stolen cars and drugs through the border. Others knew the military was often directly involved. As one resident explained, "Many traffickers are in with the military bosses. They call the boss and are told they can't pass because the army is there. So the boss will call his men to get out or let them pass. Everything continues to pass." A Mexican politician further dismantled any association between official surveillance and security. He told me in relation to then President Calderón's goal to increase military presence at the border, which explained the soldiers I encountered in the Introduction, "More vigilance and units have been sent to the border here. But they are the same ones complicit with what goes on here . . . many are paid [by traffickers]. It's a delicate situation." The choice between security, in the form of official state presence, and the *cadena* becomes obvious in a context where official security has been seen as corrupt, arbitrary, or in direct collusion with illicit actors.

Ambivalent Autonomy

Residents defend their right to the *cadenas* according to the internal laws of their communities. According to Edwin, a former community president of El Nance, who also smuggles corn, clothing, and gasoline, "We don't need [the government's] permission to have the *cadena*. It is an [internal matter]." He believed more state vigilance could generate larger problems. In his view, smugglers respected the authority of the border communities more than the government, and the people did a better job of providing security. Edwin debated the consequences of rumors that the Mexican government would regularize this crossing, including installing customs and immigration posts:

> We could not do anything if [the government regularizes this crossing]. They would not consult us. This would not be security. It would be unjust. It is against our laws [as a community]. We would not benefit at all.

I prompted a few informants with an article I found that mentioned regularizing this route. They had heard this may times before. They doubted the sincerity or capacity of the government to do this. Some feared officializing the crossing would lead to the removal of the *cadenas*, whereas others did not see any contradiction in pursuing their tax collection scheme alongside government regulation. One man in Santa Rosa asserted:

> If it happens, the *ejido* is autonomous and will fight to keep the *cadena*. [We have the] right to keep it even if [the government] puts in a customs post. The *ejido* lives from [the *cadena*] taxes. The government does not help us much, so the *cadena* does. It cost us a lot of work here . . . maintaining the road, building the assembly building. We spent a lot of time and effort trying to get the government to help, but nothing. It is better to do projects from the *cadena*.

Others pointed to the inefficacy of regularizing the border crossing to achieve security and stem illicit flows. One man related, "We have been hearing that [the government] will close this border for years, and nothing ever happens. And if they close the border over here, we will go over there," pointing to a proverbial and practical "*allá*," or "over there," indicating the vast geographic terrain of the borderlands.

Some residents believed they could fight official regularization and prevent authorities from interfering. However, most recognized that, although they had the power to unite to contest local and regional officials, they had little power if the federal government intervened. They grasped their limited ability to negotiate. In fact, even as they protested official corruption and interference in the border route, residents maintained respect for the general authority, or idea of, the state. Many residents criticized the Zapatistas for lacking this very respect. Edwin noted, "Autonomy can be good . . . people in the communities now have more education. But it can also be a bad thing to declare to do whatever you want. You need to respect the government."

Residents' interpretations of territorial sovereignty and local autonomy do not, in effect, undermine state logics of control based on jurisdiction over a demarcated territory, where the "boundaries of territorial competence [also] define the sovereignty of the state."[31] Though they threaten to take over state functions by regulating border entry and taxing commerce, they do so by interpreting statist logics that base sovereignty on territoriality literally. They reason that because the route was constructed through border residents' land, they should control it. Local conceptualizations of territoriality enable the border communities to ascribe the same rights to the state on federal land; they generally support the state's right to patrol the border at officially sanctioned posts. Such perceptions of territoriality influence how borderlanders view the dynamic of shared, albeit contested, authority at the border. Edwin argued, "People who use our road respect us more than the government since we are the ones [who live] here. We control the traffic and make the rules. It works because we are united." Yet he admitted:

> We control some things, but not everything. The government also [controls some things and makes some rules] like the schools, the highways . . . A little bit us; a little bit the government. It's the best of both because there is help from the government and the community.

Residents consider the international geopolitical line, where the monuments are erected, to be federal territory. However, border residents control the access path. Anyone must traverse local territory to approach either side of the international dividing line. Residents' understandings of border control illustrate the need to understand borders beyond dividing lines as larger regions of social interaction where multiple logics of territoriality, membership, and authority intertwine.[32] Their interpretations reveal the principle of territorial sovereignty as a contested sociopolitical construction with internal inconsistencies and multivalent interpretations rather than as a universal truism. As Madeleine Reeves argues, territorial sovereignty is an unfinished and contested process that is constantly being worked and reworked, "not an a priori fact."[33]

Borderlanders' reterritorialization of the border is not novel. Instead, it reflects a wider pattern of dispersion, reproduction, and pluralization[34] of border control and regulatory authority from official crossings to select interior locations, whether controlled by communities, drug cartels, independent peasant and worker organizations, or the state. Just as border residents installed *cadenas* to control access to territory and lay claims to surveillance, state units from immigration to customs to sanitary and agricultural inspections to the military similarly erect temporary and semipermanent checkpoints throughout Mexico's interior. It is not uncommon in Chiapas for official checkpoints and highway tollbooths to be periodically usurped by peasants and independent organizations demanding their share of the profits, which they see benefiting only elite coffers and private corporate interests. The criminal group, the Zetas', mode of operation is to collect *piso*, or a criminal tax from those engaging in illegal activities within their areas of control.[35]

Although challenging the state's sovereign authority over the border, residents' local control represents a strategic interaction with the state while it also illuminates how territorial integrity and state sovereignty are reproduced through their very disruptions.[36] Despite their critique of official corruption, residents' abilities to control border flows depend on maintaining good relationships with officials. As residents seek official approval for, or a strategic blind eye to, their local control, they reinforce the "idea of the state" and its unitary authority while obscuring its everyday assemblage of heterogeneous practices, inconsistences, and contestations.[37] According to Monique Nuijten, peasant communities historically viewed the Mexican state as a double-edged sword—as both a protector and repressor of their communities, whereby people are at once proud to be part of the nation-state as they lament corruption.[38] Nuijten termed this dynamic the "hope-generating machine," whereby the bureaucracy has the ability:

> At certain points and in certain circumstances, to overcome people's skepticism and, indeed, to entice them to start fantasizing again about new projects, hence recommencing a never-ending cycle of high expectations followed by disillusionment and ironic laughter.[39]

Mounting economic crisis, including the devaluation of the peso in 1994, a political crisis from escalating revelations of corruption, and the inability of the Mexican state to economically sustain the corporatist patronage system led the PRI's power to unravel in the 1990s. When the PRI lost its seventy-one-year grip on the Mexican presidency in 2000 with the election of President Vicente Fox of the National Action Party (PAN), Mexicans had high hopes for democracy. Yet, the subsequent elections of conservative PAN candidates in 2000 and 2006 have not enhanced democracy and socioeconomic mobility in Mexico. Social protests erupted throughout the country as many people claimed the elections were marred by fraud and corruption. Since 2000, Mexico's commitment to the neoliberal project and its elite beneficiaries has become further entrenched. The collapse of the PRI seems to have left the "hope-generating machine" intact, providing yet another example of how claims to disassociate with a previous regime are heralded as hope for change without recognizing deep continuities with the past.[40] The reemergence of the PRI with the election of President Enrique Peña Nieto in 2012 promised a new kind of PRI, but his administration has been committed to even fuller privatization and has also been accused of corruption and repressively limiting freedom of speech, dissent, and assembly.[41]

Long Live the Bad Government

My first night at the border, September 15, 2006, the eve of Mexican Independence Day, illustrated the ambivalence through which border residents living at the margins subjectively experience the state. Santa Rosa hosted an Independence Eve party and decorated its basketball court with red, green, and white flags. The assembly president, Victor, welcomed everyone as he spoke about the pride of Mexico, the revolution, and independence. After dances by schoolchildren, Victor ended the night in a booming voice at the microphone, "*Viva* (long live)," with the crowd cheering and repeating each *viva* after he cried, "*Viva* the homeland, *viva* independence, *viva* Hidalgo,[42] *viva* Mexico! He then added, "*Viva el mal gobierno*" (long live the bad government). Silence was palpable as people were taken off guard. Then Victor quickly yelled "*Viva* Mexico," and cheers resounded.

Victor was commenting on the atmosphere of fraud, discontent, and resignation that permeated Chiapas when I arrived in September 2006. In August 2006, the conservative PAN candidate, Felipe Calderón, was narrowly declared president of Mexico over the Democratic Revolution Party's (PRD) liberal populist, Andrés Manuel López Obrador. Critics cried corruption and demanded a full recount. By October, frustration had subsided across much of Chiapas. This early ironic sentiment of "Long live the bad government" characterized how border residents (and many people in Mexico) relate to, and experience, the state as something they critique, take pride in, and become resigned to as they simultaneously express hope for a better future.[43]

Border residents are ambivalent about the state. Although they may seem resigned to its problems, they also strive toward alternatives. Residents stress their respect for the government as they simultaneously forge paths that cross legal and illegal lines to evade state regulations and fill in its gaps of exclusion. Through the *cadenas*, residents balance the everyday practice of autonomy with security at the margins of the state. Autonomy, however, is contingent on the evolving border landscape and in tension with residents' simultaneous desire for more meaningful forms of state inclusion.

Phantom Commerce

5

The gap between the state's authority to create prohibition laws and its ability to enforce such laws is the space where smuggling takes place.

—Peter Andreas, "Border Games," 2000: 22

WHEN I ASKED FÉLIX, a Mexican fiscal inspector who has worked in forty of Mexico's forty-nine customs posts, what distinguished his work in this region, he responded:

> Illegality governs. It is not so much the contraband that sticks out, but that the authorities are present and do not apply the law as they should. We learn how it is and do not want conflicts. We are more flexible because of the people. This would not happen at other customs posts.

Contraband persists at the intersection of a border region increasingly committed to facilitating international trade, as well as curtailing the northward flow of undocumented migrants and illicit goods. International trade agreements have opened the border to trade for large businesses and transnational companies, but local peasants and petty merchants have encountered more obstacles despite the historical importance of cross-border trade. Although contraband contributes to tax evasion, it can also be integral to the functioning of the regional economy and survival of the local population. Commerce between Mexico and Guatemala hovers around $5 billion, which "provokes a natural labor market" outside legal channels where "70 percent of the interchanges are via contraband."[1]

The existence of parallel flows of unregulated commerce, often occurring in plain view of official offices, appears to contradict Mexico's commitment to a secure border. As Mexico and Guatemala embrace a security agenda to combat illicit transnational flows, smuggling activities and their protagonists are increasingly encapsulated within this mandate. Yet officials also ignore, and some even enable, contraband because it can benefit select regional elite, businesses, policing units, and politicians while it provides a safety valve to dampen the economic dislocations and political discontent wrought by exclusionary trade policies and structural adjustment.[2] Simultaneously criminalizing contraband while turning a blind eye to it contributes to the state's ability to portray the image of an orderly border that is conducive to capital flows and tourism while it allows networks of state agents, illicit actors, local populations, and formal businesses to benefit from the intersections between legal and illegal commerce.[3] An ethnographic approach to the border reveals how the formal, informal, legal, and illegal economies may be mutually constituted and interdependent rather than separate or necessarily antagonistic spheres.[4] This chapter focuses on the experiences and worldviews of customs employees who patrol the frontlines to demonstrate how tensions among law and practice and security and trade unfold.

Contraband is not without contradictions. It enables petty smugglers and local inhabitants to survive and gain access to basic goods, lines the pockets of select officials, helps justify the border security agenda, and can contribute to the regional economy. However, it also undercuts transparency, tax collection, efforts for democratic change, and enterprises that follow the rules. Yet maligning contraband with little additional context furthers the criminalization of the regional peasantry, who are usually no more than foot soldiers in the extralegal economy. Governments target contraband due to its implied (yet often unproven) connection to organized crime and potential threat to private and transnational corporate sector interests, often glossed as public security.[5] According to Mexico's *El Financiero* in December 2014, private sector interests implored the Mexican government to combat the illegal economy as "a key element of the national strategy against public insecurity and organized crime . . . because this sector generates losses of more than $950,000 million pesos to the formal economy and the treasury."[6] Illicit outflows and lost tax revenues negatively affect public investment and national development as they impede the ability to collect necessary taxes. But contraband is only a threat to private sector and state interests except when it is not. As Diane Davis notes, it is necessary to analyze when, under what circumstances, and for whom the informal economy may be problematic or beneficial.[7] Because informality and illegality are defined in contradistinction to the formal and legal economy, it is vital to unpack the specific, empirical ways they affect one another.[8]

Pigeonholing contraband as a threat may detract from uncovering larger problems undermining tax revenues. For example, in Guatemala, despite corporate and top individual income tax rates of 31 percent, collection is woefully low; tax revenues are among the lowest in Latin America, and corruption, exemptions, and loopholes favor the elite and tax evasion.[9] Instead of focusing on contraband as a gateway to organized crime and a threat to public security and the private sector, in Guatemala it is necessary to examine how weak and underfunded state institutions, often debilitated by elite financial interests, contribute to corruption, insecurity, and distrust of the state.[10] Kedron Thomas similarly documents how brand pirates in Guatemala, or people who reproduce brand goods without authorization, are blamed for lost tax revenues and economic woes without accounting for how neoliberal reforms cut back state spending and services while providing "tax-and-tariff free zones for multinational corporations, media, government officials, and international businesses."[11]

Extralegal trade is part and parcel of the global economy. According to Carolyn Nordstrom, 90 percent of all trade at some point passes through extralegal channels, and two-thirds of all trade runs extra-state.[12] In Mexico, INEGI estimated in 2012 that the shadow economy accounts for 25 percent of GDP and employs between 50 and 60 percent of the population.[13] Guatemala has the highest rate of informal employment in Latin America at over 70 percent, according to a 2014 report by the International Labor Organization.[14] In Chiapas, informality approaches levels closer to that of Guatemala.[15] To separate the smuggling of illicit narcotics, weapons, and gems from the smuggling of basic commodities, as well as from the formal sector enterprises that under-declare or mis-declare goods, misconstrues how the economy actually works.[16] The disproportionate policy and public focus on high-profile illicit trades like narcotics and gems, for example, obscures how the smuggling of basic goods like gasoline, food, and clothing forms a more substantial portion of the total economy.[17] The ability to control the sustenance of local populations can generate more power and profit as it puts one at the levers of national and regional development.[18]

This chapter illustrates how the legal and illegal economy intersect through the concept of "phantom commerce," or commerce that is officially invisible but that exerts a tangible impact. The extralegal economy haunts and pokes fun at the formal economy and security measures to ostensibly reduce illicit flows in favor of orderly commerce. At the border, it is not the economy's shadow or dark side—it is the economy.

Tourism Only

At first glance the official posts at Ciudad Cuauhtémoc and Las Champas in Mexico and La Mesilla in Guatemala meet the expectations of a modern border crossing (Figure 5.1). Fiscal inspectors in Las Champas are in charge of processing imports; a few minutes down the road, the customs agent in Ciudad Cuauhtémoc processes exports. There is one customs office on the Guatemalan side in La Mesilla in charge of imports and exports. Mexico modernized this post during the administration of former President Vicente Fox (2000–2006), replete with modern office buildings, inspections vehicles, a bank to process vehicular fees, mechanical gates, and a traffic light. If the light turns red, the inspector can inspect the vehicle. If it is green, the vehicle is sent on its way.

Mexico designates this crossing as a tourist point. Beyond $1,000 of merchandise, merchants need to contract a customs agent in Ciudad Hidalgo or Mexico City for authorization. Commerce must be processed at the commercial crossing in Ciudad Hidalgo, Mexico, which is over a three-hour drive

Figure 5.1. Official border crossing at Ciudad Cuauhtémoc and La Mesilla.
SOURCE: Author photo.

to the south. After the completion of the commercial bridge and highway in Ciudad Hidalgo in 2002 and in Tecún Umán, Guatemala, Ciudad Hidalgo became the central destination for commerce between Mexico and Central America. Ciudad Cuauhtémoc is considered a subsection of Ciudad Hidalgo. And yet this cross-border region is, and has historically been, a hub for regional and cross-border commerce. Businesses have grown on both sides of the border, and people from throughout Mexico and Guatemala come to shop. To reconcile the fact that this post is largely restricted to tourism with the reality of border commercial synergy makes the conclusion obvious. Border agents claim this is not an important commercial region. Little commerce passes through, despite the fact that this is the historical overland trade route between Mexico and Central America.[19] Commerce is not important because Mexico does not officially permit it to be processed here, thereby rendering it invisible. All one has to do to understand how the regional economy works is take a short drive or look around the corner from the official offices to the mountainous passes and pathways that criss-cross the borderline.

Previously, Mexican customs agent David told me Ciudad Cuauhtémoc was authorized to conduct inspections. Since the early 2000s, however, commerce is required to be approved and inspected in Ciudad Hidalgo or authorized by a contracted customs agent. David explained:

> I do not have the authority to do the paperwork. I am mainly here to verify that [merchants] enter with the [appropriate papers] and that restricted things do not enter. Here is the last place [in the chain of inspection sites], so I expect if [merchants] are passing through here, they have already passed through the other [inspection points].

Agents at Cuauhtémoc and Las Champas, Mexico, cannot provide authorization but are stationed to verify that merchants have already completed the required inspections, paperwork, and taxes. When cars pass through, an automated light turns green or red; only if the light turns red can David inspect further.

The limitations of marginalizing Cuauhtémoc as a commercial post are apparent in La Mesilla, Guatemala. According to an agent in La Mesilla, Mexico's restrictions reflect its domination of the border agenda. "Not much enters here because Mexican customs does not authorize [commerce] here . . . just Hidalgo. It is part of the politics of Mexico." La Mesilla is authorized to inspect, document, and process tariffs on commerce, but this becomes irrelevant due to Mexico's restrictions. The Guatemalan agent believed Mexico had more power because "Guatemala consumes more from Mexico . . . our production is poorer. Some things go the other way, but almost all of the products in Guatemala are from Mexico."[20] When I inquired about the relationship between customs offices in Mexico and those in Guatemala, he told me, "Mexico feels superior." Mexico, in line with a larger hemispheric security agenda (see Introduction), also exerts more influence than Guatemala over border security matters.

Customs Reforms

Mexican customs reforms, in line with a neoliberal agenda of efficiency and modernization, also restructured border vigilance in the 1990s and 2000s. Umberto, a customs agent based in Mexico City who also works in Ciudad Hidalgo, explained that fiscal reforms in the 1990s aimed to curb corruption by modernizing and centralizing border inspections. This involved closing many small customs posts that previously dotted the border landscape, including one at the exit of, and another within, the unmonitored route in 1991. According to Umberto, "They removed [the extra posts] since the money never got to customs . . . it just went into the pockets of the police." Before the reforms, he told me, customs agents were called *celadores*, and then this changed to the fiscal police in the early 1990s. They are now called fiscal inspectors. Félix, a fiscal inspector in Las Champas, told me about the changes matter-of-factly: "Before we wore light blue and now dark blue. The functions are pretty much the same, although we now have a different manual." Previously, more customs and immigration agents were stationed throughout the region, but they were removed due to corruption. Although the old system led personnel to feel, as Félix noted, "all powerful," the new arrangement did not mean more effective control. Comprised of fewer personnel with less government support and training, customs was limited in performing its job. Similarly, while policing reform in Mexico since the 1990s had entailed significant restructuring of the federal, state, and municipal police with nearly each administration, according to Daniel Sabet, "While a new name, new uniforms, and new logos are meant to symbolize a break with the past, there is often insufficient substance to such reforms."[21]

Mexico mandated frequent rotations of agents to prevent corruption, but, in effect, rotation often meant officials had more to lose by applying the law in a region where they saw the people as organized and lacking other income opportunities.[22] Esteban was the customs agent in Ciudad Cuauhtémoc when I interviewed him in January 2007, but by the spring David was in charge. Mexico pursued a similar tactic to combat corruption through reforms to the Mexican Attorney General's Office (the PGR) since the 1990s. The PGR relocated personnel, mass fired corrupt officials, eliminated entire units, altered the geography of enforcement to decrease centralization, and shortened the timelines of officials through constant rotation of police and civilian officials.[23] These reforms backfired because they destabilized relations between the state and drug trafficking organizations whereas "the prospect of rapid removal led corrupt officials to extract as much as possible from single transactions, thereby privileging ad hoc extortion over building institutions of protection."[24] This tactic in relation to police reform has often been called the "limited discretion model," which sought to curtail corruption by limiting the discretionary power of the police through frequent rotation, "deployment in large groups . . . restricted access to information, and reductions in authority."[25] Yet these reforms did not directly address the roots of corruption and, instead, often led police to work on cases or in regions they know little about, which made them increasingly ineffective while restricting their capabilities.[26] It was evident that some customs officials, who are usually not native to the border, sought to get as much as they could out of particular deals. By negotiating with the people, they could maintain regional stability and protect themselves from organized communities and potentially dangerous actors.

At the border, modernizing customs entailed the opening and closure of specific customs posts. Brenda Chalfin, in her work on Ghana's Customs Service, points to the fact that "neoliberalism's ostensible project of political streamlining provide[s] surprising opportunities for the survival of some state institutions and expanded mandate for some state employees."[27] Despite the buildup of interior impromptu checkpoints and importation of U.S. surveillance technology and training to secure Mexico's southern border, in November 2013 the Mexican government closed twelve customs checkpoints in four border states to modernize inspections and facilitate commerce.[28] The goal, according to Luis Videgaray, the Secretary of Public Finance and Credit, was to "modernize customs infrastructure by implementing a single window, a new schema for certified companies, and strengthening and training of customs personnel to combat illegality."[29] Meanwhile, the Customs Modernization Program (2007–2012) included the installation of three new integrated inspection points in Chiapas. Comprehensive Attention Centers for Border

Transit (CAITFs), instituted in Chiapas in Huixtla, La Trinitaria, and Playas de Catazajá between 2013 and 2015 with additional ones to open in 2016 and 2017 in Palenque and Tabasco, now coordinate multiple government agencies at critical highway junctures.[30] In 2014, Mexico announced it would commit 9,300 million pesos over the next four years to modernize customs.[31] Although these efforts fall in line with the Southern Border Program, announced by Mexican President Enrique Peña Nieto in July 2014, Mexico had been developing regional development and security integration initiatives leading up to it.[32] The results at the border have been increasing polarization, including heightened securitization, restricted mobility, and unpredictability for petty merchants and peasants and the facilitation of commerce for larger businesses registered to engage in cross-border trade. Streamlining, or cutting back some state functions while bolstering others, serves the interest of securitized neoliberalism, whereby security initiatives secure multinational and elite investment interests.[33] Some of these interests include Puerto Chiapas in Tapachula. Formerly San Benito, and also known as Puerto Madero, it was streamlined in 2005 to accommodate cruise ships; it is also the site of a new Special Economic Zone, approved by Mexico in 2016, to attract foreign capital by offering special privileges and incentives.[34] Securitized neoliberalism often relies on delegitimizing and criminalizing extralegal economic alternatives, but in practice alternatives are not necessarily directly suppressed. They may be simultaneously castigated and tolerated, which serves to reinvigorate clientelistic ties between peasants and officials and reinforce the discretion of state agents to uphold, ignore, or bend the rules.

Umberto asserted that Mexico's fiscal reforms made commerce more "rapid and agile." He is accustomed to dealing with large companies like Nestlé. He related that the requirements to engage in cross-border commerce remained similar, but reforms decreased the amount of paperwork. Free trade agreements simplified and liberalized the tax structure, but not all taxes disappeared.[35] He told me that many products now just required Mexico's 15 percent VAT (value added tax), but many agricultural goods and products considered sensitive still carry tariffs. Businesses also must pay for the documents and arrange the services of a customs agent.[36]

Yet the tariff regulations on the books are for Ciudad Hidalgo, which is certified to process commerce—not Ciudad Cuauhtémoc. Umberto explained that taxes are higher for individuals and businesses who are not registered in free trade with Guatemala. According to Umberto, larger companies registered, but, for others, "there is no incentive to conduct business legally." He told me, "If someone in Mexico imports from someone in Guatemala who is not registered in free trade, contraband is more convenient since they would [otherwise] have to pay 20 percent over the value [of the product since they are not eligible for reduced or duty free rates], so then it is better to pay a 10 percent bribe." He stressed the need for businesses to register in Guatemala to receive the benefits of trade liberalization but related that "many do not want to or do not know how. They don't want to be registered . . . maybe to avoid paying other types of taxes as well." Umberto labeled this a "culture of contraband," whereby:

> People think [contraband] is cheaper than conducting commerce [the right way]. But it isn't always [cheaper]. Sometimes the bribe is higher than they would have paid for the documentation. The ideal would be for all commerce to be registered.

Umberto's statement glosses over, yet reflects, the exclusions in official trade agreements as well as how trade liberalization facilitated legal and extralegal commercial flows. Some border residents and petty merchants are unaware of the requirements or circumvent them to augment their profits, but for most peasants and petty merchants there is no legal commercial path. Moreover, for many goods they smuggle, such as white corn, sugar, and coffee, duties or restrictions remain. Rogelio, the leader of the association of corn farmers near Trinitaria, Chiapas, related his frustrations when he met with regional officials to try to sell his corn legally to Guatemala:

> Ciudad Cuauhtémoc is just a trampoline. There is nowhere to get authorization. Hidalgo is where you need to make the payments, requirements. I worked hard [talked to officials] so we could sell corn according to the law, but neither government permitted it.

Some petty smugglers surmised if they were provided with the guidance and opportunity to engage in legal trade that they would pay less, due to the increasing number of state agents to whom they paid bimonthly bribes to smuggle their goods.

To understand the ubiquity of smuggling despite the existence of trade agreements, it is necessary to explain how these agreements excluded peasants as they facilitated trade for larger businesses. The intent of the agreements is obvious to border residents. One Guatemalan resident surmised the effects of the Central American Free Trade Agreement (CAFTA), "Free trade is just for the academics and the corporations. The people will become poorer." Rather than simplifying commerce, inhabitants experienced free trade provisions as opaque and exclusionary.

Specifically, trade agreements like NAFTA were negotiated to benefit elite business and private financial interests in the United States, Mexico, and Canada. NAFTA aimed to open and integrate markets and trade but was also intended to expand private investment opportunities, facilitate free movement of capital, and convert the losses of the 1980s debt crisis into financial opportunities. The interests represented were those of bankers, corporations, politicians, and lobbyists to the exclusion of small businesses, unions, civil society, and small farmers.[37] Fernández-Kelly and Massey conclude:

> The stated objectives of NAFTA—economic development in Mexico and balanced growth throughout North America—where from the outset the opposite of those actually implemented, which served narrow economic and political interests rather than the welfare of ordinary Mexicans or Americans.[38]

Mexico has twelve free trade agreements with over forty countries, making it one of the world's most enthusiastic free trading partners and Latin America's easiest country in which to conduct business.[39] Former Mexican President Zedillo (1994–2000) characterized Mexico's approach to development as "the more [free trade agreements], the better."[40] These agreements enhance the ability of transnational corporations to gain access to the Mexican market, although they do little to enable market access for smaller merchants and peasants. NAFTA and CAFTA even contain clauses protecting the interests of multinational capital, which has a chilling effect on state regulation efforts. If a country is seen as threatening investor interests, companies can sue the government under investor-state dispute settlement procedures in Chapter 11 of NAFTA and similar provisions in DR-CAFTA's Chapter 10. Border residents and peasants generally lack the business experience, capital, and training to register. For example, to import goods into Mexico, one must register with the Secretary of Finance and Public Credit. Without access to participate in free trade, alternative economic activities are labeled as informal trade or criminalized as contraband.[41]

Peasants' sentiments that they were not made aware of or trained to participate in free trade are not a matter of ignorance but reflect exclusions embedded in the agreements. Liza Grandia reveals the lack of information disseminated about DR-CAFTA, showing that "the DR-CAFTA is not a free trade agreement, but a *corporate* trade agreement that transforms foreign investment from a privilege to an inalienable right."[42] According to Grandia, because the George W. Bush administration pushed through the "DR-CAFTA talks in less than a year . . . none of the Central American delegates had a chance to see the whole document in Spanish until after it was finalized," and texts remained secret until negotiations were finalized so that neither U.S. nor Central American civil society organizations could comment.[43] Rendering commerce more efficient appears to be mere rhetoric due to numerous "side agreements" that protect particular elite privileges.[44] Grandia argues that what DR-CAFTA accomplishes is to further the needs of transnational corporations by pushing Central American governments toward privatization of key sectors, "transform[ing] intellectual property laws . . . and undermin[ing] any environmental and social laws" that threaten the construction of an environment favorable to transnational investment.[45] Even in central regions (versus the borderlands) of Guatemala where people were more aware of DR-CAFTA's provisions, it was quickly apparent the agreement was not intended for small merchants and peasants.[46]

Mexico and Guatemala also entered into a free trade agreement as part of the Mexico–Northern Triangle Free Trade Agreement in 2000–2001. However, the agreement was not well publicized and focused on commerce at Ciudad Hidalgo, Mexico, and Tecún Umán, Guatemala. Marco Antonio Aguilar's study pointed to the lack of information; many businesses and entrepreneurs in southwestern Guatemala knew little to nothing about the agreement.[47] Inconsistencies in trade relations between Mexico and Central American countries led to a new free trade agreement to harmonize regional trade, which went into effect in 2013.[48]

As bureaucrats extoll the benefits of free trade, contraband and informal trade are stigmatized despite a long regional history of informal cross-border trade. Officials vacillate between paternalistically tolerating petty smugglers and seeing them as potential threats to the business climate. A sign in the customs office at Ciudad Cuauhtémoc warns, "The illegal introduction of merchandise can rob you of your job. Do not allow this to enter your work." The irony in this region, as well as along much of the southern border, is that contraband occurs in the open rather than in secrecy. In addition to its historical role connecting populations that span the border, it became vital in the wake of neoliberal and agricultural forms that made basic goods more expensive and eroded traditional forms of livelihood.

Mexico officially touted modernizing and centralizing inspections to visibly combat corruption, which was endemic due to the discretion of individual fiscal agents stationed throughout the border terrain. These changes fit well within the parameters of NAFTA and U.S. involvement in Mexican trade affairs, making it easier to monitor Mexican trade.[49] Meanwhile, peasants and small-scale merchants who want to engage in cross-border trade have few options. Alejandro Grimson notes similar maneuvers in the Brazil–Argentina borderlands as "regional agreements like MERCOSUR allow only one kind of circulation, that considered 'legal' by states, forgetting or prohibiting the classic local exchange of local border people."[50]

Criminalization and prohibition are critical to legitimizing the exclusions and provisions of the official agreements as beneficial and legal while devaluing competing modes of commerce as threats to the political-economic order.[51] Yet officials also tolerate, and even facilitate, smuggling. Kirsten Endres, drawing from Aiwha Ong's "neoliberal zones of exception," refers to free trade border zones as locations where particular actors gain economic privileges to the exclusion of others.[52] Endres uses the term *corrupt exception* to examine regions where corruption and illegality are normalized and acquire the semblance of law.[53] The "corrupt exception" works to include extralegal traders in routinized complicit relations with authorities through bribery while excluding them from legal protection and subjecting them to the ever-present threat of predatory enforcement.[54] At the Mexico–Guatemala border, officials implore residents to engage in commerce legally even as they recognize that the exclusions of neoliberal trade zones fuel a normalized, complementary form of extralegal trade that also economically benefits select officials and private interests. Petty smugglers and residents face the unpredictable risks of enforcement.

The Unofficial Story

It took multiple attempts to get interviews with customs agents. The first few times I tried to interview fiscal inspectors in Las Champas, they directed me to Esteban, the customs agent at the office in Ciudad Cuauhtémoc. Esteban, who looked to be in his mid-twenties with close-cropped hair, was originally from Mexico City. He had been in Ciudad Cuauhtémoc for only three weeks when I met him. He had previously worked at posts near Tapachula and at Talisman. When I asked his permission to interview the other fiscal inspectors, he took care to say that all agents worked independently, "I don't have that kind of power [or] control over them." They did not report to one another. They all report to the central office in Ciudad Hidalgo. I had the most luck when simply entering an office when an officer had little else to do. After inquiring about what kinds of questions I would ask, most agents were willing to talk, but preferred written notes rather than recordings. Expecting the official explanation, I surprisingly got the opposite. Agents said they could not officially comment, but would share their opinions. This section focuses on the experiences of frontline bureaucrats. It is through their views and representations of the border and its inhabitants that we can see how controlling the border is not only marked by tensions between trade and security, but is also accomplished through everyday negotiations and the optics of race, class, and regional difference. Agents relaxed when they realized I knew how the region worked. One customs agent stated matter-of-factly, "There is a way of working in this region . . . of giving the people what they want. If not, the [people would] repress the authorities."

Like border residents, agents noted changes since the Zapatista rebellion in 1994. According to Mexican fiscal inspector Félix:

> Before, the government would just send in the military. [They] did not listen to the people. Mexican authorities used to have more power since the government supported them. Now the authorities have no protection. What would I do if someone wanted to transport something illicit and had a weapon? In Mexico I cannot shoot unless they shoot at me first. There are a lot of federal authorities, but they earn very little . . . this is why they decided to court the people. After the [Zapatista] conflict, the government began to pay more attention to the people, especially in this region, since it was, like, fifty years behind. Many people didn't even speak Spanish. Regional leaders began orienting people, and people began acquiring more education and demanding their rights.

Félix emphasized that Mexico is now democratic, but he signaled "democratic" in quotes with his fingers:

> [The government] knows they have to purchase votes or give [people] things. Before you knew the incumbent would be chosen. Now [Mexico is] still not

"democratic," but it is less of a given to be elected without the support . . . of the people . . . which the [politicians] buy. It is corrupt, and [everything can be] purchased. [Democracy] is a long process.

Félix realized the Zapatista rebellion made the government more responsive to the people, but in ways that fostered long-standing patterns of patron-clientelism and corruption. "The people woke up, realized they matter, and the government responded. But the means by which they are doing so are corrupt." Félix lamented how rural communities used moments of crisis to take the law into their own hands:[55]

Communities make their own rules. Authorities do not intervene to avoid social conflicts. In practice, the people do almost anything they like. They have a lot of control and don't permit inspection inside their communities. They don't let us in. We need to ask local authorities for permission even just to enter to have a look. Before 2000 we didn't need to do this. After 1994, little by little, communities started denying us entry. So they can transport their contraband . . . and charge themselves. It is not convenient for any authority to enter . . . The people would unite and tie him up.

He elaborated, "I know . . . close by there is a route that is well known where supposedly goods pass, but no one interferes." "Why not?" I asked. He responded,

It is controlled by mafiosos who take care of their work and their families. We don't want to intervene since we do not want any problems. If the military doesn't even enter and they are more equipped, why would someone like us risk entering? I wouldn't risk my people like that.

A Mexican officer in the State Border Police Force (PEF), a state government initiative formed in 2007 to improve security in the border region,[56] related:

People do not respect the police as much. [The people] had some bad experiences with them . . . especially in the highlands. People won't even give [an officer] a glass of water now. They throw garbage and expect us to pick it up. People became agitated, but . . . it was too much. They don't have respect anymore. But we have to maintain relationships . . . there isn't much you can do.

Other agents attributed the growing mobilization of peasants to, in their words, "backwardness." Customs agent David provided his opinion:

> A colleague (*compañero*) of mine who occupied this post before me was tied up about ten years ago. The people here are savage like that. It hurts me to say this, but that's the way it is. I had some problems when I first arrived. Merchants from Comalapa wanted to tie me up. The merchants threatened me that they wanted to only pay 5 percent instead of 15 percent VAT [value added tax] to have goods from Guatemala. But I couldn't do this. I'm not the president. Fifty people came and threatened me, but I called in help from the military and the municipal president. But you see how people react. Many are ignorant and don't know the laws. They do not engage in dialogue. To call attention, people instead blockade highways . . . [or] come with force with machetes. Maybe it was the influence of organizations, [knowing their] rights, or it is due to the ignorance of the people.

Although David lamented the "savage" label he applied to border inhabitants, these terms further their criminalization without investigating the reasons why people evade the law—in addition to revealing how officials tolerate degrees of, and co-participate in, the construction of illegality.

Some officials objectified residents as backwards, lacking education, and angry, whereas others also understood that smuggling continues because it is one of the peasantry's few options. I asked fiscal inspector Félix, who has worked for customs for fifteen years in multiple customs posts throughout the country, what he learned from this region:

> What I learned being here is that people are angry. You cannot impose your authority. When I was [stationed] in Ciudad Carmen [he laughed], each individual would scratch his own nails. You don't have the whole community getting together like you do here. [Here people are] more united . . . and in this fashion, illegality continues. In other places authorities apply the law, and people comply, pay what they owe, and proceed. Here people unite. The custom is that people are very stubborn.

Félix admitted that working in this region requires officials to bend the rules. He told me that officials retain their authority but do not fully exercise it. Félix sometimes facilitates small amounts of commerce for people through the official border post despite the restrictions:

> We are more flexible with people if they do not try to hide from us. We often let them go if they are carrying necessities for consumption. This doesn't happen at other [customs posts]. There [the agents] are not flexible. Here, if we

don't help the people, they will not help us. They would run us all out. Here the people are very poor and angry. These are under-the-table agreements . . . not really legal, but local . . . so people are content. We often don't exercise our functions as we should. All the [other policing] units are the same. If not, the people would remove us somehow.

One morning when I attempted to interview the fiscal inspectors in Ciudad Cuauhtémoc, the office building was covered in graffiti reading "Stop Structural Adjustment, Free Trade for All . . . Get Out Calderón!" Félix recounted how the protesters had held them hostage in their office for seven hours. With 200 people outside, he asked, "How could we do anything?" The protesters even drew graffiti on the customs officers' personal vehicles. Félix pointed to himself and his colleague to demonstrate their impotence when faced with a large, organized crowd. "How easily do you think they could chase us out?" he asked me.

By separating structural adjustment policies from the demands for a free trade that is inclusive of peasants and small merchants, borderlanders critique top-down versions of corporate free trade. However, the inspectors interpreted the incident as one in which independent organizations manipulated peasants. Félix continued:

The people often do not know where the leaders come from, but the [organizations and political parties] come with their ideologies, pressure the people to organize, and threaten them . . . [that if they don't join them] they will take away their programs. You see on my car [they sprayed] PPP [Plan Puebla-Panamá]. Do you think most people in the communities know what that is? They manipulate people to follow them.

Some agents attempt to be more understanding, and others acquiesce out of fear or necessity, but official narratives often vacillated between derision and paternalism as they perpetuated a view of borderlanders as savage, uneducated, or stubborn, all of which they attributed to culture. As Félix noted, "Here the culture of the people is to protest. With pressure, they obtain what they want." Historically, the Mexican and Guatemalan elite have drawn on racist and classist discourses to justify the marginalization of the peasantry and the indigenous populations. In Mexico, regional social hierarchies place northern Mexicans in a privileged racial and class position vis-à-vis perceptions of the rural, poor, and indigenous south.[57] Customs agent David, who is originally from northern Mexico, distinguished the north from the south:

> At the northern and southern borders, the law is the same, but life is very different. That is the problem: the customs . . . the culture is very different. People who live on the border sometimes do not even know if they are Mexican or Guatemalan. It is not their custom to stop commerce and have police and customs agents interfere. They don't see any problems with transporting corn that may have flies escaping.

David illustrated how official narratives began to interrelate petty smuggling with broader concerns with transnational crime, drugs, and violence as he concluded, "The people here look for the easiest way. I don't think we should facilitate. When we facilitate, people take advantage and look for more ways to get around the law. One thing leads to another." In such lines of reasoning, the peasantry's actions and misfortunes are attributed to their character and culture, displacing attention from the reasons why they engage in extralegal activities, including a widespread atmosphere of corruption, exclusionary and nontransparent trade policies, agricultural crisis, and the lack of livelihood options. Officials recognize these problems as they simultaneously fall into blaming culture and local inhabitants. Félix reasoned:

> To make things better, people need to be given more self-worth. They need jobs, agricultural supports, and these really need to be applied. By custom, here, people do not have aspirations. They lack the culture and education.

Customs agents and fiscal inspectors repeatedly qualified that they could not speak as a representative of the government but only for themselves. They might work for the government, but their motivations and identities were diverse and often contradictory, revealing a more complex view of state institutions and their agents.[58] For many, the label of state official or agent did not define them. State employees were also victims of the neoliberal restructuring processes that disadvantaged rural border residents. In the 1990s, Mexico slashed public spending by 9.8 percent, which was accompanied by a decline in real wages and purchasing power, an increase in unemployment, and cuts in government payrolls.[59] Commitments to privatization meant reducing the public sector, which previously provided an avenue into the middle class and employed large portions of the workforce in many Latin American countries.[60] Since NAFTA, Mexico has suffered from a formal jobs deficit with a concomitant rise in informality; the percentage of the population working in the informal sector rose from 52 percent in 1992 to 57 percent in 2004.[61] According to Zepeda and his coauthors, "The real value of the minimum wage has fallen 25 percent since NAFTA," which is a "reference for setting wage adjustments in a wide range of activities."[62] It therefore is critical in setting the terms for contracts, government salaries, and worker benefits.[63] An immigration agent told me that new employees were no longer offered pensions like their predecessors, just as "half of the new jobs created in the formal sector between 1993 and 2004 did not offer the basic package of benefits—Social Security, annual bonus, and two weeks of vacation—as mandated by Mexican laws."[64] Under structural adjustment, characteristics of informality, such as lack of state protection, low pay, and insecurity also began to permeate formal sector jobs.[65]

Some border residents, like Paco, dreamed of becoming an immigration agent as a step toward the middle class. Yet many immigration and customs agents saw government posts as temporary. It was not the road to class mobility that it had provided for prior generations. Many agents, like Félix, sympathized with the reasons why people engage in contraband. He was cognizant of the fact that if informal commerce ceased, people would have no means to sustain themselves. He reasoned that people were not getting rich from this but trying to survive. "In many ways, they have nothing else," he noted. He placed contraband within a context of insufficient employment, which he also used to explain his own job decision, "This is why I work for customs and am so far away from my family. For them [border residents], it is the same reason . . . to maintain themselves." Esteban studied engineering and some English. He planned to earn some money as a customs agent so he could pursue an advanced degree in mechanical design in Canada. Fiscal inspector Uriel decided to work for customs when he was twenty-five years old "to better myself and get ahead. It is better to be a professional." Now he had doubts. He wanted to start a business to have more autonomy. I asked if there were benefits to working for the government, like pensions. He responded, "No, we don't have those rights in Mexico. There used to be pensions, but no more. There are not many benefits now. When I first started working it was enough [money]. Now it is more difficult." He mentioned that during the Salinas de Gortari administration (1988–1994), the state cut back not only government employment, but also many of its benefits. According to a 1998 World Bank report, some of the challenges facing Mexico's anticorruption and public sector reform agendas are the failure (aside from a few institutions) to create a career civil service and shortcomings in implementing performance and results-based administrative institutions.[66]

Many customs employees found their work isolating. Mexican agents worked twenty-four hours with the next twenty-four hours off. Esteban said he worked weekends and holidays and had no vacation. He believed few people wanted to work such schedules. When I asked fiscal inspectors where they lived, they pointed to a room in the office building. According to Esteban, "Each month there is a rotation of personnel. One month each place. I change places the moment I am told. I don't mind since I don't have a family. I like to get to know new places, but for others this is difficult." Uriel shared a room with three other inspectors in the office. He would be stationed there for one month and then move to another post. His wife and children live in Tapachula. He sees them once a month when he returns to nearby Hidalgo, after which he is dispatched elsewhere.

When I asked Uriel about his responsibilities as a fiscal inspector, he explained that each post had its own jurisdiction. Although other inspectors, who also report to Ciudad Hidalgo, are in charge of highway inspections, they do not communicate or report to one another. Everyone reports to Hidalgo. He told me there are only three fiscal highway inspectors for Chiapas. Félix added that each customs post has four inspectors and four mobile inspectors with only ten vehicles among all of them. When I inquired about how surveillance occurs, I felt as if I were running into a dead end. His answers kept ending with, "I couldn't tell you" or "I am not in charge of that. I am only in charge of this [office]." I realized that, rather than not wanting to divulge information, Uriel was explaining the realities of a patchwork of vigilance and the fact that, with a vast landscape and scarce resources, officials faced a losing battle. Complete vigilance was a mirage; each officer was limited to what he could do or see based on his jurisdiction. Félix could travel outside of his zone, but he questioned, "Then who would watch here?" Because it is outside the inspectors' jurisdictions to patrol highways or unmonitored crossings, they see little to no commerce.

Patchworks of jurisdiction and reporting responsibilities enable the selective (in)visibility of contraband. It can simultaneously be deplored and selectively ignored. He continued, "Look here," as he motioned to his window and pointed to the white monuments demarcating the border that seemed to climb up into the mountains reaching to the open sky. "We are so few [agents] here," as if to show me how obvious it was that the border could not be fully patrolled. "[People] who cross the border in the mountains are going at their own risk. We are only four people here. In all of Chiapas there are only thirty fiscal inspectors. And this is a big state. Look again and how big, the mountains. With thirty, what are we going to do?" Félix added that sometimes people alert them to those engaging in contraband because it affects them. Although they can catch someone on the highway, Félix said, "I have never seen it, and that is a good thing." "Why?" I asked. "Because they are not really doing bad things. They are doing this to sustain themselves. There is nothing else."

I asked Uriel if there had been more inspection posts in the past. "Yes . . . but [the government] cut them down . . . also the personnel. There was almost a 50 to 60 percent reduction in staff." "Why? Why don't they add more staff?" I asked. Uriel responded, "As a public servant I don't have the right to an opinion, but you do. Why do *you* think it is not controlled?" he implored me to ponder. "But I do think there is a need for more personnel. Imagine the dimensions of Chiapas," Uriel gestured again out the window, where contraband passes along a lower road parallel to the official road. This commerce is visible from his window. One day when I was at the immigration office in Ciudad Cuauhtémoc, I glimpsed a group of migrants running through the mountains above us. One immigration agent laughed and pointed, "There they go!"

Many agents saw their work as temporary, a necessity in the current economic climate, or feared for their own security when attempting to apply the law. Like Esteban, they were frustrated with being lumped together with all state agents. They often criticized the government as they attempted to balance doing their jobs with their own safety, fears of an organized peasantry, and their understanding of the needs of the local population. Félix lamented in response to graffiti on his office and vehicle:

> Here there will be protests, but the people take it out on [us] since they see us as representatives of a government they do not like. But we don't make the policies. I might not have voted for the PAN, but as a government employee I have to do my job. People see [us] as accessible symbols for the government.

Fishermen Catch More Fish in Cloudy Waters

"There is a lack of employment and little else. Also, this informal commerce has contributed to the growth of the city, communities, and many [people] put this money back into other businesses," Uriel told me as he motioned to the unregulated commerce he could see from his office window. Customs employees repeatedly told me "this was not an important border crossing" and "very little commerce passes through." On the other hand, state agents, politicians, and residents all attributed much of the recent growth in the region to increasing commerce, especially with Guatemala. The rise in regional and cross-border commerce led Frontera Comalapa to recently be designated a city; although Chiapas is predominantly agricultural, trade represents a significant part of Frontera Comalapa's economy. Such small border towns have grown into "trade regions" as internal and cross-border migration flows through the region increase.[67] How, I wondered, could the area benefit from increased international commerce when officially there wasn't any? Ciudad Cuauhtémoc was a tourist post.

When I inquired about the role of mobile inspectors, customs agent Esteban responded, "What they are doing is inspecting trucks to make sure everything is in order." He paused. "Supposedly. That is their function. There are trucks that pass through the hillsides, through other paths." He distinguished what is supposed to happen from the apparent reality.

Alonso, from Santa Rosa, Mexico, put me in touch with Jaime, a politician from Frontera Comalapa. Jaime understood how the region worked. He told me authorities were less concerned with contraband in basic goods than with drugs. When I asked if this was due to the value of the goods, he responded, "The more economic value, the more interest the authorities have [in detaining it]." "Was this because of the taxes?" I asked. "You can't really talk about taxes, it's all strategic. Nothing generates taxes here . . . in clandestine routes." Then he paused to assert that although contraband did not generate taxes, it did contribute to earnings, due to what he called "the agreements [smugglers have] with authorities . . . totally illegal agreements." Smugglers' fees, or bribes, are larger for higher-value goods.

Jaime spoke about Frontera Comalapa's growth as more people moved to the region due to the refugee flows of the 1980s and 1990s and hurricane damages in the Sierra in the past decade. It has become a regional commercial hub, which includes commerce in grocery goods, local and regional business, *and* commerce with Guatemala. First, he explained how this was supposed to work, "People from Guatemala come to buy things, but they need to pay a tax at the border." Then he articulated the reality, "But there are few authorities to process this commerce at the border. Most does not go through [the official post]. It passes through unmonitored routes. But this commerce aids the economy of Comalapa." Specifically, the collapse of the Mexican peso in 1994 provided an economic boon to Frontera Comalapa as it generated an incentive to the cross-border market—above and underground. Guatemalans took advantage of purchasing goods more cheaply in Mexico to sell in Guatemala.[68] Jaime explained the effects of the peso collapse:

> Before the dollar was 3 pesos and then the dollar went up, the peso fell, and since the Guatemalan currency is closely linked with the U.S. dollar, it also increased in value. This aided commerce in Guatemala. Guatemalans could purchase goods here. Before they could not afford to. This helped the economy here [in Comalapa], and it was an advantage for Guatemala.

Due to the restrictions on commerce in Cuauhtémoc and the lack of space for large trucks, Jaime admitted most cross-border commerce occurred extralegally through *extravíos*. This was not a secret, but obvious to anyone who has been to Ciudad Cuauhtémoc. "As you can see," Mexican customs agent Esteban said, "you cannot really transport [anything] here. Look how crowded it gets." The narrow road at Ciudad Cuauhtémoc–La Mesilla is especially packed with vendors and stands with colorful awnings during Friday and Saturday markets, where vendors sell anything from knockoff clothing to cell phones, stereos, pharmaceuticals, and pots and pans (Figure 5.2). La Mesilla has one of the largest flea markets in Central America;[69] people come from all over southern Mexico and Guatemala to shop. Before 1983, it was a small hamlet; now it provides a critical link to Comitán, Mexico, where "large chains of commercial centers with international capital have been set up, which encourages a daily flow of people . . . across the border."[70] I questioned how unmonitored commercial flows affected the municipality of Comalapa. Did it lose or benefit? According to Jaime, "The municipality doesn't benefit, but individuals do. It's lamentable, but it's the reality. There are always people becoming richer and others becoming poorer."

Ciro, an employee who works for the Secretaría de Hacienda in Frontera Comalapa, which is in charge of municipal tax collection, also referenced

Figure 5.2. Market day in La Mesilla, Guatemala.
SOURCE: Author photo.

Comalapa's growth in the past decade. Comalapa has become a popular location for people from throughout the cross-border region to make purchases.
Companies that have set up locations in Comalapa included Elektra, furniture stores, Ceramat, Pepsi, Superior, and Bodega Aurrera, which is owned
by Walmart. Catering to a growing transmigrant population from Central
America, the municipality is now home to "travel agencies" on nearly every
corner that advertise trips to U.S.–Mexico border cities, as well as motels, cantinas, and restaurants.

When I asked Ciro about municipal growth in the past decade, he told me
Comalapa had grown 100 percent:

> It is one of the municipalities that has grown most over this time. The only
> one [in Chiapas] I can compare that kind of growth with is Tuxtla, but that is
> because [Tuxtla] is a big city. Here, because it is a small municipality, it stands
> out. The number of businesses has grown . . . there is a great flow and fluidity
> of money, a lot of production. A lot of people also went to the U.S. and sent
> money that people invested in businesses.

I asked Ciro how contraband affected the economy: "I don't think contraband provides benefits to Comalapa. Well, it contributed to some growth. But it also damages [Comalapa] since it is a black market." He explained the tax structure of Frontera Comalapa, whereby previously people would just declare nothing, but the government enhanced standards. When collecting taxes from local businesses, the municipality does not distinguish "what is national or international . . . only what they are earning. They do need to prove where they purchase." But he explained that many businesses tend not to declare the purchase. He summed it up, "They declare what is convenient." He believed that when businesses purchased products in Guatemala in this fashion that it hurt the local economy. "However, if Guatemalans come here to buy things, it benefits those who sell to them and do not submit the receipts."

Ciro related that "contraband benefits businesses in this manner, but it is a phantom benefit. The sales do not benefit the needs of the state . . . they benefit the individual. The community does not benefit if they do not declare it." Yet Ciro extended some of the wider benefits provided by this phantom commerce that does not officially exist, but that impacts the regional economy:

> But this does contribute and relate to the flows of formal commerce, since there is more fluidity. People start looking at Comalapa and see more money, more movement. They realize they can sell so they come here. The two [together] . . . legal and illegal . . . one grows and so does the other due to greater fluidity. The underground economy grows alongside the declared economy, and that benefits here.

These are the phantom benefits of contraband: profits and their economic ripple effects seem to surface overnight. With official impediments to commerce, there is no legitimate method to explain how these effects emerged. Benefits are delivered as if from a phantom or ghost—one that, however, haunts the region as residents extol the growth of the area and critique rising insecurity and inequality. Given the prevalence of informality and its permeation into the formal economy, perhaps the formal economy is the real ghost. Contraband at once bolsters and undermines the formal economy.

Ciro phrased the interrelation between the formal and informal economy as, "*a río revuelto, ganancia de pescadores*," a proverb referring to those who take advantage of disorder to enrich themselves; literally meaning that one can catch more fish in cloudy waters. In cloudy waters, the fish cannot see the dangers, or simply rise to the surface, making them easier prey. He mentioned a similar dynamic due to the growing influence of drug and migrant smugglers in Frontera Comalapa, where "these same people invest money back into businesses in the community.[71] [Since the early 2000s] the economy here has become driven by [migrant smugglers] and traffickers." Disorder may be conducive to capital accumulation transferred between the legal and illegal economies while it simultaneously can be used to justify the need for expanded and punitive border enforcement to eradicate the underground economy.[72] Illegal activities provide a rationale for expanding the border enforcement infrastructure even as officials and experts acknowledge that increasing regulations can stimulate more smuggling to evade them.[73]

Extralegal trade is not necessarily the underside of the economy; rather legal and extralegal trade proceed hand-in-hand as economic and policy reforms to facilitate trade liberalization also aid extralegal traders and the fusion of legal and illegal flows. Smugglers also benefit from aspects of enhanced economic integration, including improved communications technologies and infrastructure, privatization, and financial liberalization. These measures not only allow extralegal actors to disguise their goods as legal, but can also enable legal businesses to blur the lines of legality, often to greater effect.[74] Yet the former receive more attention from law enforcement, policy, and the public. As Carolyn Nordstrom argues:

> Because . . . high wealth business practices [for example, offshore accounts, misdeclaring goods] rely on moving monies and commodities outside legal detection and accountability along the same pathways terrorist and extra-state organizations use, measures to control the latter are less likely to be implemented.[75]

Umberto, the customs agent based in Mexico City, told me how official free trade expanded regulated and unregulated trade. Extralegal trade not only enables petty merchants and peasants to survive, but also is integral to official trade and economic growth. Customs agents often castigated peasants and petty smugglers for engaging in contraband and not understanding the rules, but Umberto revealed, "Large companies take advantage the most. There are many interests [involved], politicians too . . . Customs will not interfere . . . they are not going to control it. They benefit. A gift." He explained the effects of free trade on stimulating unregulated flows:

> Contraband goes almost parallel to the formal commerce. But it is not a standardized activity. Large businesses engage in it too . . . more with their re-

ceipts. For example, they buy for $1,000, but make the receipt say $100. They will under- or overestimate. There is also documented contraband by making false requests. It isn't possible to verify from any side. There is no one database of prices.

Greater trade openness and increased trade ushered in by NAFTA led to an increase in trade mispricing and mis-invoicing, which is a significant contributor to illicit flows.[76] According to a Global Financial Integrity (GFI) report, from 1994 through 2010, NAFTA "facilitated illicit outflows totaling at least U.S.$561 billion through export under-invoicing and import over-invoicing."[77] Illicit outflows from Mexico rose exponentially from US$1 million in 1970 to US$68.5 billion in 2010, constituting 3.8 percent of GDP per year in the 1970s to 6.1 percent per year in the 2000s as "cross-border transfers of illicit capital outpaced economic growth."[78] The numbers would be substantially higher if the drug trade and human trafficking were included.[79] Trade mispricing accounted for 80 percent of illicit flows from Mexico in the 1990s and 2000s.[80] Privatization and deregulation not only made it easier to engage in these practices and shift profits abroad, but diminished regulations and protections in already unequal labor markets also led formal sector jobs to increasingly resemble informal ones.[81] Businesses favored temporary and informal workers and subcontracting over formally protected employment, which further blurred the lines between legal, illegal, formal, and informal.[82]

In Carolyn Nordstrom's research at ports from Cape Town to Los Angeles to Rotterdam, she illustrates the mirage of border inspections.[83] She argues that 95 percent of cargo proceeds uninspected, but the larger threat would be the "gridlock" to global trade that even a 5 percent inspection rate produces.[84] As a customs official in Cape Town explained to Nordstrom, "If you let 95 percent through unopened, why not 96% or 97%? What is the greater threat? That or gridlock?"[85] Mexican customs agent David would concur with Nordstrom's informant: "It is impossible to inspect everything. [In Veracruz] 100 percent passes through gamma rays, and then of that we revise 10 percent. Here, no. Here the volume [of commerce] is almost nothing. It is not an important crossing." Umberto explained the situation in terms of resources, "The costs don't make sense to install additional customs posts. If it costs a million and [the post] only collects $300,000 a month, it is better to have contraband. It's cheaper for the government."[86] Considering Umberto's calculations, the fact that instituting more security would slow down all commerce and that formal companies, as well as local residents, rely on informal and extralegal commerce, reproducing an image of a modern border with no commerce makes sense even when the reality is clear. Yet a study by SAT in Guatemala and the Universidad Autónoma de Chiapas (UNACH) estimated that contraband at the southern border costs 200 million pesos in tax evasion a year, amounting to 22 percent of the overall collection that customs generates in this region.[87] The study pointed to how the lack of infrastructure disincentivizes legal economic integration and development at the southern border.[88]

Port authorities explained to Nordstrom that they use computerized assessments to flag certain shipments for risk. Yet this is difficult to reconcile with the fact that Nordstrom's data, in addition to that offered by agents at the Mexico–Guatemala border, demonstrated that reputable companies were often the biggest violators and that "most commonly smuggled items and routes pass through 'clean' corporations."[89] Shipping agents confirmed to Nordstrom, as Umberto recognized, that at least 90 percent of "all shipped goods are under-declared or undeclared" with no way to verify without interrupting the flow of the entire global economy.[90]

It was not just petty merchants and border traders using unmonitored routes. I regularly saw trucks from food and beverage companies traverse the unmonitored route. Sometimes companies used their own trucks and drivers, but I also knew border residents were hired on commission to arrange these exchanges. As Ciro explained, the true benefits of phantom contraband do not belong to petty smugglers and peasants, who are often most at risk of being intercepted, but rather contribute to a growing regional elite, ranging from migrant smugglers and traffickers to business owners and politicians, all of whom have increasing power over regional affairs. Umberto mentioned that politicians benefited from this atmosphere due to fewer problems with the people. The border control apparatus benefits from a depiction of a culture of illegality, which justifies increased funding to units to control the border even as reality undermines these mandates. In the context of structural adjustment and state cutbacks, the U.S. State Department has given $24 million in equipment and training and is targeting at least $75 million more to help secure Mexico's southern border under Pillar 3 of the Mérida Initiative.[91] Ciro added, "The police are involved and benefit. Before there was more vigilance. Now what changed is that there is more money. Money calls the shots."

A striking recent example of the entanglements among illegality, transnational corporate interests, and the political and economic elite is the corruption scandal that engulfed Guatemala's Otto Pérez Molina administration. La Línea, a network of high-level political officials including members of the president's administration, SAT customs officials including its head agent, and other non-SAT officials such as lawyers, importers, and an intelligence agent colluded to cut taxes for foreign companies seeking to import into Guatemala in exchange for millions of dollars in kickbacks.[92] It was not surprising that members of the elite were involved in corruption. What was surprising was that they did not get away with it. Efforts to enhance the justice system in Guatemala instituted by CICIG and the growing protests and frustrations of civil society led to the resignation and arrest of Pérez Molina and Vice President Roxana Baldetti for corruption in the fall of 2015.

Securitized Neoliberalism

Whether I asked customs agents, local politicians, or border residents what percentage of the commerce in the region was extralegal, they all estimated between 90 and 100 percent. If the majority of cross-border flows in this region occur extralegally, why do policies focus on modernizing official points of entry? According to Ciro, "There is vigilance, but the reality is another thing." Uriel stressed that it was more than a deficiency of resources. He suggested interrogating the image of security:

> What the government wants to do most is demonstrate an image that it is controlling things, but in practice . . . if you actually see it . . . you know that isn't true. But leaders never go to these places. [They are interested] more in the image.

The public may want to believe in illusions of security and policy proclamations, but Carolyn Nordstrom draws attention to how "Security is forged [by] . . . people . . . who constantly navigate the fine line between balancing security with the necessities of trade." The agents at these ports are the ones who "get it." For them this is not an illusion, but a mundane reality of working at the frontlines of international security and trade.[93]

I paused Uriel to make sure he did not mind that I was still taking notes. My preconceptions about security made me uneasy that what he was telling me could get him into trouble. Uriel brushed off my concerns, because:

It is nothing you can't see for yourself . . . look out the window. The government likes images of control, but to actually make control implies costs. The government is not willing or able to spend this. They just like the image. Yes, there is a security presence, [but] they don't exert force since they don't want conflicts. They could send more patrols, like how the government sent the PEF this year, but it is the same. They could send ten more, and it would be the same. Just an image [versus] if you look at what they are doing.

Uriel knows the realities of security are obvious to anyone who opens his or her eyes.

The demands of market liberalization combined with the securitization of the border appear to produce a conundrum at borders.[94] Yet security and free trade are not opposed; rather, the former helps ensure the latter proceeds in a manner conducive to the interests of investors, resource extraction, and transnational capital.[95] Criminalizing contraband and conflating it with an amorphous definition of organized crime uphold the economic practices of transnational and corporate elite while perpetuating and securitizing inequality in terms of who can participate in commerce and purchase goods.[96] Yet officials simultaneously tolerate informal commerce to maintain stability,[97] while informality also pervades the "legitimate" business climate. In practice, the interrelationships among extralegal and informal economic activities, formal trade, and security are unsettled, unfolding through contingent negotiations among local actors as political and economic dynamics shift.

Whose Security?

Discussions of security require questioning whose rights are being protected and valued at the expense of the exclusion or criminalization of others.[98] In the criminalized, yet tolerated, interstices of security, trade, and contraband at the Mexico–Guatemala border, border residents and petty traders find spaces to exert agency in a context of securitized neoliberalism that otherwise excludes, and even criminalizes, their activities. Yet these gaps also subject them to the whims of individual state agents who use racially infused logics to unpredictably enable, ignore, or crack down on smuggling. Meanwhile, the discourse of border security and the drug war agenda elevate the stakes as they increasingly lump contraband together with a host of often distinct illicit activities that justify the militarization of border policing and the criminalization of local populations. The profits lining official pockets and filtering into respected businesses, who use these gaps to bend the rules and enhance profits, attract little concern. They do not exist even as they may have greater political and economic impacts (versus law enforcement's preoccupation with narcotics) on regional and national economies and faith in the law.[99] Residents' extralegal practices offer livelihood options amid a wider informalization and evaporation of work. However, these practices also contribute to an economic system that favors transnational and elite interests over local livelihoods. Often residents smuggle commodities for legitimate businesses while they bear the risks. The next chapter details the roles that border residents play in the intersection between legal and illegal trade and the effects on their communities and families.

6 Inheriting the Border

Because we live on the border, people came to work in business.
We know both sides. We learned by living here and teaching
others.

—Mexican border resident

TITO WAS BORN IN EL NANCE, MEXICO to a poor family with little farmland. He grew up crossing the border to visit family and exchange goods. Now, Tito has two houses: an old cement block one and the new, two-story house with Plexiglas windows, pillars, tiled porches and floors, and an indoor bathroom with a rare hot-water shower. Tito sees himself first as a farmer and second as a businessman. He takes pride in helping others so much so that many people on both sides of the border call him Uncle Tito. His story highlights the development of, and ethical dilemmas involved in, "business" or contraband as a way of earning a living at the border.

As a young man, Tito worked hard to buy land, little by little. He migrated seasonally to work on coffee plantations in southern Chiapas. He saved to purchase pack animals, which he later sold to acquire one of the first cars at the border in the mid-1970s to transport (or smuggle) corn to Guatemala. He became the first local taxi driver, as he drove residents and goods to nearby cities on both sides of the border. He began in the corn business, selling Mexican corn to Guatemalans, because as a farmer he knew corn well. Gradually, he became familiar with more products and entered more profitable and diverse enterprises. Both the Mexican and Guatemalan states consider his businesses illegal contraband because he uses the unmonitored road to sell goods over the border, rather than official crossings. To Tito, and many border residents, however, such practices constitute business in a region where, despite free trade policies, it is difficult for peasants to participate in cross-border commerce.

Tito acknowledges that his businesses are officially illegal but believes they are legitimate. He conducts business "the way it has to be done," he says, given limited economic opportunities and bureaucratic obstacles to legally engage in cross-border commerce. Bribes are necessary to work, performing a similar function to the procedures required to manage his legal businesses (he has a dry-goods store in his home), including acquiring permits, licenses, and social and political contacts. In fact, bribes can be more predictable and transparent than formal taxes and procuring official documents.

Although it is not necessarily a rags-to-riches narrative, residents recount Tito's story as a successful example. From a meager upbringing, he struggled to provide a good life for his family in a region where one of the few alternatives is undocumented migration to the United States. His story highlights how business developed as a way of life and work at the border. According to Javier, Tito's nephew and a university student in northern Mexico:

> Tito worked and saved. His family did well. [They] were the ones who began and continue to work in [the] coffee and sugar [businesses]. They succeeded because they were first, smart, and knew about business opportunities. Tito made money because he worked hard. Before, he was poor like the rest of us. I remember when I worked with him in his fields as a small boy. He had just started working a little in business; corn, I think. People saw that the corn business was good and started working too.

He looked at me to make sure I understood: "Business is important to people here. It is how they make a living."[1]

Cross-border intermediaries, smugglers, and residents more tangentially involved in these enterprises struggle to earn a living and justify their choices in a local economy where contraband is a major facet of everyday life. Smugglers' work practices challenge preconceived ideas of what constitutes legitimate, ethical, and worthwhile labor as they refer to contraband as "business."[2] Yet the contraband economy does not necessarily open up new economic paths. Instead, it may continue and exacerbate existing class distinctions and clientelist politics in the region. Border middlemen also help sustain the regional economy and generate profits for officials and formal companies through bribes and smuggling cheaper goods. In fact, such intermediaries may be pawns in larger regional patterns of accumulation, whereby larger-scale smugglers, businesses, and officials profit while residents bear the risks of arrest, banditry, and accidents. Stigmatizing and criminalizing border middlemen obscures the profits they generate for formal businesses and officials. It also neglects to consider how free trade policies have excluded border inhabitants from legal commercial avenues. Because the middleman smuggler's main responsibilities are to arrange transport and bribe officials, the opportunities of border residence can quickly become risks.

Business Ethics

Locals rarely use the term *contrabando*, or contraband. They mostly use the term *negocio*, or business, to characterize their legitimate economic activities, which state agents and institutions label "contraband." Business describes the work practices surrounding the cross-border sale of goods such as corn, coffee, sugar, and clothing that avoid official regulation, documentation, and taxation.[3] Business involves trading products that are not considered illicit or dangerous in and of themselves but become illegal only because they are transported through the unmonitored crossing. Business not only refers to the act of smuggling but also encompasses a wider set of practices, peoples, and ideas. Participants include legal businesses, families, agricultural producers, truckers, cargo loaders, state agents, and criminal actors, which inhabit a "gray space" that renders sharp distinctions between legal and illegal and licit and illicit problematic.[4]

I use the terms *businessmen* and *middlemen* because contraband is largely a male sphere. However, women play critical, although less visible, roles by using border differentials strategically. Women stock home stores in Guatemala with cheaper Mexican goods, and some women sell food, clothing, and drinks across the border to cargo loaders and truckers. Women aid their husbands and fathers with financial accounting and certifications. One young woman, on return from the United States, began smuggling gasoline. An exception to male domination of the contraband sector is Karina, a Guatemalan woman who collaborates with Mexican merchants to sell Mexican corn and peanuts to Guatemalan merchants. She also has a small restaurant. She believes "each has his or her clients and place [to sell]. [People] do not prefer to buy from men or women. It just depends if the product is good." She and her husband moved to the border from further in the Guatemalan interior ten years ago for the business opportunities. She explained, "Perhaps it was my inheritance; we all liked [business]," because her parents were originally from the border and her mother was an itinerant food vendor.

Border residents defend their right to engage in business, and to Tito's nephew Javier this right is sacrosanct in a region where few forms of livelihood remain. As he reminded me, "Business is what we have to work in here. It is an advantage of living at the border." Residents separate the business of smuggling daily goods like corn, sugar, and coffee from what they define as illicit enterprises, including smuggling migrants, drugs, and weapons. They draw the distinction by arguing that such goods are necessary for survival, and that they lack access to legal mechanisms to engage in cross-border trade. Residents recognize that smuggling migrants, narcotics, and weapons has become more dangerous due to the increasing involvement not only of the state, but also gangs and cartels.

The lines, however, are not always clear. Residents sometimes referred to the same enterprise as contraband and business in the same conversation as their ethical judgments shifted according to their own social position, the businessmen involved and their labor practices, the direction of the commerce, and fluctuating state vigilance. The social and economic organizations of businesses are complex, intertwine with transnational legal and illegal enterprises, and are enmeshed with, and depend on, community and kinship ethics, trust, and personal relationships. Like the northern Mexico truckers in Robert Alvarez's study, truckers, middlemen, and smugglers at the border similarly "use cultural resources of patronage, *confianza* (trust), family ties, and *compadrazgo*" (a godparent relationship that socially binds families in reciprocal obligations) to manage businesses characterized by competition and risk.[5] They use their history of border residence and the resources of cross-border family, social, and economic ties to assert their right to act as border middlemen. However, as border surveillance and the presence of transnational criminal networks intensify and local jealousies begin to manifest, claims to be conducting honest business become increasingly suspect. Frontera Comalapa is not only a destination for coffee and sugar, but has also become a regional hub in the cocaine trade.[6] Although some truckers refer to themselves as *fleteros* (those who arrange transport) or *transportistas*, in the drug trafficking landscape, Central Americans who transport drugs for drug trafficking organizations are also called *transportistas*, or transporters.[7] *Transportistas* used by drug trafficking organizations are, according to Steven Dudley, often "thieves or experts in contraband" who know important routes, have connections to officials, and may possess dual nationality, but it is important to note that they are not the ones managing the flows.[8] Although they strive to separate their business from more illicit flows, many residents now view commerce destined for Frontera Comalapa with suspicion. In 2013, Frontera Comalapa witnessed a wave of murders, and rumors abound that cartel leaders use it as an operating node.[9] Nearby cities of Camojá, La Mesilla, and La Democracia, Guatemala, are also key operating areas for drug rings based in Huehuetenango that collaborate with the Sinaloa cartel.[10]

As more residents became involved in the contraband economy in the 1990s and 2000s, they formed associations to govern prices and rules of participation. They stressed that everyone who lives along this border road has a right to work in enterprises that rely on the route. Businesses are either distributed among family and close friends or organized as rotating associations, like the corn merchants, so that members take turns transporting commerce and earning income. Local smugglers justify the contraband economy in terms of its community benefits.[11] Actions that redistribute profits help garner local legitimacy for the smugglers. However, some businesses, like coffee and sugar, have become family monopolies due to the larger amount of capital and stronger connections with officials required to engage in business. When businesses depart from redistributive community norms, they raise suspicions and jealousies.

Because many residents entered the smuggling economy when they no longer had sufficient land or resources to sustain farming in the context of an agricultural crisis, locals view border residence as their historical subsistence right and resource for survival—what they call their inheritance. Residents have exchanged goods across the border for their entire lives, whether it was a satchel of corn or, now, a ten-ton truckload of sodas. As one resident put it, "I work in business because it is my inheritance. I learned to engage in business as a part of my heritage. We are from the border, and the same border offers us this opportunity." Tito recalled his father delivering corn to friends in Guatemala on his donkey. In a volatile and risky market, business savvy is not the only required skill. One must also cultivate caution, patience, and relationships with state agents, other residents, and producers, buyers, and sellers on both sides of the border. It is necessary to be familiar with roads, currency fluctuations, different products, and policing patterns on both sides of the border. Businessmen may earn large profits, lose money at other times, or wait months with little work due to the seasonality of much of their commerce (for example, coffee and corn). Successful smugglers usually carry both a Mexican and a Guatemalan cell phone, because they know where the borders of service fluctuate.

Border residents, from a history of living their lives across the border, use their cultural capital to engage in business. Most have cross-border kin and share close cross-border ties through social events and economic relations. Tito played soccer on the Guatemalan side as a boy, and Guatemalan women used to go to the Mexican side to mill their corn. Tito's father sold satchels of corn to Guatemalan friends and later taught his sons about business. Roberto, the former community president of El Girasol, Guatemala, laughed when I asked him how he met his business partners in El Nance, Mexico, "We all grew up together. About 90 percent of El Nance are relatives of mine." Other rural communities may have resources such as rich soil, but for border residents, their inheritance is based on a history of close cross-border relationships and knowledge that enables them to conduct business.

Many businessmen claim their work provides an alternative to U.S. migration in a region where northward migratory flows surged in the 1990s following agricultural reforms and the collapse in international coffee prices. Yet migration plays an integral role in fostering and sustaining businesses. Migrant earnings or remittances can be used to purchase a truck, begin a smuggling business by purchasing goods, and to pay an entry fee to a local association of businessmen or truckers to work. Previously, to start a smuggling business, residents needed access to capital from land or livestock sales or had to take out loans with high interest rates from local banks or fellow residents. When I visited in 2011, there was a new Internet cafe in Santa Rosa, Mexico, called La Grange, named after the Georgia town where the owner, Ernesto, spent many years. Ernesto stressed the multiple strategies critical to his success including smuggling a variety of products, trucking, his store, and U.S. earnings. Although it is difficult to assess the validity, he asserted he earned roughly US$100,000 during the previous year from his diverse enterprises.[12] Not only did U.S. connections provide necessary capital to start a business, but many smugglers brought their pickup trucks to the border directly from the United States. Others met future business partners in the United States. When Mexican border residents began migrating in the 1990s, they followed Guatemalans from the border region to the same destinations in Florida, Alabama, Georgia, and North Carolina.

However, migration connections and resources do not ensure success. Many find themselves excluded from border business associations on return due to increasing competition. When I visited in 2011, twenty-one-year-old Graciela tapped me on the shoulder at a soccer match in El Nance after hearing that I spoke English. She wanted to practice. She had lived in North Carolina for ten years before returning in 2008. Her father lost his job in a factory during the economic recession. Unauthorized migrants cannot acquire driver's licenses in North Carolina, and this limited his job search. They decided to return home. She wanted to continue her education in Mexico, but found it difficult to transfer her credentials. A relative promised to get her a job in a hotel in Playa del Carmen, but after she had her daughter, she could no longer pursue this option. She said the stores in Frontera Comalapa didn't offer many jobs. What there was to do here, however, "was business." Her father bought a three-ton truck to work in the corn trade. Even though he had money and a truck, he lacked business experience and lost money after he purchased corn at a high price in Mexico and prices declined in Guatemala. Graciela decided to enter the gasoline smuggling business to help her family. She was the only woman and encountered some resistance, but it was one of the few viable jobs open to her that was also compatible with bringing her infant along.

Some smugglers specialize in products and commercial chains they know best, like coffee, sugar, or corn. The most successful smugglers and truckers are adept at commercializing multiple products to compensate for price fluctuations and seasonality. Trucking and business are not profitable if trucks carry merchandise in only one direction. Mexican corn trucks usually return with Guatemalan cement blocks and when the corn and coffee harvests end, smugglers with more resources and connections transport other goods. One Mexican smuggler noted:

> Some businessmen do better than others. You really only [earn money] if you diversify . . . corn, oranges, onions, sodas, coffee. [Many products] are seasonal, so [people] with a wider vision [succeed]. You get to know the markets, make new connections, and sell other things as well.

Middlemen Smugglers

Border residents, through their control of the border route, developed a niche role as middleman intermediaries. Experience in the cross-border corn trade facilitated other smuggling and trucking businesses. Corn merchants, often called coyotes, defend their roles:

We decided that if people come from far away to sell corn to Guatemala that they need to use a local intermediary. We realized [local work] was threatened. [Corn] has to be given to someone from here. Now merchants know they need to sell to us. They cannot just pass [through here] directly. [Otherwise] we are left without work. It is important to provide work for people here.

The term *coyote* generally refers to the abuses of migrant smugglers or middlemen merchants who exploit small producers' lack of access to markets and transportation as they purchase their goods cheaply and in bulk to transport to warehouses, companies, and other buyers.[13] Some border middlemen reject the term *coyote* and prefer to be called *negociantes* (businessmen/merchants), *camioneros* (truckers), or *fleteros*, but others embrace the term without stigma. Producers are ambivalent. They recognize that intermediaries provide critical access to markets, but also believe that middlemen exploit producers' lack of market access and profit off of their products.

Many policy makers and scholars assume that middlemen necessarily exploit the vulnerability of others. Some residents and producers argue that coffee smugglers exploit producers, depress producer prices, monopolize the market, and earn large sums of money. This can be true, but also obscures how border middlemen are pawns for larger formal-sector businesses, as well as for officials who benefit from the shadow economy. Many smaller-scale smugglers struggle to support their families in a context with little other employment and unpredictable profits.

The case of coffee illustrates the complex role that coffee smugglers play in the transnational legal and extralegal economy in the context of economic crisis. The deregulation of the international coffee market and the dismantling of Mexico's National Coffee Institute (INMECAFE) in 1989 led to a crisis and collapse in coffee prices, which was particularly acute in Chiapas. According to Marie-Christine Renard, "The National Coordinator of Coffee Growers Organizations estimated that producers lost 65 percent of their income in the first fifteen years of the crisis."[14] These factors, combined with reduced access to credit and state supports, led a few transnational corporations to dominate the coffee economy.[15] As strong national industries in both Mexico and Guatemala, the coffee and sugar industries carry high duties or prohibitions on cross-border sale. Coffee is among Mexico and Guatemala's largest exports, and 6 percent of Mexico's and 31 percent of Guatemala's economically active population depends on coffee.[16] Coffee and sugarcane are excluded from free trade arrangements between Mexico and Guatemala and still carry duties.[17] Due to these restrictions, people who smuggle coffee and sugar require more capital and connections to purchase it and bribe officials.

Locals regard coffee and sugar smuggling businesses as more controversial and risky than corn, which is a lower-value product. Border resident Rigo, who has worked for immigration throughout Mexico, explained:

> The difference between coffee and corn is that coffee is worth more . . . it has a higher price, and so the tax they are avoiding is higher. But does coffee hurt you? No. Tortillas? No. Basically they are the same. The only difference is price. What people see as having a greater value, or higher price, they will say is more illicit.

Higher-value products structure a different approach to smuggling: one that requires more capital, more connections to state agents, and more secrecy (hence less openness to more participants). Legality emerges as a sliding ethical scale, rather than a black-and-white assessment, in a context where large companies have privileged access to cross-border trade whereas poorer regional inhabitants face insurmountable restrictions and opaque guidelines. Luis Hernández Navarro (2004) further critiques the ethics of a coffee system that marginalizes the rural population and depresses the prices they receive for their harvests to the benefit of transnational traders and roasters:

> Ironically, coffee is one of the products where Mexican and Central American farmers should be profitable according to the theory of comparative advantages. But instead of a bonanza, coffee cultivation under current conditions has condemned the growers to poverty, exile, death, or charity. Meanwhile transnational traders and international investment funds accumulate huge fortunes.[18]

Coffee smuggling, which many residents view as a relatively lucrative business, poses risks as it simultaneously intersects with the formal regional economy. Tito and his sons, along with a few other families, control most of the coffee smuggling through this route. Coffee is smuggled in both directions, depending on the year, prices, currency differentials, and demands for specific varietals. The warehouses to which he smuggles coffee distribute it throughout Mexico and even export it abroad to the United States and Europe.

Tito's coffee business provides employment that ripples through his extended family and community. Without Tito, the truckers and cargo loaders

Figure 6.1. Coffee cargo loader waiting for work.
SOURCE: Author photo.

he employs would be out of work (Figure 6.1). Tito pays a commission to his mother-in-law to use her land as one of his depots for truck exchanges, which is her only source of income. His sister-in-law sells food and drinks to the cargo loaders and truckers. Through his friendship with the municipal president, Tito receives certificates to document that the coffee he transports from Guatemala to Mexico is produced in Mexican communities. His daughter Nanci fills out the forms in their home storefront. Tito distributes the certificates to other truckers, who either work with him or must gain his permission to work to receive the documents and official tolerance. Some people may see him as monopolizing this business, but most view him as a benevolent patron fulfilling obligations that tie wealthier and poorer residents together. It is difficult and costly to establish relations with clients and state agents. Tito helps others by lending his name and managing the risks. The certificates confirm the coffee is Mexican, provide market access, and protect truckers from state agents. They are with Don Tito.

Another border resident reminded me that, rather than a smuggler or businessman, Tito is a *comisionista*, meaning he usually does not purchase or sell coffee. Instead, he works on commission for warehouses, individual speculators, and even regional warehouses of corporations such as AMSA (Agro Industries of Mexico), which is Mexico's strongest commercial firm.[19] AMSA, which belongs to ECOM Industrial Agroindustrial Corp., "a global commodity merchant and sustainable supply chain management company,"[20] finances coyote intermediaries who purchase coffee from small producers at low prices.[21] Some coyotes, like Tito, extend these practices across the border. They help companies supplement their inventories for export and acquire different or cheaper varietals from across the border while evading taxes, documentation, and inspection. ECOM is responsible for nearly 70 percent of Mexico's coffee exports, with AMSA alone contributing half of Mexico's coffee exports.[22] Searching for coffee at the lowest price is complemented, and mimicked, by extralegal strategies whereby coyotes depress the prices of rural producers and contribute to corporate profits. Coffee corporations, through their relations with border smugglers and middlemen, also weave between legal and illegal lines at the border, but they can easily distance themselves from accountability or knowledge of these practices.[23]

As a *comisionista*, Tito brokers coffee sales across the border and arranges transport and official collusion. Some *comisionistas* become smugglers when they acquire more resources, but most remain *comisionistas* because their risks and vulnerabilities to price and demand fluctuations are lower. Tito may seem to control local border flows, but his work is intimately related to larger companies and officials who reap more substantial benefits and face little risk.

Border middlemen are tied to prevailing arrangements of state and commercial power even as they seek to subvert it through smuggling. In addition to bribes, Tito and other local smugglers help finance local politicians and purchase the votes of their neighbors. In return, officials facilitate smuggling, help forge permits, and repay smugglers double after elections. The communities can benefit when wealthier residents encourage the municipality to provide projects. In other instances, though, in exchange for turning a blind eye to smuggling, some officials ignore community needs. The municipality of Frontera Comalapa, Mexico, has largely been a PRI stronghold known for conservatism and allegations of official corruption. In March 2016, Jorge Antonio Aguilar Lucas, the PRI municipal president, was ousted and arrested for alleged implication in the murder of councilman and former municipal presidential candidate for the Ecological Green Party of Mexico (PVEM)[24]

Jesus Alaín Anzueto Roblero.[25] Other colluding municipal employees were arrested as they attempted to use this border route to escape to Guatemala. Aguilar Lucas has since been declared innocent and was reinstated in September 2016. Collusion between residents and officials depresses desire for change in this context. An opposition candidate who came to El Nance to campaign invited women to a meeting about resisting corruption. When Tito's wife saw her sister returning from the meeting, she half-jokingly asked, "Are you betraying Tito?" At the end of my fieldwork, when I left my car at Tito's, his son had covered the entire back window with a picture of the PRI candidate.[26]

Tito may provide social, political (in terms of votes and local support), and economic capital to state officials, but he also occupies the more vulnerable position in these patron–client relations. About ten years ago, he was arrested for smuggling, and each year his business depends on the willingness of officials to cooperate. His wife lamented that the officials allow him to work, "but there are always more people to pay . . . They just keep paying. The authorities think he earns more than he does." Many smugglers and middlemen reinvest profits directly back into the business. Some barely earn enough to pay back monthly bank loans and bribes. Many lose money. Due to the exclusion of border peasants from formal trade venues, as specified in Chapter 5, some surmise it might be less expensive to conduct business, if they could, legally.

In this interpretation, some local smugglers merely get by (and also are being taken advantage of) in a larger commercial system that marginalizes them alongside the producers they purportedly exploit. Smugglers help sustain the livelihoods of underpaid officials through bribes while they contribute to the expansion of the policing apparatus to combat smuggling. Others point out that residents have work because companies want to avoid the taxes and prohibitions. As another resident put it:

> If companies paid taxes, they would not need Tito. He does not manage the money to purchase coffee since he is just the *comisionista*, but he knows who sells it . . . and they come looking for him. Some work with warehouses or particular buyers, the rich people who hoard and speculate, and the companies who have permits to export abroad.

Tito asserts his important role:

> [Mexican and Guatemalan buyers and sellers] cannot interchange directly since the place of exchange is here [because the road is unmonitored]. They

do not want to go through the official border. They need us in between. People come looking here because it is a border.

Another resident summed up the benefits and lack of risks for the coffee companies, as well as the wider economic processes in which Tito and border middlemen are embedded: "[The companies] do not care where the coffee is from. They only care about the quality. They do not check where the bags are from. It does not matter. They just mark it all as [being from] Comalapa." In this fashion, warehouses and companies benefit from smugglers who circumvent regulations and taxes to supplement company quotas. Similarly, Carolyn Nordstrom highlights how the legal and extralegal intertwine as companies profit from extralegal practices while maintaining plausible deniability about how contracts and goods are obtained.[27] As one CFO of a multinational company told Carolyn Nordstrom:

> I guess we know how it works. But we don't. Because this all works by not asking. We don't ask the site manager how we got a system up and running. He does, or he doesn't. We ask for the formal reports. We know not to ask for the, ah, details.[28]

Such extralegal strategies do not threaten the formal economy, but instead dovetail with the prevailing ethics of accumulation and business practices in the legal economy.[29] According to Marie-Christine Renard, overproduction, which led to price declines for farmers and increased profits for roasters, branders, and exporters, is due to specific global corporate strategies whereby:

> Firms . . . save on raw materials by substituting coffee from one region with that from another without alterations in the taste of the final product. For example, Proctor & Gamble substituted the 500,000 bags of washed mild coffee from Mexico with *robust* coffee from Vietnam.[30]

Tito's fashioning of certificates that label Guatemalan coffee as Mexican and the warehouses' tactics of supplementing their inventories with cheaper smuggled coffee from across the border both mimic and supplement this legitimate corporate strategy.

Trucking as a Way of Life

Tito's brother Virgilio told me, "Now my truck is my machete." In light of the lack of options for corn farming, his pickup truck is essential for him to earn a living smuggling corn, beans, and peanuts. Residents believe that business allows them to migrate to the United States less often than others in the countryside. Many residents capitalized on U.S. migrant remittances or earnings to first purchase trucks but believe that, when there is business at the border, "we can stay here, and there is work." Owning a truck enables an individual to enter the contraband economy to transport goods. Becoming a trucker requires less capital and official connections than becoming a middleman or businessman. Residents regard truck ownership with pride and as an avenue for economic mobility.

Robert Alvarez notes the aura of masculine pride surrounding trucking in Mexico:

> Throughout Mexico, truckers partake of the image and reputation of the macho folk hero of the road . . . The trucker seems to command the highway, disdaining the danger for which Mexican highways are notorious, and relishing adventure, spontaneity, women, and tequila, all the while sacrificing for the good of the family he maintains and supports.[31]

At the border, on the Day of the Virgin of Guadalupe, truckers lead the parade. Red, white, and green (the colors of the Mexican flag) balloons and placards of the Virgin adorn trucks. Some drivers attach speakers to their trucks to blast music and prayers. Truckers proudly emblazon their trucks with the names of their children or with refrains such as, "The Solitary Coyote" or "All of this for not having studied" (*Todo por no estudiar*). Trucking is a niche job specialty of border residents. The truckers' parking lot, established in 2011, enforces truckers' claims to the border as their inheritance, or their historically given means of livelihood.

When I returned in 2011, I noticed the loading depot near where the unmonitored border road meets the Mexican highway was no longer occupied by merely a few trucks and trailers exchanging cargo. Instead it was a parking lot for nearly 100 ten-ton trucks, all owned by Mexican border residents. Two women had established a storefront to sell snacks and drinks, and the truckers had constructed a roofed patio area with tables and two toilet and shower stalls. When I had last visited in 2008, some truckers had begun parking at the entryway to more rapidly capitalize on incoming business opportunities, but the sheer scale of the new parking lot was surprising.

Mexico's recent crackdown on border security and drug cartels, which was beginning to be felt when I conducted my fieldwork in 2006 and 2007, contrasted sharply with what border residents continued to experience. As local, national, and international media, policy makers, scholars, and human rights advocates document increasing clashes among the Mexican military, police, and rival drug cartels, as well as the abuses and deportations of Central American migrants in nearby towns and municipalities, this crossing appeared more open than ever—at least for residents.

The truckers' parking lot physically displayed local monopolization of border commerce. In 2008 border truckers were organizing into an association to control this route and fend off a competing trucking association in Comitán.[32] Border truckers perceived this competition as a threat to their livelihoods. One trucker explained, "We are the ones who work here. We take turns to unload whatever arrives here. Truckers have to unload and give us the cargo to transport over the border." Now organized into an association of *camioneros*, or truckers, they visibly assert their right as middlemen truckers in cross-border commerce. They no longer permit long-distance truckers to transport goods directly to Guatemala. They must transfer cargo to local truckers and their cargo loaders.

If residents own multiple trucks, as do Tito's sons Samuel and Gerardo, they become *fleteros*. *Fleteros* are people who own trucks, arrange transports, and rent their trucks to businessmen and smugglers. Being a *fletero* is an increasingly lucrative and often less financially risky business than smuggling. However, risk assessments are changing as residents surmise that drug traffickers seek out local truckers to transport goods. Samuel and Gerardo each own two trucks, which they either drive themselves, rent out, or employ other residents to drive as chauffeurs to deliver merchandise. They distinguish themselves as *fleteros* rather than businessmen, arguing that despite appearances, they do not have enough money to be full-fledged businessmen. Poorer residents see little difference between the two. Samuel earns about US$80 to US$100 per coffee truck transport between the border and Frontera Comalapa. When he employs a driver, he pays him $10 to $20. *Fleteros* with multiple trucks earn a commission from smugglers and arrange transports without running the risks associated with transport, including interception by officials, banditry, and accidents, because many trucks are old and in disrepair. They earn commissions independent of the price fluctuations of commodities that businessmen face. Chauffeurs tend to be younger nephews and cousins and poorer residents. Samuel's wife is nervous when her husband drives, because a few years ago his truck flipped over near a mountainside. Another time, Tito's nineteen-year-old nephew went on a transport from their community to Tapachula, which is about a four-hour drive. The boy's mother waited anxiously by the phone for hours with her sister, Tito's wife, until she confirmed his arrival. Businessmen assert that the owner of the product and truck are responsible for the risks and for bribing the officials, but they do not occupy the front lines.[33] Chauffeurs assured me if they encountered officials, they could call the businessman and truck owner to help. However, one instance illustrated the hierarchy of vulnerability.

In one year, in addition to follow up visits, I heard very few instances of violence in an area conducive to illicit flows even though Frontera Comalapa, Mexico, and nearby Camojá and La Democracia, Guatemala, have become more dangerous in recent years. Many smugglers and truckers own guns for protection, and I sometimes heard them go off late at night after drunken fiestas as men shot their guns into the night sky. In general, though, violence was bad for business. Just before Christmas 2006, however, my neighbors in Santa Rosa were discussing some of the negative aspects of living at the border. They told me about a neighbor, Darinel, a chauffeur who worked for Pedro, a border resident who owns four ten-ton trucks and a large dry-goods store and is one of the larger corn merchants. Darinel was shot in the eye while driving one of Pedro's trucks to deliver corn to Guatemala. A few days later I visited Darinel's family.

Darinel lost his eye, but he was preparing to return to trucking. His family was not worried. They believed this was a rare occurrence, one they never imagined could happen. They were not afraid because, as his mother stated, "We do not owe anyone anything." They thought he had been mistaken for someone else. Most residents believe such violence occurs when there is jealousy or an unsettled debt. Some thought he was mistaken for the truck's owner, Pedro. The family could not afford a doctor, but they were grateful to Pedro, his *patrón*, for taking care of the expenses. Like other residents, Darinel's family believes the owner of the truck or product is responsible for any accidents or problems. Darinel's wife reasoned, "Usually there is more danger for them [businessmen] and not for the drivers. The [businessmen] are the ones with money so they are usually the targets." However, Darinel suffered the physical costs.

Vulnerability and Exploitation

Narratives of exploitation are also too simplistic to describe relations between more successful residents and poorer counterparts. Most residents share kinship, patron–client, and close emotional relationships with local smugglers. Darinel's family continued to respect and work for Pedro because Pedro fulfilled his obligations as a good *patrón*. Darinel has work, and Pedro maintained his profitable enterprise and respect. Paco's case illustrates how the contraband economy sharpens and normalizes class differences even as increasingly unequal relatives continue affectionate and economically vital relations. Paco is Tito's nephew and the son of a landless farmer who works as a field hand and coffee cargo loader for Tito.

Businessmen like Tito help poorer family members and provide employment, but most benefits remain concentrated within the nuclear family (as other family resources are allocated). One Mexican resident related, "Businessmen provide employment . . . chauffeurs, cargo loaders. But most of the money is for themselves." Businessmen's children are prepared for more success not only in the extralegal economy, but also in the formal sector. Tito helped his sons purchase trucks, provided them with initial clients, and gave them money to construct their homes, enabling them to become full-fledged businessmen and truckers. None of them felt economically obligated to migrate to the United States. Tito purchased a house for his other children in the capital of Tuxtla Gutiérrez, so that they could attend a private university. He assists his nephews and siblings in different ways that reflect existing relations of patronage between more powerful community members and poorer neighbors and relatives. Community and kinship patron–client hierarchies extend to the contraband sector. Just as Tito employs extended family as field hands and cattle drivers, he also employs them as cargo loaders and truck drivers. They have necessary employment they would otherwise lack, but the type without opportunities for upward mobility. Cargo loaders earn the equivalent of US$5 per truck, which is the same as a full day's wage as a field hand. Cargo loaders can load multiple trucks each day, but there are also days and seasons where there is little to no commerce. As mentioned in Chapter 3, the work can be onerous. One girl told me her father injured his shoulder loading corn. He could not load cargo or work his fields for over a month. Trucking and cargo loading enable residents to get by, but the income is not enough to purchase a truck or become a businessman.

Paco did not question these inequalities and defended his relatives' hard work and generosity, but his experience growing up at the border sharpened his criticisms of the contraband economy. He decided to pursue an accounting degree rather than drive a truck or load cargo like many of his peers. He saw the illusion of the profits of business; although many tout the success stories, he recounted the risks and those who (especially without smuggler parents to help them) fail. Paco displayed ambivalence about the contraband economy in a limited employment context. His experience demonstrates how individuals negotiate the legal and illegal economy and their benefits and risks.

Paco was left back in school twice, but he persevered to attend vocational high school in accounting in Comitán. He hopes to find a job nearby, although there are few, so he can live in the *campo* (countryside). According to Paco:

> I've always liked it here and want to be with my family. Maybe I could work in the fields from time to time and also learn to drive a truck. I would like to get a professional job nearby. When you have one, it is easier to get a loan from the government . . . to build my own house here.

Paco thought it is preferable and more stable to pursue a career, but, to even have the option of entering business, he told me, "You need money and trucks."

Paco could not afford to attend the better high schools and universities in the capital like his cousins—Tito's children and grandchildren. Paco's mother's house was so flooded from the summer rains that she took refuge in a migrant relative's house. We all crouched one August afternoon into a corner of the flooded porch to talk. His mother, once fearful Paco would attempt to migrate to the United States, was proud and, like Paco, believed there were jobs if he persevered. At the same time, he and his mother acknowledged the reality that for many border residents, trucking supplemented the wages of poorly paid professionals. Patron–client relations with wealthier neighbors and relatives could help. Paco reflected:

> Some people think business is an easier and faster way to earn more money, but in reality it is not as reliable. Sometimes you make a lot, but sometimes you lose. It is better to have a career, to acquire skills to prepare you for a job. But a lot of people don't think like that and want what is faster and easier. But I think it is also a good idea to learn how to drive a truck, to have that option.

The contraband economy weaves together residents engaged in smaller-scale extralegal activities, border middlemen, migrants, larger-scale smugglers, and families and neighbors. Such interconnections make rendering simple distinctions between illegal/legal, exploitation/generosity, and ethical/unethical problematic although they also help explain why residents simultaneously unquestioningly support and express misgivings about the contraband economy.

The (Extra)Legal Economy

One particularly hot day, I was walking up hill on the Guatemalan side of the border, and I saw a woman wave and motion for me to come in for lemonade.[34] This was my first encounter with Francisca, a loquacious woman with a large heart. In addition to her eight biological children, she adopted two children from migrant women en route from Central America to the United States. As a midwife, she delivered their babies. When their mothers were reluctant to carry the newborns on the journey north, Francisca adopted them and treated them as her own. In the next few weeks, I repeatedly ran into Francisca at soccer games selling drinks and then again at my neighbor's house in Santa Rosa on the Mexican side. This is where I learned that Francisca was a used clothing vendor. However, her business is technically extralegal, because she takes advantage of price and currency differentials by purchasing the clothing at the border in La Mesilla, Guatemala, and using the unmonitored crossing to resell on the Mexican side.

Oppositions between the legal/illegal or between a socially embedded versus a market-based economy are too restrictive to explain how border commerce is embedded in social, kinship, and community relations, as well as how it fluidly intersects with formal economic ventures. Tito and his family smuggle coffee from Guatemala to Mexico, and then companies legally export this coffee to Europe and the United States as Mexican coffee. Without the international border, most of these border smuggling businesses would be legal. Francisca sells clothing door-to-door much like many women all over the world, except that working over the international border renders her work illegal, as well as more profitable. A more permissive attitude toward contraband as a result of local mobilizations in the late 1990s gave Francisca what she calls "the freedom to work." Her case further illustrates how cross-border businesses intertwine with one another and with cross-border social and family networks. Her situation details how, amid intensifying inequalities and the presence of drug trafficking in the region, some residents are beginning to suspect wealthier businessmen of collusion with more illicit actors.

Francisca is an astute businesswoman. She chooses to work in Mexican pesos or Guatemalan quetzales, depending on currency fluctuations and purchasing power. Prior to the late 1990s, when Guatemalan civil patrols and the military were stationed at the border and various state agents policed the Mexican side, conducting business was difficult. Francisca related that for the past ten to fifteen years she has been more free to work. Recent informal agreements between border residents and regional state agents protect the free movement of border residents (from either side) within the border route up to the Mexican federal highway on one side and the Guatemalan highway on the other. Previously, Francisca either needed a border crossing card (obtainable only at the official crossing for a limited area) or she risked detention. Because of these changes, Francisca's border experience moved from the white monuments marking the geopolitical border to the intersection of the border road with the Mexican federal highway. Both national governments consider her business illegal because she crosses an unmonitored border to purchase and sell goods. She evades inspection, taxes, and documentation. But she sees herself as a vendor who sells to her neighbors. Before officials were removed, however, she was leery about engaging in commerce she considered to be "more illegal."

When she sells clothing in Mexico, Francisca purchases her household necessities with her earned pesos to avoid getting cheated on the exchange. Her husband has experience in construction, but he also works as a cargo loader. Because he earns only about US$5 for each truck and they lack cultivable land, her income is vital. Through her husband's construction work and cargo loading, her two eldest children's U.S. migrant remittances, her clothing sales, and a small store in her home, Francisca's family struggles to make ends meet. She purchases goods for her store on both sides of the border depending on currency differentials, prices, and availability of goods. Making a living at the border entails amalgamating multiple work strategies that cross legal and illegal lines.

One of Francisca's sons works for her brother, a sugar smuggler. He loads Guatemalan sugar into Mexican trucks for sale in Mexico. In the sugar business, she says, one can "really make money." Sugar businessmen purchase sugar from warehouses in Camojá, La Democracia, and Huehuetenango; transport it to their homes in their trucks; and repackage it in bags from Mexican sugar companies.[35] Some, like Emanuel, a successful Guatemalan sugar businessman, work primarily with one Guatemalan company (he works with one company in Huehuetenango but with various buyers in Mexico). Outside his depot, which was his old small cement home, Emanuel employs teenage boys, including his nephews, to use a machine to zipper-seal Guatemalan

Figure 6.2. Packaging Guatemalan sugar into Mexican bags.
SOURCE: Author photo.

sugar into Zucarmex (a Mexican multinational and one of the largest sugar conglomerates in North America) bags[36] (Figure 6.2). Mexican border business partners—his main partner is Tito's son Gerardo—pick up the sugar in their trucks and deliver it to Mexican stores and warehouses that sell the sugar throughout the country and even ship it abroad. Throughout the years, due to kinship, social, and business connections, Tito and Emanuel's fathers became *compadres* (they are godparents to each other's children). Now their sons are business partners. Emanuel and Gerardo learned business from their fathers. As Emanuel's father remembers, "He came with me to deliver corn to the border as a boy. He made his contacts through business and through me." Emanuel arranges sales with Mexican stores, and Gerardo is in charge of the *flete*, or transport, and arranging bribes with Mexican officials. Although Gerardo is more of a *fletero* (transporter) and Emanuel the businessman who arranges the purchases and sales, both built new two-story homes and purchased ATVs for their sons. Emanuel faces risks when prices fluctuate, but he safely exchanges cargo at his home. In contrast, Gerardo does not deal with price volatility, but he is responsible for transport risks when moving Guatemalan sugar into Mexico.

Francisca is uncertain how these men recently become relatively wealthy: "They all started out poor like us. In the past few years they all built large houses. Sugar does not [provide] like that." She lamented that her brother did not help her, and she, like others, was beginning to suspect the real source of his earnings. Yet sugar businessmen attribute their recent wealth to large price differentials between Mexican and Guatemalan sugar and the averted customs taxes. Emanuel insisted it was not sudden wealth that enabled him to build a large house. He asserted, "As a child, we all lived in straw houses. Making money took years of hard work and saving." He discussed the risks when prices and demands fluctuated. His wife insisted that he invested money wisely and much of it was used to construct their home. Many businessmen and *fleteros* underplay their wealth to maintain notions of respectability, arguing their income is seasonal. In 2008, Emanuel explained his profits in a way that reflected how legal trade dynamics affected the smuggling economy:

> The sugar business is good now. The price went up in Mexico since they do not have much sugar because they send it to the U.S. But Guatemala has many mills, and the price is not as high—about [US$50] a bag in Mexico and [US$35] in Guatemala now.

Because Emanuel, like Tito, helped his family and poorer residents, he escaped the suspicions levied at businessmen, like Francisca's brother, who defied community redistributive norms. Emanuel supported his sister's family after her husband's death.

Illusory Promises

Most border residents believe contraband benefits them in terms of employment opportunities and the taxes the communities collect at the tollbooths. However, many began to doubt the positive impacts as it became increasingly difficult to establish legitimate businesses not affected by the competition from illegal ones. For example, Nueva Vida's border tried to open a community cooperative store. The store failed; residents argued it could not compete with stores that supplemented their inventories with cheaper smuggled goods from Mexico. Most smugglers and middlemen like Tito work in smuggling to provide better opportunities for their children. Even the relatively successful often struggle. For most, it was not their desired occupation, nor what they wanted for their children. Tito was proud that he sent four of his six children to university and two became teachers. However, both struggle to find employment, and Samuel, trained as a secretary in vocational school, left the profession for the more lucrative coffee and trucking businesses. As a secretary, he had to commute to a nearby municipality (or pay rent to live there). He realized he could remain home and earn more money following his father—US$150 a month in his prior job versus US$500 a month in trucking. Emanuel sent his son to university in Guatemala City to study business, and he hoped to study in the United States. Francisca laughed when I asked about Emanuel's son's plans to work for a company. Many parents hoped that their work as smugglers could provide a path for their children to earn a degree and enter the formal sector that long eluded them. Francisca told me matter-of-factly about the lack of formal sector opportunities, "Of course he will return and work with his father. He will help *his* business do better!" Guatemalan teacher Fani, whom we met in Chapter 2, related the illusory promise of mobility:

> Wilmer [a past community president] worked hard as a [businessman] to send his son to study. He became a teacher and then left to become a cargo loader. He could earn more money. Many study and then realize they can earn more loading cargo.

As profits rise and more long-distance business opportunities present themselves at the border, businessmen are less likely to abide by redistributive norms and, instead, create family monopolies. The change in the past few years from small cement homes to smugglers who build homes that may have pools, indoor bathrooms, high surrounding walls, tiled floors, two stories, and even a few with air conditioning units makes others suspicious of what they perceive to be all-of-a-sudden earnings. When I returned in 2011, one businessman had installed broadband Internet access in his home. One sugar smuggler's older two-room cement home stands in stark contrast adjacent to his two-story pillared home, where he is contemplating installing air conditioning (Figure 6.3). He uses the old house as a depot to store sugar satchels. According to Alonso, a teacher:

> It is no coincidence that the drug trade increased in the same three to four years that these houses were built. Sugar cannot be worth that much. These people were poor before. They might be transporting something else. After all, the sugar path [toward Mexico] is the same as the drug route.[37]

Figure 6.3. A sugar smuggler's home on the Guatemalan side of the border.
SOURCE: Author photo.

Residents prefer not to ask where this wealth comes from. Emanuel's neighbor iterated, "Who knows what his work is? They say it is sugar. He also transports sodas. Maybe it's money laundering. My husband worked in sugar some years ago, but it is risky, and he lost a lot when the peso fell." Under conditions of increasing inequality and secrecy, and as Frontera Comalapa and Huehuetenango become central transshipment locations for the drug trade,[38] local terminologies begin to shift from business to contraband. Shaylih Muehlmann documents how hiding drugs among legitimate commerce in trucks is a well-known method of smuggling at the northern border as NAFTA increased truck traffic across the border.[39] She details the risk calculus of a trucker who willingly transported drugs underneath his trailers while carrying goods like vegetables on top.[40] Because trucking was so intertwined with the drug trade, he felt safer knowing what he was smuggling and getting paid for it versus risking the uncertainty of being a "blind mule," meaning that traffickers stash drugs in a truck without the driver's knowledge.[41] At the time, I did not know if border residents willingly did this or ran the risk of being "blind mules," but rumors indicated this could be occurring.

A Fraught Struggle

Border residents like Tito, who once worked harvesting corn and coffee, rather than being consigned to a life of despair or migration appear to contest the economic order that excludes peasants and the poor by positing smuggling as a legitimate economic enterprise. In the context of economic liberalization, the corporatization of agriculture and industry, and crisis in the countryside, the activities of small-scale border smugglers lead us to question designations of ethical, legitimate work. They redefine the smuggling of basic goods as business and challenge the state's role to define legitimate and illegitimate activities based on arbitrarily imposed and policed national borders.

Other scholars argue that informal and extralegal traders can embody a type of grassroots resistance to the exclusions and humiliations of the formal economy.[42] Gilberto Rosas, in his work with youth at the U.S.–Mexico border, argues that violent youth behaviors constitute a political act of "delinquent refusal" of the conditions of neoliberalism.[43] Kathleen Millar, in her work with recyclers, known as *catadores*, at the Jardim Gramacho garbage dump in Rio de Janeiro, however, challenges assessments of informal work as a reactionary form of resistance or as a mere survival strategy.[44] She stresses the tensions for *catadores* who choose to work on the dump as an alternative to the indignities of waged labor options as they recognize that working on the dump is also "pure suffering."[45] She argues that their decisions do not necessarily constitute a form of resistance, or an "oppositional stance"; instead, she posits that *catadores*' strategies are a form of "relational autonomy."[46] Working on the dump enables recyclers to respond to the daily insecurities of the poor as well as pursue other social and "life projects," which constitute a form of release, if not resistance, to the conditions of neoliberal labor available to the poor.[47] In a neoliberal context where deregulation and the dismantling of protected work have led the formal sector to resemble the informal sector in terms of insecure and low-paid work, the informal sector is no longer a "cushion" for times of economic hardship but may be a preferable alternative.[48]

At the border, smugglers, who largely see themselves as merchants, truckers, and businessmen, sometimes articulate their actions as a form of resistance to the exclusions of the formal economy and trade policies. Yet despite the increase in smuggling in the past two decades, smuggling maintains a strong continuity with economic activities that border residents have relied on to supplement subsistence for generations. Like the *catadores* in Millar's study, the more flexible conditions of work, as well as the embeddedness of this work in their communities, enable businessmen to engage in smuggling while fulfilling familial and community obligations. Smugglers can work other jobs or farm when business is low, remain home with their families, and incorporate family and friends into businesses. Businessmen express pride in their work, but they also view their work with a degree of anxiety and ambivalence.

Being a smuggler does not necessarily constitute a form of politics or a refusal of the dominant economic system. Nor should smugglers be written off as criminals. Instead, smuggling is a way for residents to stake out a piece of the prevailing economy for themselves and their families amid risk and uncertainty.[49] Border businessmen may challenge the structures of international trade that exclude them by justifying their own participation through extralegal avenues. However, their actions do not tend to destabilize business as usual nor do they amplify space to address underlying problems of socioeconomic exclusion that condition their limited choices. The risks of seizure and arrest are always present even when smugglers have good relationships with officials. Businessmen know that their activities do not necessarily undermine the formal economy, as their work often contributes to prevailing arrangements of capital accumulation and state power in the region.[50] In contrast to analysts who argue that extralegal activities subvert the state and formal institutions,[51] extralegal activities can also be critical to the state and formal regional economy even as they undermine people's faith in them.[52]

Taking Contraband Seriously

Border businessmen embody ambivalent positions among the formal economy, the extralegal economy, and their rural communities.[53] As residents smuggle coffee for corporate warehouses, they simultaneously contribute to the impoverishment of rural producers by further depressing their prices. Some middlemen and truckers certainly exploit others, but they also provide opportunities for those with little access to employment or market access. Community members rely on Tito and Emanuel for loans with lenient repayment conditions and for economic support. At the same time, the contraband economy offers scant economic mobility. Residents with prior access to land, migrant remittances, political connections, and livestock are better positioned to enter, and succeed in, the contraband economy. Smugglers, as a local elite, often further tie their communities into patronage relationships with corrupt politicians who see little desire for change. Residents express uncertainty as they see the contraband economy benefiting some more than others. Yet most people still believe they benefit and maintain close kinship, social, and economic relations with these wealthier residents. Businessmen are respected community members as long as they abide by local redistributive norms and community and kinship obligations.

Taking contraband seriously, or understanding the work practices of smugglers from their standpoints and within its particular context, can illuminate how politics of neoliberalism, free trade, and security come together to criminalize and exclude the poor as neoliberal policies also frustrate the state's ability to provide substantive policing and institutional reforms and meaningful and secure employment.[54] Taking contraband seriously entails not only contextualizing extralegal activity, but also attuning to its effects on shifting individual subjectivities and personal relationships. Even as businessmen exhibit pride in their work and express macho bravado, these same sentiments produce anxiety, uncertainty, and sometimes fear—a fraught and double-edged variant of struggle.

Border middlemen are usually not the winners, but rather their practices end up contributing to existing forms of capital accumulation, rural dispossession, and insecurity in the region. Demonizing middlemen may blind us to who acts, or even pulls the strings, on either side. At the border designations of legality and illegality often serve as lofty discourses, while developing configurations of power and profit may benefit from their blurring.

Recently, residents have directly and indirectly facilitated the growing penetration of illicit enterprises by colluding either directly with drug traffickers to transport their goods or indirectly by turning a blind eye and closing their eyes and ears out of concern for their own safety. Residents seldom spoke directly about drug trafficking, which was relegated to the realm of whispers, jokes, and rumors. Suspicions arose around a large home with a horse race track and multiple cars, residents who attended horse races and hosted cockfights, and others who seemed to have built new homes too quickly and without ever migrating to the United States. Residents occasionally used humor to accuse a friend of being a narco. They grasped the influence of drug trafficking; as a Guatemalan resident told me, "Narcos pass through here, but the people do not pay attention, do not ask, and do not get involved . . . because they will kill you." A Mexican border resident added, " If there are [or aren't] narcos, this does not interest us as long as they do not bother us." As Shaylih Muehlmann notes at Mexico's northern border, however, in some areas dominated by narcotrafficking, it is riskier to abstain than to participate.[55] Their position leaves them with few choices.

Border middlemen, smugglers, truckers, and everyday residents may benefit from this lucrative crossing, which they describe as their inheritance right based on their residence. But they also bear the risks while larger legal (for example, businesses, state officials) and illegal (such as drug traffickers) players reap unfettered and unblemished profits. It is through rumors, humor, and whispers that residents make sense of their anxieties and ambivalence about the border economy more generally, which may bring more inequality and uncertainty but also access to new commodities and opportunities in a region that has long been neglected.[56] By following a conflict over the local gasoline smuggling business, Chapter 7 reveals these larger transnational power dynamics into which residents are now inserted.

7 Strike Oil

AT FIVE IN THE EVENING IN EARLY SEPTEMBER 2007, as the heat began to subside and the sky threatened to storm, Alonso gathered forty men around the table they had set up on the grass adjacent to Santa Rosa's community *cadena*, or tollbooth, where residents levy tolls on passing smugglers. Alonso designated Félix, who had worked in a restaurant in Georgia, the "cook," and he began to simmer coffee in a large pot over a fire. The group had just entered the gasoline smuggling business and were using the *cadena* as a site to wait for cargo from Guatemalan trucks, socialize, and plan group strategies. Each member took a turn driving the empty Guatemalan canisters to the Mexican PEMEX gasoline station two miles down the road and transporting the gasoline back to the Guatemalans waiting at the *cadena*, who would then distribute the gasoline to suppliers throughout Huehuetenango, Guatemala.

Alonso had never imagined he would smuggle gasoline. Many people in Santa Rosa look up to him as a university-educated primary school teacher and consider him to be successful. However, realizing the corruption in the educational establishment and meager wages, he quickly saw the economic disparities and the ironies in what the state deems legal and illegal work. He earned the equivalent of $700 per month as a teacher, but learned he could earn $1,600 a month in the gasoline business without going more than a few miles from his home.

In 2007, a conflict over the gasoline smuggling trade erupted between two competing groups of border resident smugglers and truckers. Most border residents believe everyone who lives along this border road has the right to share in the work and profits of smuggling businesses that depend on the unmonitored route. This conflict represented a rupture in such locally accepted understandings by revealing the balance between valuing community benefits and the demands of profit and competition in a limited economy. The conflict began as a local dispute between gasoline smugglers that escalated into an intercommunity conflict. It then attracted unprecedented regional attention and revealed the multiple stakes involved in the lucrative, controversial gasoline trade in a region where contraband provides invisible benefits to commercial growth, authority figures have fragmented, and Mexico and Guatemala militarize security. The escalating situation surrounding gasoline smuggling culminated in a military raid in 2008. This conflict illustrates evolving dynamics of governance at the border, which are increasingly complex as security becomes increasingly militarized and drug cartels, gangs, and criminal groups gain regional influence. Desmond Enrique Arias and Daniel Goldstein use the term *violent pluralism* to describe the coexistence of democracy and violence in Latin America.[1] They argue that violence is integral to the maintenance of state institutions and the rule of law, as well as to those who work to undermine, parallel, or contest them.[2] At the border, violence, rights-based discourses, and lawmaking rationales are pluralized and embraced by multiple actors, including state officials, border residents, smugglers, and criminal gangs, to justify their modes of control in ways that extend regional insecurity.[3] Residents believe they embody the law within this route and, in some respects, have disrupted the state's ability to control trade across its borders. As the gasoline dispute attracted larger regional attention, though, it became clear that alternative border authorities engage in a complex symbiosis with the state and are increasingly embedded in an evolving and uncertain landscape.

Returning to Alonso and his group, Alonso was telling Felipe to find a Mexican flag to erect at the *cadena*. "We will call our group La Independencia," Alonso announced. He associated the upcoming Mexican Independence Day with his group's struggle to gain a foothold in the gasoline smuggling business that was, in their opinion, unfairly monopolized by men in El Nance. To members of La Independencia, monopolizing the business violates the local ethic that "everyone who lives here has the right to work here." The border communities usually do not need to raise their *cadena* chains to block the road against uncooperative smugglers and officials, because most smugglers obey the community rules. Yet, during the first week of September 2007, Santa Rosa kept its chain raised to blockade their section of the road. They united to block the flows of smuggled gasoline from Mexico to Guatemala and clothing from Guatemala to Mexico (these were often the same business contacts controlled by men in El Nance) until El Nance permitted them to also work in these businesses. In response, El Nance blocked their section of the road to prevent Santa Rosa from working. Because El Nance prevented access to Guatemala and Santa Rosa to the Mexican highway, the entire unmonitored route was shut down.

Fuel Surge

Gasoline and diesel were significantly cheaper in Mexico than in Guatemala in the few years leading up to the 2006–2007 rise in gasoline smuggling at the border. Guatemalan prices began to soar in the summer of 2007 to some of the highest in Central America, reaching almost twice that of Mexican prices, paralleling global concerns in 2007 over rising crude oil prices.[4] According to *El Periódico*, in May 2007 Guatemalans encountered the highest gasoline prices in their history.[5] The price for a gallon of gasoline in Guatemala rose by 11.46 percent between July and August 2007,[6] which made it increasingly profitable for Guatemalans to smuggle gasoline from Mexico. When price differences grew, the bribes to authorities in Mexico also rose from the equivalent of about US$900 to $1,400 biweekly, but the trade remained lucrative. Even when price differentials between Mexican and Guatemalan gasoline were modest, contraband was desirable. As one gasoline smuggler in El Nance told me:

> Even when the price difference is not much, the Guatemalans prefer to purchase gasoline from the [smugglers] who buy from us. The gas stations in Guatemala are not trustworthy. They charge more and often don't even fill the tank the entire way. They add water or air. There is an alliance between the Guatemalan government and the gasoline companies. People do not trust either.

I asked, "Do smugglers also inflate the prices, though?" He responded, "No. In Guatemala, the government and the companies are the thieves. People prefer to buy from [smugglers] instead. They end up getting better quality gasoline at a better price." Although this man wanted to defend his business, he also spoke to a pervading sense that legitimate business in the borderlands suffers from corruption and serves elite interests. If smugglers did not deliver quality gasoline, they would lose business.

Previously, gasoline smuggling was an occasional, small-scale business. When price differentials between Mexican and Guatemalan gasoline increased, a group of border residents saw the opportunity to harness the business. They learned of potential Guatemalan clients from their connections in the smuggled clothing trade. On May 3, 2006, nine men from El Nance organized to control this trade. According to one PEMEX employee, one gasoline station began to receive deliveries of two to three tankers per day, each carrying 35,000 liters. During the previous year, they received only one or two such shipments per week. The group expanded from working with one gas station to three. In the smuggling chain, the Guatemalan merchants delivered empty 200-liter canisters to the Mexicans at their community depot hidden in the unmonitored route. Group members in El Nance then loaded the canisters into their pickup trucks and drove to the PEMEX station, located at the intersection of the border crossing with the Mexican highway. A Mexican truck loading gasoline is subject to less scrutiny than a Guatemalan one, which would need to be checked for the proper permits to even be present in Mexican territory. Loading gasoline gradually into pickups lessened the visibility of the growing trade. The men then collaborated to transfer the full canisters to the Guatemalans at the group's depot in El Nance. The exchange within the unmonitored route provided necessary cover to the smuggling business, because the Mexican gasoline would then enter Guatemala in Guatemalan trucks. The Guatemalans appeared to be simply conducting national commerce. Within their group, the men in El Nance followed community ethics to distribute work equally through a rotation system and to collaborate to pay biweekly bribes to the head of each policing unit—eleven in total.

As the trade became more lucrative, Guatemalan merchants no longer brought only pickup trucks but began arriving in ten-ton trucks, which could hold eighty to ninety gasoline canisters in addition to filling their own tanks to siphon off. None of the men in the El Nance group owned a ten-ton truck, so they paid a commission to another community member to rent his trucks. Because this arrangement cut into their profits, they negotiated with the colluding state officials to permit Guatemalan ten-ton trucks to proceed directly to the gas station on condition that a group member accompany the truck. This change rapidly increased the visibility of the trade's growing volume.

This change in transportation structure also began to spark debate and jealousy among other border residents who desired a share of the business. Yet the group refused to expand their membership, arguing there was not enough business or sufficient money. Many residents doubted this reasoning. They saw the trade grow from being conducted in pickups to ten-ton trucks and waited to fill their own personal car tanks at the gas station in increasingly long lines behind the ten-ton trucks filling eighty to ninety canisters full of gasoline. The breaking point for many was that the group no longer even used their own vehicles. Residents generally respect that they cannot enter a business if they do not have the contacts, resources, or required transportation, but they now saw the men were not even providing transport. As some said, "They are just going for a ride. That is something anyone can do." These debates began to highlight diverging ideas about the "right to work" and the community benefits of contraband residents otherwise value.

Going for a Ride

The problems started when pickup truck drivers in Santa Rosa wanted to enter the gasoline business. Due to U.S. migration and remittances, more border residents now owned trucks, especially pickups, and desired an opportunity to engage in business. The pickup drivers in Santa Rosa believed it was unfair to monopolize the business in a region where there was little else. Alonso remarked, "El Nance has been eating the whole cake, and that is unfair." Alonso's group mobilized to demand a role in the related gasoline and clothing businesses. As truckers and border residents, they believed they deserved a share in these businesses, because the commerce traversed their road. In contrast to other businesses, these trades did not involve selling or purchasing products or negotiating prices. The only work involved was bribing officials and arranging transport. According to the excluded men, "They get paid to go for a ride," and the refusal to share work was unethical.

The two groups held three meetings to discuss the problems. Although some in El Nance were open to sharing the business, more vocal members protested, "Why should we give them our business? We made the contacts and did the work [to establish clients and connections to state officials]." They believed if more men entered, it would destroy their business. As more residents acquired capital to engage in trucking and business, many feared oversaturation of the contraband market, which can already readily contract due to fluctuating prices, trends in legal commodity markets, supply and demand,

and official tolerance.[7] In contrast, the men in Santa Rosa argued, "We want equality; everyone in the community has rights." Stressing the community benefits of contraband, they argued it was preferable for more people to benefit a little than for a few people to benefit a lot. Rumors circulated in Santa Rosa that El Nance was monopolizing work and in El Nance that Santa Rosa was trying to steal their business. Some in El Nance believed the men in Santa Rosa merely wanted a cut in the business without the corresponding obligation to pay bribes to officials.

In the incipient stages of the dispute, opinions within the communities varied. However, the group in Santa Rosa quickly turned to discourses of community to unite fellow community members behind their plight. At first, the community president of Santa Rosa was hesitant to become involved, but as the members of La Independencia framed the issue as a community one, the local authorities decided the issue should be resolved at the monthly community assembly meeting.

La Independencia group representatives submitted a document to be read at the community assembly, which requested the community's support and permission to raise the *cadena* chain, and hence block all commerce, if the group in El Nance refused to share the business. Because the *cadena* profits benefit the entire community, the decision to halt commerce lies with the community. To convince fellow residents, representatives of La Independencia associated their group's struggle with popular notions of community, rights, economic justice, and family. This discourse is particularly appealing in Santa Rosa, which is structured as an *ejido*. Many still view community obligations (such as serving the *cadena*) as collective responsibilities. Accordingly, many believe smuggling and trucking businesses should be run as associations to distribute the benefits of the contraband economy as much as possible.

At the beginning of the meeting, many community members were unaware of how many members were involved in this conflict. When called on, members of La Independencia gradually raised their hands and then one by one, as if to stress their solidarity in numbers, stood up and walked to the front of the assembly so thirty men stood before the community. One man asserted, "We work for the community," and the business "benefits the *ejido*." He argued, "By not allowing us to work, the economic interests of the community as a whole will suffer. We invited the [group] from El Nance many times to come here to discuss an agreement, but they do not want one." Another man continued:

We are the people who live here. For many years we, and the people of El Nance, worked on the border road. We also have the right to benefit. They should not be the only ones benefiting. [Building the road] cost us a lot, and others are benefiting. We are asking for work and your [the community's] help to accomplish this goal. We are not organizing to engage in vandalism or anything bad . . . but to work. We want your support to be able to work. We want to unite with the group in El Nance, but they do not want us to. We are within our rights to demand this since this is our land. We want an agreement. We asked the advice of the most educated people in the community, and they informed us that we have the right to work. Our group is open to anyone from here to sign up. We want help from our people and dialogue, not conflict. We should not be afraid since we have rights. We will talk, and they [El Nance] will understand. We only want half of the truck transport price . . . we do not want to get involved in anyone's business. We want permission from the assembly that if El Nance does not agree to our mutual agreement then we have the support of the community to proceed by other means. [Our group is] organized now as you see with a secretary, treasurer, and a board. Many of us bought pickup trucks so that we could work at home and be with our families. If we cannot work, many of us will be forced to migrate to the U.S. and leave our families and community.

According to La Independencia, they did not want to interfere in anyone's business but wanted to only participate as truckers. The distinction between business and trucking is important. Residents believe that a business belongs to someone because he or she invests personal resources in it and purchases and sells products. In contrast, they view a truck transport as a job that does not require the same intensive involvement or right to sole ownership. Trucking unions at the border are usually run as rotating associations to distribute work and profits. Residents view the right to participate in transport as conditional on border residence and owning a truck. However, many, like detractors in El Nance, doubt there is enough work for all. The preceding speech, along with community members' reactions, illustrates how the group in Santa Rosa envisioned the struggle to smuggle gasoline as (1) a community issue, (2) integral to family and community solidarity in the face of widespread U.S. migration, (3) a form of employment open to the community, (4) a way to assert their rights as border residents, and (5) necessary to protect the security of the community and its children due to risks posed by trucks traveling at high speeds transporting a flammable substance.

Because all community members take turns patrolling the *cadena* and use the border road daily, the potential dangers posed by the gasoline trade were readily apparent. Most people preferred the business to be in the hands of trusted community members rather than outsiders. Others asserted the trade should be abolished entirely. Although most realized the potential economic opportunities, many (especially those not involved in smuggling businesses) believed it was not worth the risks. As one resident stated, "If El Nance does not agree to share the business, we should issue a denouncement, or call the state officials in Tuxtla to terminate this business altogether." Others worried that simply blocking the *cadena* would prompt El Nance to do the same and stifle important community revenues. A member of La Independencia contested this reasoning by arguing that because toll revenues were so critical, El Nance would quickly realize they were wrong and the "conflict would last five minutes." It was imperative that El Nance realize they could not monopolize the benefits of business. The majority resolved to support the group and block the *cadena* if El Nance did not agree to a settlement. The assembly sent a message to El Nance and awaited the reply. The communities have disagreed in the past, but this was the first time one community threatened to block the other's commerce. La Independencia doubted the conflict would go this far and saw blockading the road as a measure of last resort. As Alonso reassured many, "We will talk. We will have a dialogue and reach an agreement. But this situation [of the communities fighting with one another] is new."

The following night, as it neared midnight and I sat in bed writing field notes, I heard loud music and laughter outside my window, which was directly above El Nance's gasoline depot and close to the *cadena*. I went outside to see what was transpiring. About thirty-five men were gathered at El Nance's *cadena*. Samuel told me Santa Rosa had blocked their section of the road at the *cadena*; in response, they did the same. "We will not allow them to work. There are too many people already and not enough money to permit this . . . Because we cannot work, we decided to drink," Samuel laughed. The men turned blocking the road into a party that lasted into the wee hours of the night. Samuel laughed, "Now you will need a visa to pass through here; no one will pass."

As the conflict escalated and both groups blocked their sections of the road, they effectively shut down commerce. Both parties believed this was just a local conflict, but it soon rippled outward to provoke consternation from Guatemalan border residents. As one Guatemalan border resident remarked, "There is no work here now because they both closed their *cadenas*. People here are upset since it affects us, too." Some Mexican residents advised business contacts in Mexico that the road would be temporarily closed and commerce halted, but they did not see a need to inform their Guatemalan neighbors. As one man stated, "They are another country; we don't need to tell them."

However, the evening after the road closure went into effect, the five-man leadership of Nueva Vida, Guatemala, drove their pickup down the hill to Santa Rosa. Upset that they were not notified of the road closure, one man stated:

> We may be from another country, but we are neighbors and are affected by the same things as you are. If something happens here, it affects us. If we were to close our road, it would also affect you, the money coming into your *cadena*, and employment in your community.

They received few answers as to how long the conflict would last, and the Guatemalan men offered to mediate the dispute. Alonso related their perspective to justify the closure, "We want 50 percent [of the business] because we built this section of the road, and only El Nance is benefiting. We finally woke up. We realized . . . what they are doing is not right. We are well within our rights to close the road, because the *ejido* is autonomous to enforce its laws. We should be equal since the gasoline trade is not a business, but a transport." Another member continued, "We still need an agreement. We are all a little chain. We need to unite the communities on both sides since commerce affects all of our interests [and] . . . in order for the chain to function." Through the conflict, it became apparent how the border communities within the route depended on one another regardless of the country in which they were located.

Escalation and the Law

A few moments later, Félix, a resident of El Nance who also works for the municipality of Frontera Comalapa, Chiapas, approached Alonso's group in Santa Rosa with an article in the local newspaper. The article featured a denouncement of gasoline smuggling that named the communities of Santa Rosa and El Nance. One man was surprised: "We [our communities] are never in the paper. Usually the newspapers are bribed." They tried to figure out who had denounced them. It is locally understood that reporting in this vein is not due to good investigative journalism, but rather the result of paying someone to divulge or not to divulge information that serves their interests. Another member lamented, "Now people know about us; maybe now [gasoline smuggling] will just end." I later talked with the men in El Nance about the article. They suspected regional taxi drivers, who resented the long lines at the gas station created by the business, of issuing the denouncement. Both groups blamed outsiders, quickly realizing that what they saw as an internal conflict had caught unwanted regional attention. Despite the intercommunity nature of the conflict, they realized their little chain did not operate in isolation.[8] Many feared the article might attract attention from state officials from Tuxtla, or even Mexico City, who were unfamiliar with the area and the dynamics of smuggler–official relations. Yet, one experienced businessman wryly commented:

> [The government] always says the law will be stricter and that they will send more enforcement. So we are careful for a few days, and then the new officials take our money, too. It is always the same, and things will return to how they were.

In the next few days, as the Guatemalans in Nueva Vida and El Girasol attempted to mediate the conflict, there was a strange turn of events. El Nance decided to cede the entire gasoline and clothing businesses to Santa Rosa. In Santa Rosa, many believed El Nance was trying to set them up to be caught. Others surmised that El Nance's group was temporarily working in another border route. One group member was cautious:

> We suspect their motives. They are liars. Why would they give everything to us? So we have decided not to commercialize anything. The group in El Nance probably knows where the officials are. They are waiting to see us working so that they can call the police to catch us.

In fact, residents witnessed the increasing presence of police near the gas stations, whom they believed were collaborating with El Nance.

The following Thursday was the first time La Independencia would take charge of the clothing business, which El Nance also abdicated to them. When the Guatemalan merchants arrived, the men in Santa Rosa were apprehensive because they suspected El Nance was trying to trick them. Alonso and his group were also having trouble arranging meetings with the customs inspector. Alonso repeatedly told me he had to find what he termed "the law" before they could work, but he had little knowledge of who embodied that authority and expressed frustration with his inability to locate the appropriate representatives. The law, in this sense, referred to the diverse regulatory authorities at the border including state police, federal police, customs inspectors, immigration agents, the military, the highway patrol, and the border police force. The vagueness with which Alonso employed this term reflected the degree to which he was unfamiliar with dealing with these authorities. The group selected Alonso as their leader due to his intelligence and knowledge of human rights and because he is articulate. These skills, however, did not translate into knowing which officials were in charge of arranging bribes to smuggle gasoline. Alonso told the merchants they needed to wait until tomorrow when he planned to talk with the customs inspector's office, although he was uncertain if the customs inspector was the highest authority responsible. However, if the merchants did not transport their goods that evening in time to set up for the Friday market, they would lose a week's worth of business. They resolved to send a few people to the highway to verify the situation. Sure enough, the military had erected a temporary roadblock, and one man reported, "When I saw the military there, I also saw Juan [gasoline smuggler from El Nance] with them! They want to scare us [from working]." The military allowed them to pass, but only in exchange for a bribe that was higher than if they had arranged a preestablished agreement.

After this incident, it became imperative that Alonso's group, as he said, "find the law" so they could work. Although residents take the law into their own hands in some respects, they are also dependent on agents of the law for their livelihoods. They depend on such officials to either turn a blind eye to their activities or to indirectly or directly collude with them. Residents may envision themselves as alternative regulatory authorities, but their strategies highlight the interdependence between smugglers and the state.[9] Officials not only receive bribes from smugglers, but they may also derive essential benefits for their units, including gifts of gasoline. In return, smugglers receive approval to conduct their businesses and may also garner official protection against rivals (for example, the threat to rat out others) or other policing units. Through rituals that seek out officials in their offices, search the highways for police, or use relationships with local officials to remain informed about more distant policing efforts, residents redramatize the authority of the state to rule and its power to enforce, neglect, or bend the rules in a region where it may otherwise appear that authority is increasingly fragmented.[10]

The struggle to smuggle gasoline demonstrates how legality at the border has little to do with the letter of the law. Instead it has to do with relationships, perceived economic necessity, and evolving power configurations in a region where officials balance Mexico's focus on security with the realities of trade, their own meager salaries, lack of sufficient personnel, the spread of cartels and criminal groups, and the regional embeddedness of contraband. Alonso, as a teacher relatively unfamiliar with the world of contraband, remained confounded as to where the law was located so it could be purchased and controlled.

Fieldwork Dream and Nightmare

My friendship with Alonso over the course of my fieldwork enabled unique access to La Independencia's struggles. As a teacher, Alonso often identified with my work and was excited to help me formulate and test research questions. Alonso was also interested in how smuggling worked, both as a relative outsider to the business who wanted to participate to benefit economically and as someone interested in smuggling analytically and politically. We spent many afternoons talking during the gasoline conflict as we both learned how locals engage in contraband and about the different players. Alonso and his group's openness and ideals of inclusivity (part of their appeal to garner community support) extended to me in a context where contraband is often the domain of men, making it difficult to fully participate in their meetings. The men met most evenings at the *cadena* in a festive atmosphere of music and communal eating.

To be included in their group was simultaneously an anthropologist's dream and an ethical nightmare. On the one hand, I observed the inner workings of the group's business dynamics and negotiations. I witnessed how they discussed ideas about equality and negotiated among themselves as they positioned themselves vis-à-vis smugglers, community members, and state officials. I learned from the inside how contraband actually worked and how newcomers start a business and collude with state agents. There were, however, limits to my participation in a business that was still illegal and controversial even though group members framed their efforts in terms of a struggle for their rights.[11] Moreover, I could not alienate residents of El Nance, lest they think I was spying on them or actually smuggling gasoline myself! Because the groups portrayed the conflict as two-sided despite the fact that it was more complex, I could not be perceived as favoring either side, especially because I lived in El Nance at the time. I lived next door to El Nance's gasoline exchange depot where transfers between the group and Guatemalan merchants occurred.

Santa Rosa's La Independencia group solicited my input as an educated (and U.S.) professional to help them organize, articulate their rights, and understand El Nance. In fact, recruiting me to their cause may have been a strategy to sanction their claims. It sometimes seemed all too easy to become seduced by their inclusive rhetoric of fighting for their rights. However, I could not fully engage without compromising my research, personal friendships, and safety. I therefore attempted to understand both groups' perspectives. Santa Rosa's openness provided me with more access to information than El Nance, where those involved in gasoline smuggling remained more guarded. The manner in which each group incorporated me reflected how Santa Rosa structured the conflict in a more inclusive and communitarian manner, whereas El Nance perceived the dispute as an individual and small group business issue. Generally, throughout the research process, residents of El Nance were more hesitant to trust me than people in Santa Rosa. In contrast to the *ejido* communal structure of Santa Rosa, El Nance is a smaller community of private property owners, where residents generally regard work concerns (whether farming, cattle raising, or contraband) as individual matters even though, in practice, wealthier residents share work with relatives. When I lived in Santa Rosa during the first half of my fieldwork, neighboring children often shouted in our glassless (and therefore quite useless) windows to remind us to attend the monthly assembly meetings. In contrast, cultivating enough rapport to attend El Nance's assembly meetings took months. Assembly meetings in Santa Rosa are open to the entire community, but only male adults are invited to El Nance's meetings (except that the elderly are excused, and widows and wives of migrants are included). El Nance's community president during the first half of my fieldwork was excited about my research and extended invitations, but the authorities who succeeded him were more guarded.

Because the gasoline conflict occurred at the end of my fieldwork, I had already cultivated a sense of trust in both communities, but I acknowledge that how the communities and groups perceived me, as well as the conflict, may have influenced my interpretations of events. For example, at first, I mistakenly did not think twice about the fact that Alonso arranged my going away party at Santa Rosa's *cadena* during the gasoline conflict. Because I spent significant time in the communities on both sides of the border, I invited friends and contacts on both sides and naively assumed my relationships would transcend the dispute. Yet, it was during these weeks that I heard people in El Nance asking me if I were a member of La Independencia, if I were smuggling gasoline, or why I was working with them. Some people became hesitant in our other conversations as they suspected I might relay information to Santa Rosa. Tito's daughter-in-law, Clara, mentioned that the men did not want to come to the party because they were still fighting with Santa Rosa. Clara wanted to come but was nervous about what others would think. She suggested a separate party at their home. As she told me:

> Women are different. We don't have any problems with them [people in Santa Rosa]. But now we are not getting along so well. They [Santa Rosa] are behaving badly because they took away our work. It is not right to be working and have a job and for others to just take it away from you. They do not understand.

Clara did attend with her mother-in-law and their children, nieces, and nephews, but they stayed briefly. What seemed to dispel these perceptions (in addition to time and distancing myself more from La Independencia) was when the trade attracted official attention. The conflict came to a halt when both parties became afraid to work.

Fueling Power

The conflict over gasoline smuggling revealed fissures in the local dictum that "everyone who lives here has the right to work here." It made clear that such ethics no longer characterized most business practices in a climate of increasing business competition. More broadly, the conflict illustrated the ironies of treating transnational contraband as a local issue. Residents focused on their interpretations of rights, but neglected to note how their trade was enmeshed in larger regional and transnational political and economic dynamics. In this larger context, residents are more often pawns than authority figures in the evolving power and economic landscape in the borderlands.

Was there something particular about gasoline that sparked such a divisive conflict? Although denouncements, infighting, and manipulations by powerful smugglers or state officials might be expected in the realm of contraband, this was unusual. Contraband in most other items remains relatively open to border residents, unproblematic, and institutionalized in daily life. The disputes and suspicions surrounding gasoline smuggling were not the rule, but the exception.

It is therefore important to examine the product of gasoline itself, for what it means in daily and national life. First, at the time, Mexico's oil industry was nationalized, and much of Mexico's petroleum originates from southern states like Chiapas. In Mexico, the state-owned company, PEMEX, dominated the distribution and production of petroleum. Meanwhile, Guatemala imports most of its petroleum, and transnational companies distribute gasoline and diesel.[12] Many Mexicans at the border firmly believe that they have the right to distribute their gasoline as a national product. In contrast, others espoused a nationalist argument to condemn the traffic, arguing, "[Smuggling gasoline] risks depleting our national resource, and then we may not have any left for us." Many of their opinions reflect recent debates regarding the privatization of PEMEX in the context of the Mexican oil sector's growing inefficiency and President Peña Nieto's commitment to deeper privatization.[13] In 2013, President Peña Nieto's energy and financial reforms paved the way for the privatization of PEMEX, which contributed 40 percent of state income and 70 percent of the "total national budget" in a country with a history of dismal tax collection.[14] Previously, the Mexican Constitution established that "hydrocarbons are the patrimony of all Mexicans."[15] Critics argue that, although privatization will provide a boon to oil investors and private oil companies, the consequences may be disastrous for the working poor, generating economic shocks, environmental damage, and rural displacement to facilitate and expand extraction.[16] In early 2017, protests against the effects of privatization, called "el gasolinazo," erupted throughout Mexico as a falling peso and subsidy cuts led prices to surge by 20 percent.[17]

In 2006–2007 Guatemalan border residents had fewer connections to the gasoline business, perceived it to be risky, and were hesitant to become involved. For one, states tend to police goods entering the country more intensively than those exiting. Logistically, Mexican smugglers had to go only two miles to their own gasoline station, whereas Guatemalan merchants transported the smuggled gasoline long distances. Guatemalan residents viewed gasoline smuggling as something reserved for the rich and powerful and perhaps even linked to sophisticated criminal groups and multinational corporations that employed paramilitaries or other corrupt agents. Some suspected the gasoline companies hired smugglers to bear the risks for them to supplement their gasoline. Others believed that companies employed powerful individuals who would harm them if they were caught smuggling gasoline that interfered with their business. A 2007 *La Prensa* article cited death threats against the mayor of the local municipality for attempting to investigate gasoline trafficking.[18] In contrast, in Mexico, residents knew the local gasoline station owners, and many residents worked there. The owner gifted the group in El Nance PEMEX T-shirts and appreciated the boost in business.

On the Mexican side, residents reasoned gasoline was a national product to which they had rights. In contrast, Guatemalan residents were unfamiliar with the gasoline business, which they feared was linked to transnational companies, powerful foreign investors, or organized mafias. The high premium for gasoline, and the multiplicity of actors involved in its trade and distribution, revealed that gasoline smuggling was by no means a local issue, but rather a transnational one. It reached far beyond border residents. As private companies, foreign investors, the military, criminal gangs, and long-distance powerful smugglers entered the equation, the gasoline conflict illustrated how petty smuggling is becoming more unpredictable for border residents.

Spiraling Governance

To cope and thrive in the gaps of the legal and extralegal economy, residents rely on their strategic location and cross-border networks and knowledge to engage in, manipulate, and benefit from cross-border flows. However, local knowledge and residents' cultural capital, which enable them to occupy critical roles in the contraband economy, may be becoming less relevant as such knowledge and connections increasingly become transnational commodities accessible to those beyond the border and the agents of protection and predation at the border spiral. Long-distance truckers still collaborate with border residents or arrange connections via cell phones, but residents' roles in making business and official connections are less necessary in the climate of transnational illegal and legal business. Perhaps this is why residents are now trying more vehemently to assert their position by blocking the pathway to external merchants who do not use them as truckers and intermediaries. In this context, residents' control of the border can also quickly turn from resource to liability as they stand at the crossroads of multiple actors seeking to profit from the border. At this juncture, a focus on mutual profits in a region that depends on contraband enables officials, residents, cartels, legitimate businesses, and smugglers to coexist relatively peacefully and symbiotically.

However, conflicts, such as the one between the gasoline smugglers, highlight the vulnerability of border residents in a region where authority and violence have fragmented among various actors while the state also works to reassert its sovereignty, at times violently. When I visited in 2011, I learned that a border gasoline smuggler was murdered close to Frontera Comalapa. Some feared the trade was now increasingly dangerous and becoming connected to the spreading influence of drug traffickers. Most, however, were not frightened and believed this to be a case of jealousy, theft, or mistaken identity or that he was involved in something else.

Residents' agreements with authorities can quickly and unpredictably fizzle, especially when officials change. In 2008, I learned the gasoline smugglers were surprised in the route by a rare bust by a military unit from Comitán, Chiapas. The military confiscated five Guatemalan trucks full of canisters of gasoline and held them ransom for about US$20,000. Gasoline smuggling eventually resumed, and larger-scale Guatemalan smugglers continue to operate with impunity.[19] Locally, this has become a quieter business monopolized by a few wealthier resident smugglers with stronger official connections or by small groups of people smuggling smaller quantities more rapidly (repeated pickup trips instead of using a ten-ton truck). Interestingly, the few wealthier, more powerful residents who smuggled gasoline independent of the groups escaped scrutiny in the conflict between the two groups, as well as official attention. They largely continued smuggling gasoline the entire time. Although some group members approached these community members for advice on contacts and official relations, others believe that perhaps they ratted them out to the military. The gasoline conflict, in many respects, deflected attention from the fact that despite residents' rhetoric about the inclusivity of border smuggling, the risks and benefits of smuggling remain unequal as a few reap the large rewards and those with the fewest connections bear the risks.

Periodically, due to continued media and political attention, police and military come to investigate, and the traffic stops. They usually turn a blind eye while local policing and military units receive fuel subsidies from smugglers. Within a few days, trade resumes due to the multiple actors who profit. The bust may have been a disruption in the everyday order of things, whereby closing official eyes to contraband is profitable for many in the region. At the same time, such dramatic displays of state authority maintain the very system whereby smuggling proceeds, but the state maintains a foothold in defining its trajectory and form despite the growing salience of alternative forms of governance. In his ethnography of smuggling and migration from Morocco to Spain, David McMurray points to how attempts to evade the state may enhance its legitimacy:

> Ruses and subterfuges [of evading official control] miss . . . the interesting process by which the dominated often become complicitous in legitimizing state power . . . [They] can succeed at what they are doing while simultaneously confirming the legitimacy of the state's monopoly on ceremony and violence.[20]

Border residents have gained some control by negotiating with, rather than simply trying to evade, state authorities. Yet, in doing so they reaffirm the state's legitimacy and "right to rule."[21] The state and its agents retain a credible threat to enforce the law, and therefore smugglers need to purchase the selective, or non-, enforcement of the law.[22] Peter Andreas calls this a "corruption tax"; corruption prices increase with escalating enforcement.[23] When new truckers wanted to engage in gasoline smuggling, they went on a runaround search for the law to purchase and subvert it, often complaining they could not find the law, personalized in the agents who embody and enact it at the border. Rituals of evading the state combined with periodic intense displays of state power, therefore "dramatize the legitimacy" of state authority and its effects on how individuals situate themselves in relation to the state.[24] Border smugglers' phone calls to police friends who advise them of local (as well as more distant) policing movements, positioning of spies, and routine checks for officials on the highway all constitute ways of reinstantiating state power and their relations to it. Official contacts not only permit smugglers to operate, but they also protect them (and warn them) from other policing units.[25] Officials and smugglers benefit symbiotically when officials crack down on rival groups.[26] Smugglers monopolize more business for themselves while officials can earn profits and demonstrate success with evidence of arrests and confiscations. Specifically, the group in Santa Rosa suspected that El Nance's stronger relationships with police would be used to arrest them and protect El Nance's control of the gasoline smuggling trade. In this case, officials can manage and manipulate unpredictability. The group in El Nance trusted the police to protect them and target the group in Santa Rosa but instead learned that policing units preferred to receive the additional bribes.[27] Local and regional units could also do little once federal authorities became involved. Despite a status quo where smugglers seem relatively free to operate, the military's dramatic arrest of gasoline smugglers served to remind smugglers why they need to keep performing their search for the law.

Richard Snyder and Angelica Duran-Martinez argue that Mexican policing reforms since the 1990s, including decentralization and shortening the timetables of particular officials, were intended to reduce corruption and collusion with organized crime.[28] When the PRI exerted hegemonic control, criminal organizations and the state-protection racket existed in a relatively stable and predictable symbiosis.[29] Destabilizing this racket has led to a proliferation of criminal groups as well a more complex and unpredictable geography of law enforcement.[30] Conflicts and uncertainty ensued over whom to bribe in addition to competition among criminal groups over market share and territory. Without a stable and reliable means of official protection, crime groups increasingly turn to violence and acquire and enact their own privatized means of predation and protection.[31]

At this point, the border communities have maintained their niche in the contraband economy independent from the criminal groups and cartels that establish controls along other border passages. Border smugglers can also still negotiate with officials, but this is becoming an increasingly costly and unpredictable enterprise. Each year the bribe prices increase and the addition of more security to the border has translated into more policing units to bribe. When the newly created State Border Police (PEF) arrived at the border in early 2007 to control drug trafficking and organized crime at the border, local smugglers stopped their work for a few days.[32] However, they soon realized that many of the officers were the same ones they knew from the local police force. They just had new uniforms and were yet another unit that needed to be added to the roster to bribe.

Rural gasoline smugglers and border residents are small players in this complex unraveling and respiraling of violence and governance. In effect, they become pawns in a shifting landscape of law enforcement where criminal groups and drug traffickers have carved out their own areas of control. Drug traffickers have increased their power in this region in the past decade, and even more so since I left the field in 2007. As more drugs began coming through Central America, the Sinaloa cartel and the Zetas moved into Central America to "better manage and guarantee the 'safe' passage of their inventory."[33] The Zetas gained a presence in Huehuetenango in 2007,[34] and increasingly in 2008, as border regions became battlegrounds for turf wars where locals could do little but avoid these locations and close their eyes. In November of 2008, in a region where residents in 2006 and 2007 believed that drug traffickers passed through but caused few problems, a cell affiliated with the Zetas (still associated with the Gulf Cartel before separating in 2010), murdered nearly twenty people in a nearby border crossing in Agua Zarca, Guatemala, in a confrontation with the Sinaloa cartel. The shootout occurred during horse races, which I learned at the border were notorious locations to cover for drug exchanges. When I read the news while writing my dissertation back in the United States, I phoned Tito's family to check on them because I knew one of his daughters-in-law had family in Agua Zarca. They responded, "Everyone is fine. Nobody went there. It is tranquil." Francisca from El Girasol also informed me, "No one from here went. We *knew* not to go." This last comment is particularly illustrative of the importance of border knowledge and networks. Border residents asserted that they were safe and did not worry extensively about violence because they were intimately familiar with the occasions and locations where violence and narco turf wars tended to break out. A *Prensa Libre* article articulated similar responses; its title stated that the residents of Agua Zarca preferred not to speak. According to the article, residents said either that they did not know anything, they were not present, or they shut off their cell phones.[35]

I learned in 2014 that one of Guatemala's most wanted narcotraffickers, Eduardo Villatoro Cano, known as "El Guayo," had fled through a nearby unmonitored crossing before capture in Tuxtla Gutiérrez, where he was discovered in a plastic surgery clinic attempting to alter his appearance. Prior to his capture, residents reported nearby towns like Camojá had become more dangerous, soldiers patrolled the entrance to the Guatemalan side of the crossing from the highway, and daily fears of robbery or assault were heightened. The delicate relationships among state units, criminal groups, petty smugglers, and residents continue to unfold; residents maintain their silence to retain a degree of autonomy and livelihood, but their position is increasingly precarious as drug groups have established influence throughout the region and over other corridors. The Zetas' critical mode of operation is to take control over territory and establish a monopoly over crime so that anyone engaging in extralegal activity must pay them a "criminal tax" or "*piso*."[36] At this point, they have not taken over this corridor, the communities retain their own *cadena* taxes, and daily life remains relatively tranquil. Yet residents are also useful for maintaining an open and traversable pathway and for serving as possible transporters. Violence has improved in Guatemala's borderlands in the last few years, but much of this can be attributed to different agreements among the Sinaloa cartel, the Zetas, and Guatemalan narcofamilies rather than to dismantlement of these groups.[37] In 2008, the Zetas pursued a surge to control vital points in Guatemala for drug purchase and transfer,[38] but the Guatemalan attorney general's office under Claudia Paz y Paz led efforts to weaken their presence.[39] Yet other groups have struggled to fill the holes, and the Sinaloa cartel remains powerful in the region as it forms flexible alliances with Guatemalan transport and criminal groups.[40] Chiapas is currently relatively less violent than some other Mexican states; some argue this is because cartels have established their own zones of influence rather than clashing.[41]

Conclusion

The Illicit Trio: Drugs, Arms, and Migrants

The line between "legal" and "illegal" is held to be clear
and definitive inside a given state, a hegemonic claim. Yet
the actual practice is ambiguous and subject to resourceful
manipulation. Legality and illegality are thus simultaneously
black and white, and shades of gray.

—Josiah McC. Heyman and Alan Smart, "States and
Illegal Practices: An Overview," 1999: 11

THROUGH DETAILING THE LIVES OF BORDER INHABITANTS and petty smugglers, *Contraband Corridor* illuminates the context in which people define smuggling goods as honest work. Rather than taking contraband and illegality for granted, it problematizes how and why certain economic activities, along with their protagonists, are labeled "contraband" and "crime" as others enjoy greater mobility and access. The lens of securitized neoliberalism reveals how regional security and trade policies proceed in tandem to sanction certain flows of goods, peoples, and logics and restrict others. Yet regional trade integration and an escalation of border security coexist with an extension of extralegal activities that enjoy increasing legitimacy among regional inhabitants. Without understanding why people engage in extralegal activities,[1] and how and under what conditions these activities become illegalized, aggressive approaches to crime are not only likely to fail, but also may further distrust in the state and its institutions and foster more insecurity and inequality.

Border residents are relatively marginal players in a region experiencing the recent influx of drug cartels, criminal groups, and militarized policing to strengthen border security. Yet, local residents' control over the unmonitored border road on which they reside positions them as gatekeepers in an evolving landscape of contested governance between state units, criminal groups, and local inhabitants. Residents' patterns of interaction with state officials, which are characterized by patron–client ties and a critical interdependence, reveal the contradictions of escalating enforcement to combat the drug trade and a climate of rising violence and insecurity.

In the context of the decline of corn farming, socioeconomic and political crisis, and the lack of alternative livelihood options, border residents reason that smuggling daily goods may be illegal, but it is socially acceptable and critical to their survival.[2] Even so, smuggling rarely enables individuals to surmount their deeper economic, social, and geographic marginalization. Although residents and border smugglers told me that state authorities were now more understanding and enabled them to work, smugglers remain dependent on, and in many ways bolster, the power of the state and the discretion of its agents. Border residents strategize creative ways to earn a living and bypass official trade regulations, but their activities are more likely to benefit larger formal businesses, regional politicians, more powerful illicit traders, and corrupt law enforcement officials. Border residents embody the risks. They must evade or pay off state agents and personally risk robbery, accidents, and arrest. Even when smuggling may provide benefits to segments of the regional economy, petty smugglers are increasingly stigmatized in an official landscape that mistakenly lumps together rural peasants, youth, terrorists, delinquents, criminals, and migrants as potential threats to public and national security.[3]

In the neoliberal context, applying a security lens to informal commerce and conflating contraband with transnational crime serves not only to elevate and protect the elite transnational and corporate profits with which it is contrasted, but also to exert control over the activities and mobility of marginalized groups.[4] Local and transnational business interests view the informal economy as a threat to their profits even as they also rely on, and may profit from, it. According to Alain Basail Rodríguez, economic and political interests converge to render the border "a space of criminalization and militarization in the name of a modern ideal of security . . . and a moralistic ideal of social life for the control, vigilance, discipline, and containment of migratory flows and informality."[5] Kedron Thomas argues in her work on brand pirates in Guatemala that "international legal frameworks provide a sanctioned discourse to transfer blame [for underdevelopment and poverty] onto groups of citizens cast as illicit and problematic," which further reproduces inequality and criminalization of the poor.[6] In turn, marginalized groups, who may purchase counterfeit or contraband goods because they cannot afford to purchase the legitimate versions, or who engage in contraband and unauthorized reproduction because they are excluded from legitimate commercial opportunities, call out these inequities to legitimate their own practices.[7]

Maintaining a tough official stance against contraband not only fuels the expansion of the border security apparatus and the exclusion and criminalization of marginal border inhabitants, but it also obscures the ways in which contraband is embedded in business as usual. Contraband's symbiosis with the formal economy and state policing agencies can help contextualize how law enforcement, politics, and illicit actors often merge in the borderlands. Categories of licit and illicit, and even the term *contraband* itself, are revealed as politically laden as they also fail to explain the complex, unfolding social and economic reality. Although it is a mistake to group corn smugglers with drug cartels and human smugglers, the logics of criminalization paint them with a wide brushstroke in the fight against illicit activity.[8] In contrast, contraband is often detached for examination from the global political economy. Contraband and unmonitored crossings must be understood not as the underside of trade or as deviations but as integral parts of the formal economy and the state.[9]

Because border residents justify smuggling basic commodities across the border, I wondered what they considered to be illicit, or unacceptable, as well as illegal. This conclusion examines the relatively recent securitization of migration, or rendering migration a security concern and threat, at the Mexico–Guatemala border to illustrate the effects of the social and political construction of illegality. Securitization refers to how the state socially constructs migration and migrants as threats, which it uses to justify the militarization and violent surveillance of certain spaces and peoples in the name of security.[10] As Mexico cracks down on undocumented migration, corruption and violence have increased while migration continues. The case of migration is instructive for what a heavy-handed approach to extralegal activities without addressing underlying causes may portend.

The Illegalization of Migration

Guatemalan border resident Francisca and I always had lively fast-paced conversations; we both have reputations for talking too quickly. Sometimes I had to pause her to parse the different words she used to describe cross-border business. She usually spoke about the cross-border sale of daily goods as "business"; however, she occasionally slipped into using the word *contraband*. She was adamant that selling corn, coffee, and other daily goods across the unmonitored border might be illegal but still business. I asked her what she considered to be illicit when, in passing, she mentioned the existence of other types of "illicit contraband." "Drugs, arms, and migrants," she rattled off quickly as if they all naturally belonged together. Many people explained that smuggling drugs, arms, and migrants was illegal and illicit—both politically and socially unacceptable and risky[11]—because the state more actively patrolled these activities, or at least they supposedly did. Yet Francisca had never thought about why they were illicit. This time, she thought for a few moments, repeating similar responses to other border residents who stated that drugs were bad for your health and a bad influence on society whereas weapons posed a palpable risk of harm. But when it came to explaining *why* smuggling migrants was illicit, residents hesitated. Francisca paused and threw her hands up in the air, "*Saber?*"—a popular local refrain meaning, "Who knows?" A Mexican border resident elaborated, "The authorities are concerned because [migrants] cross the border without documents, but who knows why they are bothering them? They don't bother us."

Border residents connected the Mexican state's crackdown on undocumented Central American migrants to a U.S.-designed migration agenda. As one migrant shelter staff member in Tecún Umán, Guatemala explained, "[Previous President] Bush asked Mexico to help detain migrants going north. Mexico is doing dirty work [of the United States]."

In contrast, population movements were historically porous along the Mexico–Guatemala border due to kinship connections, social relations, and refugee flight and return movements during and following the Guatemalan counterinsurgency conflict in the 1980s and 1990s. Alonso, a teacher in Santa Rosa, Mexico remembers, "When I was a teenager [in the early 1980s], we gave Guatemalans rides to Comitán [nearby Mexican city] for a small fee all the time. It was no problem. I was kind of a coyote," he laughed.[12] However, few residents express interest in doing this now. Alonso has hosted Central American migrant women in his house, who worked as domestics until they accumulated enough money to continue their journey north. He taught them the Mexican national anthem, Mexican slang, and even advised them to dye their hair. However, he no longer provides rides. Many border residents relate the story of a local corn merchant and storeowner who was arrested for providing rides to Central American migrants. Rumors circulate that a few residents leveraged their connections to U.S. employers to serve as coyotes and manufacture work visas for migrants in the 1990s, but such stories remain either rumors or situated in the past. Few currently talk about working as migrant smugglers in contrast to the degree of openness with which they discuss the smuggling of corn, coffee, fruits and vegetables, sugar, gasoline, and clothing.

Yet is there anything inherently more dangerous about a migrant than a satchel of coffee? If anything, it would seem that most residents would more readily help migrants because they empathize with their plight due to their own experience migrating to the United States. Residents not only see that the state enacts stiffer penalties and directs more policing efforts toward migrant flows, but they are also beginning to repeat the state's racialized depictions of migrants as threats. Residents refer to Guatemalans as *paisanos*, or countrymen, but many fear Hondurans and Salvadorans due to a proliferation of media on gang violence perpetrated by the Mara Salvatrucha and Barrio 18 gangs in these countries, as well as in urban border cities like Tapachula and Tecún Umán. Some border residents associate stories of gang violence with people from El Salvador and Honduras, whom they gloss as *maras*, despite the fact that these gangs trace their roots to the streets of Los Angeles and were then deported and transnationalized to Central America.[13] There was little evidence at the time that these gangs had a significant presence in this particular region. However, factions associated with the Zetas and Sinaloa cartel were beginning to spread and Huehuetenango and Frontera Comalapa have become territorial lynchpins in the drug trade.[14] As Jennifer Burrell notes, the term *mara* has come to unite, and gloss over, varying kinds of criminality despite their actual distinctions; the fear the label inspires comes to justify tough-on-crime and violent approaches to deal with insecurity.[15]

A few Hondurans and Salvadorans now reside in the border communities after they became frustrated with the journey north. They found work loading cargo for smugglers or married locals. Due to land pressures and fears of delinquency, Santa Rosa, Mexico, decided to expel Central Americans from their community in 2007. They were unable to implement the expulsion, but many argued that Central Americans were potentially dangerous because they came from "conflictive countries." Raids on undocumented migrants have become more frequent in the municipality of Frontera Comalapa, Chiapas, as well as in cantinas (bars) in nearby Camojá, Guatemala. A local pastor, who wished to open a migrant hostel in Frontera Comalapa faced resistance and even threats from local authorities and residents who associated migrants with criminality.

Although many residents blame migrants for perceptions of rising insecurity, prior to the intensification of Mexico's efforts to contain illicit narcotics and migrants in the late 1990s and early 2000s, neither posed a significant risk to border populations. Drugs and migrants passed through with minimal fanfare amid other flows. Residents noted they were not the ones with a drug problem; the United States was the nation with high addiction rates. Yet this has shifted in recent years as Mexico commits itself to a militarized approach to containing the northward flows of narcotics, illicit goods, and unauthorized migrants. Due to the mounting difficulty of passing through Mexico, more migrants and drugs are remaining in Mexico, and especially in border regions, hence justifying more policing. When I visited the border in 2008, this was the first time I heard concerns about youth becoming involved in drugs. Between 2002 and 2008, cocaine usage in Mexico increased from 1.4 percent of the population to 2.4 percent.[16]

States shape the forms that smuggling takes through the power to regulate, facilitate, or criminalize particular flows.[17] Enhanced security measures led migrants to rely more heavily on smugglers who could avoid or pay off state agents, gangs, and other criminal actors. Migrants in southern Mexico responded to a proliferation of highway checkpoints by hopping aboard a moving freight train, dubbed "the Beast," risking life and limb to migrate northward.[18] When U.S. concern over a Central American migrant "crisis" in 2014 led Mexico to focus policing efforts on the train, migrants turned to riskier routes and smuggling fees increased from US$6,000–$8,000 to US$9,000–$10,000 accordingly.[19] The inability to substantively reform the police and judicial system means that heightened border security also translates into corruption acting as what Peter Andreas calls "an informal form of taxation," so that bribes rise as security escalates.[20]

Responses to Mexico's security challenge and police corruption have included legal reforms and professionalization, "militarization [of policing], consolidation of existing police forces, and creation of new forces."[21] Militarized policing, or using military discipline and leaders in policing,[22] and the militarization of drug and migrant surveillance have backfired by creating more insecurity among the population, which adds to the motivations to migrate northward. Policing reforms have sought to upgrade policing through improved salaries, benefits, and training and enhanced monitoring, but accountability measures have not been priorities, lack of institutional change dampens the effectiveness of reforms, and corruption and lack of public trust in the police remain serious challenges.[23] Specifically, a culture of informal rules and patronage politics continue to guide policing, making it difficult to translate and institutionalize reforms in practice.[24]

Dawn Paley critically points to how policing reform under the Mérida Initiative has failed to eradicate corruption.[25] Efforts toward specialization, decentralization, and professionalization of policing distanced specialized units from modes of central authority and accountability, which contributed to escalating violence and human rights violations.[26] She further contends that policy reforms under the Mérida Initiative to improve law enforcement and reform the judicial system have proceeded hand-in-hand with the Mérida Initiative's militarization and counterinsurgency components, working to enforce public order and secure a climate conducive to transnational investment rather than improving democratic accountability.[27] Militarization may help discipline the police, but it does little to reform it or make it accountable.[28] Moreover, without addressing wider problems plaguing governance, an inadequate and overwhelmed criminal justice system, and complicity between organized crime and the politicians to whom police leadership are responsible and are appointed by, policing reform risks remaining largely ornamental.[29]

As Mexico, with U.S. support, militarizes the southern border to combat the smuggling of drugs and undocumented migrants, violence, insecurity, and human rights abuses have increased. According to Human Rights Watch, Mexico heavily depends on the military to wage the drug war; Mexico's Commission on Human Rights has received 9,000 reports of abuses by the military since 2006.[30] Mexico's murder rate rose by 50 percent per year from 2008 to 2010, human rights violations against migrants escalated, and efforts to reform the criminal justice system remain insufficient.[31] In 2015, according to the Global Impunity Index, Mexico had the second highest impunity rate of fifty-nine countries measured.[32] Only 7 percent of crimes are reported, of which only 4.46 percent result in convictions.[33] Taking into consideration unreported crimes, this means that less than 1 percent of crimes in Mexico are punished.[34] Few citizens trust authorities, and an inadequate justice system and underfunded state institutions impede access to justice.[35] The U.S. Congress has placed human rights conditions on portions of Mérida assistance, but the Consolidated Appropriations Act of Fiscal Year 2017 stipulates no such conditions on Mérida funds.[36]

The Inter-American Commission of Human Rights reported in 2013 that, in the past few years, migrants have been more likely to face disappearance, kidnapping, extortion, assault, murder, and robbery perpetrated by gangs, police, and immigration officials alike.[37] Despite Mexican legislation intended to decriminalize migration in 2008 and to improve the protection of migrants' human rights through the 2011 Migration Law (Ley de Migración), abuses have continued. Despite some reforms, the institutional structure of Mexico's migration system remained unchanged with "the INM retaining most policy and operational responsibilities."[38] The root causes propelling migration, such as poverty, political and economic violence, insecurity, and impunity in Mexico and Central America, as well as the economic and social pulls for migrant labor in the United States, remain inadequately addressed.

In 2013, Mexico's National Institute of Migration (INM) ranked eighth in the number of human rights abuses reported to Mexico's National Human Rights Ombudsman, with the military and federal police tallying even more abuses.[39] According to a Casa del Migrante report in Saltillo, Mexico, the most denunciations for migrant abuses were charged at the federal police, even ahead of the Zetas cartel and gangs.[40] As the gasoline smugglers in Chapter 7 illustrated, the addition of a new police force, the PEF, did not mean more surveillance, but another unit to bribe. When gasoline smuggling caught state attention, it did not cease. Instead, officials demanded higher bribes. Similarly, a merchant in southern Mexico told the journalist Manu Ureste, "As there are more checkpoints, there is more corruption."[41] Securitizing migration further empowered smugglers and corrupt officials.

Mexico is recently bearing the effects of a U.S. proclaimed migrant "crisis," after thousands of Central American minors arrived at the U.S.–Mexico border in the summer of 2014. The U.S., Mexican, and Central American governments sought to address the problem through enhancing border security, as well as targeting root causes of migration through the Plan of the Alliance for Prosperity in the Northern Triangle of Central America. In 2014, Mexican President Enrique Peña Nieto implemented the Southern Border Program. The program claimed to "protect and safeguard the human rights of migrants," but included sending additional security units to the southern border, including the military, federal, state, and municipal police and more than 300 members of the gendarmerie, "a force of military police with the approach to protect strategic economic interests."[42] The U.S. State Department plans to provide US$86 million in International Narcotics Control and Enforcement funds to bolster the program to install more checkpoints and naval bases and enhance technology along Mexico's southern border.[43] Apprehensions of Central American children at the U.S.–Mexico border plummeted by 45 percent from the fall of 2014 to September 2015, but Mexico's deportations of Central American minors rose by 67 percent, merely displacing rather than resolving the issue.[44] By the summer of 2015, the number of apprehensions of minors at the U.S.–Mexico border was going back up.[45] Since 2012, the number of crimes committed against migrants in border states has risen 200 percent.[46] In 2014, over half of these crimes were committed by criminal organizations, but the next biggest culprit was the federal police, responsible for 20 percent of assaults against migrants according to the Documentation Network Defenders Migrant Organizations.[47]

To address the propellants of migration in Central America—namely social exclusion, poverty, and insecurity—the presidents of Guatemala, Honduras, and El Salvador; the Inter-American Development Bank; and former U.S. Vice President Joe Biden met in Guatemala City in March 2015 to support implementation of the Plan of the Alliance for Prosperity in the Northern Triangle of Central America.[48] Central American leaders requested US$1 billion; the U.S. Congress allocated US$750 million in December 2015.[49] The plan contains development and security objectives ranging from investment in health and education to the expansion of policing, support of microenterprise, facilitation of regional trade, and stimulation of public-private partnerships.[50] It seeks to involve public and private sectors and civil society, although the process is not specified.

The plan is comprehensive, including investing in economic and educational opportunity in marginal areas and supporting local initiatives, dismantling trade barriers within Central America, professionalizing the civil service, and reforming the judicial and policing systems. Yet the joint statement brief also reads a bit like a laundry list,[51] making it difficult to discern which policies will be prioritized, especially if aspects conflict. Questions remain regarding who will have a say in what kinds of security and development initiatives are implemented and in what fashion. Will trade be facilitated for all or just for investors and developers as concretized in NAFTA and CAFTA? Historian and Honduras expert Dana Frank warns:

> [The plan's] actual content, though will only exacerbate the problems, since it . . . rewards the very elite and transnational corporate interests whose policies and practices have produced the crisis of poverty and security the proposal offers to address.[52]

Critics point to how development is interpreted to mean the implementation of more free trade zones, increasing privatization, and fewer worker protections, all policies that have enhanced the profits of transnational corporations, eroded the livelihoods of the poor, and heightened insecurity.[53] The plan also endorses the expansion, rather than the revision, of current security approaches. Because such policies have compounded the insecurity that causes people to flee, this should give pause to accepting the plan at face value. The United States has continued to fail to reform its immigration system, which means that the pulls for migration—the demand for cheap labor, family ties, and insufficient legal visa mechanisms—remain. The plan proceeds alongside increased funding to secure the U.S–Mexico and Mexico–Guatemala borders, which has only enhanced insecurity, human rights violations, and the power of human smugglers.

Given the reputations of the leadership in Guatemala and Honduras for repressing dissent to the dominant security and neoliberal economic models, it remains to be seen if the Alliance for Prosperity will chart a new path toward social inclusion and public security or if it constitutes a further step toward securitized neoliberalism, or the usage of security forces, the military, and police to secure transnational investments to the exclusion of local inhabitants.[54] Critics suspect the latter; the majority of proposed funds were targeted toward trade integration and security, with US$400 million to trade integration and US$300 million to security under the Central American Regional Security Initiative (CARSI).[55] CARSI funds in 2016 doubled from 2015 despite the fact that CARSI reintroduced militarized policing into Guatemala and increased human rights violations.[56] Human rights take back stage, with just four mentions in the twenty-five-page plan prepared by El Salvador, Honduras, and Guatemala, and largely focus on the rights of migrant minors of concern to U.S. border security.[57] There is no mention that equipping corrupt governments, where insecurity is propagated by collusion between illicit actors and state elements, may exacerbate the problem.[58] Good governance reforms depend largely on Central American leaders, rather than independent international monitoring units like the UN International Commission against Impunity in Guatemala, which achieved some success fighting impunity in Guatemala, despite the fact that in Guatemala and Honduras political figures have been associated with the very problems of poor governance.[59]

The securitization of migration also does not deter migrants; it is a windfall for criminal and drug organizations, who can capitalize on ransom payments from U.S. family members and prey on migrant desperation.[60] Drug and migrant smuggling were previously more distinct enterprises, but the securitization of migration produced states' own fears. Drug and migrant smuggling networks increasingly intersect as migrants are forced to carry drugs in exchange for safe passage, smugglers must pay off drug cartels for route access, or migrants seek out drug cartels and violent entrepreneurs to cross the border.[61] As the Mexican state targeted cartel leadership, fragmentation generated increased competition, violence, and unpredictability. This approach has led to the *cucaracha*, or cockroach, effect; as drug cartels are targeted by the military, operations and associated violence pop up elsewhere, often with more layers of intermediation making them more difficult to eradicate.[62] Noelle Brigden notes how this uncertain landscape, where control of territory is constantly shifting, led former relatively "trustworthy smugglers . . . to defect from their clients, unexpectedly breaking their contracts and selling their human cargo to another potentially unreliable carrier."[63] Criminal groups like the Zetas have benefited from migrant vulnerability as they diversified into kidnapping, human trafficking, illicit commerce, and extortion.[64] Criminal organizations have created belts of control in Mexican territory to demand quotas for passage, further complicating the landscape of immobility and vulnerability.[65] Militarized efforts through the Mérida Initiative have also failed to stem the drug trade and related violence. In the first half of 2015, the U.S. State Department found that about 90 percent of cocaine en route to the United States was transported through Central America and Mexico, up from 80 percent in 2012.[66]

The Illicit and the War on Drugs

Why have drug and migrant smuggling increasingly intersected and become more lucrative and violent? The answers largely lie with the forms of policing that generated their own nightmare: the securitization of migration and the militarization of the drug war. These approaches proceed without effective police, judicial, and military reform; reconsideration of neoliberal reforms that render large portions of the population vulnerable and expendable; the exclusive development model of securitized neoliberalism embraced by Mexico, the United States, and Guatemala that disproportionately benefits transnational elites and criminalizes opposition; and entrenched corruption and impunity. Moreover, the United States has failed to curb demand for drugs and cheap labor or enact effective gun control. In 2010, almost 80 percent of confiscated assault weapons in Mexico were traced to the United States.[67] Because viewing undocumented migration as illicit is historically recent and still perplexing to many border residents, examining the illegalization of migration helps illustrate the social, political, and economic process by which an activity or group of people is designated as illicit and the concordant material effects.

It is more difficult for border residents, as well as policy makers in Mexico, Guatemala, and the United States, to question the illegalization of drugs. However, as Peter Andreas notes, early border functions in the United States were more concerned with customs controls; drugs and migrants were not of concern.[68] Paul Gootenberg historicizes the criminalization of cocaine by demonstrating how it was once a relatively small, peaceful, and legal trade restricted to a remote part of the Andes and often used in various countries for medical purposes like anesthesia.[69] For border populations, smuggling, whether of food, medicine, or drugs, has long been accepted as an historical inevitability.[70]

Drugs became a concern of moral crusaders in the United States in the early twentieth century, but the United States had little power to influence world policy on drug issues until it emerged as a dominant global power after World War II. The Cold War context enabled the United States to criminalize cocaine and influence Latin American governments to comply with eradication mandates. The criminalization of cocaine in the 1950s is what inaugurated an "illicit culture and circuit of cocaine production" as it spread throughout South America and the Caribbean. U.S. President Nixon's declaration of a War on Drugs in 1969 institutionalized the hardline hemispheric approach to containing the drug trade, which led it to become only more illicit, violent, lucrative, and harder to contain as smugglers became more sophisticated, inventory and profits rose, street prices declined, and the geography of the trade shifted northward.[71]

As the United States militarized the war on drugs, it shifted the epicenter of the drug trade closer to the United States.[72] Chasing out Chilean traffickers in the 1970s in coordination with the Pinochet coup government moved the trade to Colombia, and the militarization of Colombia and Caribbean air routes in the 1980s and early 1990s rerouted the trade to Mexico and Central America.[73] By the late 1990s, more than 90 percent of cocaine flowed into the United States via Mexico.[74] The illegalization of drugs generated more criminality and violence, but this did little to stem the drug trade, whose supply ballooned to over 100 times the market in the early twentieth century.[75] Recently, Latin American leaders and U.S. critics, including the former U.S. Attorney

General Eric Holder, have called for decriminalization and a reassessment of militarization as an avenue to control the drug problem. Even though Mexican and Guatemalan leaders, including former Presidents Calderón and Pérez Molina, spoke out on behalf of drug reform, both governments continue to receive funds, training, and equipment, continuing militarized approaches.[76]

Border residents increasingly view smuggling drugs and migrants as illicit and dangerous as the state puts a mediatized focus on combating them. However, residents also recognize the holes in the state's rhetoric. Residents stressed that although they circumvent legal trade requirements by smuggling goods like corn, coffee, sugar, and gasoline, these activities were not illicit because state policing units did not actively pursue them. According to residents, the mandate of the police and military, regardless of the actual division of responsibilities, was to conduct vigilance against the smuggling of arms, drugs, undocumented migrants, and stolen goods like cars. Residents resented official interference in their businesses, but they welcomed the military and police to do, as they said, "their jobs." Local assessments were often contradictory, though, as Alonso noted, "The military occasionally enters the route to search for drugs, arms, and migrants. They say they are here to provide security. But you will see . . . they are usually working directly with the criminals. Drug traffickers will drive through the border road right behind the military vehicle," escorting it. Residents related how drug traffickers passed through highway checkpoints by being embedded with military leaders. When they are detained, they simply call up their contacts and are allowed to proceed. Border merchants usually considered the Mexican military less corruptible than the police. Yet in many instances they believed the military was above corruption because it was in league with the traffickers. To propose that the solution to insecurity and violence lies with increased funding to the Mexican military and militarizing policing is deeply problematic when "the lines between the state and criminal groups are murky."[77] As Dawn Paley notes in *Drug War Capitalism*, the massive deployment of federal police and military to Juárez in 2008 to contain drug violence was followed by escalating homicide rates; when the same strategy was applied to Acapulco it took over from Juárez to become Mexico's most dangerous city in 2012.[78]

The Same Rats

Employing a militarized state response to curtail extralegal activities assumes there is a sharp division between the state and illegal actors. Yet the state has historically existed in a tense symbiosis with extralegal actors in the region. Residents often refer to police as *rateros*, literally meaning "rats," to signify thieves, or even *maras*, the term they use to refer to gangs. As Michael Taussig writes of the uncertainty generated by the blurring between violent extralegal and state actors during the *limpieza* in Colombia, "Aren't the [paramilitaries] just another gang, indeed the most violent one in town, whose code—if we may call it that—has merged with the code of 'law and order'? . . . Maybe that's how it is all over the world now—a hierarchy of gangs, some legal, others not."[79] To ostensibly battle crime and drug violence, the state begins to mimetically mirror the criminals, employing its own criminal actions or even using criminal groups in the name of security.[80]

Interdependency historically characterized relations between illicit armed groups and the state in Mexico and Guatemala, where clandestine units, paramilitaries, or death squads were used to accomplish the state's dirty work without a direct association.[81] In Mexico, many police continue "double dipping . . . from criminal organizations and the state"; fierce criminal organizations like the Zetas were formed from special forces deserters to conduct protection and enforcement for the Gulf Cartel before splitting off in 2010.[82] Howard Campbell questions the term *cartel*, because it not only implies that drug organizations are static and hierarchically organized, but it also neglects how "organized crime and official government are so tightly interwoven."[83] The revelations surrounding the disappearance of the forty-three university students from the Ayotzinapa Rural Teachers' College in Iguala, Guerrero, Mexico in 2014, illustrates the collusion among government officials, the police, and criminal elements. The mayor of Iguala and his wife, who has family ties to the Guerreros Unidos crime cartel, were found to have orchestrated the disappearances in collusion with the cartel.

The drug war atmosphere augments a history of state violence against youth and the poor, symbolized vividly by the state-orchestrated massacre of students in Tlateloco, Mexico in 1968. When searching for the missing Iguala students in 2014, the discovery of mass graves that did not belong to these students brought to light the mass problem of disappearance, impunity, and official collusion in Mexico, where over 40,000 Mexicans and 70,000 migrants have disappeared since 2006.[84] Botched investigations and missing evidence characterized the search. Jonathan Gibler states that this case demonstrates that the term *corruption* is no longer adequate, because what exists now is a "full merger between police forces and local governance and organized crime . . . and the confluence of two forms of violence—the classic state violence of repression and the kind of newish forms of narcobrutality."[85] The independent investigation by the Inter-American Commission on Human Rights revealed inconsistencies in the state's official report, which may reveal higher levels of complicity among gangs, the drug trade, the military, and the federal and local police.

In Chiapas, Victor Hugo López, former director of the Fray Bartolomé de las Casas Human Rights Center (Frayba), reported that the pretext of the drug war reintroduced the presence of the military into indigenous communities, which only recently experienced a wane in militarization from the Zapatista conflict.[86] Criminalization has proceeded alongside militarization as Chiapas has witnessed a return to legalized forms of torture, detention, and disappearance.[87] Despite official adherence to international accords respecting human and indigenous rights, conflicts have arisen between foreign extractive industries and indigenous communities throughout the state.[88] In January 2015 in Agua Azul reserve, the federal and state police forcibly evicted peasants defending their territory.[89] Similar to border residents, the *ejido* San Sebastián Bachajón set up a tollbooth to charge tourists to enter the nearby Agua Azul waterfalls.[90] To counteract their resistance, the municipality and police organized "shock groups" to instill fear and violence.[91]

Border residents grasp the intersection between the increasing penetration of transnational capital in the region, securitization, and their own dispossession. For example, Plan Puebla-Panamá (PPP), spearheaded by former Mexican President Vicente Fox (2000–2006), was a regional initiative to connect Mexico's nine poorest southern states and Central American countries in a regional development initiative that would essentially convert the region into a free trade corridor.[92] The proposal provoked vociferous protests from human rights observers, indigenous communities, and environmentalists, leading the project to officially recede. In fact, though, many of the projects, ranging from the construction of hydroelectric dams to resource extraction and highway extensions, continued as the government diffused protest by not drawing attention to the existence of a unified project. Due to the unpopularity of the PPP, many projects proceeded without mentioning the PPP as the agenda's formulation, as well as its execution, has been surrounded by secrecy and exclusion.[93] The plan was revived with few changes under then Mexican President Calderón in 2009. It merely received a new moniker, the Mesoamerican Integration and Development Project.[94] When discussing the prospect of the PPP, Fredy, the former community president of El Nance, Mexico, expressed doubts. In the same discussion, he worried about proposals to regularize the unmonitored crossing by installing security personnel. According to Fredy, "There will be no benefits for us. Just for the businesses . . . there will be security for them. If Plan Puebla-Panamá [is implemented], they will install authorities, businesses for rich people, just [benefits for the] large business owners. Nothing for us. We will be their garbage men." In Chiapas, regional economic integration agendas have gone hand in hand with security initiatives, which have been targeted at securing transnational investments, resource extraction, and highways and special economic zones to facilitate the transportation of resources to international markets, contributing to a climate of securitized, or militarized, neoliberalism.[95]

In Guatemala, the return of the military to the public security realm to fight the drug war is especially troubling in a country that recently emerged from a brutal counterinsurgency conflict and where impunity for wartime, as well as current acts of, violence is extremely high.[96] The United States cut off funding to Guatemala's military in 1990 due to human rights abuses. Despite this, conditions have loosened, and these restrictions do not apply to Defense Department funds, from which $27.5 million was given to Guatemalan security forces for counternarcotics control from 2008 to 2012.[97]

War-era connections among the state elite, organized crime, the military, and police persist in Guatemala.[98] According to the Center for International Policy (CIP), former military hold 40 percent of government positions in the security sector.[99] The Guatemalan Kaibiles exemplify the blurring among the military, state special forces, and illicit actors. The Kaibiles are a Guatemalan elite special forces unit, trained by the United States in counterinsurgency warfare, which committed atrocities during the counterinsurgency war. Especially concerning are links among former Kaibiles and drug traffickers and criminal organizations, such as Mexico's Zetas, who recruit former Kaibiles.[100] The Mexican military detained former Kaibiles in the unmonitored route in El Nance in 2005. Sources revealed that the Kaibiles, found heavily armed, were part of former Guatemalan President Alfonso Portillo's (2000–2004) security circle. Portillo was living in Mexico and was facing embezzlement charges in Guatemala.[101] Guatemala is using the Kaibiles to militarize the jungle areas of the Petén to promote "citizen security," but, as Megan Ybarra argues, the Kaibiles remain empowered to act above the law to inflict violence in the name of security.[102] Ironically, they are tasked with combating the incursions of the Zetas, who recruited from the Kaibiles' former ranks.[103] The Guatemalan state's response to crime and violence has been criminalization and harsh policing, which are "productive of what it is supposed to defeat, namely, criminal enterprise."[104]

Questioning Illegalization

By questioning how certain people and activities become designated as illegal or criminal, and how this serves to justify militarized state responses, we can reveal the political, social, and economic processes undergirding dominant assumptions of what is considered legal or illegal. In the discourse of border security, petty contraband, drug trafficking, migrant trafficking, and the arms trade are increasingly interconnected and suspected for potential links to terrorism.[105] Despite the fact that illicit narcotics and smuggled papayas can traverse the same routes, they are often trafficked by different persons for distinct reasons. In recent security directives, however, rural peasants are painted as potential criminal and terrorist threats. John F. Kelly, former U.S. Marine Corps Commander of the U.S. Southern Command, stated in a brief before the 113th Congress in 2014, "Terrorist organizations could seek to leverage [these] same smuggling routes to move operatives with intent to cause grave harm to our citizens or even quite easily bring weapons of mass destruction to the United States."[106] Proclamations equating Mexico's porous southern border with crime and a potential terrorist threat ignore that Chiapas has the twelfth lowest homicide rate in the nation; roadside billboards advertise it as "Mexico's third safest state."[107] Despite rumors, border contraband continues to be largely pursued by family and social groups with long historical ties seeking to stake out a livelihood.[108] There is no clear evidence that it is linked to drug trafficking even as traffickers might seek out truckers and some individuals may decide to become involved.

Criminal actors may benefit from a climate where the state has lost its authority and illegality and bending the rules are the norm,[109] but how and under what conditions the tolerance of extralegal activities is a boon to organized crime is a question for investigation rather than a truism.[110] Border residents repeatedly fetishized the law as a thing you could purchase; in this region it remains to be seen how the sums of money associated with the drug trade will shift the relations among informality, the state, criminal organizations, and local inhabitants. Yet targeting informality through a criminal lens without examining the reasons why people turn away from, distrust, or are excluded from the state and formal sector, may generate a dangerous dynamic of escalation that reproduces criminalization while making criminal structures more challenging to eradicate. The losers in spirals of mutual escalation between criminal actors and state units charged with combating them are everyday people caught up in their midst.[111]

We begin to question who and what all of this security is really for—who is being made more secure or insecure—even as many rural peasants ardently defend aggressive approaches out of fears for their own safety. The lessons provided by the securitization and criminalization of drugs and undocumented migrants are that trends toward criminalizing petty smugglers, although also enabling contraband to proceed, may lead these trades to also shift from being relatively small, benign, and sometimes regionally beneficial to being more illicit, dangerous, and tied to more violent groups. Victor Hugo López from Frayba in Chiapas asserts that the current approach to enhancing security has:

> Hardened measures not against crime, but against the population . . . The protection of the border, the reinforcement of security, and the combat against organized crime have meant greater social control and a great index of repression against the population as a whole.[112]

In Chiapas, Mexico's commitment to security exacerbated human rights violations; Frayba's cases doubled from about 400 to 500 in 2011 to 1,000 in 2014.[113] Almost half of reported human rights cases resulted from the effects of criminalization, including inadequate access to justice, arbitrary detention, and torture.[114]

Despite the fact that border residents are implicitly or even explicitly criminalized by the security state, many express the desire for a strong security presence to prevent violence and crime. This is particularly the case in Guatemala. The resounding support for the resurgence of the military, or militarized policing, to contain criminal violence and delinquency in a country recently emerged from violent military rule appears puzzling. When former Guatemalan President Otto Pérez Molina, remembered by many for orchestrating genocidal violence during the counterinsurgency war, first campaigned in 2006 on the *mano dura*, or tough on crime platform, many border residents welcomed this approach despite a lack of crime in their own communities. Only a few former refugees in Nueva Vida, Guatemala, were dubious as they saw the parallels to the violence they experienced in the 1980s. Guatemala reframed its security approach to focus on public and citizen security, meaning the freedom from fear of crime and violence. In practice, however, this sanctions remilitarization, which has only enhanced insecurity for marginal populations.[115] The result is an escalation and privatization, or what Daniel Goldstein refers to as a "neoliberalization of violence," whereby violence is dispersed across social actors operating to preserve their own security.[116] The urban and rural poor have often suffered the brunt of militarized security policies in both Mexico and Guatemala, as they are the most likely to inhabit crucial transit corridors or territory conducive to transnational development initiatives.[117]

Trade and security policies that criminalize marginal residents and escalate police and military enforcement have not curtailed violence in the region, but rather have extended corruption, insecurity, and the criminalization of society. Instead of merely adding more security, we need to question whom prevailing definitions of security serve, revisit misguided trade and security policies, pay attention to the reasons why people engage in extralegal trade, and consider the absence of meaningful livelihood options.

Specifically, *Contraband Corridor* draws attention to how security and trade policies work together to valorize and facilitate transnational corporate cross-border commerce and movement as they criminalize informal trade and restrict the movements of marginal border inhabitants and migrants. Border residents attempt to turn designations of the legal and illegal on their heads as they decry state corruption and the exclusion of formal trade policies. They claim it is legitimate to acquire multiple national documents through extralegal means, smuggle goods across the border, and assert their control over the unmonitored border crossing along which they live while taxing smugglers to use the road. However, their moral justifications are beginning to unravel as some smuggling businesses become more lucrative and exclusionary, local inequalities intensify, and the smuggling of daily goods intertwines with the drug trade and networks of official corruption. In a context of corruption, the informalization of the economy,[118] and lack of opportunity, it is tempting for some border truckers to carry other merchandise northward. Border residents' practices do not address the roots of their exclusion, namely lack of development and gainful employment in the countryside and Mexico's and Guatemala's commitments to a securitized neoliberalism that favors capital and profits over people and subsistence.

Although extralegal practices at the border may constitute small forms of everyday resistance, or "weapons of the weak,"[119] they do not undermine or question the prevailing order that excludes them. Smuggling does little to contest the advance of securitized neoliberalism at the Mexico–Guatemala border. Smuggling enables border residents to earn a living in a context with few alternatives, but it does not provide the majority with enough to surmount their own circumstances. Many take immense risks. In exchange for being able to minimally support one's family and basic expenses, one risks large financial losses, possible arrest if officials decide to change their minds, or violence from criminal actors.

Gordon Mathews and Carlos Alba Vega employ the term *globalization from below* to describe the informal, and often extralegal, transnational practices that characterize how much of the world experiences globalization in contrast to the sphere of "high-end" globalization, or "globalization from above," which encompasses states, international institutions, and corporations.[120] The difference between globalization from above and that from below is one of power dynamics and differentiated political, social, and economic access as the two realms interrelate in unequal fashions.[121] Although they stress the critical interdependence between globalization from above and below, the term continues to imply that globalization from below is an "alternative," and often stigmatized, variant of the dominant form of globalization.[122] Yet at the border, risking separating out "globalization from below" may detract from focusing on the common interests that both forms of globalization serve and the actors they criminalize. Border residents often perceive their own smuggling of basic goods as a form of resistance to an economy that excludes them. However, their efforts are often contradictory, because they reinforce the border security agenda while their smuggling activities may also benefit larger formal businesses and state agents, as well as more dangerous criminal actors. Meanwhile, residents run higher risks and increasing criminalization as violence and insecurity in the region spread.

We usually hear only the success stories. Few people talk about the failures, as Paco urged me to consider in Chapter 6. In subsequent visits to the border, I met men who spent over a decade in the United States and returned to the border convinced they could make a living trucking contraband. It was rarely what they imagined. Few become relatively wealthy, and these individuals usually had previous advantages such as more substantial U.S. migrant earnings or remittances, an inheritance, or land and cattle to offset costs and provide a financial cushion.

At the Mexico–Guatemala border, border smugglers enjoy local support amid a lack of political confidence, crisis in the countryside, and the lack of alternatives as long as they appear to act on behalf of their communities, even if they are largely benefiting themselves, illicit actors, or corrupt politicians and businesses. Smugglers must evade state officials as they actively seek them out to strike deals to enable their businesses and remove competitors. Petty border smugglers are not stealing from or attacking anyone and rarely use violent means. Smuggling can damage national industries by undercutting tariffs or prohibitions meant to protect them from international competition, depress local producer prices by creating additional competition, and introduce potential risks to health and safety due to lack of regulation and inspection. However, smuggling also provides peasants with alternative forms of livelihood when they are left with little else, offers markets for producers and consumers who cannot afford, or are excluded from, legitimate options, and can stimulate parts of the formal economy. Smugglers are at once individualistic and socially dependent and damaging to and supportive of state policing bodies and segments of the formal economy.

Smuggling enterprises may travel an alternate geographic route to official commerce, but their goods and profits do not flow in separate economic channels. More often than not, smuggled goods travel into the inventories of respected national and transnational businesses, which can earn substantial profits by evading duties, paperwork, and inspections. Businesses supplement their inventories when selling the goods domestically or exporting abroad, as illustrated by Tito and the coffee warehouses in Chapter 6. Smugglers are not necessarily contesting the neoliberal trade system, but rather, are often subsidizing it. They internalize the logic of "selling to the best buyer" and run the risks of official arrest, robbery, or assault while other private interests accrue risk-free benefits.[123] Meanwhile, producers in the region face an uphill battle competing to sell corn and coffee. The neoliberal mandates of deregulation, privatization, and liberalization in societies plagued by inequality and a small elite (that also benefits from a blind eye toward blurring between the illegal and legal) prevent states from being able to collect sufficient taxes and seize the policy space to bolster the formal economy and state institutions in ways that would inspire confidence and security.[124] Instead of looking at how elite actors benefit from current arrangements and revising underlying structural inequalities and free market policies that destabilize work more broadly, informality and criminality become red herrings that are symptoms of the very dynamics they are charged with destabilizing.

Chapter 4 documented how border residents united to expel corrupt officials from their border route. They capitalized on a climate of a political crisis, when social movements were advocating for the rights of peasants, the indigenous, and the poor. Yet autonomy is illusory as locals bear the risks of surveillance and continue to perpetuate patron–client ties and corruption that deliver community votes to the prevailing municipal authorities in exchange for facilitating extralegal commerce that disproportionately benefits a few. In the PRI patronage system, the state tied itself to *ejidos* through local authorities or local elites, *caciques*, who granted allegiance and delivered votes in exchange for land and state resources.[125] With the decline of the system of state corporatism, efforts for democratic change, accountability, and social and economic inclusion are stifled as the figure of the *cacique* is reincarnated in powerful local smugglers and clientelistic politics are reproduced. Although many smugglers work on behalf of their communities, their business interests often hold sway. In Chapter 4, when the municipality offered more assistance in return for removing the *cadenas*, local smugglers turned down this deal despite community support for it. It remains to be seen if smuggler and community interests will continue to align or if more powerful smugglers will become more distant from their community members.

Border smugglers also do not avoid or subvert the state. Instead, they actively seek out state agents and gain their approval to begin and maintain a smuggling business, as described in Chapters 6 and 7. Smugglers line the pockets of individual state agents through bribes, as well as provide the rationale for the expansion of border policing and militarization despite the fact that this has not reduced smuggling, the drug trade, or violence. Would-be smugglers, like Alonso, reinforce the mythic power, or magic of the state,[126] as he obsessed over needing to "look for the law" to work in gasoline smuggling. His language invokes the power and aura of the state that is everywhere and nowhere, all-powerful yet impossible to locate.[127]

Understanding the complex interdependence between the state and extralegal practices renders thinking about alternatives to illegalization and criminalization imperative. These discourses not only do not produce the intended results of reducing crime and illegality, but, in fact, they may produce and escalate it. As the compounding effects of illegalization, criminalization, and militarization touch down in already marginalized communities, extralegal activities garner more social legitimacy and sanction. In a spiral of mutual escalation between the state and extralegal actors, who increasingly blur together, illegality is used to demand more state enforcement whereas more enforcement, and its often harsh face, gives more local credence to extralegal alternatives.

Border Boomerang

The interrelations among neoliberal economic policies, anti-immigration policies in the United States, and border and drug security policies have produced a vicious border boomerang effect.[128] As neoliberal policies destabilized local livelihoods, people began to migrate to the United States. Anti-immigration policies that increased deportable offenses and instilled fear have led more migrants from this border crossing to return home, where they find the extralegal economy to be one of the few remaining options. At this juncture, violence perpetrated by both criminal actors and escalating state forces to combat them, alongside the lack of opportunity, reanimate the necessity to migrate.

When I returned to the border in 2011, I sat with Fani in El Girasol, Guatemala, contemplating her future. She had completed her teaching certification. She had only part-time work teaching after-school classes to local youth. Despite the desires of their parents, who worked in the smuggling economy so their children could obtain an education and become professionals, she related how many youth say they want to be cargo loaders for smugglers. When I visited Fani in 2014, she had lost her job and was debating using her Mexican birth certificate to travel to Cancún to work in hotels. Her brother, Julián, had been deported for the second time from the United States. Julián's wife was recently detained and arrested on felony charges for using false Social Security documents in Georgia to pay her electric bill and keep herself and her children afloat after Julián's deportation. In the context of the criminalization of immigration, or governing migration through crime, more immigrants are getting funneled into the criminal justice system not because they are committing more crimes, but because more of the daily activities that unauthorized immigrants rely on to merely get by are elevated to the level of criminally punishable and deportable offenses.[129] Fani seemed resigned to the situation. I felt the need to investigate when I returned home. Perhaps it was not hopeless. I found out his wife had been in jail for two years. Their six U.S.-born children were transferred from the care of a friend to the Georgia Department of Human Services. I communicated with a local social worker to obtain more information about her release to Immigration and Customs Enforcement (ICE) custody, find a pro bono lawyer, and explore options to reunite her with her children. The situation is further complicated by the fact that Julián, their father, is Guatemalan whereas their mother is from Chiapas, Mexico. We made little headway. During the final edits for this book, however, I learned that she was released on humanitarian grounds and was able to have visitations with her children. The last I heard, she was waiting for her immigration court date.

When I visited the border in 2014, residents expressed hope for a change in the immigration climate for their relatives in the United States. However, the election of Donald Trump, and his plans to build a wall along the United States–Mexico border and ramp up the criminalization and deportation of immigrants, has halted many of the dreams of migrants and their families—at least for now. U.S. immigration policies, combined with continued pressure on Mexico to militarize its southern border in the name of security and stopping "illicit flows," may lead more border residents to befall a similar fate to Fani's family as they undergo desperate measures across legal lines, criminalized by livelihood strategies across multiple borders, to support their families. Even during my summer 2014 visit, more people seemed to be returning to the border after over a decade in the United States due to lingering effects of the 2008 economic recession combined with heightened anti-immigration policies in Florida, North Carolina, Georgia, and Alabama, where most border residents tend to migrate. On return, many decide to give business a go.

Notes

Introduction

1. *El Financiero.* September 7, 2006.

2. I do not reference these articles because doing so would reveal the identities of the border communities.

3. Isacson, Meyer, and Morales 2014: 7, 10. Seven are located on the Chiapas–Guatemala border (Basail Rodríguez 2016b: 5).

4. Isacson, Meyer, and Morales 2014: 10 and Secretaría de Seguridad y Protección Ciudadana 2015. The number of vehicular crossings varies across sources.

5. I do not cite this report, so as to preserve the anonymity of the crossing.

6. See description of incident in Galemba 2013.

7. See Andreas 1999.

8. See Goldstein 2010, 2012; Zilberg 2011; Jusionyte 2015; Aguiar 2014; and Arroyo 2006.

9. Also see Zilberg 2011: 6, 4; and Goldstein 2012: 17.

10. See Andreas 1999: 96, 2010, and 2011.

11. See Villafuerte Solís 2009.

12. Gúzman Mérida 2004: 138, translation mine.

13. Just as security discourses are repeatedly interrupted, Goodale and Postero (2013: 1–2) point to the contested and interrupted nature of neoliberalism in Latin America to demonstrate how new possibilities emerge even alongside the continued dominance of neoliberalism.

14. IFAD 2012

15. Vázquez Olivera 2010 and Clot 2013.

16. Clot 2013: 16 and Andreas 1999.

17. Clot 2013: 8; Mathews and Vega 2012; Gauthier 2007; and Basail Rodríguez 2016b.

18. All names are pseudonyms unless specified to protect identities. Some individual traits are also altered, or I created composite characters to protect informants.

19. Highway expansion in the 1990s has also been linked to surveillance against the Zapatistas (Hernández Castillo 2001 and Nash 2001: 93).

20. In its most basic facets, neoliberalism refers to an assemblage of political and economic practices guided by a belief that individual and societal well-being can be best guaranteed by advancing the free market (Harvey 2005: 2).

21. Thomas, O'Neill, and Offit 2011: 9 and Burrell 2013.

22. Grindle 1996: 1.

23. Kelly 2008: 11.

24. De Ita 1997.

25. Fox and Haight 2010: 11 and Wise 2011.

26. Morales 1999: 990 and McCune et al. 2012.

27. Kelly 2008: 12.

28. Nash 2001.

29. Hernández Castillo 2001 and Kelly 2008.

30. Nash 2001.

31. Villafuerte Solís 2005: 479.

32. CONEVAL 2015 and World Bank Data 2014.

33. Bradford 2011.

34. CONEVAL 2015 and Villafuerte Solís 2015.

35. Villafuerte Solís 2005, 2009 and Secretaría de Economía 2016: 24.

36. Paláez-Herreros 2012: 207; Villafuerte Solís and García Aguilar 2006; and Villafuerte Solís 2005. Also see Fábregas Puig and Ponciano 2014.

37. Thomas, O'Neill, and Offit 2011: 8.

38. Thomas, O'Neill, and Offit 2011: 8; Fischer and Benson 2006; Little 2013; Goldín 2011; and Thomas 2011.

39. Benson, Thomas, and Fischer 2011.

40. Schneider 2012: 179.

41. USAID 2010: 1.

42. Kelly 2008: 64.

43. Economist David Lozano, cited in Conn 2014; and Villafuerte Solís 2005.

44. See Centeno and Portes 2006 on the role of the informal economy.

45. U.S. Census Bureau 2017; also see Paley 2014.

46. Cruz Burguete 1998.

47. Casillas 2008: 144.

48. Hristoulas 2003: 40 and Andreas 2003: 13.

49. Pickard 2005. See Gilberto Rosas (2006: 344) on thickening the border, which can also be applied to the expansion of U.S. border policing to the Mexico–Guatemala border.

50. Birson 2010 and Jaramillo 2001.

51. Hristoulas 2003: 41 and Hufbauer and Vega-Cánovas 2003: 128.

52. Benitez-Manaut 2004: 14 and Sandoval Palacios 2006.

53. Andreas 2003: 12.

54. Villafuerte Solís 2014: 127–128. This later became the Mexico–Guatemala High-Level Security Group.

55. Johnson 2008; also see Nevins 2014.

56. Ogren 2007: 210; Sandoval Palacios 2006; and Villafuerte Solís and Leyva Solano 2006.

57. Benítez-Manaut 2004 50 and Villafuerte Solís and Leyva Solano 2006.

58. Tenuto-Sánchez 2014 and Pickard 2003.

59. Isacson, Meyer, and Morales 2014: 5.

60. Villafuerte Solís 2004: 67, translation mine.

61. See Sandoval Palacios 2006.

62. For example, see Hufbauer and Vega-Cánovas 2003: 128.

63. Benítez-Manaut 2004: 50.

64. Andreas 2003: 4.

65. Ibid.: 5–6; also see 2002, 2000.

66. Andreas 2003: 6 and Figueroa, Lee, and Schoik 2011.

67. Nevins 2002: 138.

68. Ibid.

69. Gomberg-Muñoz 2011: 34, 303.

70. Seelke 2016.

71. Isacson, Meyer, and Morales 2014: 21.

72. Castro Soto 2015.

73. Henríquez 2016.

74. INEGI 2011.

75. Ibid.

76. Isacson, Meyer, and Morales 2014: 31 and Paley 2014.

77. Alianza Mexicana contra el Fracking 2015.

78. Seelke and Finklea 2017: 1

79. Isacson, Meyer, and Morales 2014.

80. Seelke and Finklea 2017 and Isacson, Meyer, and Morales 2014: 5.

81. CIP Americas Program in MAWG 2013: 18.

82. Paley 2014: 25–26, 35. See Conclusion for updates on impunity in Mexico.

83. U.S. Department of State 2017; MAWG 2013; and Abrego 2014.

84. MAWG 2013: 3 and Paley 2014.

85. Grann 2011.

86. Paley 2014.

87. MAWG 2013.

88. Isacson, Meyer, and Morales 2014, citing a 2010 State Department cable.

89. Hart 1973; see Goldstein 2016: 19–20; Castells and Portes 1989; and Centeno and Portes 2006: 25–26.

90. Centeno and Portes 2006: 26. They draw from Castells and Portes 1989.

91. Ibid., drawing from Castells and Portes 1989.

92. See Goldstein (2016: 21, 23), drawing from Gandolfo (2009) on fluidity between formality and informality.

93. Donnan and Wilson 1999: 105.

94. Aguiar 2014; Heyman and Smart 1999; Smart 1999; Galemba 2013; Davis 2012; and Goldstein 2016.

95. Andreas 2011: 7; Friman 2009a; and Heyman and Smart 1999.

96. Also see Basail Rodríguez 2016b: 13.

97. Abraham and Van Schendel 2005: 4, 25; Martínez 1994; Clot 2013; Grimson 2002; and Jusionyte 2015.

98. Abraham and Van Schendel 2005.

99. See Donnan and Wilson 1999 and Martínez 1994.

100. Donnan and Wilson 1999; Abraham and Van Schendel 2005; Wilson and Donnan 1998; and Galemba 2013: 276.

101. See Karibo 2011: 85.

102. See Thomas and Galemba 2013; Heyman 2013; and Jusionyte 2015.

103. Marx 1990 [1867].

104. See Comaroff and Comaroff (2006) on the fetishization of the law in the postcolony where calls for the "rule of law" or more law are often used to justify corruption, violence, and illegality. Also see Penglase 2011.

105. For example, Bacon 2008 and Gomberg-Muñoz 2011.

106. Heyman and Smart 1999; and also see Martínez (1994: 10) on the "borderlands milieu."

107. Ybarra 2016: 195; Goldstein 2010, 2012; and Jusionyte 2015.

108. See Benjamin 1986 and Aretxaga 2003: 405–406 for the law as a tautology.

109. See Goldstein 2012: 25; Goldstein 2016: 104; Benson, Thomas, and Fischer 2011; and Burrell 2013.

110. Seelke and Finklea 2017: 4–5.

111. Goldstein 2012: 14; Ybarra 2016; Jusionyte 2015; and Buzan, Waever, and de Wilde 1998.

112. Goldstein 2016: 103; Goldstein 2010, 2012: 23–25; and Jusionyte 2015: 17.

113. Goldstein 2012: 25.

114. Ibid.: 13, 26; Goldstein 2005; and Goldstein 2010: 498.

115. Goldstein 2010: 487; Burrell 2013: 16; and Benson, Thomas, and Fischer 2011.

116. Zilberg 2011: 10.

117. Ibid.: 4.

118. Thomas, O'Neill, and Offit 2011: 16 and Camus 2012.

119. Thomas, O'Neill, and Offit 2011: 16.

120. Grann 2011 and Burrell 2013: 5. The impunity rate declined from around 95 percent to 70 percent, and justice advanced with the arrival of the International Commission against Impunity in Guatemala (CICIG) in 2007 and under Claudia Paz y Paz's leadership as attorney general in 2010 (B. Reeves 2014). However, conservative business and political elite succeeded in shortening Paz y Paz's term on a legal challenge in 2014 (Lakhani 2014).

121. Thomas, O'Neill, and Offit 2011; Thomas 2011; Benson, Thomas, and Fischer 2011; Burrell 2013; Burrell and Moodie 2013; and Goldstein 2012.

122. Benson, Thomas, and Fischer 2011: 140.

123. Benson, Thomas, and Fischer 2011: 141; Goldstein 2010, Dickens de Girón 2011; Godoy 2004, 2006; and Burrell 2013.

124. Godoy 2004, 2006; Burrell and Moodie 2013; Goldstein 2010; and Burrell 2013.

125. Burrell 2013: 181n6, citing Grupo de Apoyo Mutual and the National Civil Police (PNC) on statistics from the Guatemalan Supreme Court compiled by Carlos Mendoza at the Ministerio de Gobernación. Also see p.117.

126. See ibid.

127. Goldstein 2012: 17; Jusionyte 2015: 17; Isacson, Meyer, and Morales 2014: 21; and Paley 2014.

128. Goldstein 2012: 17.

129. Isacson, Meyer, and Morales 2014: 31.

130. Goldstein 2012: 17, 2010 and Centeno and Portes 2006: 37, 40.

131. Centeno and Portes 2006: 37, 40 and Goldstein 2012: 22–23.

132. See Goldstein 2016: 24; Dent 2012: 31–32, 44 ; and Thomas 2013.

133. Dent 2012: 32, emphasis in original.

134. See Goldstein 2010, 2012; Burrell 2013; and Jusionyte 2015.

135. Heyman and Campbell 2011: 189.

136. Das and Poole 2004: 4; also see Ferme 2004 and M. Reeves 2014.

137. See Coutin 2005.

138. Nordstrom 2007: 73.

139. Ibid.

140. In addition to tax functions, SAT is responsible for administration of customs.

141. Arriola Vega 2009: 33; also quoting Naím 2005: 25.

142. Das and Poole 2004 and M. Reeves 2014: 145.

143. See critique of the term migrant crisis in Sánchez 2014.

144. Schneider and Schneider 2008.

Chapter 1

1. Regional inhabitants often refer to Frontera Comalapa as "Comalapa."

2. I use his real name to credit him for his assistance and work at the border.

3. See Kauffer and Velasco 2002.

4. See Hernández Castillo 2012.

5. I disguise the names of the border communities and some of their identifying characteristics to protect the identities of residents.

6. Clot 2013.

7. "We are all named Hernández."

8. Gupta and Ferguson 1997 and Coutin 2005: 195; also see M. Reeves 2014.

9. See parallels in Andreas 2010.

10. See Andreas 2010; McMurray 2001; Coutin 2005; and Nevins 2002.

11. See parallels in Muehlmann 2014.

12. Vázquez Olivera 2010; Martínez 1994; and Clot 2013.

13. See Goldstein 2012: 28, 29; Goldstein 2016; and Das and Poole 2004.

14. Das and Poole 2004: 9.

15. Martínez 1994: 25.

16. Scott 2009: 9.

17. Clot 2013: 4–5, drawing from Canales et al. 2010, 37.

18. Das and Poole 2004: 9, 20.

19. Border residents had picked up on a long nationalist, as well as U.S., tradition of anthropological study of Mexican indigenous communities (see critique in Kelly 2008: 32).

20. A hot drink made with corn *masa*, cinnamon, and sugar.

21. Lewis 2005: 3.

22. Ibid.: 6.

23. Ibid.: 7.

24. Ibid.: 7.

25. Vázquez 2010: 112.

26. Lewis 2005: 6.

27. Hernández Castillo 2001: 34.

28. Nolan-Ferrell 2005: 302.

29. Ibid.

30. Ibid., translation mine. Nolan-Ferrell 2005 draws from Knight 1986, I: 8–9.

31. Hernández Castillo 2001: 21.

32. Ibid.

33. Lewis 2005: 6–7 and Hernández Castillo 2001.

34. Hernández Castillo 2001: 24 and Lewis 2005: 7.

35. Lewis 2005: 7.

36. Hérnandez Castillo 2001: 24.

37. Ibid.: 24.

38. Ibid.

39. Ibid.

40. INEGI 2010.

41. UNHRC 2001 and Freyermuth Enciso and Hernández Castillo 1992.

42. Ludy 1998 and García García 2002.

43. Freyermuth Enciso and Hernández Castillo 1992.

44. Montejo 1999.

45. Seventy-five percent of refugees lived outside of designated camps (Jonas 2013)

46. Also see Montejo 1999 and Manz 2004.

47. Freyermuth Enciso and Hernández Castillo 1992.

48. Montejo 1999.

49. Cutts 2000: 130; also see Montejo 1999 and Manz 1988.

50. Cutts 2000: 130 and Montejo 1999.

51. Montejo 1999.

52. Kauffer 2002 and Fabila Meléndez 2002.

53. M. A. Castillo 2006.

54. García 2006: 83.

55. Ibid.: 83.

56. Kauffer and Velasco Santos 2002.

57. See Kauffer 2002.

58. M. A. Castillo 2006 and Alba and Castillo 2012.

59. Stephen 1999; and Swords 2010: 120, citing Centro de Derechos Humanos 2005.

60. Hernández Castillo 2001 and Hale 2005.

61. SIPAZ 2001.

62. Stephen 1999.

63. Ibid.: 830, 838.

64. Smith 1990; Warren 2001: 10; and Little-Siebold 2001.

65. Montejo 1999: 37.

66. Grandin 2000: 199 and Schlesinger and Kinzer 1999: 19.

67. Immerman 2010.

68. Schlesinger and Kinzer 1999: 17 and Immerman 2010: 14.

69. Thomas, O'Neill, and Offit 2011: 5 and Montejo 1999: 4.

70. Ibid.: 40.

71. Schirmer 1998; and Manz 2004: 21–23. Funds were suspended in 1977 due to reports of human right violations, but resumed as covert CIA operations under President Reagan to contain communism after the fallout from Vietnam. The 1996 Peace Accords suspended military aid to Guatemala, but President Bush resumed aid to combat drug violence after Guatemala promised to respect human rights (Guatemalan Human Rights Commission/USA Factsheet 2015).

72. Burrell 2013: 26 and Schirmer 1998.

73. Montejo 1999: 42; Burrell 2013: 24; and Manz 2004.

74. Manz 2004.: 155 and Burrell 2013: 34.

75. United States Institute of Peace 1997.

76. Hale 2006: 6 and Burrell 2013.

77. IFAD 2012.

78. SEDESOL 2014.

79. García 2006: 51 and Gómez 2002.

80. ENCOVI 2011, cited in INE 2013b.

81. Gúzman Mérida 2004: 62.

82. INE 2013.

83. Gúzman Mérida 2004 and Camus 2012.

84. INE 2013a and González 2011: 5, cited in Camus 2012: 85.

85. COMAR is a Mexican government agency in charge of refugee assistance and protection. It was created in 1980 to work with the UN High Commissioner for Refugees (UNHCR) to address the refugee situation in Mexico.

86. SEDESOL 2013.

87. Rousseau, Morales, and Foxen 2001; Manz 2004; and Nolin Hanlon 1999.

88. See Worby 2001 and Bradley (2013: 111) on the FORELAP program used to aid returning refugees acquire land.

89. Watanabe 1992 and Gúzman Mérida 2004.

90. Nevins 2002.

91. Donnan and Wilson 1999 and Martínez 1994.

Chapter 2

1. The Guatemalan army created mandatory civil patrols in each community to force all adult males to monitor their communities against the guerillas, effectively destroying local forms of community authority, culture, and solidarity (Montejo 1999 and Manz 1988). Many residents of El Girasol internalized the army's rhetoric that "the patrol would allow a village to protect itself from the *guerillas*" (Montejo 1999: 66 and Manz 1988: 38).

2. The survey intended to capture youth's notions of the border and their ethnic and national identities. I chose fifth and sixth graders because this was the oldest

age group for which I could gather comparable samples in the border communities. Informed consent for the survey was obtained from students, parents, and teachers.

3. Consulate General of Guatemala in Denver, Colorado, U.S.; personal communication with an anonymous employee, August 12, 2016

4. Fitzgerald 2008: 58.

5. Hoyo 2015: 11 here draws from Hubbard Urrea 2010: 130–131.

6. Hoyo 2015: 10–11. Mexico also considers the first generation of individuals born abroad to a Mexican parent to be Mexican by birth because it recognizes both *jus sanguinis* (blood rights) and *jus soli* (soil rights or birthright citizenship) rights to nationality (Ibid.: 11).

7. Ibid.: 11.

8. Ibid.: 12. They cannot obtain another nationality and waive the right to use their birth citizenship in Mexico.

9. Sarazua 2016.

10. See Martínez 1994 and Sahlins 1989 on the navigation of multiple nationalities in border regions. See Kelly 2006 on manipulation of documents.

11. See Ferme 2004 and Reeves 2013.

12. Reeves 2013: 509.

13. Mitchell 1999.

14. Ibid.: 85, 89; M. Reeves 2014: Das and Poole 2004; and Ferme 2004: 82, 94.

15. Hernández Castillo 2001: 6.

16. See Hondagneu-Sotelo and Avila 1997 on how "neither here nor there" also characterizes the plight of transnational mothers in Los Angeles. See Anzaldúa 1999 and Martínez 1994: 310.

17. See Martínez (1994: 20) on the "versatility" embodied by border populations.

18. De Vos 2002; Basail Rodríguez 2005; Hernández Castillo 2001; and Rosaldo 2001: xi.

19. See Anzaldúa 1999; Alvarez 1995; Heyman 1994; and Rosaldo 1993 [1989].

20. See M. Reeves 2014 for an excellent processual account of borders that examines when and where borders become pertinent and socially meaningful.

21. Ibid.

22. This shifted with the installation of a multiagency CAITF (Comprehensive Attention Centers for Border Transit) checkpoint in La Trinitaria preceding Comitán in 2015 (see Chapter 5).

23. Isacson, Meyer, and Morales 2014.

24. See Reeves (2013: 515) on learning how to "perform residence" and legality.

25. Das 2007: 162–163; Kelly 2006: 90; Gordillo 2006; Benjamin 1986; Ferguson 2006; and Comaroff and Comaroff 2006.

26. Das 2007: 168, 172.

27. Goldstein 2012: 98.

28. Ibid.: 83, drawing from Abrams 1988 [1977] on the state as an "illusion" or "mask" for the power dynamics it conceals; Das 2007: 162, 166–167 argues that the state "oscillates between a rational and magical mode of being."

29. Das 2007: 166, 162. See Aretxaga 2003 and M. Reeves 2014.

30. Goldstein 2012: 98 and Reeves 2013: 520; see Das and Poole 2004 and Ferme 2004.

31. Das 2007: 178; Reeves 2013; and Kelly 2006: 92.

32. See Reeves 2013: 517 and Brigden 2016.

33. Fitzgerald 2008 and Hoyo 2015.

34. See Hernández Castillo 1992; Fábregas Puig 1996; and Cruz Burguete 1998.

35. Hoyo 2016a: 108.

36. See Montejo 1999 on these labels.

37. Hoyo 2015 and Sarazua 2016.

38. Some residents still lack documents because they missed the opportunity to process their forms while in the United States.

39. See Ludy 1998.

40. See Hernández Castillo 2001.

41. See Molyneux 2006.

42. Hoyo 2015.

43. Hoyo 2016b and Sarazua 2016: 11.

44. Manz 2004; Egan 1999; and Rousseau, Morales, and Foxen 2001 document the tensions refugees experienced when returning because the military had given many of their lands to those who had collaborated with them.

45. See Foucault 1990.

46. See Das and Poole 2004; Das 2007; and Goldstein 2012.

47. Since 2013, the Personal Identification Document (Documento Personal de Identificación, or DPI) replaced the cédula (*Latino News* 2012).

48. INI stands for Instituto Nacional Electoral and is often used to refer to the elector's credential. INE was previously called IFE (Instituto Federal Electoral)

49. Asencio 2012.

50. Ibid.

51. See Reeves 2013: 516.

52. See Vila 1999 and Stephen 1999.

53. Goldstein 2012: 95.

54. Hoyo 2015.

55. Hoyo 2016b.

56. Hoyo 2015: 20.

57. Sarazua 2016: 13.

58. Nevins 2002: 10, 139, 166; also drawing from Sack 1986: 33 on relation among territoriality, nationality, and law.

59. See Foucault 1990. See Scott (1998) on how states render populations legible and governable.

60. See Sahlins 1989: 225.

61. Goldstein 2012 and Mitchell 1999.

62. See Das and Poole 2004, Das 2007; and Taussig 1997.

63. Reeves 2013: 512, also drawing from Fassin and d'Halluin 2005; also see Andersson 2014.

64. Lakhani 2016.

65. Ibid. The author quotes Gretchen Kuhener, who is the Director of the Institute of Women in Migration.

Chapter 3

Portions of this chapter appear in Rebecca B. Galemba, 2012a. "'Corn Is Food, Not Contraband': The Right to 'Free Trade' at the Mexico–Guatemala Border." *American Ethnologist* 39(4): 716–734.

1. This number is likely a gross underestimate because it refers only to amounts recorded by the municipality. According to the Guatemalan Corn Truckers Association, closer to 10,000 tons per month of corn enter Huehuetenango from Mexico (Bolaños and Castillo 2010). This route is the principal entrance for corn from Mexico into Huehuetenango but varies seasonally.

2. Wise 2011: 48.

3. The establishment of this association is discussed further in Chapter 6.

4. See Edelman 2005; Scott 1976; and Abraham and Van Schendel 2005.

5. Fischer and Benson 2006 and Watanabe 1992.

6. This corn trade is conducted in Mexican pesos on both sides of the border. I use rough dollar equivalents from the 2007 exchange rate to put the amounts in perspective.

7. *People's World* 2007. Tortilla prices increased between 42 percent and 67 percent in 2007 from 6 to 8.5 pesos (De Ita 2007).

8. Agribusiness claimed there were shortages as they hoarded the 2006–2007 harvests, augmented prices through speculation, and amassed large profits (De Ita 2007).

9. Narco accusations reflect the permeation of the drug trade and commentaries on what border residents suspect as ill-gotten wealth. Here, however, the accusation is used to tease Ramón as part of the atmosphere of banter at the depots.

10. See Naylor 2002. Employing Mexican and Guatemalan cargo loaders can be explained by the need to exchange corn between trucks in the unmonitored route so that the Mexican corn appears Guatemalan by exiting the route to Guatemala in a Guatemalan truck. However, the presence of often separate Mexican truckers and merchants, border merchants' and truckers' monopolization of the route's commerce, the presence of Mexican and Guatemalan border intermediaries, as well as

the agreement within the merchant association and with the association of irrigation canal producers to establish fair prices to purchase corn, all lend themselves to a more complex explanation. This explanation must take into account local moral justifications that all border residents should have the opportunity to work and that corn is necessary to regional livelihoods.

11. Recinos 1991.

12. Fitting 2011: 114 and Villafuerte Solís 2009.

13. Fittting 2011.

14. Ibid..: 14.

15. Ibid.: 95.

16. Yúnez-Naude 2003: 1.

17. Ibid: 2–3.

18. Bartra and Otero 2005 and De Ita 1997. However, broader social movements, including the Zapatistas, La Vía Campesina, In Defense of Corn, and Movimiento el Campo no Aguanta Más (MCAM), go beyond the state and invoke both corn as a cultural symbol and the right to food sovereignty to protest the liberalization of the corn trade and the introduction of genetically modified corn as well as the neoliberal model itself (Bartra and Otero 2005; Edelman 2005; and Fitting 2011).

19. De Ita 1997 and Hewitt de Alcantará 1992.

20. Bartra 2003.

21. He may also have been referring to the fact that most corn exported from the United States is yellow corn, generally used in Mexico and Guatemala for animal feed. In Mexico and Guatemala, white corn is preferred for human consumption.

22. De Ita 1997 and Fuentes et al. 2005.

23. Fuentes et al. 2005.

24. Camus 2012: 75.

25. See Watanabe 1992. Some Guatemalan border residents work on nearby coffee plantations, but because of their border proximity many supplement or replace agriculture with commerce, trucking, and cargo loading (see Gúzman Mérida 2004).

26. Fuentes et al. 2005: 78, translation mine.

27. De Ita 2007.

28. Merry (2006) uses the term *vernacularization* to describe how people interpret and translate global discourses on women's human rights in specific cultural contexts. In this case, the form of vernacularization falls into Merry's (2006: 44) analysis of subversion, where "the name and transnational referent are retained but the content of the ideas and the structure of the organization is dramatically changed."

29. Nash 2001: 86.

30. De Ita 1997: 2, translation mine.

31. Harvey 1998.

32. Wise 2011: 47.

33. King 2006, 9 and Nadal 2000.

34. Wise 2011: 47.

35. Ibid.: 47; 2010: 169. Wise (2011: 47) calculates the losses by looking at how dumping affects their prices in relation to what they would otherwise receive.

36. Harvey 1998 and King 2006: 6–7.

37. SARH-CEPAL 1992: 92, cited in Harvey 1998: 182–183.

38. Harvey 1998: 182–183.

39. Wise 2011: 48. About 3 million people moved into seasonal agriculture, but the loss of 2.3 million obscures the larger effects (Wise 2016).

40. World Bank 2015.

41. Zepeda, Wise, and Gallagher 2009: 10, 12–13.

42. Wise 2011: 47; De Ita 2007; *People's World* 2007.

43. King 2006.

44. Ibid.: 43.

45. SAT 2015: 70. Guatemala has a quota of 150,000 metric tons of yellow corn from Mexico that can enter duty free (World Trade Organization 2015: 34). The duty is 15 percent for yellow corn above the quota (SAT 2015: 70).

46. He noted how people in Ciudad Hidalgo and Tecún Umán have long referenced river contraband as a form of free trading. See Staudt 1998, 2001; Mathews and Vega 2012; and Gauthier 2007.

47. Bartra and Otero 2005; De Ita 1997; Hernández 1992; and Hewitt de Alcantará 1992.

48. De Ita 1997.

49. In the latter part of the 1990s, the state saw the former leaders of the corn mobilizations of the 1980s as key allies in efforts to reconstitute state power and contain the Zapatistas (see De Ita 1997 and Pérez Ruiz 2004).

50. See Hernández Castillo 2001 and Pérez Ruiz 2004.

51. Sabet 2015: 508, also drawing from Fox 1994.

52. Cross 1998; Sabet 2015: 509; and Davis 2012.

53. Preston 1998.

54. Centeno and Portes 2006: 28.

55. See Goldstein 2012.

56. Ibid.; Das 2007; and Aretxaga 2003.

57. Residents and producers believe the military's job should be only to ensure they are not transporting anything illegal or dangerous, such as drugs.

58. Abraham and Van Schendel 2005: 4.

59. See Taussig 1998 and Comaroff and Comaroff 2006: 5 on how the legal and illegal, the transgression and the norm, define and redefine one another.

60. Comaroff and Comaroff 2006: 5.

61. See Agamben (2005) on the state of exception. Penglase (2009) demonstrates how drug traffickers in Brazil manipulate the uncertainty of whether they will uphold the rules to generate fear and power in the favelas.

62. John Watanabe (2000) illustrates how assertions of municipal autonomy in Guatemala have historical roots in the nineteenth century.

63. The document was, however, not readily accessible. It took the mayor's assistants some time to find it. Officials and residents hinted that the agreement was not publicized because it would outrage Guatemalan producers who may compete for this market.

64. See Figure 3.1 for yearly taxes collected by La Democracia since 1998.

65. Bolaños and Castillo 2010 and Radio en Linea 2011.

66. Coyoy 2011 and Ministerio de la Economía 2011.

67. See Fitting 2011 and Villafuerte Solís 2009.

68. Villafuerte Solís 2009: 79.

69. See Edelman 2005 and Fitting 2011.

70. See Van Etten and Fuentes 2004: 54.

71. See Mathews and Vega 2012 and Ribeiro 2012.

72. Goldín 2011.

Chapter 4

1. See parallels in Flynn 1997.

2. The Mexican peso has fallen dramatically against the U.S. dollar in recent years, but at the time the conversion to U.S. dollars was roughly 10.7 pesos per US$1; I use the rough ratio of 10 pesos per US$1 in this book. See Index Mundi 2016.

3. See Galemba 2012b. Some portions of this chapter appear in Rebecca B. Galemba. 2012b. "Remapping the Border: Taxation, Territory, and (Trans) National Identity at the Mexico–Guatemala Border." *Environment and Planning D: Society and Space* 30(5): 822–841.

4. Regional tax collection has a long history on both sides of the border, dating back to the *alcabala* tax during Spanish rule (Wallace Wilkie, Meyer, and Monzón de Wilkie 1976). These taxes, however, were usually levied by regional elite/strongmen; not by local communities.

5. Claudio Lomnitz (1995: 42) relates Mexico's challenge to create a professional bureaucracy and public sphere. In the colonial era officials were supposed to earn money from their positions (Elliot 1984: 195, 299, cited in Lomnitz 1995: 23). Mexico's bureaucracy continues to experience a blending of "rational bureaucracy with '*caciquismo*,'" referring to governance based on relations of patronage between local elites and their communities (Lomnitz 1995: 25).

6. Sieder 2002 and Nash 2001, drawing from Nugent and Alonso 1994: 229.

7. See Nuijten 2003 and Harvey 1998.

8. Lewis 2005: 4–5.

9. Although the end of the war also spurred local mobilizations on the Guatemalan side of the border, residents on both sides tend to focus on changes in Mexico, which has historically imposed tougher border vigilance.

10. Rus, Hernández Castillo, and Mattiace 2003: 7.

11. Ibid.: 9.

12. See Doyle 2003 on investigation into Mexico's Dirty War (1968–1982) and government-enforced disappearances. Also see Gutmann 2002.

13. Nash 2001: 79.

14. Ibid.

15. Rus, Hernández Castillo, and Mattiace 2003: 11. The National Indigenous Congress (CNI) of 1974, organized by Bishop Samuel Ruiz García, helped spur the spread of independent organizations (Nash 2001: 95).

16. Hernández Castillo 2001 and Pérez Ruiz 2004.

17. Hernández Castillo 2001: 224, 225.

18. See Gutmann 2002: 151 and Stephen 1999.

19. Rus, Hernández Castillo, and Mattiace 2003: 18. The armed group responsible for the atrocities was checked through the military checkpoint by state security forces under the mandate of a nearby army general (Rus, Hernández Castillo, and Mattiace 2003: 20). Also see Gutmann 2002.

20. Rus, Hernández Castillo, and Mattiace 2003: 18.

21. Ibid.: 15.

22. Ibid.

23. Formed in 1982 by campesinos who had broken ties with government-sponsored National Confederation of Campesinos (CNC) and agitates around land rights (Nash 2001: 95).

24. Rus and Vigil 2007: 163–164.

25. See Andreas 1999; and Abraham and Van Schendel 2005.

26. See Andreas 1999, 2010.

27. See Burrell 2013 and Godoy 2004, 2006. Also see Goldstein 2010, 2004, 2005.

28. Burrell 2013; Godoy 2004, 2006; and Goldstein 2010.

29. See Scott's 2009 work, in contrast, of how hill populations in Southeast Asia have resisted state incorporation. Border residents' claims to autonomy must be situated within their symbiotic relationship with state control and their ambivalent desire for more state incorporation and avoidance.

30. See Goldstein 2004 for a discussion of lynchings as a performative means of engaging with the state.

31. Sahlins 1989: 3. Also see Nevins 2002; Sack 1986: 33; and M. Reeves 2014.

32. See Sahlins 1989: 4 and Nevins 2002.

33. M. Reeves 2014: 180.

34. See Roitman 2005, 2006 on the pluralization of regulatory authorities.

35. Dudley 2011. The Zetas were former Special Forces of the Mexican military who deserted in the late 1990s to work as the enforcement arm of the Gulf Cartel. They split to form their own violent criminal organization in 2010. In the 1990s, they received training from the United States in counterinsurgency and counternarcotics operations (Paley 2014: 120).

36. See Das and Poole 2004 and M. Reeves 2014.

37. Nuijten 2003: 15. See descriptions of the "idea of the state" as articulated by Abrams 1988 [1977]; Alonso 1994; Mitchell 1999; and M. Reeves 2014.

38. Nuijten 2003: 196.

39. Ibid.: 197.

40. Ibid. In contrast to a climate of co-optation and cycles of fear, hope, and contestation that permeate much of Chiapas, the Zapatistas have consciously opted out of this system by creating autonomous communities that reject association with, and even recognition by, the government.

41. Ackerman 2016 and Paley 2014.

42. Priest Miguel Hidalgo instigated the first call to overthrow the Spanish and begin the revolution, through the *Grito* (cry) of Dolores in 1810. He played an integral role in leading the struggle for independence until his execution in 1811. Many Mexicans refer to him as the father of Mexico and the independence movement.

43. See Gutmann 2002; Gledhill 2004; and Nuijten 2003; see Lomnitz (1995: 35) on ritual as a form of "political expression and . . . conflict resolution" in Mexico.

Chapter 5

1. *El Orbe* 2015; translation mine.

2. Andreas 2002, 1999.

3. See Andreas 2002 and Heyman and Cambell 2007.

4. See Clot 2013: 14; Clot also cites Adler-Lomnitz 2013: 136.

5. Paley 2014 and Goldstein 2010.

6. Becerril 2014.

7. Davis 2012: 14.

8. Ibid.: 13 and Goldstein 2016: 23. Also see Meagher (2014) on the need for empirical studies.

9. Gagne 2016 and Schneider 2012: 172.

10. Gagne 2016 and Schneider 2012.

11. Thomas 2013: 147.

12. Nordstrom 2007: 162.

13. Chávez 2014 and ILO 2014.

14. González 2015b and ILO 2014.

15. Clot 2013: 10, citing INEGI 2013.

16. Nordstrom 2007: 21.

17. Ibid.: 40.

18. Ibid.

19. Castillo, Ribot, and Olivera 2006.

20. As of 2012, Mexico is the fifth most important destination of Guatemala's exports and second for imports, whereas Guatemala is only twelfth as a source for Mexico's exports and twenty-sixth for imports (WTO 2015: 8).

21. Sabet 2010: 266.

22. Friman (2009b: 54, 57) posits reasons that policy makers may be unwilling to enforce the law from a more macro perspective, demonstrating that policy mandates are nested in "higher-level systems" such as security or international trade as they also need to contend with how policies are embedded in social "expectations concerning the legitimate use of state power." At the Mexico–Guatemala border, officials balance applying mandates to enhance security with commitments to facilitating trade and regional social discontent.

23. Snyder and Duran-Martinez 2009: 263–264.

24. Ibid.: 263.

25. Sabet 2012: 37.

26. Ibid.: 37–38.

27. Chalfin 2010: 9.

28. AnimalPolitico 2013.

29. Ibid.

30. Isacson, Meyer, and Morales 2014 and Isacson, Meyer, and Smith 2015.

31. Muciño 2014.

32. See Isacson, Meyer, and Smith 2015: 32. Also see Pickard (2005) on the Security and Prosperity Partnership (2005–2009) to deepen security and regional integration between the United States, Mexico, and Canada.

33. See Paley 2014; also see Goldstein 2010, 2012 and Jusionyte 2015.

34. Dorset Chiapas Solidarity 2016.

35. By the end of 2015, Mexico and Guatemala had liberalized between 96 and 98 percent of their tariff lines; "only 216 tariff lines for Mexico (1.8% of the Tariff) were to remain subject to duties . . . [and] only 3.2% of Guatemala's tariff lines [were] subject to duties." (World Trade Organization 2016: 33).

36. Small businesses under the limits of $1,000 per day do not need a customs agent.

37. Fernández-Kelly and Massey 2007: 102. Opportunities for opening investment were seen as key to protecting investor interests and ensuring that Mexico was a credit-worthy, secure investment (102).

38. Ibid.: 106.

39. Díaz 2001; Villareal 2012; Figueroa, Lee, and Van Schoik 2011; and World Bank Group 2015.

40. Díaz 2001.

41. Ieva Jusionyte 2013, 2015 documents similar exclusions and privileges around the MERCOSUR agreement. MERCOSUR, the Common Market of the South, is a subregional political and economic block established among Argentina, Paraguay, Uruguay, and Brazil in 1991 with additional associate countries. Venezuela's membership was suspended in 2016. As the countries entered official trade integration through MERCOSUR, local forms of traditional commerce were increasingly restricted and criminalized (2013: 234).

42. Grandia 2012: 187.

43. Ibid.

44. Ibid.

45. Ibid.

46. Little 2013.

47. Aguilar 2003: 4; translation mine.

48. Azurdia 2013 and WTO 2016.

49. Fernández Casanueva, 2014.

50. Grimson 2002: 167. Also see Jusionyte 2013: 236.

51. See Gallant 1999 and Heyman and Smart 1999.

52. Endres 2014: 3 and Ong 2006: 5, cited in Endres 2014: 3.

53. Endres 2014: 12.

54. Ibid.: 3; also see Goldstein 2012.

55. See parallels in Goldstein 2004.

56. Border residents misinterpreted this force as coming directly from the orders of President Calderón because it dovetailed with his rhetoric regarding the border, even though it was a state initiative under Juan Sabines Guerrero (Basail Rodríguez 2016a).

57. In the eyes of northern Mexicans, southern Mexico is often associated with disparaging assumptions and stereotypes of indigeneity and backwardness (see Vila 1999 and Stephen 1999). Many customs agents stationed in Chiapas are from the north or have been trained in institutions that may perpetuate these stereotypes.

58. Also see Heyman 1995; Chalfin 2010; and M. Reeves 2014.

59. Nash 2001: 85.

60. Centeno and Portes 2006: 38.

61. Zepeda, Wise, and Gallagher 2009: 12–13.

62. Ibid.: 14. These authors cite data from CONSAMI n.d. and Fairris, Popli, and Zepeda 2008.

63. Zepeda, Wise, and Gallagher: 14.

64. Ibid.

65. Centeno and Portes 2006: 40 and Basail Rodríguez 2016.

66. Giugale, Lafourcade, and Nguyen 2001: 730.

67. Fábregas Puig and Ponciano 2014: 17.

68. Mérida Gúzman 2004: 134; translation mine.

69. QuimiNet.com 2006.

70. Fábregas Puig and Ponciano 2014: 17.

71. See Muehlmann 2014: 155 on the integration of the legal and illegal economy in relation to drug trafficking.

72. See Andreas 1999, also 2010; and Comaroff and Comaroff 2006.

73. Andreas 1999 and Díaz 2015.

74. Nordstrom 2007 and Naylor 2002: 10.

75. Nordstrom 2007: 179.

76. Kar 2012: 33.

77. Ibid.

78. Ibid.: 19.

79. Ibid.: 5.

80. Ibid.: 5.

81. Centeno and Portes 2006: 38-40.

82. Ibid.: 38.

83. Nordstrom 2007.

84. Ibid.: 119.

85. Ibid.

86. See Scott 2009 on costs of governing spaces distant from state control.

87. *El Orbe* 2015.

88. Ibid.

89. Nordstrom 2007: 195.

90. Ibid.: 120.

91. Seelke and Finklea 2017: 11.

92. Daugherty 2015.

93. Nordstrom 2007: 202.

94. Andreas 2002: 39.

95. Paley 2014; Goldstein 2010, 2012; and Jusionyte 2015.

96. See Thomas 2013.

97. Cross 2011.

98. Goldstein 2010, 2012.

99. Nordstrom 2007; Naylor 2002: 33–34 argues that it is prohibition that forces up prices in the drug market and that the size of the market is often overstated from politicized guestimates (see Andreas 2010). Naylor 2002: 10 asserts that "the real threat to economic morality comes from seemingly legitimate business types intent on seeing how far they can bend the rule before they have to pay politicians to rewrite them."

Chapter 6

1. Preceding segments also appear in Rebecca B. Galemba, 2012c. "Taking Contraband Seriously: Practicing 'Legitimate Work' at the Mexico–Guatemala Border." *The Anthropology of Work Review* 33(1): 3–14.

2. Also see Basail Rodríguez 2016b: 13.

3. See Galemba 2012c.

4. See Reeves 2013, drawing from Yiftachel 2009.

5. Alvarez 2005: 44. Truckers, middlemen, and smugglers are increasingly integrated into larger transnational legal and illegal markets, although they still remain embedded in their small, collectivist, and kin-oriented communities.

6. Martín Pérez 2006.

7. Dudley 2010: 69. They also act as local distributors.

8. Ibid.

9. Isacson, Meyer, and Smith 2015: 31.

10. These groups supposedly work with the Sinaloa cartel; to maintain their territorial power they have assassinated members of the Zetas who have sought to establish influence in the region since 2008 (Los Chapincitos 2013).

11. Alvarez (2005: 64) attributes the corporate organization of trucking in southern Mexico to various factors including the post-1980s withering of the economy that limited commercial employment options in addition to the fact that truckers often balance business with farming demands. Like Tito, even though they spend most of their time conducting commerce, the truckers in Alvarez's study continue to primarily identify as farmers (Alvarez 2005: 64).

12. I did not know this individual well enough to assess the truth of the statement. However, his statement illustrates the perceptions of grandeur and pride that often surround the contraband economy in contrast to other employment options. Although many businessmen downplay their wealth to deflect attention and scrutiny, others boast.

13. See Watanabe 1992; Fischer and Benson 2006; Goldín 2011; and Renard 2011.

14. Renard 2011: 153 and Celis 2005, cited in Renard.

15. See Hernández Navarro 2004 and Renard 2011.

16. Hernández Navarro 2004.

17. SAT 2015.

18. Hernández Navarro 2004.

19. Renard 2011: 154.

20. See description at www.ecomtrading.com/

21. Renard 2011.

22. Ibid., drawing from Pérez Grovas et al. 2002: 50.

23. I do not know to what degree the companies knew about these practices, but border residents insinuated that they either knew, were directly facilitating, or at least benefited from turning a blind eye.

24. He was previously municipal president from 1991 to 1995, but as a member of the PRI. The PVEM has attempted to win elections in municipalities using former PRI representatives (Escalona Victoria 2016).

25. *Cuarto Poder* 2016. On his arrest, many inhabitants mobilized to demand his release (Gaceta Mexicana 2016).

26. Tito's son from Tuxtla purchased the car.

27. Nordstrom 2007.

28. Ibid.: 111.

29. See ethics of illegality in Roitman 2006.

30. Renard 2011: 153.

31. Alvarez 2005: 39.

32. In southern Mexico, Alvarez argues that forming an association or union enables truckers to acquire licenses to operate, or monopolize, particular routes. Chiapas trucking unions are often embedded in PRI clientelistic politics because they depend on state officials for permits (Alvarez 2005: 65, 69).

33. This assumption parallels norms in legal commerce whereby merchants are the ones who "have the major responsibility for all tasks associated with distribution and marketing" including transport (Alvarez 2005: 46).

34. Some parts of this section appear in Galemba 2012c.

35. Yet, when prices and demands change, the trade may reverse directions.

36. Zucarmex was founded in Mexico in 1992 after the privatization of the sugar industry and has five mills in Mexico. See Gúzman Mérida 2004.

37. Galemba 2012c.

38. Dudley 2010.

39. Muehlmann 2014: 12.

40. Ibid.

41. Ibid.: 13, 166.

42. MacGaffey and Bazenguissa-Ganga 2000; Ribeiro 2006; and Bourgois 1995.

43. Rosas 2012: 119.

44. Millar 2014: 49.

45. Ibid.: 39.

46. Ibid.: 49, 47.

47. Ibid.: 35–36.

48. Centeno and Portes 2006: 40; and Itzigsohn 2000.

49. See Matthews and Vega 2012 and Roitman 2006.

50. See Roitman 2006.

51. See Naím 2005 and Arriola Vega 2009.

52. Also see Nordstrom 2007; Heyman and Smart 1999; and Abraham and Van Schendel 2005.

53. Title cited from Galemba 2012c.

54. Centeno and Portes 2006.

55. Muehlmann 2014: 166.

56. See Malkin 2001.

Chapter 7

1. Arias and Goldstein 2010: 4.

2. Ibid.

3. See parallels in Goldstein 2004 and Rus and Vigil 2007.

4. World demand for oil was increasing for several years, with a peak of 86 million barrels a day in 2007. This declined during the onset of the 2008 recession but began to increase with recovery (see Gas Prices Explained, n.d.). Even when crude oil prices dropped in 2008, Guatemala's prices remained high. In contrast, Mexico's government established fuel prices and often kept gas and diesel prices artificially low and subsidized gasoline to quell discontent (Plante and Jordan 2013). In June of 2007, a liter of gasoline was 6.88 pesos in Mexico and the equivalent of 10 Mexican pesos in Guatemala.

5. A gallon of regular gas cost 27.79 quetzales (about US$3.45), and it cost drivers 20 quetzales more to fill a tank than the previous week. See Quinto, May 24, 2007.

6. See El Fronterizo, September 4, 2007.

7. Market structures for smuggling often relate to trade restrictions, demands, and supplies in the legal market (see Andreas 1999).

8. Such focus on regional aspects reflects the fact that, in southern Mexico, trucking has generally been a regional, rather than national, enterprise (Alvarez 2005).

9. See Andreas 1999; also see Roitman 2005, 2006.

10. See McMurray 2001.

11. See Robben 1996 and Osburg 2013 on ethnographic seduction.

12. OCR 2006.

13. Since 2004, oil production has declined as domestic demand has grown (Melgar 2012). According to Lourdes Melgar (2012), 35 percent of government income derives from oil revenues, but "despite being one of the top petroleum companies in the world, PEMEX is technically bankrupt, sharply curtailing the possibilities for growth and investment."

14. Paley 2014: 100.

15. Ibid.

16. Ibid. and Carlsen 2014.

17. Okeowo 2017.

18. Mike Castillo 2006.

19. Barrientos 2012.

20. McMurray 2001: 127–128.

21. Ibid.: 130.

22. Snyder and Duran-Martinez 2009: 255 and Andreas 1999: 94.

23. Andreas 1999: 94.

24. McMurray 2001: 129. Also see Andreas 2011 and Endres 2014.

25. See Andreas 1999 and Snyder and Duran-Martinez 2009: 255.

26. Andreas 1999 and Snyder and Duran-Martinez 2009: 255.

27. In their work on state-sponsored protection rackets, Snyder and Duran-Martinez (2009: 261, 259) argue that state protectors prefer multiple criminal organizations over exclusive protection because competition drives up costs of protection. Meanwhile, criminal groups prefer many protectors and one organization to lower protection expenses (ibid.: 259). At the border, having multiple protectors does not reduce prices for smuggling groups because each agency (for example, federal police, state police, customs, sanitary inspections, and the military) charges to selectively enforce or not enforce the authority under its jurisdiction See Snyder and Duran-Martinez (2009) on the implications of changing and overlapping jurisdictional authority in Mexico.

28. Ibid.: 267, 270.

29. Ibid.: 263.

30. Ibid.: 267.

31. Perret 2012; Snyder and Duran-Martinez 2009; Paley 2014; Vogt 2013; and Brigden 2016.

32. This is a small state unit within the structure of the Chiapas state public security ministry (Isacson, Meyer, and Smith 2015: 14). It has not acquired much force; in 2012 they had only fifty members, even though currently they have 135 and fifty equipped units (Basail Rodríguez 2016a; Secretaría de Seguridad y Protección Ciudadana 2015; and Isacson, Meyer, and Smith 2015: 14).

33. Olson, Shirk, and Selee 2010: 7–8.

34. López 2013.

35. *Prensa Libre* 2008.

36. López 2013 and Dudley 2011.

37. Isacson, Meyer, and Morales 2014: 9, drawing from López 2013.

38. According to InSight Crime, the Zetas have fewer connections than the Sinaloa cartel to source countries, so they rely on purchasing drugs in Honduras and Guatemala (Dudley 2013).

39. Ibid.

40. Ibid.

41. Velasco Santos 2016.

Conclusion

1. Dua and Menkhaus 2012.

2. Abraham and Van Schendel 2005.

3. See parallels in Jusionyte 2015.

4. Aguiar 2014: 3, 26; Cross 2011; Dent 2012; and Thomas 2013.

5. Basail Rodríguez 2016b: 15–16, translation mine; and Aguiar 2014.

6. Thomas 2013: 157.

7. Thomas 2013; Dent 2012. See Cross 2011: 321 on "pirate populism."

8. See Cross 2011 and Aguiar 2014.

9. Nordstrom 2007: 21–23.

10. See Goldstein 2012; Ybarra 2016: 195; and Jusionyte 2015.

11. See Abraham and Van Schendel 2005.

12. See Galemba 2012c.

13. Zilberg 2007, 2011 and Burrell 2013: 143.

14. Dudley 2010, 2013.

15. Burrell 2013: 143.

16. Instituto Nacional de Psiquiatría Ramón de la Fuente Muñiz 2012: 2, citing from Secretaria de Salud 2009: 173.

17. Andreas 2000: 23.

18. See Nazario 2014 and Kovic 2008.

19. Isacson, Meyer, and Morales 2015: 22.

20. Andreas 2011: 8.

21. Sabet 2012: 23.

22. Ibid.: 38. Sabet (drawing from Galán 2011), notes that in 2011 more than half of Mexico's states had "current of former military leaders in their top public-security positions."

23. Sabet 2010: 252, 267 and 2012: 20–21.

24. Ibid.: 23–24.

25. Paley 2014.

26. Ibid.: 140.

27. Ibid.: 85–86, 89.

28. Galán 2011, citing Ernesto López Portillo Vargas, founding director of the Institute for Security and Democracy (Insyde).

29. Sabet 2010: 266 and Bargent 2016.

30. Human Rights Watch 2015. Because jurisdiction for investigating these claims is restricted to the military justice system, it is challenging to hold the military accountable.

31. Paley 2014: 114 and Human Rights Watch 2015.

32. Le Clercq, Rodíguez, and Lara 2016.

33. Ibid., no page, executive summary.

34. Ibid., no page, executive summary.

35. Ibid.: 25 and Bargent 2016.

36. Seelke and Finklea 2017: 12.

37. Inter-American Commission on Human Rights 2013: 48, cited in HRW 2015.

38. Alba and Castillo 2012: 15.

39. Isacson, Meyer, and Morales 2014: 32.

40. Ureste 2014b; see Galemba 2014.

41. Ureste 2014a, translation mine; see Galemba 2014.

42. Ureste 2015 and Carlsen 2015.

43. Lakhani 2015 and Isacson, Meyer, and Smith 2015: 16. The Pentagon provides additional assistance, but overall the amounts "appropriated, allocated, or spent" remain somewhat unclear, although there is consensus that U.S. funding has increased (Isacson, Meyer, and Smith 2015: 16)

44. Isacson, Meyer, and Smith 2015: 7; also Sorrentino 2015.

45. Isacson, Meyer, and Smith 2015: 32.

46. Ureste 2017.

47. Tourliere 2015.

48. U.S. Department of State 2015.

49. This still represents a large jump in funding to the region (García 2016).

50. U.S. Department of State 2015.

51. Ibid.

52. Frank 2015.

53. Main 2015.

54. Since the coup against Manuel Zelaya in Honduras in 2009, Honduras has become one of the most violent countries in the world. Zelaya had been rolling back neoliberal economic reforms and curbing privatization. The current administration has been accused of direct collusion with traffickers even as Honduras asserts its commitment to combating drugs and crime. Honduras has not only militarized policing, resulting in increases in human rights abuses, but has also employed violence to facilitate the expansion of transnational capital. Rights Action reported eighty-eight murders in the Aguán valley between 2010 and 2013 of members of peasant associations perpetrated by the Honduran military and police in coordination with palm oil plantations seeking to displace them (Bird 2013). In Guatemala, the government has justified states of siege and militarization of policing to quell peasant protests against resource extraction by foreign companies (for example, see Nolin and Stephens 2010).

55. Gonzalez 2015a.

56. Ibid. and MAWG 2013.

57. Inter-American Development Bank 2014; also see Frank 2015.

58. The one mention of human rights abuses refers to reparations to Guatemalan communities that suffered abuses during the construction of the Chixoy Dam. This

is mentioned in isolation from ongoing abuses in the name of transnational development (for example, see Nolin and Stephens 2010).

59. Main 2015.

60. Paley 2014: 148.

61. See Slack and Whiteford 2011.

62. Villafuerte Solís 2014.

63. Brigden 2016: 3.

64. Paley 2014: 148.

65. Ibid.: 149.

66. U.S. Department of State 2016: 182; U.S. State Department 2013; and Lohmuller 2016. According to Dudley 2010: 63, pressure on the drug trade in Mexico has intensified violence in Central America.

67. COHA 2011.

68. Andreas 2003: 86.

69. Gootenberg 2012: 159, 161; also see critique in Paley 2014.

70. Campbell 2009: 31, drawing from Dugan 1997.

71. Gootenberg 2012: 162, 163.

72. Ibid.

73. Ibid.: 165.

74. Ibid.: 172.

75. Gootenberg 2008: 306, 313–314, cited in Gootenberg 2012: 160.

76. Gootenberg 2012: 178 and MAWG 2013.

77. Paley 2014: 28.

78. Ibid.: 111, 125.

79. Taussig 2003: 112, 158.

80. Schneider and Schneider 2008: 366. Also see Zilberg 2011; Taussig 2003; and Aretxaga 2003.

81. Also see Sluka 2000.

82. Paley 2014: 28.

83. Campbell 2009: 19, 7.

84. Paley 2014: 25.

85. Gibler 2014.

86. Flores 2014.

87. Ibid.

88. Ibid.

89. Dorset Chiapas Solidarity 2015.

90. Ibid.

91. Ibid.

92. Pickard 2002.

93. Tenuto-Sánchez 2014 and Pickard 2003.

94. Carlsen 2009.

95. Alberto Arroyo (2006) termed the conjoining of neoliberal corporate interests to regional security policies "militarized neoliberalism." Otros Mundos, maps shared on January 18, 2017.

96. Guatemala Human Rights Commission/USA in MAWG 2013: 20.

97. Isacson, Meyer, and Morales 2014: 29 and MAWG 2013.

98. Guatemala Human Rights Commission/USA in MAWG 2013, 20.

99. MAWG 2013.

100. Ibid.

101. After being cleared of charges by a Guatemalan court in 2011, he was extradited to the United States to face money laundering and conspiracy charges in 2013. He pled guilty in 2014 (*The Tico Times* 2014).

102. Ybarra 2016: 203.

103. Ibid.: 203.

104. Schneider and Schneider 2008: 367.

105. Also see Aguiar 2014; parallels in Jusionyte 2015.

106. U.S. Southern Command 2014: 4.

107. Isacson, Meyer, and Morales 2014: 8. Drug violence is more prevalent on the Guatemalan side of the border, where drugs spend more time as they are prepared for transshipment (9).

108. See Cross 2011.

109. Sabet 2015.

110. See Andreas 2011 on selectivity bias in connecting illicit flows to violence, for example.

111. Carey and Marak 2011: 8; Heyman and Campbell 2011; Paley 2014; Muehlmann 2014; and Andreas 1999, 2000.

112. Flores 2014.

113. Ibid.

114. Ibid.

115. Ybarra 2016; Burrell 2013; and Thomas, O'Neill, and Offit 2011.

116. Goldstein 2010.

117. See Paley 2014.

118. Centeno and Portes 2006.

119. Scott 1985.

120. Mathews and Vega 2012: 1.

121. Ribeiro 2012: 222, 223.

122. Ibid.: 230, 221. Ribeiro (2012) and Mathews and Vega (2012) stress that "globalization from below" should *not* be seen as a separate system. My concern for applying this term at the border is the risk in romanticizing these strategies as alternative even as they enable residents to earn a livelihood.

123. See Mathews and Vega 2012: 11 on how such actors "out-neoliberalize" those who institute "globalization from above."

124. Centeno and Portes 2006.

125. Nash 2001 and Rus 1994.

126. Taussig 1997.

127. See Goldstein 2012 on "phantom state" and Aretxaga 2003.

128. I borrow the *boomerang* term from Elana Zilberg's 2007 work on the transnational boomerang effects among tough on crime and criminalization of immigration policies in the United States, stringent gang abatement measures in Central America, and cycles of unauthorized northward migration.

129. Inda and Dowling 2013.

References

Abraham, Itty, and Willem van Schendel. 2005. "Introduction: The Making of Illic-itness." In *Illicit Flows and Criminal Things: States, Borders, and the Other Side of Globalization*, edited by Willem van Schendel and Itty Abraham, 1–37. Indianapolis: University of Indiana Press.

Abrams, Philip. 1988 [1977]. "Notes on the Difficulty of Studying the State." *Journal of Historical Sociology* 1(1): 58–89.

Abrego, Leisy J. July 9, 2014. "Rejecting Obama's Deportation and Drug War Surge on Central American Kids." *The Huffington Post*. Retrieved on November 9, 2015, from www.huffingtonpost.com/leisy-j-abrego/rejecting-obamas deportat_b_5568358.html.

Ackerman, John M. February 23, 2016. "Mexico is Not a Functioning Democracy." *Foreign Policy*. Retrieved on July 26, 2016, from http://foreignpolicy.com/2016/02/23/obama-pena-nieto-mexico-corruption/.

Adler-Lomnitz, Larissa. 2013. *Redes Sociales, Cultura y Poder: Ensayos de Antropología Latinoamericana*. México: FLACSO.

Agamben, Giorgio. 2005. *State of Exception*, translated by Kevin Attell. Chicago: University of Chicago Press.

Aguiar, José Carlos G. 2014. "Estados de Simulación: Piratería, contrabando, neoliberalismo y el control de la ilegalidad en América Latina. *Perspectivas, Insyde Ideas*.

Aguilar, Marco Antonio. 2003. "Consecuencias del Tratado de Libre Comercio Triángulo Norte de Centroamérica y México." Facultad de Ciencias Económicas y Empresariales, Facultades de Quetzaltenango, Universidad Rafael Landívar.

Alba, Francisco, and Manuel Ángel Castillo. October 2012. "New Approaches to Migration Management in Mexico and Central America." San Diego: Woodrow Wilson International Center for Scholars. Migration Policy Institute, 1–24.

Alianza Mexicana contra el Fracking. December 17, 2015. "Nueva ley para criminalizar la protesta social y limitar el libre flujo de información en el marco de las reformas estructurales." Retrieved on April 27, 2017, from http://nofrackingmexico .org/nueva-ley-para-criminalizar-la-protesta-social-y-limitar-el-libre-flujo-de -informacion-en-el-marco-de-las-reformas-estructurales/.

Alonso, Ana María. 1994. "The Politics of Space, Time and Substance: State Formation, Nationalism and Ethnicity." *Annual Review of Anthropology*: 379–405.

Alvarez, Robert R. Jr. 2005. *Mangos, Chiles, and Truckers: The Business of Transnationalism*. Minneapolis: University of Minnesota Press.

———. 1995. "The Mexican–U.S. Border: The Making of the Anthropology of Borderlands." *Annual Review of Anthropology* 24(4): 447–470.

Andersson, Ruben. 2014. "Hunter and Prey: Patrolling Clandestine Migration in the Euro-African Borderlands." *Anthropological Quarterly* 87(1): 119–149.

Andreas, Peter. 2011. "Illicit globalization: Myths, Misconceptions, and Historical Lessons." *Political Science Quarterly* 126(3): 403–425.

———. 2010. "The Politics of Measuring Illicit Flows and Policy Effectiveness." In *Sex, Drugs, and Body Counts: The Politics of Numbers in Global Crime and Conflict*, edited by Peter Andreas and Kelly M. Greenhill, 23–45. Ithaca, NY: Cornell University Press.

———. 2003. "A Tale of Two Borders: The U.S.–Canada and U.S.–Mexico Lines after 9-11." In *The Rebordering of North America: Integration and Exclusion in a New Security Context*, edited by Peter Andreas and Thomas J. Biersteker, 1–23. New York and London: Routledge.

———. 2002. "Transnational Crime and Economic Globalization." In *Transnational Organized Crime and International Security: Business as Usual?*, edited by Mats R. Berdal and Mónica Serrano, 37–52. Boulder, CO: Lynne Rienner Publishers.

———. 2000. *Border Games: Policing the U.S.–Mexico Divide*. Ithaca, NY: Cornell University Press.

———. 1999. "Smuggling Wars: Law Enforcement and Law Evasion in a Changing World." In *Transnational Crime in the Americas*, edited by Tom Farer, 85–98. New York: Routledge.

AnimalPolítico. November 28, 2013. "Hacienda cierre 12 garitas aduanales en 4 estados fronterizos." Retrieved on October 21, 2015, from www.animalpolitico.com /2013/11/hacienda-cierra-12-garitas-aduanales-en-4-estados-fronterizos/.

Anzaldúa, Gloria. 1999 [1987]. *Borderlands/La Frontera*. San Francisco: Aunt Lute.

Arias, Enrique Desmond, and Daniel M. Goldstein. 2010. "Violent Pluralism: Understanding the New Democracies of Latin America." In *Violent Democracies in Latin America*, edited by Enrique Desmond Arias and Daniel M. Goldstein, 1–34. Durham, NC: Duke University Press.

Aretxaga, Begoña. 2003. "Maddening States." *Annual Review of Anthropology*. 32: 393–410.

Arriola Vega, Luis Alfredo. 2009. "Security and Migration in the Tabasco-El Petén Border Region." *Migración y Desarollo* 13: 25–40.

Arroyo, Alberto. November 30, 2006. "ASPAN y la pérdida de soberanía." *Memorias del X Congreso internacional sobre integración regional, fronteras y globalización*. Chiapas, México: San Cristóbal de las Casas.

Asencio, Karen Mercado. April 12, 2012. "The Under-Registration of Births in Mexico: Consequences for Children, Adults, and Migrants." *Migration Policy Institute*. Retrieved on August 12, 2016, from www.migrationpolicy.org/article/under -registration-births-mexico-consequences-children-adults-and-migrants.

Asturias, Miguel Ángel. 1993. Translated by Gerald Martin. *Men of Maize*. Critical Edition. Pittsburgh and London: University of Pittsburgh Press.

Azurdia, Mercedes. September 2, 2013. "New Free Trade Agreement with Mexico Takes Effect in Guatemala." *PanAm Post*. Retrieved on July 28, 2016, from https:// panampost.com/mercedes-azurdia/2013/09/02/new-free-trade-agreement-with -mexico-takes-effect-in-guatemala/.

Bacon, David. 2008. *Illegal People: How Globalization Creates Migration and Criminalizes Immigrants*. Boston: Beacon Press.

Bargent, James. February 4, 2016. "Mexico Impunity Levels Reach 99%: Study." *InSight Crime*. Retrieved on August 24, 2016, from www.insightcrime.com/component /content/article?id=7447:mexico-impunity-levels-reach-99-study.

Barrientos, Ricardo. October 30, 2012. "Contrabando: expresión de poder real e impunidad." *Plaza Pública*. Retrieved on October 22, 2015, from www.plazapublica .com.gt/content/contrabando-expresion-de-poder-real-e-impunidad.

Bartra, Armando. January 21, 2003. "Para que sirve la agricultura?" *La Jornada*. México.

Bartra, Armanda, and Gerardo Otero. 2005. "Contesting Neoliberal Globalism and NAFTA in Rural Mexico: From State Corporatism to the Political-Cultural Formation of the Peasantry." *Journal of Latino/Latin American Studies* Special Edition 1:164–190.

Basail Rodríguez, Alain. August 8, 2016a. Personal Communication.

———. 2016b. "Relaciones comerciales transfronterizas, anclajes y fugas en Chiapas, entre Guatemala y México." Paper presented at the XXXIV Latin American Studies Congress. New York: 1–23.

———. 2005. "Gobernar en frontera: Desafíos de la Gobernabilidad y el Desarrollo en el Sur Mexicano." In *Fronteras Des-Bordadas: Ensayos Sobre la Frontera Sur de México*, Coordinated by Alain Basail Rodríguez, 153–188. Chiapas, México: Universidad de Ciencias y Artes.

Becerril, Isabel. December 2, 2014. "Economía ilegal genera pérdidas por 950,000 mdp." *El Financiero*. Retrieved on May 14, 2015, from www.elfinanciero.com.mx /archivo/economia-ilegal-genera-perdidas-por-950-000-mdp.html.

Benítez-Manaut, Raúl. 2004. *Mexico and the New Challenges of Hemispheric Security*. Woodrow Wilson Center Reports on the America. Washington, DC: Woodrow Wilson Center for Scholars. Latin America Program.

Benjamin, Walter. 1986. "Critique of Violence." In *Reflections: Essays, Aphorisms, Autobiographical Writings*, edited by P. Demetz, translated by E. Jephcott, 277–301. New York: Harcourt Brace Jovanovitch.

Benson, Peter, Kedron Thomas, and Edward F. Fischer. 2011. "Guatemala's New Violence as Structural Violence: Notes from the Highlands." In *Securing the City. Neoliberalism, Space, and Insecurity in Postwar Guatemala*, edited by Kevin Lewis O'Neill and Kedron Thomas, 127–146, Durham, NC: Duke University Press.

Bird, Annie. February 20, 2013. "Human Rights Abuses Attributed to Military Forces in the Bajo Aguán Valley in Honduras." *Rights Action*. Retrieved on December 1, 2015, from http://rightsaction.org/sites/default/files/Rpt_130220_Aguan_Final .pdf.

Birson, Kurt. September 23, 2010. "Mexico: Abuses against U.S. Bound Migrant Workers." *NACLA*. Retrieved on December 11, 2014, from https://nacla.org/news /mexico-abuses-against-us-bound-migrant-workers.

Bolaños, Rosa M., and Mike Castillo. March 24, 2010. "Conflicto por ingreso de maíz blanco desde México." *Prensa Libre*. Retrieved on July 9, 2012, from www.prensalibre .com/economia/Conflicto-ingreso-maiz-blanco-Mexico_0_230976910.html.

Bourgois, Philippe. 1995. *In Search of Respect: Selling Crack in El Barrio*. Cambridge, UK: Cambridge University Press.

Bradford, Harry. May 24, 2011. "10 Countries with the Worst Income Inequality: OECD." *The Huffington Post*. Retrieved on October 20, 2015 from www.huffington post.com/2011/05/23/10-countries-with-worst-income-inequality_n_865869 .html.

Bradley, Megan. 2013. *Refugee Repatriation: Justice, Responsibility, and Redress*. Cambridge, UK: Cambridge University Press.

Brigden, Noelle. 2016. "Improvised Transnationalism: Clandestine Migration at the Border of Anthropology and International Relations." *International Studies Quarterly* 60(2): 1–12.

Burrell, Jennifer L. 2013. *Maya after War: Conflict, Power, and Politics in Guatemala*. Austin: University of Texas Press.

Burrell, Jennifer L., and Ellen Moodie, eds. 2013. "An Introduction: Ethnographic Visions of Millennial Central America." In *Central America in the New Millennium: Living Transition and Reimagining Democracy*, vol. 102, 1–32. New York and Oxford, UK: Berghahn Books.

Buzan, Barry, Ole Waever, and Jaap de Wilde. 1998. *Security: A New Framework for Analysis*. Boulder, CO, and London: Lynne Rienner Publishers.

Campbell, Howard C. 2009. *Drug War Zone: Frontline Dispatches from the Streets of El Paso and Juárez*. Austin: University of Texas Press.

Camus, Manuela. 2012. "Fronteras, comunidades, indígenas y acumulación de violencias." *Desacatos* 38, enero-abril: –94.

Canales, Alejandro I., Jorge Martínez Pizarro, Leando Reboiras Finardi, and Felipe Rivero Polo. 2010. *Migración y Salud en Zonas Fronterizas: Informe Comparativo sobre Cinco Fronteras Seleccionadas*. Santiago de Chile: Naciones Unidas.

Carey, Elaine, and Andrae Marak. 2011. "Introduction." In *Smugglers, Brothels, and Twine: Historical Perspectives on Contraband and Vice in North America's Borderlands*, edited by Elaine Carey and Andrae M. Marak, 1–9. Tuscon: The University of Arizona Press.

Carlsen, Laura. July 7, 2015. "Deportación, detención ilegal y abusos en la frontera de EEUU con Guatemala." *Programa de las Américas*. Retrieved on December 1, 2015, from www.cipamericas.org/es/archives/15407.

———. May 27, 2014. "Mexico's Oil Privatization: Risky Business." *Foreign Policy in Focus*. Retrieved on October 22, 2015, from http://fpif.org/mexicos-oil-privatization -risky-business/.

———. September 10, 2009. "Plan Puebla-Panamá Advances: New Name, Same Game." *Americas Program*. Retrieved on October 20, 2015, from www.cipamericas .org/archives/1834.

Casillas, Rodolfo R. 2008. "The Routes of Central Americans through Mexico: Characterization, Principal Agents and Complexities." Translated by Ana María D'amore y Marueen Harkins. *Migración y Desarrollo*.10: 141–157.

Castells, Manuel and Alejandro Portes. 1989. "World Underneath: The Origins, Dynamics, and Effects of the Informal Economy." In *The Informal Economy: Studies in Advanced and Less Developed Countries*, edited by Alejandro Portes, Manuel Castells, and Laura Benton, 11–37. Baltimore, MD: Johns Hopkins University Press.

Castillo, Manuel Ángel. April 1, 2006. "Mexico: Caught between the United States and Central America." *Migration Policy Institute*. Retrieved on October 21, 2015, from www.migrationpolicy.org/article/mexico-caught-between-united-states-and -central-america.

Castillo, Manuel Angel, Mónica Toussaint Ribot, and Mario Vázquez Olivera. 2006. *Espacios Diversos, Historia en Común: México, Guatemala y Belice: La Construcción de una Frontera*. México, Frontera Sur: Secretaría de Relaciones Exteriores.

Castillo, Mike. September 7, 2006. "Amenazado por denunciar contraband: Francisco Hidalgo, Alcalde de la Democracia, Huehuetenango. *Prensa Libre*. Retrieved on

May 20, 2009, from www.prensalibre.com/pl/2006/septiembre/07/lectura_dept .html#151072 (link no longer available).

Castro Soto, Gustavo. January 7, 2015. "La Mineria en Chiapas 2015." El Escaramujo No. 49. *Otros Mundos*, A.C/Rema-M4. Chiapas, México: San Cristóbal de las Casas.

Celis, Fernando. 2005. Presentation at the V. Congress of the Mexican Association for Rural Studies, Oaxaca, Mexico.

Centeno, Miguel Angel, and Alejandro Portes. 2006. "The Informal Economy in the Shadow of the State." In *Out of the Shadows: Political Action and the Informal Economy in Latin America*. Edited by Patricia Fernández-Kelly and Jon Shefner, 23–48. University Park: Pennsylvania State University Press.

Centro de Derechos Humanos Fray Bartolomé de las Casas. 2005. "Balance annual 2005 sobre la situación de lo derechos humanos en Chiapas." San Cristóbal de las Casas, Chiapas Mexico: CDHFB.

Chalfin, Brenda. 2010. *Neoliberal Frontiers: An Ethnography of Sovereignty in West Africa*. Chicago: University of Chicago Press.

Los Chapincitos. June 21, 2013. "En Guatemala: Cae Hermano de Jefe Narco que Ordenó la Matanza de 9 Policías." Retrieved on April 19, 2017, from https:// loschapincitos.wordpress.com/2013/07/21/en-guatemala-cae-hermano-de-jefe -narco-que-ordeno-la-matanza-de-9-policias/.

Chávez, Fernando. August 13, 2014. "The Threat of Mexico's Massive Underground Economy." *Worldcrunch*. Retrieved on October 22, 2015, from www.worldcrunch .com/business-finance/the-threat-of-mexico-o-s-massive-undergound-economy /c2s16698/.

Clot, Jean. 2013. "Acercamiento conceptual a las prácticas económicas informales en los pasos fronterizos entre México y Guatemala." *Diacronie. Studi di Storia Contemporanea* 13(1).

Comaroff, Jean, and John Comaroff. 2006. "Law and Disorder in the Postcolony: An Introduction." In *Law and Disorder in the Postcolony*, edited by Jean Comaroff and John Comaroff, 1–6. Chicago: University of Chicago Press.

Comisión Nacional de Salarios Mínimos (CONASAMI). n.d. Retrieved from www .conasami.gob.mx/formatestimonios.aspx?ID=10∫=0 (link no longer available).

Conn, Clayton. August 8, 2014. "Informal Economy Makes up 26% of Mexico's GDP." Telesur.tv.net. Retrieved on October 20, 2015, from www.telesurtv.net/english /news/Informal-Economy-Makes-Up-26-of-Mexicos-GDP-20140808-0044.html.

Consejo de Evaluación de la Política de Desarrollo Social (CONEVAL). July 23, 2015. "CONEVAL Informa los Resultados de la Medición de Pobreza 2014." Dirección de Información y Comunicación Social. Comunicado de Prensa No.005. Retrieved on December 3, 2015, from www.coneval.gob.mx/SalaPrensa/Documents /Comunicado005_Medicion_pobreza_2014.pdf.

Council on Hemispheric Affairs (COHA). June 27, 2011. "Mexican Drug Violence Fueled by U.S. Guns." Retrieved on December 1, 2015, from www.coha.org /mexican-drug-violence-fueled-by-u-s-guns/.

Coutin, Susan Bibler. 2005. "Being En Route." *American Anthropologist* 107(2): 195–206.

Coyoy, Alexander. July 29, 2011 "Aumento en el maíz fomenta contrabando." *Prensa Libre*. Retrieved on July 9, 2012, from www.prensalibre.com.gt/san marcos/Aumento -maiz-fomenta-contrabando 0 508149232.html

Cross, John C. 2011. "Chapter 6: Mexico." In *Media Piracy in Emerging Economies*, edited by Joe Karaganis, 305–326. New York: Social Science Research Council.

———. 1998. *Informal Politics: Street Vendors and the State in Mexico City*. Stanford, CA: Stanford University Press.

Cruz Burguete, José Luis. 1998. *Identidades en Fronteras, Fronteras en Identidades: Elogio a la Intensidad de los Tiempos en los Pueblos de the Frontera Sur*. D.F. Mexico: El Colegio de Mexico.

Cuarto Poder. March 8, 2016. "Exalcalde de Frontera Comalapa no ofrece pruebas." Retrieved on August 31, 2016, from www.cuartopoder.mx/exalcaldedefronter acomalapanoofrecepruebas-152524.html.

Cutts, Marc, ed. 2000. *The State of the World's Refugees: Fifty Years of Humanitarian Action*. United Nations High Commission for Refugees. Oxford, UK: Oxford University Press.

Das, Veena. 2007. *Life and Words: Violence and the Descent into the Ordinary*. Berkeley: University of California Press.

Das, Veena, and Deborah Poole. 2004. "State and its Margins: Comparative Ethnographies." In *Anthropology in the Margins of the State*, edited by Veena Das and Deborah Poole, 3–34. Santa Fe, NM: School of American Research Advanced Seminar Series.

Daugherty, Arron July 20, 2015. "Guatemala's Big Corruption Scandal, Explained." *InSight Crime*. Retrieved on October 21, 2015, from www.insightcrime.org /news-analysis/guatemala-la-linea-customs-scandal-explained.

Davis, Diane. 2012. "Prólogo: Fundamentos analíticos para el estudio de la informalidad: una breve introducción." In *Informalidad, Incertidumbre, Metrópolis y Estado: Como Gobernar la Informalización?*, edited by Felipe de Alba and Frederic Lesemann, 11–37. Mexico: PUEC-UNAM, INRS, Collegium de Lyon (EURIAS).

De Ita, Ana. August 2007. "Fourteen Years of NAFTA and the Tortilla Crisis." *Bilaterals.org*. Retrieved on October 21, 2015, from www.bilaterals.org/?fourteen -years-of-nafta-and-the.

———. 1997. "Impunidad local en el mercado global: Los maiceros entre el filo del gobierno mexicano y el libre comercio." Ponencia presentada en el Congreso de LASA 97, en Guadalajara, México, del 17 al 19 de abril de 1997.

Dent, Alexander S. 2012. "Piracy, Circulatory Legitimacy, and Neoliberal Subjectivity in Brazil." *Cultural Anthropology* 27(1): 28–49.

de Vos, Jan. 2002. "La Frontera Sur y sus Fronteras: Una Visión Histórica." In *Identidades, Migraciones, y Género en la Frontera Sur de México*, edited by Edith F. Kauffer Michel, 49–67. Chiapas, Mexico: ECOSUR.

Díaz, George T. 2015. *Border Contraband: A History of Smuggling across the Rio Grande*. Austin: University of Texas Press.

Díaz, Miguel. 2001. "Mexico: Free Trade Agreements Anyone?" *United States–Mexico Chamber of Commerce. NAFTA Series*. Retrieved on October 21, 2015, from www.usmcoc.org/b-nafta2.php.

Dickens de Girón, Avery. 2011. "The Security Guard Industry in Guatemala: Rural Communities and Urban Violence." In *Securing the City. Neoliberalism, Space, and Insecurity in Postwar Guatemala*, edited by Kevin Lewis O'Neill and Kedron Thomas, 103–126. Durham, NC: Duke University Press.

Donnan, Hastings, and Thomas M. Wilson. 1999. *Borders: Frontiers of Identity, Nation and State*. Oxford, UK: Berg.

Dorset Chiapas Solidarity. April 22, 2016. "Senate Passes Federal Law for Special Economy Zones (SEZ.) Retrieved on April 25, 2017, from https://dorsetchiapas solidarity.wordpress.com/2016/04/22/senate-passes-federal-law-for-special -economic-zones-sez/.

———. January 31, 2015. "Ejidatarios of San Sebastián Bachajón Continue to Defend Their Territory against the Threat of Dispossession from the Government of Chiapas." Retrieved on December 1, 2015, from https://dorsetchiapassolidarity .wordpress.com/2015/01/.

Doyle, Kate. October 10, 2003. "The Tlateloco Massacre: U.S. Documents and the Events of 1968." *The National Security Archive*. Washington DC: The George Washington University. Retrieved on May 3, 2017, from http://nsarchive.gwu.edu /NSAEBB/NSAEBB99/.

Dua, Jatin, and Ken Menkhaus. 2012. "The Context of Contemporary Piracy: The Case of Somalia." *Journal of International Criminal Justice* 10(4): 749–766.

Dudley, Steven. September 16, 2013. "Guatemala's New Narco-Map: Less Zetas, Same Chaos." *InSight Crime*. Retrieved on July 29, 2016, from www.insightcrime.org /news-analysis/guatemalas-new-narco-map-less-zetas-same-chaos.

———. September 8, 2011. "The Zetas in Guatemala." *InSight Crime*. Retrieved on July 29, 2016, from www.insightcrime.org/media/k2/attachments/insight_crime_the _zetas_in_guatemala.pdf.

———. October 2010. "Drug Trafficking Organizations in Central America: *Transportistas*, Mexican Cartels and *Maras*." In *Shared Responsibility: U.S.–Mexico Policy Options for Confronting Organized Crime*, edited by Eric L. Olson, David A. Shirk, and Andrew Selee, 63–94. San Diego: Woodrow Wilson International Center for Scholars, Mexico Institute, Trans-Border Institute, UCSD.

Dugan, Richard. 1997. *Benefit of Location: The National Rationing System and El Paso, Texas, 1942–1945.* Master's thesis, ETD Collection for University of Texas, El Paso.

ECOM Agroindustrial Corp. Ltd Website. Available at www.ecomtrading.com/.

Edelman, Marc. 2005. "Bringing the Moral Economy back in . . . to the Study of 21st Century Transnational Peasant Movements." *American Anthropologist* 107(3): 331–354.

Egan, Brian. 1999. "Somos de la Tierra: Land and the Guatemalan Refugee Return." In *Journeys of Fear: Refugee Return and National Transformation in Guatemala*, edited by Liisa L. North and Alan B. Simmons, 95–111. Montreal, PQ, and Kingston, ON: McGill-Queen's University Press.

Elliot, John H. 1984. "Spain and America in the Sixteenth and Seventeenth Centuries." In *Cambridge History of Latin America. Vol. I*, edited by Leslie Bethell, 287–340. New York: Cambridge University Press.

Encuesta Nacional de Condiciones de Vida (ENCOVI). 2011. Guatemala.

Endres, Kirsten W. 2014. "Making Law: Small_Scale Trade and Corrupt Exceptions at the Vietnam–China Border." *American Anthropologist* 116(3): 611–625.

Escalona Victoria, José Luis. September 2, 2016. Personal Communication.

Fabila Meléndez, Antonio. 2002. "Perspectiva Histórica del Refugio Guatemalteco en México y los Retos para su Integración." In *La Integración de los Exrefugiados Guatemaltecos en México: Una experiencia con rostros múltiples*, edited by Edith F. Kauffer Michel, 21–27. San Cristóbal de las Casas, Chiapas, México: ECOSUR.

Fábregas Puig, Andrés. 1996. "Desde el Sur: Una Revisión del Concepto de Frontera." *Fronteras* 1(1): 10–15.

Fábregas Puig, Andrés, and Ramón González Ponciano. 2014. "The Mexico-Guatemala, Guatemala–Mexico Border: 1983–2013." *Frontera Norte* 26(3): 7–35.

Fairris, David, Gurleen Popli, and Eduadro Zepeda. June 2008. "Minimum Wages and the Wage Structure in Mexico." *Review of Social Economy.* LXVI(2): 181–208.

Fassin, Didier, and Estelle d'Halluin. 2005. "The Truth from the Body: Medical Certificates as Ultimate Evidence for Asylum Seekers." *American Anthropologist* 107(4): 597–608.

Ferguson, James. 2006. *Global Shadows: Africa in the Neoliberal World Order.* Durham, NC: Duke University Press.

Ferme, Mariane C. 2004. "Deterritorialized Citizenship and the Resonances of the Sierra Leonean State." In *Anthropology in the Margins of the State*, edited by Veena Das and Deborah Poole, 81–116. Santa Fe, NM: School of American Research Advanced Seminar Series.

Fernández Casanueva, Carmen. August 2014. Personal communication.

Fernández-Kelly, Patricia, and Douglas S. Massey. 2007. "Borders for Whom? The Role of NAFTA in Mexico–US Migration." *The ANNALS of the American Academy of Political and Social Science* 610(1): 98–118.

Figueroa, Alejandro, Erik Lee, and Rick Van Schoik. 2011. "Realizing the Full Value of Transborder Trade with Mexico." North American Center for Transborder Studies. New Policy Institute. Tempe: Arizona State University.

El Financiero. September 7, 2006. "Frontera Sur, Paraíso del Contrabando." Retrieved on September 8, 2016, from www.sintesiscaaarem.org.mx/COM/SPRENSA.NSF /edd9fcf3e268b3c606256d94006eab12/c4e289a329bbe924862571e200633e85?

Fischer, Edward F., and Peter Blair Benson. 2006. *Broccoli and Desire: Global Connections and Maya Struggles in Postwar Guatemala*. Stanford, CA: Stanford University Press.

Fitting, Elizabeth. 2011. *The Struggle for Maize: Campesinos, Workers, and Transgenic Corn in the Mexican Countryside*. Durham, NC: Duke University Press.

Fitzgerald, David. 2008. *A Nation of Emigrants: How Mexico Manages Its Migration*. Berkeley: University of California Press.

Flores, Nancy. June 20, 2014. "Chiapas: Militarization and Looting Threaten Indigenous." *Chiapas Support Committee*. Retrieved on December 1, 2014, from http:// compamanuel.com/2014/06/20/chiapas-militarization-and-looting-threaten -indigenous/.

Flynn, Donna K. 1997. "'We Are the Border': Identity, Exchange, and the State along the Bénin Nigeria Border." *American Ethnologist* 24(2): 311–330.

Foucault, Michel. 1990. *The History of Sexuality. Volume 1: An Introduction*. New York: Vintage.

Fox, Jonathan. 1994. "The Difficult Transition from Clientelism to Citizenship: Lessons from Mexico." *World Politics* 46(2): 151–184.

Fox, Jonathan, and Libby Haight. 2010. "Preface and Synthesis of Research Findings: Farm Subsidy Policy Trends" and "Mexican Agricultural Policy: Multiple Goals and Conflicting Interests." In *Subsidizing Inequality: Mexican Corn Policy since NAFTA*, edited by Jonathan Fox and Libby Haight, 5–22. Mexico City and Santa Cruz: Woodrow Wilson International Center for Scholars' Mexico Institute, the University of California, Santa Cruz, and Centro de Investigación y Docencia Económicas.

Frank, Dana. March 9, 2015. "Just Like Old Times in Central America: Why the U.S. Needs to Stop Funneling Money to Honduras and Start Treating Its President like the Corrupt Ruler He Really Is." *Foreign Policy*. Retrieved on December 1, 2015, from http://foreignpolicy.com/2015/03/09/just-like-old-times-in-central -america-honduras-juan-orlando-hernandez/.

Freyermuth Enciso, Graciela and Rosalva Aída Hernández Castillo, compil. 1992. *Una Década de Refugio en México: Los Refugiados Guatemaltecos y los Derechos Humanos*. Hidalgo y Matamoros, Tlalpan D.F.: CIESAS.

Friman, H. Richard. 2009a. "Crime and Globalization." In *Crime and the Global Political Economy*, edited by H. Richard Friman, 1–19. Boulder, CO, and London: Lynne Rienner Publishers.

———. 2009b. "Externalizing the Costs of Prohibition." In *Crime and the Global Political Economy*, edited by H. Richard Friman, 49–65. Boulder, CO, and London: Lynne Rienner Publishers.

El Fronterizo. September 4, 2007. "Trafican con gasolina en la zona fronteriza con Guatemala." Comitán de Domínguez, Chiapas, México. Web link no longer available.

Fuentes, López, Mario Roberto, Jacob van Etten, José Luís Vivero Pol, and Álvaro Ortega

Aparicio. 2005. *Maíz para Guatemala, Propuesta para la Reactivación de la Cadena Agroalimenaria de Maíz Blanco y Amarillo*. SERIE "PESA Investigación", no. 1, FAO Guatemala, Guatemala, C.A.

Gaceta Mexicana. April 7, 2016. "Libera al ex president municipal de Frontera Comalapa." Retrieved on August 31, 2016, from www.gacetamexicana.com/libera-al-ex-presidente-municipal-comalapa/.

Gagne, David. June 27, 2016. "Death but No Taxes: How Guatemala's Elite Foster Crime, Impunity." *InSight Crime*. Retrieved on June 29, 2016, from www.insightcrime.org/news-analysis/death-but-no-taxes-how-guatemala-elites-foster-crime-impunity.

Galán, Marcelo. February 28, 2011. "Militares, a cargo de seguridad en 17 entidades." *El Universal*. Retrieved on August 4, 2016, from http://archivo.eluniversal.com.mx/primera/36411.html.

Galemba, Rebecca B. 2014. "Mexico's Border (In)Security." *The Postcolonialist*. 2(2). Retrieved on November 9, 2015 from http://postcolonialist.com/academic-dispatches/mexicos-border-insecurity/.

———. 2013. "Illegality and Invisibility at Margins and Borders." *PoLAR: Political and Legal Anthropology Review* 36(2): 274–285.

———. 2012a. "'Corn Is Food, Not Contraband': The Right to 'Free Trade' at the Mexico Guatemala Border." *American Ethnologist* 39(4): 716–734.

———. 2012b. "Remapping the Border: Taxation, Territory, and (Trans) National Identity at the Mexico–Guatemala Border." *Environment and Planning D: Society and Space* 30(5): 822–841.

———. 2012c. "Taking Contraband Seriously: Practicing 'Legitimate Work' at the Mexico–Guatemala Border." *The Anthropology of Work Review* 33(1): 3–14.

Gallant, Thomas W. 1999. "Brigandage, Piracy, Capitalism, and State-Formation: Transnational Crime from a Historical World-Systems Perspective." In *States and Illegal Practices*, edited by Josiah McC. Heyman, 25–62. Oxford, UK: Berg.

Gandolfo, Daniella. 2009. *The City at Its Limits: Taboo, Transgression, and Urban Renewal in Lima*. Chicago: University of Chicago Press.

García, María Cristina. 2006. *Seeking Refuge: Central American Migration to Mexico, the United States, and Canada*. Berkeley: University of California Press.

García, Mercedes. March 3, 2016. "Alliance for Prosperity in the Northern Triangle: Not a Likely Final Solution for the Central American Migrant Crisis." Washington, DC: Council on Hemispheric Affairs (COHA).

García García, Antonino. 2002. "La Integración de los Refugiados Guatemaltecos en Chiapas." In *La Integración de los Exrefugiados Guatemaltecos en México: Una experiencia con rostros múltiples*, compiled by Edith Michel Kauffer et al., 207–224. San Cristóbal de las Casas, Chiapas: ECOSUR.

Gas Prices Explained. n. d. Retrieved on October 22, 2015 from http://gasprices explained.org/.

Gauthier, Melissa. 2007. "Fayuca Hormiga: The Cross-Border Trade of Used Clothing between the United States and Mexico." In *Borderlands: Comparing Security in North America and Europe*, edited by Emmanuel Brunet-Jailly, 95–116. Ottawa: University of Ottawa Press.

Gibler, John. November 13, 2014. Comments Cited/Interviewed in "Are Mexico's Missing Students the Victims of U.S.-Backed Drug War?" *Democracy Now*. Retrieved on December 1, 2015, from http://www.democracynow.org/2014/11/13/are _mexicos_missing_students_the_victims.

Giugale, Marcelo, Olivier Lafourcade, and Vinh H. Nguyen, eds. 2001. *Mexico, A Comprehensive Development Agenda for the New Era*. Washington, DC: World Bank Publications.

Gledhill, John. 2004. "Corruption as a Mirror of the State in Latin America." In *Between Morality and Law: Corruption, Anthropology and Comparative Society*, edited by Italo Pardo, 155–179. Aldershot, Hampshire, UK: Ashgate.

Godoy, Angelina Snodgrass. 2006. *Popular Injustice: Violence, Community, and Law in Latin America*. Stanford, CA: Stanford University Press.

———. 2004. "When 'Justice' Is Criminal: Lynchings in Contemporary Latin America." *Theory and Society* 33(6): 621–651.

Goldín, Liliana R. 2011. *Global Maya: Work and Ideology in Rural Guatemala*. Tucson: University of Arizona Press.

Goldstein, Daniel M. 2016. *Owners of the Sidewalk: Security and Survival in the Informal City*. Durham, NC: Duke University Press.

———. 2012. *Outlawed: Between Security and Rights in a Bolivian City*. Durham, NC: Duke University Press.

———. 2010. "Toward a Critical Anthropology of Security." *Current Anthropology* 51(4): 487–517.

———. 2005. "Flexible Justice: Neoliberal Violence and Self-Help Security in Bolivia." *Critique of Anthropology* 25(4): 389–411.

———. 2004. *The Spectacular City: Violence and Performance in Urban Bolivia.* Durham, NC: Duke University Press.

Gomberg-Muñoz, Ruth. 2011. *Labor and Legality: An Ethnography of a Mexican Immigrant Network.* Oxford, UK: Oxford University Press.

Gómez, Pedro Joaquin Ortiz Guzmán. 2002. Comité Coordinador de Integración y Desarrollo Comunitario en Chiapas, México (CIDECH), y su Papel en el Proceso de la Integración de los Refugiados Guatemaltecos en Chiapas. In *La Integración de los Exrefugiados Guatemaltecos en México: una experiencia con rostros múltiples,* edited by Edith F. Kauffer Michel, 111–121. San Cristóbal de las Casas, Chiapas: ECOSUR.

González, Elizabeth. February 6, 2015a. "Central America Update: Unpacking $1 Billion in U.S. Assistance to the Northern Triangle." *Council of the Americas.* Retrieved on December 1, 2015, from www.as-coa.org/articles/central-america -update-unpacking-1-billion-us-assistance-northern-triangle.

———. April 2, 2015b. "Weekly Chart: Latin America's Informal Economy." *Council of the Americas.* Retrieved on October 20, 2015, from www.as-coa.org/articles /weekly-chart-latin-americas-informal-economy.

Gonzáles, Mariano. 2011. "Violencia en Guatemala: aproximaciones al panorama estadístico e hipótesis sobre su aumento en postguerra." *Diálogo* 29, Tercera Época. Guatemala: Facultad Latinoamericana de Ciencias Sociales–Guatemala.

Goodale, Mark, and Nancy Postero. 2013. "Revolution and Retrenchment: Illuminating the Present in Latin America." In *Neoliberalism. Interrupted: Social Change and Contested Governance in Contemporary Latin America,* edited by Mark Goodale and Nancy Postero, 1–22. Stanford, CA: Stanford University Press.

Gootenberg, Paul. 2012. "Cocaine's Long March North, 1900–2010." *Latin American Politics and Society* 54(1): 159–180.

———. 2008. *Andean Cocaine: The Making of a Global Drug.* Chapel Hill: University of North Carolina Press.

Gordillo, Gastón. 2006. "The Crucible of Citizenship: ID-paper Fetishism in the Argentine Chaco. *American Ethnologist* 33(2): 162–176.

Grandia, Liza. 2012. *Enclosed: Conservation, Cattle, and Commerce among the Q'eqchi' Maya.* Seattle: University of Washington Press.

Grann, David. April 4, 2011. "A Murder Foretold: Unraveling the Ultimate Political Conspiracy." *The New Yorker.* Retrieved on October 20, 2015, from www .newyorker.com/magazine/2011/04/04/a-murder-foretold.

Grandin, Greg. 2000. *The Blood of Guatemala: A History of Race and Nation*. Durham, NC: Duke University Press.

Grimson, Alejandro. 2002. *El Otro Lado del Río: Periodistas, Nación y Mercosur en la Frontera*. Buenos Aires: Eudeba. University de Buenos Aires.

Grindle, Merilee Serrill. 1996. *Challenging the State: Crisis and Innovation in Latin America and Africa*. Cambridge, UK: Cambridge University Press.

Guatemala Human Rights Commission/USA Fact Sheet. Washington, DC. Retrieved on October 20, 2015, from www.ghrc-usa.org/Publications/factsheet_USassistance_Guatemala.pdf.

Gupta, Akhil, and James Ferguson. 1997. *Culture, Power, Place: Explorations in Critical Anthropology*. Durham, NC: Duke University Press.

Gutmann, Matthew. 2002. *The Romance of Democracy: Compliant Defiance in Contemporary Mexico*. Berkeley: University of California Press.

Guzmán Mérida, Pedro Alberto. 2004. *Olas en la Sierra: Eventos, Casos y Observaciones de Huehuetenango*. Huehuetenango, Guatemala: CEDFOG.

Hale, Charles R. 2006. *Más que un Indio: Racial Ambivalence and Neoliberal Multiculturalism in Guatemala*. Santa Fe, NM: School for Advanced Research Press.

———. 2005. "Neoliberal Multiculturalism: The Remaking of Cultural Rights and Racial Dominance in Central America." *Political and Legal Anthropology Review* 28(1): 10–28.

Hart, Keith. 1973. "Informal Income Opportunities and Urban Employment in Ghana." *Journal of Modern African Studies* 11(1): 61–89.

Harvey, David. 2005. *A Brief History of Neoliberalism*. Oxford, UK: Oxford University Press.

Harvey, Neil. 1998. *The Chiapas Rebellion: The Struggle for Land and Democracy*. Durham, NC: Duke University Press.

Hernández, Luis. 1992. "Maiceros: De la Guerra por los precios al desarrollo rural integral." In *Reestructuración Económica y Subsistencia Rural: El maíz y la crisis de los ochenta*, coordinated by Cynthia de Alcantará, 87-107. México, D.F.: El Colegio de México.

Hernández Castillo, Rosalva Aída. 2012. "Cross_Border Mobility and Transnational Identities: New Border Crossings Amongst Mexican Mam People." *The Journal of Latin American and Caribbean Anthropology* 17(1): 65–87.

———. 2001. *Histories and Stories from Chiapas: Border Identities in Southern Mexico*. Austin: University of Texas Press.

———. 1992. Los Refugiados Guatemaltecos y la Dinámica Fronteriza en Chiapas. In *Una Década de Refugio en México: Los Refugiados Guatemaltecos y los Derechos Humanos*. Compiled by Graciela Freyermuth Enciso and Rosalva Aida Hernandez Castillo, 93-105. Chiapas, México: CIESAS. Instituto Chiapaneco de Cultura.

Henríquez, Elio. April 10, 2016. "Rechazan 60 poblados de Chiapas hidroeléctrica en el río Usumacinta." *La Jornada*. Retrieved on December 7, 2016, from www .jornada.unam.mx/2016/04/10/estados/024n1est.

Hewitt de Alcantará, Cynthia. 1992. "Introducción: Reestructuración económica y subsistencia rural." In *Reestructuración Económica y Subsistencia Rural: El maíz y la crisis de los ochenta.* coordinated by Cynthia de Alcantará, 15–61. México, D.F.: El Colegio de México.

Heyman, Josiah McC. 2013. "The Study of Illegality and Legality: Which Way Forward?" *PoLAR: Political and Legal Anthropology Review* 36(2): 304–307.

———. 1995. "Putting Power in the Anthropology of Bureaucracy: The Immigration and Naturalization Service at the Mexico–United States Border." *Current Anthropology* 36(2): 261–287.

———. 1994. "The Mexico–United States Border in Anthropology: A Critique and Reformulation." *Journal of Political Ecology.* 1(1): 43–66.

Heyman, Josiah McC., and Howard C. Campbell. 2011. "Afterword: Crime on and across Borders." In *Smugglers, Brothels, and Twine: Historical Perspectives on Contraband and Vice in North America's Borderlands*, edited by Elaine Carey and Andrae M. Marak, 177–190. Tuscon: University of Arizona Press.

———. 2007. "Corruption in the U.S. Borderlands with Mexico: The 'Purity' of Society and the 'Perversity' of Borders." In *Corruption and the Secret of Law: A Legal Anthropological Perspective*, edited by Monique Nuijten and Gerhard Anders, 191–218. Aldershot, Hampshire, UK: Ashgate.

Heyman, Josiah McC., and Alan Smart. 1999. "States and Illegal Practices: An Overview." In *States and Illegal Practices*, edited by Josiah McC. Heyman, 1–24, Oxford, UK: Berg.

Hondagneu-Sotelo, Pierrette, and Ernestine Avila. 1997. "'I'm Here, but I'm There': The Meanings of Latina Transnational Motherhood." *Gender & Society* 11(5): 548–571.

Hoyo, Henio. 2016a. "Nationals, but Not Full Citizens: Naturalisation Policies in Mexico." *Migration Letters* 13(1): 100–115.

———. August 18, 2016b. Personal Communication.

———. August 2015. "Report on Citizenship Law: Mexico." EUDO Citizenship Observatory. Robert Schuman Centre for Advanced Studies in collaboration with Edinburgh University Law School. Country Report, RSCAS/EUDO-CIT-CR 2015/2016. San Domenico di Fiesole, Italy: Badia Fiesolana.

Hristoulas, Athanasios. 2003. "Trading Places: Canada, Mexico, and North American Security." In *The Rebordering of North America: Integration and Exclusion in a New Security Context*, edited by Peter Andreas and Thomas J. Biersteker, 24–45. New York and London: Routledge.

Hubbard Urrea, E. 2010. *Nacionalidad, Ciudadanía y Voto en el Extranjero*. Culiacán: Comisión Estatal Electoral Sinaloa.

Hufbauer, Gary Clyde and Gustavo Vega-Cánovas. 2003. "Whither NAFTA? A Common Frontier." In *The Rebordering of North America: Integration and Exclusion in a New Security Context*, edited by Peter Andreas and Thomas J. Biersteker, 128–152, New York and London: Routledge.

Human Rights Watch (HRW). 2015. "World Report 2015: Mexico. Events of 2014." Retrieved on December 1, 2015, from www.hrw.org/world-report/2015/country -chapters/mexico.

Instituto de Investigaciones Económicas y Sociales (IDIES). August. 2012. "Estudio de potencial económico y propuesta de mercado territorial de Huehuetenango," coordinated by María Frausto. Universidad Rafael Landívar. With ONU Mujues and MDGIF-Fondo para el Logro de los ODM, Guatemala. Retrieved on December 3, 2015, from www.url.edu.gt/PortalURL/Archivos/56/Archivos /HUEHUETENANGO%20Estudio%20de%20potencial%20econ%C3%B3mico .pdf.

Immerman, Richard H. 2010. *The CIA in Guatemala: The Foreign Policy of Intervention*. Austin: University of Texas Press.

Index Mundi. 2016. "Mexican Peso to US Dollar Exchange Rate. August 28, 2006– August 19, 2016." New York: United States Federal Reserve Bank of New York. Retrieved on August 24, 2016 from www.indexmundi.com/xrates/graph.aspx?c1 =MXN&c2=USD&days=3650.

Inda, Jonathan Xavier, and Julie A. Dowling. 2013. "Introduction: Governing Migrant Illegality." In *Governing Immigration through Crime: A Reader*, edited by Julie Dowling and Jonathan Inda, 1–36. Stanford, CA: Stanford University Press.

Instituto National de Estadística (INE). November 2013. "Caracterización Departmental de Huehuetenango 2012." Gobierno de Guatemala, 1–76. Retrieved on December 3, 2015, from www.ine.gob.gt/sistema/uploads/2013/12/09/Rg8LuLRvK4e MdsJ1Ox2RArHwzDBRC6YD.pdf.

———. December 2013. "Caracterización Huehuetenango 2012." Gobierno de Guatemala, 3–37. Retrieved on April 8, 2017, from www.ine.gob.gt/sistema/uploads /2013/12/10/c17rorHI84x540Kpu3DPOYlXVfVJ4VLt.pdf.

Instituto Nacional de Estadística y Geografía (INEGI). 2011. "Perspectiva Estadística Chiapas." December 2011. Aguascalientes, México: INEGI.

Instituto Nacional de Estadística y Geografía (INEGI).

———. 2010. "Estados Unidos Mexicanos. Censo de Población y Vivienda 2010. Resultados definitivos. Tabulados básicos. www.inegi.org.mx (4 de marzo de 2011). Aguascalientes, México: INEGI.

Instituto Nacional de Psiquiatría. 2012. Ramón de la Fuente Muñiz; Instituto Nacional de Salud Pública; Secretaría de Salud. Encuesta Nacional de Adicciones

2011: Reporte de Drogas. J. A. Villatoro-Velázquez, M. E. Medina-Mora, C. Fleiz-Bautista, M.M. Téllez-Rojo, L. R. Mendoza-Alvarado, M. Romero-Martínez, J. P. Gutiérrez-Reyes, M. Castro-Tinoco, M. Hernández-Ávila, C. Tena-Tamayo, C. Alvear-Sevilla, and V. Guisa-Cruz. D.F., México: INPRFM; 2012. "Encuesta Nacional de Adicciones 2011" Reporte de Drogas."

Inter-American Commission on Human Rights. December 30, 2013. "Human Rights of Migrants and Other Persons in the Context of Human Mobility in Mexico." *Organization of American States.*

Inter-American Development Bank. September 2014. "Plan of the Alliance for Prosperity in the Northern Triangle: Regional Plan Prepared by El Salvador, Guatemala, and Honduras." Retrieved on December 1, 2015, from http://idbdocs.iadb .org/wsdocs/getdocument.aspx?docnum=39224238.

International Fund for Agricultural Development (IFAD). May 2012. Enabling Poor Rural People to Overcome Poverty in Guatemala. Rome, Italy. Retrieved on April 17, 2017, from www.ifad.org/documents/10180/16e68b93-2e7f-4804-8385 -b8d53d784130.

International Labor Organization (ILO). 2014. "Thematic Labour Overview: Transition to Formality in Latin America and the Caribbean." Regional Office for Latin America and the Caribbean. Retrieved on October 22, 2015, from http:// ilo.org/wcmsp5/groups/public/---americas/---ro-lima/documents/publication /wcms_314469.pdf.

Isacson, Adam, Maureen Meyer, and Gabriela Morales. August 2014. "Mexico's Other Border: Security, Migration, and Humanitarian Crisis at the Line with Central America." Washington, DC: *Washington Office on Latin America*, pp. 2–44.

Isacson, Adam, Maureen Meyer, and Hannah Smith. November 9, 2015. "Increased Enforcement at Mexico's Southern Border: An Update on Security, Migration and U.S. Assistance." *Washington Office on Latin America.* Retrieved on August 8, 2016 from www.wola.org/analysis/new-report-increased-enforcement-at -mexicos-southern-border/.

Itzigsohn, José. 2000. *Developing Poverty: The State, Labor Market Deregulation, and the Informal Economy in Costa Rica and the Dominican Republic.* University Park: Pennsylvania State University Press.

Jaramillo, Velia. June 26, 2001. "Mexico's Southern Plan: The Facts. Crackdown Underway on Migration from Central America." *World Press Review.* Retrieved on December 1, 2015, from www.worldpress.org/0901feature22.htm.

Johnson, Jennifer. January 2008. "The Forgotten Border: Migration & Human Rights at Mexico's Southern Border." Washington, DC: Latin America Working Group Education Fund, 1–24.

Jonas, Susanne. March 27, 2013. "Guatemalan Migration in Times of Civil War and Post-War Challenges." *Migration Policy Institute.* Retrieved on November 18,

2015, from www.migrationpolicy.org/article/guatemalan-migration-times-civil-war-and-post-war-challenges.

Jusionyte, Ieva. 2015. *Savage Frontier: Making News and Security on the Argentine Border*. Berkeley: University of California Press.

———. 2013. "On and off the Record: The production of legitimacy in an Argentine border town." *PoLAR: Political and Legal Anthropology Review* 36(2): 231–248.

Kar, Dev. 2012. "Mexico: Illicit Financial Flows, Macroeconomic Imbalances, and the Underground Economy," 1–81. Washington DC: Global Financial Integrity (GFI). A Program of the Center for International Policy.

Karibo, Holly. 2011. "Detroit's Border Brothel: Sex Tourism in Windsor, Ontario, 1945–1960." In *Smugglers, Brothels, and Twine: Historical Perspectives on Contraband and Vice in North America's Borderlands*, edited by Elaine Carey and Andrae M. Marak, 83–100. Tuscon: University of Arizona Press.

Kauffer, Edith F. Michel. 2002. "Introducción." In *La Integración de los Exrefugiados Guatemaltecos en México: Una experiencia con rostros múltiples*, edited by Edith F. Kauffer Michel, 13–18. San Cristóbal de las Casas, Chiapas, México: ECOSUR.

Kauffer, Edith F. Michel, and Juan Carlos Velasco Santos. 2002. *En el Camino de la Integración: Exrefugiados y Mexicanos en Chiapas*. San Cristóbal de las Casas, Chiapas, México: ECOSUR.

Kelly, Patty. 2008. *Lydia's Open Door: Inside Mexico's Most Modern Brothel*. Berkeley: University of California Press.

Kelly, Tobias. 2006. "Documented Lives: Fear and Uncertainties of law during the Second Palestinian Intifada." *The Journal of the Royal Anthropological Institute* 12(1): 89–107.

King, Amanda. 2006. "Ten Years with NAFTA: A Review of the Literature and an Analysis of Farmer Responses in Sonora and Veracruz." CIMMYT Special Report 06-01. Mexico, D.F.: CIMMYT/Congressional Hunger Center.

Knight, Alan. 1986. *The Mexican Revolution*, vol. I.. Cambridge, UK: Cambridge University Press.

Kovic, Christine. 2008. "Jumping from a Moving Train: Risk, Migration and Rights at NAFTA's Southern Border." *Practicing Anthropology* 30(2): 32–36.

Lakhani, Nina. April 4, 2016. "Mexico Tortures Migrants—and Citizens—in Effort to Slow Central American Surge. *The Guardian*. Retrieved on June 13, 2016, from www.theguardian.com/world/2016/apr/04/mexico-torture-migrants-citizens-central-america.

———. February 4, 2015. "Mexico Deports Record Numbers of Women and Children in US_Driven effort." *The Guardian*. Retrieved on December 1, 2015, from www.theguardian.com/world/2015/feb/04/mexico-deports-record-numbers-women-children-central-america.

———. February 19, 2014. "Claudia Paz y Paz Ousting Puts Spotlight on Guatemalan Justice System." *The Guardian*. Retrieved on April 17, 2017, from www .theguardian.com/global-development/poverty-matters/2014/feb/19/claudia -paz-y-paz-guatemala-justice-system.

Latino News. December 1, 2012. "Información Valiosa sobre la 'Nueva Cédula de Guatemala.'" *Latino Alabama/Tennessee*. Retrieved on August 2, 2016, from www .latino-news.com/informacion-valiosa-sobre-la-nueva-cedula-de-guatemala/.

Le Clercq Ortega, Juan Antonio, Gerardo Rodíguez, and Sánchez Lara, coordinators. February 2016. "Índice Global de Impunidad México IGI-MEX 2016." *Centro de Estudios Sobre Impunidad (CESIJ)*. Puebla, México: Universidad de las Américas Puebla.

Lewis, Stephen E. 2005. *The Ambivalent Revolution: Forging State and Nation in Chiapas, 1910–1945*. Albuquerque: University of New Mexico Press.

Little, Walter E. 2013. "Maya Handicraft Vendors' CAFTA Discourses, 'Free Trade Is Not For Everyone in Guatemala.'" In *Central America in the New Millennium: Living Transition and Reimagining Democracy*, edited by Jennifer L. Burrell and Ellen Moodie, 181–195. Oxford, UK, and London: Berghahn Books.

Little-Siebold, Christa. 2001. "Beyond the Indian-Ladino Dichotomy: Contested Identities, Ethnicities, Class and the Emergent National State." *Journal of Latin American Anthropology* 6(2): 176–197.

Lohmuller, Michael. March 5, 2016. "CentAm Still Dominant Cocaine Route into US: State Dept." *InSight Crime*. Retrieve on April 17, 2017, from www .insightcrime.org/news-analysis/central-america-still-dominant-cocaine-route -us-state-department-report.

Lomnitz, Claudio. 1995. "Ritual, Rumor and Corruption in the Constitution of Polity in Mexico." *Journal of Latin American Anthropology* 1(1): 20–24.

López, Julie. July 18, 2013. "Guatemala: la cambiante cara del narco." *Plaza Pública*. Retrieved on July 29, 2016, from www.plazapublica.com.gt/content/guatemala-la -cambiante-cara-del-narco.

Ludy, Virgina Molina. 1998. "Migración, Historia e Identidad. El Caso de los Guatemaltecos en Chiapas." In *Diversidad Etnica y Conflicto en América Latina. Vol. III: Migración y Etnicidad: Reflexiones Teóricas y Estudios de Caso*, coordinated by Raquel Barcelo and Martha Judith Sanchez, 201–216. D.F., México: UNAM, Instituto de Investigaciones Sociales.

MacGaffey, Janet, and Rémy Bazenguissa-Ganga. 2000. *Congo-Paris: Transnational Traders on the Margins of the Law*. Bloomington: Indiana University Press.

Main, Alexander. February 27, 2015. "Will Biden's Billion Dollar Plan Help Central America?" *NACLA*. Retrieved on December 1, 2015, from https://nacla.org /news/2015/02/27/will-biden's-billion-dollar-plan-help-central-america.

Malkin, Victoria. 2001. "Narcotrafficking, Migration, and Modernity in Rural Mexico." *Latin American Perspectives* 28(4): 101–128.

Manz, Beatriz. 2004. *Paradise in Ashes: A Guatemalan Journey of Courage, Terror, and Hope*. Berkeley: University of California Press.

———. 1988. *Refugees of a Hidden War: The Aftermath of Counter-Insurgency in Guatemala*. Albany: State University of New York Press.

Martín Pérez, Fredy. February 2006. "Las pistas del narco." *Contralínea*. Retrieved on October 21, 2015, from http://chiapas.contralinea.com.mx/archivo/2006/febrero /htm/LasPistasNarco.htm.

Martínez, Oscar J. 1994. *Border People: Life and Society in the U.S.–Mexico Borderlands*. Tucson: University of Arizona Press.

Marx, Karl. 1990 [1867]. "The Fetishism of the Commodity and Its Secret." *Capital: A Critique of Political Economy*, Vol. 1, 163-177, translated by Ben Fowkes. London: Penguin.

Mathews, Gordon, and Carlos Alba Vega. 2012. "Introduction: What Is Globalization from Below?" In *Globalization from Below: The World's Other Economy*, edited by Gordon Mathews, Gustavo Lins Ribeiro, and Carlos Alba Vega, 1–16. London and New York: Routledge.

McCune, Nils Max, Francisco Guevara-Hernández, Jose Nahed-Toral, Paula Mendoza-Nazar, Jesus Ovando-Cruz, Benigno Ruiz-Sesma, and Leopoldo Medina-Sanson. 2012. "Social-Ecological Resilience and Maize Farming in Chiapas, Mexico." In *Sustainable Development-Authoritative and Leading Edge Content for Environmental Management*, edited by Sime Curkovic, 485–512. Rijeka, Croatia: INTECH.

McMurray, David. 2001. *In and Out of Morocco: Smuggling and Migration in a Frontier Boomtown*. Minneapolis: University of Minnesota Press.

Meagher, Kate. 2014. "Smuggling Ideologies: from Criminalization to Hybrid Governance in African Clandestine Economies." *African Affairs* 113(453): 497–517.

Melgar, Lourdes. Summer 2012. "The Future of PEMEX." *Americas Quarterly*. Retrieved on August 5, 2016, from www.americasquarterly.org/node/3781.

Merry, Sally Engle. 2006. "Transnational Human Rights and Local Activism: Mapping the Middle." *American Anthropologist* 108(1): 38–51.

The Mesoamerican Working Group (MAWG). November, 2013. "Rethinking the Drug War in Central America and Mexico." Retrieved on December 11, 2014, from www.ghrc-usa.org/wp-content/uploads/2013/12/Mesoamerica-Working-Group _Rethinking-Drug-War-Web-Version.pdf.

Millar, Kathleen. 2014. "The Precarious Present: Wageless Labor and Disrupted Life in Rio de Janeiro, Brazil." *Cultural Anthropology* 29(1): 32–53.

Ministerio de la Economía (MINECO). February 9, 2011. *Comunicado: Se autoriza la importación de contingentes de harina de trigo y maíz blanco.* Guatemala City: MINECO

Mitchell, Timothy. 1999. "Society, Economy, and the State Effect." In *State/Culture: State-Formation after the Cultural Turn,* edited by George Steinmetz, 7–97. Ithaca, NY, and London: Cornell University Press.

Molyneux, Maxine. 2006. "Mothers at the Service of the New Poverty Agenda: Progresa/Oportunidades, Mexico's Conditional Transfer Programme." *Social Policy & Administration* 40(4): 425–449.

Montejo, Victor. 1999. *Voices from Exile: Violence and Survival in Modern Maya History.* Norman: University of Oklahoma Press.

Morales, Isidro. 1999. "NAFTA: The Institutionalisation of Economic Openness and the Configuration of Mexican Geo-Economic Spaces." *Third World Quarterly* 20(5): 971–993.

Muciño, Francisco. July 10, 2014. "SAT invertirá 9,300 mdp para modernizer aduanas." Forbes, México. *Forbes.* Retrieved on October 21, 2015, from www.forbes.com.mx/sat-invertira-9300-mdp-para-modernizar-aduanas/.

Muehlmann, Shaylih. 2014. *When I Wear My Alligator Boots: Narco-Culture in the U.S.–Mexico Borderlands.* Berkeley: University of California Press.

Nadal, Alejandro. 2000. "The Environmental and Social Impacts of Economic Liberalization on Corn Production in Mexico." Oxford, UK: Oxfam-GB-WWF-International.

Navarro, Luis Hernández. December 15, 2004. "To Die a Little: Migration and Coffee in Mexico and Central America." *Counterpunch.* Retrieved on December 1, 2015, from www.counterpunch.org/2004/12/15/migration-and-coffee-in-mexico-and-central-america/.

Nazario, Sonia. 2014. *Enrique's Journey.* New York: Random House.

Naím, Moises. 2005. *Illicit: How Smugglers, Traffickers, and Copycats Are Hijacking the Global Economy.* New York: Anchor Books and Random House.

Nash, June. 2001. *Mayan Visions: The Quest for Autonomy in an Age of Globalization.* New York: Routledge.

Naylor, R. T. 2002. *Wages of Crime: Black Markets, Illegal Finance, and the Underworld Economy.* Ithaca, NY, and London: Cornell University Press.

Nevins, Joseph. 2014. "Policing the Workplace and Rebuilding the State in 'America's Finest City': US Immigration Control in the San Diego, California–Mexico Borderlands." *Global Society* 28(4): 462–482.

———. 2002. *Operation Gatekeeper: The Rise of the "Illegal Alien" and the Making of the U.S.–Mexico Boundary.* New York: Routledge.

Nolan-Ferrell, Catherine. 2005. "El desarrollo de una región sin una identidad nacional: La Zona del Soconusco, Chiapas, 1880–1920." In *Chiapas: De la Independencia a La Revolución*, rdited by Mercedes Olivera and María Dolores Palomo, 301–312. México, D.F. and Tuxtla Gutiérrez, Chiapas: Centro de Investigaciones y Estudios Superiores an Antropología Social (CIESAS) y Consejo de Ciencia y Technología del Estado de Chiapas (COCyTECH).

Nolin, Catherine, and Jaqui Stephens. 2010. "'We Have to Protect the Investors': Development & Canadian Mining Companies in Guatemala." *Journal of Rural and Community Development* 5(3): 37–70.

Nolin Hanlon, Catherine. 1999. "Guatemalan Refugees and Returnees: Place and Maya Identity." In *Journeys of Fear: Refugee Return and National Transformation in Guatemala*, edited by Liisa North and Alan B. Simmons, 213–236. Montreal, PQ, and Kingston, ON: McGill-Queen's University Press.

Nordstrom, Carolyn. 2007. *Global Outlaws: Crime, Money, and Power in the Contemporary World*. Berkeley: University of California Press.

Nugent, David, and Ana María Alonso. 1994. "Multiple Selective Traditions in Agrarian Struggle: Popular Culture and State Formation in the *Ejido* of Namiquipa, Chihuahua." In *Everyday Forms of State Formation: Revolution and the Negotiation of Rule in Modern Mexico*, edited by Gilbert M. Joseph and Daniel Nugent, 209–246. Durham, NC: Duke University Press.

Nuijten, Monique. 2003. *Power, Community, and the State: The Political Anthropology of Organization in Mexico*. London, UK: Pluto Press.

Objective Corporate Research (OCR). May 12, 2006. Taghmen Energy (TAG). An Exposure to Oil Exploration and Production in Colombia and Guatemala. Sam Kiri, analyst. London: Objective Capital Limited: 1–40.

Ogren, Cassandra. 2007. "Migration and Human Rights on the Mexico–Guatemala Border." *International Migration* 45(4): 203–243.

Okeowo, Alexis. January 24, 2017. "The Gas-Price Protests Gripping Mexico." *The New Yorker*. Retrieved on April 19, 2017, from www.newyorker.com/news/daily-comment/the-gas-price-protests-gripping-mexico.

Olson, Eric L., David A. Shirk, and Andrew Selee. October 2010. "Introduction." In *Shared Responsibility: U.S.–Mexico Policy Options for Confronting Organized Crime*, edited by Eric L. Olson, David A. Shirk, and Andrew Selee, 1–30. San Diego, CA: Woodrow Wilson International Center for Scholars, Mexico Institute, Trans-Border Institute, UCSD.

Ong, Aiwha. 2006. *Neoliberalism as Exception: Mutations in Citizenship and Sovereignty*. Durham, NC: Duke University Press.

El Orbe. April 1, 2015. "Imparable el Contrabando en la Frontera Sur." Retrieved on August 8, 2016, from http://elorbe.com/portada/2015/04/01/imparable-el-contrabando-en-la-frontera-sur-2.html.

Osburg, John. 2013. "Meeting the 'Godfather': Fieldwork and Ethnographic Seduction in a Chinese Nightclub." *PoLAR: Political and Legal Anthropology Review* 36(2): 298–303.

Otros Mundos. January 18, 2017. Maps shared from organizers.

Paley, Dawn. 2014. *Drug War Capitalism*. Oakland, CA: AK Press.

Peláez-Herreros, Óscar. 2012. "Análisis de los Indicadores de Desarrollo Humano, Marginación, Rezago Social y Pobreza en los Municipios de Chiapas a Partir de una Perspectiva Demográfica." *Economía, sociedad y territorio* 12(38): 181–213.

Penglase, Ben. 2011. "Lost Bullets: Fetishes of Urban Violence in Rio de Janeiro, Brazil." *Anthropological Quarterly.* 84(2): 411–438.

———. 2009. "States of Insecurity: Everyday Emergencies, Public Secrets, and Drug Trafficker Power in a Brazilian Favela." *PoLAR: Political and Legal Anthropology Review* 32(1): 47–63.

People's World. February 9, 2007. "Mexico's Tortilla Crisis: Harvest of NAFTA." Retrieved on October 21, 2015, from http://peoplesworld.org/mexico-s-tortilla-crisis-harvest-of-nafta.

Pérez Grovas, Victor, Edith Cervantes, John Burstein, Laura Carlsen, and Luis Hernández. 2002. *El Café en México, Centroamérica y el Caribe: Una Salida Sustentable a la Crisis.* Mexico City: Coordinadora de Pequeños Productores de Café de Chiapas/Coordinadora Nacional de Organizaciones Cafetaleras.

Pérez Ruiz, Maya Lorena. 2004. "Cerco Antizapatista y Lucha por la Tierra en Chiapas: El Caso de CEOIC." In *Tejiendo Historias: Tierra, Género y Poder en Chiapas,* edited by Maya Lorena Pérez Ruiz, 31–70. D.F., México: Conaculta-INAH.

Perret, Antoine. 2012. "Privatization of the War on Drugs in Mexico and Colombia." *Interdisciplinary Journal of Human Rights Law* 7(1): 45–67.

Pickard, Miguel. August 24, 2005. "Trinational Elites Map North American Future in 'NAFTA Plus.'" Americas Program. *Americas Program.* Silver City, NM: International Relations Center.

———. March 1, 2003. "Grassroots Protests Force the Mexican Government to Search for a New PPP Strategy." *Americas Program Policy Report.* Silver City, NM: Interhemispheric Resource Center.

———. September 19, 2002. "PPP: Plan Puebla-Panamá, or Private Plans for Profit?" CorpWatch. Retrieved on December 1, 2015, from www.corpwatch.org/article.php?id=3953.

Plante, Michael D., and Amy Jordan. 2013. "Getting Prices Right: Addressing Mexico's History of Fuel Subsidies." *Southwest Economy. Federal Reserve Bank of Dallas.* Third Quarterly: 10–13.

La Prensa Libre. December 2, 2008. "Pobladores de Agua Zarca prefieren callar." Retrieved in May 2009 from www.prensalibre.com/pl/2008/diciembre/02/280467.html (page no longer available).

Preston, Julia. January 8, 1998. "Mexican Governor Resigns in Aftermath of Indians' Massacre." *The New York Times.* Retrieved on October 21, 2015, from www.nytimes.com/1998/01/08/world/mexican-governor-resigns-in-aftermath-of-indians-massacre.html.

Quiminet.com. September 7, 2006. "Frontera Sur. Paraiso del Contrabando." Retrieved on October 22, 2015, from www.quiminet.com/noticias/frontera-sur-paraiso-del-contrabando-2275020.htm.

Quinto, Ricardo. May 24, 2007. "Los Precios de Combustible Llegaron a su Nivel Más Alto de la Historia de Guatemala." *El Periódico.* Retrieved in May 2009 from www.elperiodico.com.gt/es/20070524/actualidad/39945 (site no longer available).

Radio en Linea. February 8, 2011. Emisoras Unidas 89.7. "Manifestantes bloquean rutas de Huehuetenango por controles de maíz de contrabando." With information from Mike Castillo. Retrieved on July 9, 2012, from http://noticias.emisorasunidas.com/noticias/nacionales/manifestantes-bloquean-rutas-de-huehuetanango-por-controles-al-maiz-de-contraban.

Recinos, Adrián. 1991. Translated into English by Delia Goetz and Sylvanus G. Morley. *Popol Vuh: The Sacred Book of the Ancient Quiché Maya.* Norman: University of Oklahoma Press.

Reeves, Benjamin. March 11, 2014. "Attorney General Out in May, Says Guatemalan Court." *The Tico Times News.* Retrieved on October 20, 2015, from www.ticotimes.net/2014/03/11/attorney-general-out-in-may-says-guatemala-court.

Reeves, Madeleine. 2014. *Border Work: Spatial Lives of the State in Rural Central Asia.* Ithaca, NY: Cornell University Press.

———. 2013. "Clean Fake: Authenticating Documents and Persons in Migrant Moscow." *American Ethnologist* 40(3): 508–524.

Renard, Marie Christine. 2011. "Free Trade of Coffee, Exodus of Coffee Workers: The Case of the Southern Mexican Border Region of the State of Chiapas." In *Research in Global Sociology and Development: Globalization and the Time–Space Reorganization: Capital Mobility in Agriculture and Food in the Americas, Vol. 17,* edited by Alessandro Bonanno, Josefa Salete Barbosa, and Terry Marsden, 147–165. Somerville, MA, and Bingley, West Yorkshire, UK: Emerald Group Publishing Limited.

Ribeiro, Gustavo Lins. 2012. "Conclusion: Globalization from Below and the Non-Hegemonic World-System." In *Globalization from Below: The World's Other Economy,* edited by Gordon Mathews, Gustavo Lins Ribeiro, and Carlos Alba Vega, 221–235. London and New York: Routledge.

———. 2006. "Economic Globalization from Below." *Etnográfica* 10(2): 233–249.

Robben, Antonius. 1996. "Ethnographic Seduction, Transference, and Resistance Dialogues about Terror and Violence in Argentina." *Ethos* 24(1): 71–106.

Roitman, Janet. 2006. "The Ethics of Illegality in the Chad Basin." In *Law and Disorder in the Postcolony*, edited by Jean Comaroff and John Comaroff, 247–272. Chicago: University of Chicago Press.

———. 2005. *Fiscal Disobedience: An Anthropology of Economic Regulation in Central Africa*. Princeton, NJ: Princeton University Press.

Rosaldo, Renato. 2001. "Foreword." In *Histories and Stories from Chiapas: Border Identities in Southern Mexico*, edited by Rosalva Aída Hernández Castillo, ix–xi. Austin: University of Texas Press.

———. 1993 [1989]. *Culture and Truth: The Remaking of Social Analysis*, with a new Introduction. Boston: Beacon Press.

Rosas, Gilberto. 2012. *Barrio Libre: Criminalizing States and Delinquent Refusals of the New Frontier*. Durham, NC: Duke University Press.

———. 2006. "The Thickening Borderlands Diffused Exceptionality and 'Immigrant' Social Struggles during the 'War on Terror.'" *Cultural Dynamics* 18(3): 335–349.

Rousseau, Cecile, María Morales, and Patricia Foxen 2001. "Going Home: Giving Voice to Memory: Strategies of Young Mayan Refugees Who Returned to Guatemala as a Community." *Culture, Medicine, and Psychiatry* 25(2): 135–168.

Rus, Jan. 1994. "The 'Comunidad Revolucionaria Institucional': The Subversion of Native Government in Highland Chiapas, 1936–1968." In *Everyday Forms of State Formation: Revolution and the Negotiation of Rule in Modern Mexico*, edited by Gilbert M. Joseph and Daniel Nugent, 265–300. Durham, NC: Duke University Press.

Rus, Jan, Aída Hernández Castillo, and Shannon L. Mattiace, eds. 2003. *Mayan Lives, Mayan Utopias: The Indigenous Peoples of Chiapas and the Zapatista Rebellion*. Lanham, MD: Rowman and Littlefield Publishers.

Rus, Jan, and Diego Vigil. 2007. "Rapid Urbanization and Migrant Indigenous Youth in San Cristóbal, Chiapas, Mexico." In *Gangs in the Global City: Alternatives to Traditional Criminology*, edited by John Hagedorn, 152–184. Urbana: University of Illinois.

Sabet, Daniel M. 2015. "Informality, Illegality, and Criminality in Mexico's Border Communities." *Journal of Borderland Studies* 30(4): 505–517.

———. 2012. *Police Reform in Mexico: Informal Politics and the Challenge of Institutional Change*. Stanford, CA: Stanford University Press.

———. October 2010. "Police Reform in Mexico: Advances and Persistent Obstacles." In *Shared Responsibility: U.S.–Mexico Policy Options for Confronting Organized Crime*, edited by Eric L. Olson, David A. Shirk, and Andrew Selee, 247–270. San Diego: Woodrow Wilson International Center for Scholars, Mexico Institute, Trans-Border Institute, UCSD.

Sack, Robert David. 1986. *Human Territoriality: Its Theory and History*. Cambridge, UK: Cambridge University Press.

Sahlins, Peter. 1989. *Boundaries: The Making of France and Spain in the Pyrenees.* Berkeley: University of California Press.

Sánchez, Gabriella. June 2014. "Contextualizing the Discourse of Unaccompanied Minors: Postcards from the Frontlines." *Anthropology News: Postcards from the Frontlines* 55(6): 10.

Sandoval Palacios, Juan Manuel. 2006. "Migración y seguridad nacional en las fronteras norte y sur de México." In *Geoeconomía y geopolítica en el área del Plan Puebla-Panamá*, edited by Daniel Villafuerte Solís and Xochitl Leyva Solano, 237–264. D.F., México: CIESAS.

Sarazua, Juan Carlos. March 2016. "Informe sobre la Ciudadanía Guatemala." EUDO Citizenship Observatory. Robert Schuman Centre for Advanced Studies in collaboration with Edinburgh University Law School. Country Report, RSCAS/EUDO-CIT-CR 2016/2. San Domenico di Fiesole, Italy: Badia Fiesolana.

Schirmer, Jennifer G. 1998. *The Guatemalan Military Project: A Violence Called Democracy.* Philadelphia: University of Pennsylvania Press.

Schlesinger, Stephen, and Stephen Kinzer. 1999. *Bitter Fruit: The Story of an American Coup in Guatemala.* Cambridge, MA: Harvard University Press.

Schneider, Aaron. 2012. *State-Building and Tax Regimes in Central America.* New York: Cambridge University Press.

Schneider, Jane, and Peter Schneider. 2008. "The Anthropology of Crime and Criminalization." *Annual Review of Anthropology* 37: 351–373.

Scott, James C. 2009. *The Art of Not Being Governed: An Anarchist History of Upland Southeast Asia.* New Haven, CT: Yale University Press.

———. 1998. *Seeing Like a State: How Certain Schemes to Improve the Human Condition Have Failed.* New Haven, CT: Yale University Press.

———. 1985. *Weapons of the Weak: Everyday Forms of Peasant Resistance.* New Haven, CT: Yale University Press.

———. 1976. *The Moral Economy of the Peasant: Rebellion and Subsistence in Southeast Asia.* New Haven, CT: Yale University Press.

Secretaría de Agricultura y Recursos Hidráulicos and Comisión Económica para América Latina y el Caribe (SARH-CEPAL). 1992. Primer informe nacional sobre tipología de productores del sector social. México: Subsecretaría de Política Social y Concertación and SARH.

Secretaría de Desarrollo Social (SEDESOL,). CONEVAL. 2014. Informe Annual Sobre la Situación de Pobreza y Rezago Social. Frontera Comalapa, Chiapas. Retrieved on December 3, 2015, from www.sedesol.gob.mx/work/models/SEDESOL/Informes_pobreza/2014/Municipios/Chiapas/Chiapas_034.pdf.

———. 2013. Catálogo de Localidades. Unidad de Microregiones. Dirección General Ajunta de Planeación Microregional. Retrieved on December 3, 2015, from www

.microrregiones.gob.mx/catloc/LocdeMun.aspx?tipo=clave&campo=loc&ent=07 &mun=034.

Secretaría de Economía. June 1, 2016. "Inversión Extranjera Directa en México y en el Mundo. Carpeta de Información Estadística." DGIE-Dirección General de Inversión Extranjera. Retrieved on March 8, 2017, from www.gob.mx/cms/uploads /attachment/file/99366/Carpeta_IED_2015_0601.pdf.

Secretaría de Salud. 2009. "Consejo Nacional contra las Adicciones." Instituto Nacional de Psiquiatría Ramón de la Fuente, Instituto Nacional de Salud Pública. *Publicación Especial. Encuesta Nacional de Adicciones.* Reporte de Resultados Nacionales.

Secretaría de Seguridad y Protección Ciudadana. May 27, 2015. Fronteriza. Gobierno de Estado de Chiapas. Available at https://sspc.chiapas.gob.mx/Secciones/fronteriza.

Seelke, Clare Ribando. March 9, 2016. "Mexico's Recent Immigration Enforcement Efforts." *Congressional Research Service: In Focus.*

Seelke, Clare Ribando, and Kristin Finklea. January 18, 2017. "U.S.-Mexican Security Cooperation: The Mérida Initiative and Beyond. *Congressional Research Service.* CRS Report for Congress. R41349. Washington, DC.

Sieder, Rachel. 2002. "Recognizing Indigenous Law and the Politics of State Formation in Mesoamerica." In *Multiculturalism in Latin America: Rights, Diversity, and Democracy,* edited by Rachel Sieder, 184–207. New York: Palgrave Macmillan.

SIPAZ. August 2001. "UPDATE: Indigenous Rights Law, A New Obstacle to the Peace Process in Chiapas." Vol. VI, no. 3. Retrieved on April 17, 2017, from www .sipaz.org/update-indigenous-rights-law-a-new-obstacle-to-the-peace-process-in -chiapas/?lang=en.

Slack, Jeremy, and Scott Whiteford. 2011. "Violence and Migration on the Arizona–Sonora Border." *Human Organization.* 70(1): 11–21.

Sluka, Jeffrey. 2000. "Introduction: State Terror and Anthropology." In *Death Squad: The Anthropology of State Terror,* edited by Jeffrey A. Sluka, 1–45. Philadelphia: University of Pennsylvania Press.

Smart, Alan. 1999. "Predatory Rule and Illegal Economic Practices." In *States and Illegal Practices,* edited by Josiah McC. Heyman, 99–128. Oxford, UK: Berg.

Smith, Carol A. 1990. *Guatemalan Indians and the State: 1540–1988,* 99–128. Austin: University of Texas Press.

Snyder, Richard, and Angelica Duran-Martinez. 2009. "Does Illegality Breed Violence? Drug Trafficking and State-Sponsored Protection Rackets." *Crime, Law and Social Change* 52(3): 253–273.

Sorrentino, Joseph. June 20, 2015. "Cómo Estados Unidos "Resolvió" La Crisis de Migración Centroamerica." *La Jornada del Campo.* 93. Retrieved on December 1, 2015, from www.jornada.unam.mx/2015/06/20/cam-crisis.html. Originally published in *In These Times.*

Staudt, Kathleen A. 2001. "Informality Knows No Borders: Perspectives from El Paso–Juárez." *SAIS Review* 21(1): 123–130.

———. 1998. *Free Trade? Informal Economies at the US–Mexico Border.* Philadelphia: Temple University Press.

Stephen, Lynn. 1999. "The Construction of Indigenous Suspects: Militarization and the Gendered and Ethnic Dynamics of Human Rights Abuses in Southern Mexico." *American Ethnologist* 26(4): 822–842.

Superintendencia de Administración Tributaria (SAT). July 2015. "Arancel Centroamericano de Importación." Retrieved on July 27, 2016, from http://portal.sat .gob.gt/sitio/index.php/tramites-o-gestiones/aduanas/para-importar.html.

Swords, Alicia. 2010. "Teaching Against Neoliberalism in Chiapas, Mexico: Gendered Resistance via Neo-Zapatista Network Politics." In *Contesting Development: Critical Struggles for Social Change*, edited by Philip McMichael, 116–131. New York and London: Routledge Press.

Taussig, Michael. 2003. *Law in a Lawless Land.* Chicago: University of Chicago Press.

———. 1998. "Transgression." In *Critical Terms for Religious Studies*, edited by Marc C. Taylor, 349–364. Chicago: University of Chicago Press.

———. 1997. *The Magic of the State.* New York and London: Routledge.

Tenuto-Sánchez, Mary Ann. March 25, 2014. "The Plan Puebla-Panamá Is Changing Chiapas." *Chiapas Support Committee.* Retrieved on October 20, 2015, from http:// compamanuel.com/2014/03/25/the-plan-puebla-panama-is-changing-chiapas/.

Thomas, Kedron. 2013. "Brand 'Piracy' and Postwar Statecraft in Guatemala." *Cultural Anthropology* 28(1): 144–160.

———. 2011. "Spaces of Structural Adjustment in Guatemala's Apparel Industry." In *Securing the City. Neoliberalism, Space, and Insecurity in Postwar Guatemala*, edited by Kevin Lewis O'Neill and Kedron Thomas, 147–164. Durham, NC: Duke University Press.

Thomas, Kedron, and Rebecca B. Galemba. 2013. "Illegal Anthropology: An Introduction." *PoLAR: Political and Legal Anthropology Review* 36(2): 211–214.

Thomas, Kedron, Kevin Lewis O'Neill, and Thomas Offit. 2011. "Securing the City: An Introduction." In *Securing the City. Neoliberalism, Space, and Insecurity in Postwar Guatemala*, edited by Kevin Lewis O'Neill and Kedron Thomas, 1–24. Durham, NC: Duke University Press.

The Tico Times. March 18, 2014. "Guatemala ex-President Alfonso Portillo Pleads Guilty Money Laundering Conspiracy Charges in New York." *AFP: The Tico Times.* Retrieved on December 1, 2015, from www.ticotimes.net/2014/03/18 /guatemala-ex-president-alfonso-portillo-pleads-guilty-to-money-laundering -conspiracy-charges-in-new-york.

Tourliere, Mathieu. July 29, 2015. "Policía Federal, la institución que más roba y extorsiona a migrantes: Redodem." *El Proceso*. Retrieved on December 1, 2015, from www.proceso.com.mx/?p=411839.

United States Agency for International Development (USAID). August 2010. "USAID Country Profile: Property Rights and Resource Governance: Guatemala. Retrieved on April 17, 2017, from www.land-links.org/wp-content/uploads/2016/09 /USAID_Land_Tenure_Guatemala_Profile_0.pdf.

UNHRC. The UN Refugee Agency. November 29, 2001. "From Refugee to Citizen: A Guatemalan in Mexico." Retrieved on November 18, 2015, from www.unhcr .org/3c064aab4.html

United States Census Bureau. February 2017. Top Trading Partners: February 2017. Washington, DC: U.S. Department of Commerce. Retrieved on April 21, 2017, from www.census.gov/foreign-trade/statistics/highlights/toppartners.html.

United States Department of State. January 20, 2017. Central American Security Initiative: Fact Sheet: Bureau of International Narcotics and Law Enforcement Affairs. Retrieved on April 17, 2017, from www.state.gov/j/inl/rls/fs/2017/260869 .htm.

———. March 2016. "International Narcotics Control Strategy Report. Volume I: Drug and Chemical Control." Bureau of International Narcotics Law Enforcement Affairs. Retrieved on August 12, 2016, from www.state.gov/documents /organization/253655.pdf.

———. March 3, 2015. "Joint Statement by the Presidents of El Salvador, Guatemala, and Honduras, and the Vice President of the United States of America Regarding: The Plan for the Alliance for Prosperity of the Northern Triangle." Retrieved on December 1, 2015, from www.state.gov/r/pa/prs/ps/2015/03/238138.htm.

———. March 1, 2013. "International Narcotics Control Strategy Report (INCSR)— Country Reports—Afghanistan through Costa Rica." Diplomacy in Action. Retrieved on August 11, 2016, from http://www.state.gov/j/inl/rls/nrcrpt/2013 /vol1/204048.htm#Costa_Rica.

United States Institute of Peace. February 1, 1997. Truth Commission: Guatemala. Retrieved on October 20, 2015, from www.usip.org/publications/truth -commission-guatemala.

United States Southern Command. March 13, 2014. "Posture Statement of General John F. Kelly, United States Marine Corps Commander, United States Southern Command. Before the 113th Congress." Senate Armed Services Committee. 1–45. Retrieved on April 17, 2017, from www.armed-services.senate.gov/imo/media /doc/Kelly_03-13-14.pdf.

Ureste, Manu. January 13, 2017. "Peña prometió protegerlos, pero delitos contra migrantes en la frontera sur se disparan 200%." *AnimalPolítico*. Retrieved on April 19,

2017, from www.animalpolitico.com/2017/01/pena-prometio-protegerlos-delitos
-migrantes-la-frontera-sur-se-disparan-200/.

———. July 7, 2015. "Plan Frontera Sur: un año después, los robos de migrantes se disparan 81% en los estados del sur." *AnimalPolítico*. Retrieved on December 1, 2015,
from www.animalpolitico.com/2015/07/plan-frontera-sur-prometia-proteger-a
-migrantes-un-ano-despues-robos-se-disparan-81-en-estados-del-sur/?utm_
source=Hoy+en+Animal&utm_campaign=59254541ae-ga&utm_medium=email
&utm_term=0_ae638a5d34-59254541ae-392950997.

———. December 15, 2014a. "Especial: De Tonalá a Tapachula, 224 kilómetros de
retenes y corrupción." *AnimalPolítico*. Retrieved on December 1, 2015, from
www.animalpolitico.com/2014/12/especial-de-tonala-tapachula-224-kilometros
-de-retenes-y-corrupcion/.

———. January 30, 2014b. "Federales extorsionan a más migrantes que el crimen or-
ganizado." *AnimalPolítico*. Retrieved on December 1, 2015, from www.animal
politico.com/2014/01/federales-con-mas-denuncias-de-extorsion-migrantes
-que-el-crimen-organizado/#axzz37BroGA9m.

Van Etten, Jacob and Mario R. Fuentes. 2004. "La Crisis del Maíz en Guatemala:
Las Importaciones de Maíz y la Agricultura Familiar." *Anuario de Estudios Cen-
troamericanos*. Universidad de Costa Rica 30(1–2): 51–66.

Vázquez Olivera, Mario. 2010. *Chiapas, Años Decisivos. Independencia, Unión
a México y Primera República Federal*. Tuxtla Gutiérrez, Chiapas, México:
UNICACH, Colección Selva Negra.

Velasco Santos, Juan Carlos. December 6, 2016. Personal communication.

Vila, Pablo. 1999. "Constructing Social identities in Transnational Contexts: The Case
of the Mexico–US border." *International Social Science Journal* 51(159): 75–87.

Villafuerte Solís, Daniel. 2015. "Crisis Rural, Pobreza y Hambre en Chiapas." *Revista
LiminaR: Estudios Sociales y Humanísticos* vol. XIII(1): 13–28.

———. 2014. "Security Issues on the Mexico–Guatemala Border and Their Relationship to the New National Security Policy of the United States." In *US National Security Concerns in Latin America and the Caribbean: The Concept of Ungoverned
Spaces and Failed States*, edited by Gary Prevost, Harry E. Vanden, Carlos Oliva
Campos, and Luis Fernando Ayerbe, 113–141. New York: Palgrave Macmillan.

———. 2009. Cambio y continuidad en la economía chiapaneca. In *Chiapas después de
la tormenta: Estudios sobre economía, sociedad y política*. Edited by Marco Estrada
Saavedra, 25-94. D.F., México: El Colegio de México.

———. 2005. "Rural Chiapas Ten Years after the Armed Uprising of 1994: An Economic Overview." *The Journal of Peasant Studies* 32(3-4): 461–483.

———. 2004. *La Frontera Sur de México: Del TLC México-Centroamérica al Plan
Puebla-Panamá*. México: UNAM.

Villafuerte Solís, Daniel, and María del Carmen García Aguilar. 2006. "Crisis Rural y Migraciones en Chiapas. *Migración y Desarollo.* 102–130.

Villafuerte Solís, Daniel, and Xochitl Leyva Solano, coord. 2006 *Geoeconomía y geopolítica en el área del Plan Puebla-Panamá.* D.F., México: CIESAS.

Villareal, M. Angeles. July 3, 2012. "Mexico's Free Trade Agreements." *Congressional Research Service. CRS Report for Congress.* 7-5700. Washington, DC: U.S. Government Printing Office.

Vogt, Wendy. 2013. "Crossing Mexico: Structural Violence and the Commodification of Undocumented Central American Migrants." *American Ethnologist* 40(4): 764–780.

Wallace Wilkie J., Meyer M. C., and Monzón de Wilkie E., 1976. *Contemporary Mexico: Papers of the 4th International Congress of Mexican History.* Berkeley: University of California Press.

Warren, Kay. 2001. "Introduction: Rethinking Bipolar Constructions of Ethnicity." *Journal of Latin American Anthropology* 6(2): 90–105.

Watanabe, John M. 2000. "Cultural Identities, the State, and National Consciousness in Late Nineteenth-Century Guatemala." *Bulletin of Latin American Research* 19: 321–340.

———. 1992. *Maya Saints and Souls in a Changing World.* Austin: University of Texas Press.

Wilson, Thomas M., and Hastings Donnan, eds. 1998. *Border Identities: Nation and State at International Frontiers.* Cambridge, UK: Cambridge University Press.

Wise, Timothy A. August 10, 2016. Personal Communication.

———. January/February 2011. "Mexico: The Costs of U.S. Dumping." *NACLA Report on the Americas* 44(1): 47–49.

———. 2010. "The Impact of U.S. Agricultural Policies on Mexican Producers." In *Subsidizing Inequality: Mexican Corn Policy since NAFTA*, edited by Jonathan Fox and Libby Haight, 163–172. Mexico City and Santa Cruz: Woodrow Wilson International Center for Scholars' Mexico Institute; the University of California, Santa Cruz; and Centro de Investigación y Docencia Económicas.

Worby, Paula. 2001. "Security and Dignity: Land Access and Guatemala's Returned Refugees." *Canada's Journal on Refugees* 19(3): 17–24.

The World Bank. September 24, 2015. "World Development Indicators." Mexico: Employment in Agriculture (% of total employment). Retrieved on August 10, 2016, from https://knoema.com/WBWDIGDF2015Aug/world-development-indicators-wdi-september-2015?tsId=2423740.

World Bank Data. 2014. "Gross Domestic Product 2014." Retrieved on December 3, 2015 from http://databank.worldbank.org/data/download/GDP.pdf.

World Bank Group. 2015. "Doing Business: Measuring Business Regulations." Retrieved on July 6, 2016, from www.doingbusiness.org/rankings.

World Trade Organization (WTO). September 28, 2016. "Trade Policy Overview of Guatemala." Report by the Secretariat. Trade Policy Review Body. WT/TPR/S/348. Submitted by Guatemala.

———. September 7, 2015. "Factual Presentation: Free Trade Agreements between Mexico and Central America—Costa Rica, El Salvador, Guatemala, Honduras, and Nicaragua." Report by the Secretariat. Geneva: Committee on Regional Trade Agreements. WT/REG349/1.

Ybarra, Megan. 2016. "'Blind passes' and the Production of Green Security through Violence on the Guatemalan border." *Geoforum* 69: 194–206.

Yiftachel, Oren. 2009. "Critical Theory and 'Gray Space': Mobilization of the Colonized." *City* 13(23): 240–256.

Yúnez-Naude, Antonio. 2003. "The Dismantling of CONASUPO, A Mexican State Trader in Agriculture." *The World Economy* 26: 97–122.

Zepeda, Eduardo, Timothy A. Wise, and Kevin P. Gallagher. 2009. "Rethinking Trade Policy for Development: Lessons from Mexico under NAFTA." Washington, DC: Carnegie Endowment for International Peace: Policy Outlook: 1–22.

Zilberg, Elana. 2011. *Space of Detention: The Making of a Transnational Gang Crisis between Los Angeles and San Salvador.* Durham, NC: Duke University Press.

———. 2007. "Refugee Gang Youth: Zero Tolerance and the Security State in Contemporary US–Salvadoran Relations." In *Youth, Globalization, and the Law*, edited by Sudhir Alladi Venkatesh and Ronald Kassimir, 61–90. Stanford, CA: Stanford University Press.

Index

Abraham, Itty, 16–17, 98
Abrams, Philip, 242n28
Acapulco, 221
Acteal massacre, 96, 113, 247n19
Agamben, Giorgio, 246n61
agriculture, 5, 25, 102; in Guatemala, 10,
    42–43, 59, 86, 92, 98–99, 100; in Mexico,
    8–9, 74, 77, 85, 86–89, 90–91, 100, 146
Agua Azul reserve, 223
Agua Zarca, 207
Aguilar, Marco Antonio, 140
Aguilar Lucas, Jorge Antonio, 170
Altar Sonora, 28
Alvarez, Robert R., Jr., 163, 173, 252n11,
    253nn32,33, 254n8
AMSA (Agro Industries of Mexico), 170
Andreas, Peter, 130, 205, 214, 220, 251n99,
    254n7, 259n110
anthropology, 32, 36, 38
Anzueto Roblero, Jesus Alaín, 171, 253n25
Arbenz, Jacobo, 42
Arias, Desmond Enrique, 189
arms smuggling: attitudes of border residents
    regarding, 121, 123, 125, 163; as illicit,
    15, 35, 119, 121, 132, 163, 212, 221; and
    terrorism, 225
Arroyo, Alberto, 259n95
Asturias, Miguel Ángel, 74
Avila, Ernestine, 241n16
Ayotzinapa Rural Teachers' College, 222

Baldetti, Roxana, 157
Barrio 18, 213

Bartra, Armando, 244n18
Basail Rodríguez, Alain, 210, 233n3, 250n56,
    255n32
Bersin, Alan, 11
Bird, Annie, 257n54
birth certificates, 50–51, 52, 65–66, 67, 68
border boomerang effect, 231, 260n128
border citizenship, 61
border demarcations, 1, 3, 28, 29, 37, 50, 83,
    110, 127, 149, 179
border residents, 31–35, 157, 244n25;
    associations among, 76–77, 78, 80,
    81, 82, 83, 84, 93, 94–95, 138, 164, 165,
    174, 193, 243n1, 244n10, 253n32; birth
    certificates of, 50–51, 52, 65–66, 67, 68;
    community interdependence, 35–36, 196;
    cultural capital of, 165; currency usage
    by, 57, 179; dual nationality among, 25,
    50–54, 58, 61, 63, 64–65, 67–72; economic
    inequality among, 5, 48, 107, 121, 124,
    151, 153, 161, 175–77, 178, 183, 185–86,
    187, 204, 210, 227; education, 44, 45,
    176–77, 182, 188, 231; family relationships
    among, 175–77; as gatekeepers, 209;
    legal documents of, 60–62, 63, 64–66,
    67–69, 70, 72–73, 227, 242nn47,48;
    local redistributive norms, 78, 164,
    181, 182, 186, 193; as marginalized, 5,
    18, 20, 25, 29, 36, 38, 39, 61, 63–64, 72,
    73, 77, 100, 113, 124, 145, 210, 211, 227,
    230–31; means of communication, 7;
    mobilizations of, 92–93, 103, 110, 113–17,
    118–19, 142–45, 178, 230, 245n49, 247n9;

border residents (*continued*)
national identity of, 50–51, 54–56, 60–73, 240n2; as *negociantes* (businessmen/middlemen), 16, 34, 122, 160–62, 163, 165, 166–67, 175, 179–81, 184–86, 194, 252nn5,12; restricted economic opportunities of, 1, 5–6, 7, 8–10, 25, 36, 73, 98, 146, 158, 163, 210, 227, 228, 229, 231–32; state agents expelled by, 7, 93, 103, 109, 111–12, 114, 116, 143, 230. *See also* cargo loaders; tollbooths; truckers
border residents' views: on border residence as inheritance, 162, 164–65, 173, 187; on corruption, 110–11, 115–16, 119–20, 122, 125, 128, 129, 138, 161, 190–91, 197, 205, 230–31; on drug smuggling, 20, 121, 123, 125, 150, 163–64, 174, 186–87, 206–7, 213–14, 220, 221, 227, 243n9, 245n57; on Guatemalan state, 18–19, 25–26, 48, 56, 60, 65, 226; on Mexican state, 18–19, 25–26, 35, 40, 48, 56, 60, 65, 74, 96, 97–98, 124, 125, 129, 149, 197–99, 201, 202, 203, 205, 210, 221–22, 225, 226, 230, 245n59, 247n29; on migrant smuggling, 121, 125, 163, 212–14, 219–20, 221; on right to work, 62, 77, 85, 86, 93, 94, 95, 100, 103, 163, 164, 188–89, 192, 194, 199, 200, 201, 203, 244n10; on territoriality, 126–27; on trade agreements, 77, 103, 137–39, 145, 158; on Zapatistas, 114, 115, 126, 142–43
border security, 21, 22, 25–26, 36, 73, 210–11, 225; corruption in, 15, 56–58, 77, 110–11, 115–16, 119–20, 122, 125, 128, 135–36, 138, 141, 146, 150, 161, 168, 170, 171, 175, 190, 191, 192, 193, 197, 198, 205, 206, 214–15, 216, 227, 230–31, 255n27; of Guatemala, 4, 7, 8, 10–11, 13–14, 16, 111, 130–31, 178–79, 189, 208, 218, 220, 226–27; of Mexico, 3–4, 7, 8, 10–11, 12–15, 16, 35, 58–59, 76, 111, 125, 130–31, 134–41, 149, 155–58, 163, 173–74, 178–79, 189, 197, 198–99, 204–6, 213–16, 218, 220, 227, 230, 232, 235n49, 247n9, 258n66; relationship to illegality, 3–5, 16, 17–18, 26, 30, 154; relationship to trade agreements, 4–5, 12, 18, 26, 130, 141, 186; relationship to violence, 18, 26, 209, 219, 221; transnational corporations benefited by, 158, 210, 215, 219, 224, 227. *See also* corruption; state agents
brand pirates, 132, 210

Brazil, 246n61
Brazil–Argentina borderlands, 141
bribery. *See* corruption
Brigden, Noelle, 219
Burrell, Jennifer, 213
Bush, George W., 13, 140, 212, 240n71

CAFTA. *See* Central American Free Trade Agreement
Calderón, Felipe, 3, 125, 129, 145, 221, 223, 250n56
Camojá, 48, 164, 175, 179, 207, 213
Campbell, Howard, 20, 222
cargo exchanges, 21–24, 34
cargo loaders, 176–77, 213, 231, 243n10; in coffee smuggling, 168–69, 176; in corn smuggling, 7, 21–22, 26, 34, 48, 76, 81–82, 84, 98, 101, 102, 176; earnings, 22, 81–82, 176, 179, 182
CARSI. *See* Central American Regional Security Initiative
Casa del Migrante, 216
Casillo Armas, Carlos, 42–43
cell phones, 7, 57
Centeno, Miguel Angel, 15–16, 97
Center for International Policy (CIP), 224
Central American Free Trade Agreement (DR-CAFTA/CAFTA), 11, 91, 92, 139–40, 217
Central American Regional Security Initiative (CARSI), 14, 218
Chalfin, Brenda, 136
Chamic, 58, 59, 120
Chiapas, 36–37, 67, 208; Acteal massacre, 96, 113; coffee plantations, 38; economic conditions, 6, 8, 9, 13, 20, 38, 44, 45, 100, 132, 151, 252n11; education in, 44, 45; Fronteriza region, 44; highlands, 86; highway expansion, 7; homicide rate in, 225; land reform in, 9; Mexican government policy in, 41–42, 96–98, 110, 113, 142–43, 245n49; Mexican military in, 41–42, 97, 111, 113, 204, 206, 223, 224, 245n57; mining concessions in, 13; oligarchy in, 110; poverty in, 6, 9, 44; resource extraction in, 20; San Andrés Accords, 41; Soconusco region, 37, 38; State Border Police Force (PEF), 143, 158, 206, 216, 250n56, 255n32; Usumacinta River, 13; Zapatista rebellion, 41–42, 96, 107, 112–15, 117, 126, 142–43, 223, 234n19, 245n49, 248n40

Chicomuselo, 78

Chile, 220

CICIG. *See* International Commission against Impunity in Guatemala

Ciudad Cuauhtémoc, 2, 116, 137, 138, 150; customs office at, 91, 134, 136, 140, 141–42, 151; immigration office at, 30, 57, 58, 149; official border crossing at, 1, 57, 116, 133, 151; politics in, 145

Ciudad Hidalgo, 15, 133–34, 137, 140, 142, 245n46

clientelism, 96, 112, 113, 137, 143, 161, 230, 253n32. *See also* patronage or patron-client relations.

Clot, Jean, 6

clothing smuggling, 132, 162, 178, 191, 197–98, 213

cocaine criminalization, 220

coffee prices, 165, 167, 168, 170, 172, 185

coffee smuggling, 48, 166, 167–70, 211, 213, 221, 229, 253n23; as business, 162, 163; capital requirements, 101, 164, 168; cargo loaders, 168–69, 176; coffee brokers (*comisionistas*), 168–70, 171–72, 176, 178; coffee producers, 185, 229; vs. corn smuggling, 168; truckers, 168–69

Cold War, 43, 112, 220

Colombia, 220, 222

COMAR (Mexican Commission for Refugee Assistance), 45, 51, 63, 64, 240n85

Comaroff, Jean and John: *Law and Disorder in the Postcolony*, 98, 236n104, 245n59

Comitán de Domínguez, 2, 27, 57, 66, 116, 174, 204, 212, 241n22; economic conditions, 151; immigration office in, 59

CONASUPO (National Company of Popular Subsistence), 74, 81, 83, 85, 87, 88, 90–91, 92, 93

Copenhagen school, 18

corn: corn producers, 78, 81, 82, 84, 87, 89–90, 93–95, 96, 97, 101, 102, 103, 167, 229; as cultural symbol, 85–86; Guatemalan tariff on, 91, 99–100; from Mexico vs. US, 86, 87, 244n21; and NAFTA, 74–75, 85, 87–88, 90–91, 92; prices of 80–81, 82, 84–85, 86, 87, 88–89, 92, 94, 97, 98, 101, 102, 166, 168m, 243nn7,8, 244n10, 245n35; as subsistence crop, 25, 45, 77, 86, 88, 89, 244n10; U.S. export of, 86, 87, 88–89, 100–101

corn smuggling, 119, 138, 160, 211, 213, 221, 243n6; amount smuggled, 74, 243n1; as business, 162, 163, 164; cargo loaders, 7, 21–22, 26, 34, 48, 76, 81–82, 84, 98, 101, 102, 176; vs. coffee, 168; as "free trade," 25, 74, 76, 77, 83, 87–88, 89–98, 119; Guatemalan brokers, 78, 83–84, 94, 95, 100, 102, 103; levels of intermediation in, 84, 243n10; local ethics in, 84–85; Mexican merchants (*coyotes*), 76, 77, 78–81, 82, 83–84, 87, 90, 94, 95, 97–98, 99, 100, 101, 102–3, 164, 166–67, 175; and NAFTA, 74–75, 85, 86, 87–89, 90–91, 92; as subsistence right, 86, 93, 94, 95, 164; vs. sugar smuggling, 168; tolls levied on, 75, 83, 91, 93–94, 95, 99, 101; truckers, 7, 16, 22, 26, 34, 75, 76, 78–79, 84, 166

corruption: attitudes of border residents regarding, 110–11, 115–16, 119–20, 122, 125, 128, 129, 138, 161, 190–91, 197, 205, 230–31; in border security, 15, 56–58, 77, 110–11, 115–16, 119–20, 122, 125, 128, 135–36, 138, 141, 146, 150, 161, 168, 170, 171, 175, 190, 191, 192, 193, 197, 198, 205, 206, 214–15, 216, 227, 230–31, 255n27; bribery of state agents, 115–16, 119–20, 124, 125, 138, 141, 150, 161, 168, 170, 171, 175, 190, 191, 192, 193, 197, 198, 204, 205, 206, 210, 214, 216, 225, 229, 230, 251n99, 255n27; in Guatemala, 24, 56–58, 117, 132, 157, 190–91; and limited discretion model, 136; in Mexico, 18, 56–58, 67, 96, 112, 129, 135–36, 142–43, 150, 170, 190, 191, 192, 211, 214, 216, 221, 222–23, 230

Coutin, Susan: on clandestinity, 30–31

criminal groups, 209, 213, 216, 217, 219, 221–22, 224–25, 226. *See also* Gulf cartel; Sinaloa cartel; Zetas

currency usage, 57

Das, Veena, 242n28; on illegibility of state power, 60

Davis, Diane, 131

Democratic Revolution Party (PRD), 129

Dent, Alexander: on piracy, 20

Díaz, Porfirio, 38

Documentation Network Defenders Migrant Organizations, 217

drug cartels, 26, 189, 206–7, 209, 211, 219, 222–25; Gulf Cartel, 207, 222, 248n35; Sinaloa cartel, 164, 206, 207, 208, 213, 252n10, 255n38. *See also* Zetas

drug smuggling, 1, 59, 155, 182, 209, 230;
attitudes of border residents regarding,
20, 121, 123, 125, 150, 163–64, 174,
186–87, 206–7, 213–14, 220, 221, 227,
243n9, 245n57; in Frontera Comalapa,
28, 44, 154, 163–64, 183, 213; as illicit,
15, 35, 119, 121, 132, 212, 221; Mérida
Initiative regarding, 13–14, 157, 215,
219; militarization of drug war, 12,
14, 158–59, 214–15, 219–21, 223,
226, 230–31; relationship to migrant
smuggling, 154, 213–14, 218–19, 221,
225, 226; relationship to terrorism, 225;
relationship to violence, 14, 26, 120, 204,
206–8, 222, 226, 259n107
dual nationality, 25, 49, 50–54, 58, 61, 63,
64–65, 67–71
Dudley, Steven, 163–64, 255n38, 258n66
Duran-Martinez, Angelica, 206, 255n27

Echeverría Alvarez, Luis, 112
Ecological Green Party of Mexico (PVEM),
170–71, 253n24
ECOM Industrial Agroindustrial Corp., 170
ECOSUR (El Colegio de la Frontera Sur), 27
Edelman, Marc, 244n18
Eisenhower, Dwight, 43
ejidos, 9, 45, 105, 109–10, 223, 230. See also
Santa Rosa
El Girasol, 2, 49, 56, 68, 81, 165, 197, 207, 231;
corn smuggling in, 78, 81, 83–84, 99,
102; economic inequality in, 48; during
Guatemalan civil war, 47–48, 117–18,
240n1; nationality in, 52; politics in,
48; returned refugees in, 46; tollbooth
(cadena) at, 28, 118; tolls levied by, 28,
111, 118
Elliot, John H., 246n5
El Nance, 2, 29, 37, 44, 50, 60, 111, 165,
171, 224; conflict with Santa Rosa,
190, 193–97, 199–202, 204, 205;
gasoline smuggling in, 189, 190, 191,
192–97, 198, 204, 205; nationality in,
68, 72; subsistence corn farming in, 45;
tollbooth (cadena) at, 28, 105, 116, 121;
tolls levied by, 28, 104, 105, 109, 124,
125–26
El Periódico, 190
El Salvador, 213, 218
Endres, Kirsten, 141
Escalona Victoria, José Luis, 253n24
extravíos, 20–21

Ferguson, James, 30
Fernández-Kelly, Patricia, 139
Financiero, El, 131; on Mexico-Guatemala
border, 1
fincas, 47
Fitting, Elizabeth, 85, 244n18
Florida, 5–6, 49, 80, 165, 232
food smuggling, 21–24, 119, 132, 213. See also
coffee smuggling; corn smuggling
Fox, Vicente, 10, 11, 128, 133, 223
Foxen, Patricia, 242n44
Frank, Dana, 217
Fray Bartolomé de las Casas Human Rights
Center (Frayba), 226
Friman, H. Richard, 249n22
Frontera Comalapa, 1, 2, 13, 39, 59, 67,
68, 73, 78, 95, 105, 121, 124–25, 175,
204; document forging in, 66; drug
smuggling in, 28, 44, 154, 163–64, 183,
213; economic conditions, 28, 44,
150–52, 153; growth of, 150–52;
indigenous Guatemalan refugees in,
39, 44; migrant smuggling in, 44, 154,
213; politics in, 170–71

gasoline prices, 190, 191, 202, 254nn4,5
gasoline smuggling, 26, 132, 162, 166, 187,
188–208, 213, 221; earnings from, 188; in
El Nance, 189, 190, 191, 192–97, 198, 204,
205; in Mexico vs. Guatemala, 202–3;
vs. other smuggling, 201–2, 204; role of
bribery in, 119, 190, 191, 197, 198, 205,
206, 216, 230; in Santa Rosa, 188, 189–90,
192, 193–201, 204, 205
gem trafficking, 132
gender, 16, 32–33, 71–72, 162, 166, 200
General Agreement on Tariffs and Trade
(GATT), 8
Georgia, 6, 165, 188, 231, 232
Gibler, Jonathan, 222–23
Global Financial Integrity (GFI), 155
Global Impunity Index, 215
globalization from below, 228, 259n122
Goldín, Liliana, 102
Goldstein, Daniel, 18, 60, 70, 189, 227
Goodale, Mark, 333n13
Gootenberg, Paul, 220
Grandia, Liza, 139–40
Grupo Gruma, 87
Guadalupe Grijalva, 78
Guatemala: agriculture in, 10, 42–43, 59;
amount of commerce with Mexico, 130,

151; border security policies, 4, 7, 8, 10–11, 13–14, 16, 111, 130–31, 178–79, 189, 208, 218, 220, 226–27; and CAFTA, 11; CEAR (Special Commission for Attention to the Displaced, Returnees, and Refugees), 46; Chixoy Dam, 257n58; civil defense patrols (PACs), 43, 47, 48, 49, 117, 178–79, 240n1; civil police (PNC), 76, 111, 118; civil war, 9–10, 14, 19, 39, 43, 46, 47–48, 49, 62, 64, 69, 76, 111, 117–18, 212, 224, 226, 240n71, 247n9; corruption in, 24, 56–58, 117, 132, 157, 190–91; drug war policies, 224–25; economic conditions, 10, 25, 135, 167–68, 249n20; exports from Mexico, 135, 249n20; FONAPAZ (National Fund for Peace), 46; FORELAP (Fund for Labor and Productive Reinsertion of the Returnee Population), 46; highlands, 86; homicide rate in, 19; impunity rate in, 19, 237n120; indigenous people in, 9, 19, 36–37, 39, 42–43, 44, 45, 46, 47, 48, 49, 145; La Línea in, 157; lynchings in, 19; military, 14, 40, 43, 47, 49, 76, 117–18, 224, 226–27; municipal autonomy in, 99, 246n62; national identity in, 61; neoliberalism in, 8, 9–10, 219, 227, 257n54; paramilitaries in, 222; poverty in, 10, 43, 44; public security firms in, 19; refugees from, 10, 27, 39–41, 44, 46–47, 61, 70, 239n45; relations with United States, 11, 42–43, 224, 240n71; RENAP (National Registry of Persons), 51, 61; returned refugees in, 40, 46–48, 49, 51, 70, 102, 117, 242n44; Superintendencia de Administración Tributaria (SAT), 24, 91, 99, 156, 157, 237n140, 245n45; taxation in, 131, 246n4; Truth Commission for Historical Clarification Report, 43; Venceremos 2001, 10–11

Guatemalan Corn Truckers Association, 243n1

Guerrero, 41

Guerreros Unidos cartel, 222

Gulf Cartel, 207, 222, 248n35

Gupta, Akhil, 30

Guzmán Mérida, Pedro Alberto, 244n25

Hart, Keith, 15

Harvey, David, 234n20

Harvey, Neil, 89

Hernández Castillo, Rosalva Aída, 39, 54, 113, 247n19, 334n19

Hernández Navarro, Luis, 168

Heyman, Josiah McC., 20, 209

Hidalgo, Miguel, 129, 248n42

Hidalgo, 41

Holder, Eric, 221

Hondagneu-Sotelo, Pierrette, 241n16

Honduras, 24, 213, 217, 218, 255n38 257n54

Huehuetenango department, 24, 46, 48, 111, 164, 188; agriculture in, 86–87; amount of corn smuggled into, 243n1; corn shortages in, 98–99; Huehuetenango city, 2, 57, 61, 99, 179, 183; poverty in, 6, 44; violence in, 19; Zetas in, 206, 213

Huixtla, 137

human rights abuses, 215–16, 217, 218, 223, 224, 226, 240n71, 257nn54,58

Human Rights Watch, 215

human trafficking, 155, 219

Hurricane Mitch, 99

Iguala disappearances, 222

illegality: illegality fetishism, 17; vs. illicitness, 15–17, 98, 121, 132, 158–59, 162, 163–64, 178, 186, 211–12, 219–20, 221; myth of, 30–31; relationship to border security, 3–5, 16, 17–18, 26, 30, 154; relationship to legality, 6, 16, 17, 21–22, 23–24, 26, 52, 54, 69, 70–72, 98–99, 119, 129, 130–31, 132, 153, 154, 155, 162, 163, 167, 168, 170, 172, 177–79, 181–82, 184–85, 186, 209, 211, 225, 227, 229–31, 245n59, 250n41, 253n33, 254n7; as social and political process, 17, 56; social context of, 31–32; transnational corporations benefited by, 159, 202, 210, 229

illicit commerce, 5, 7, 11, 12, 18, 26, 123, 131; vs. illegal commerce, 15–17, 98, 121, 132, 158–59, 162, 163–64, 178, 186, 211–12, 219–20, 221. See also arms smuggling; drug smuggling; migrant smuggling

In Defense of Corn, 244n18

indigenous people: in Guatemala, 9, 19, 36–37, 39, 44, 45, 46, 47, 48, 49, 145; in Mexico, 32, 36–37, 38–42, 44, 48, 61–63, 70, 73, 102, 113, 145, 223, 238n19, 247n15

INEGI (Mexico's National Institute of Statistics and Geography), 13, 132

informal economy, 131, 139; defined,
  15; piracy in, 20; relationship to
  neoliberalism, 5, 8–10; vs. formal
  economy, 5, 8–10, 15–16, 17, 20, 26,
  153–55, 158, 184–85, 211, 225–26,
  228, 229–30. *See also* illegality; illicit
  commerce
InSight Crime, 255n38
Institutional Revolutionary Party (PRI), 109,
  112, 128–29, 170, 206, 220, 230, 253n24
Inter-American Commission on Human
  Rights, 215, 223
International Commission against Impunity
  in Guatemala (CICIG), 157, 218, 232n120
International Commission of Limits and
  Water, 37, 110
International Monetary Fund (IMF)
  structural adjustment terms, 8, 88, 147
Isacson, Adam, 255n32, 257n43

Jonas, Susanne, 239n45
Jordan, Amy, 254n4
Juárez, 221
Jusionyte, Ieva, 250n41

Kaibiles, 224–25
Kelly, John F., 225
King, Amanda, 89

La Democracia, 1, 2, 46, 48, 55, 118, 175;
  corn smuggling in, 75, 83, 99, 100; drug
  smuggling in, 164; economic conditions,
  44; homicides in, 44, 49; nationality in,
  65–66; politics in, 100; sugar smuggling
  in, 179; tolls levied on corn by, 75
La Gloria, 47
Lakhani, Nina, 237n120
La Línea, 157
La Maravilla, 2; former Guatemalan refugees
  in, 39–40, 44, 45, 61–64, 102; lack of
  tolls in, 62; nationality in, 45, 47, 51,
  62–64, 242n38; subsistence corn farming
  in, 45
La Mesilla, 2, 24, 123; customs post at, 91,
  133, 134–35; drug smuggling in, 164;
  flea market in, 59, 151, 152; immigration
  office at, 57, 58; official border crossing
  at, 1, 32, 57, 58, 133, 134–35, 151, 178
Las Champas, 59, 133, 134, 135, 141
La Trinitaria, 2, 77, 78, 137, 241n22
La Vía Campesina, 244n18
limited discretion model, 136

Lomnitz, Claudio, 246n5
López, Victor Hugo, 223, 226
López Obrador, Andrés Manuel, 129
Los Chapincitos, 252n10

Manz, Beatriz, 240n1
Mara Salvatrucha, 213
Martínez, Oscar J., 27
Marx, Karl: on commodity fetishism, 17
Maseca, 87
Massey, Douglas S., 139
Mathews, Gordon, 259n122, 260n123; on
  globalization from below, 228
Mattiace, Shannon L., 247n19
McMurray, David, 205
Melgar, Lourdes, 254n13
MERCOSUR, 141, 250n41
Mérida Initiative, 13–14, 157, 215, 219
Merry, Sally Engle 244n28, on
  vernacularization, 244n28
Mesoamerican Integration and Development
  Project, 223. *See also* Plan Puebla-
  Panamá (PPP).
Mesoamerican Working Group (MAWG), 14
methodology, 6, 25–26, 33–35, 199–201
Mexico: agriculture in, 8–9, 74, 77, 85, 86–89,
  90–91, 100, 146; amount of commerce
  with Guatemala, 130, 151; Article 27 of
  Constitution, 9; assimilationist policies,
  38–39; Attorney General's Office (PGR),
  136; border security policies, 3–4, 7, 8,
  10–11, 12–15, 16, 35, 58–59, 76, 111, 125,
  130–31, 134–41, 149, 155–58, 163, 173–74,
  178–79, 189, 197, 198–99, 204–6, 213–16,
  218, 220, 227, 230, 232, 235n49, 247n9,
  258n66; COMAR (Mexican Commission
  for Refugee Assistance), 45, 51, 63, 64,
  240n85; Comprehensive Attention
  Centers for Border Transit (CAITFs),
  136–37; CONASUPO (National
  Company of Popular Subsistence), 74, 81,
  83, 85, 87, 88, 90–91, 92, 93; corruption
  in, 18, 56–58, 67, 96, 112, 129, 135–36,
  142–43, 150, 170, 190, 191, 192, 211,
  214, 216, 221, 222–23, 230; Customs
  Modernization Program, 136; debt crisis,
  8, 112, 139; economic conditions, 8–9,
  13, 25, 38, 80–81, 85, 86–89, 112, 128,
  135, 146, 167–68, 202, 216, 249nn20,37;
  Energy Reform, 13; Federal Law to
  Prevent and Punish Crimes in the Field
  of Hydrocarbons, 13; and GATT, 8;

indigenous people in, 32, 36–37, 38–42, 44, 48, 61–63, 70, 73, 102, 113, 145, 223, 238n19, 247n15; justice system, 215; Law on Indigenous Rights, 41; Mérida Initiative, 13–14, 157, 215, 219; Migrant Stabilization Program, 40; migration policies, 26, 137, 211, 212, 213, 215–17; military, 3–4, 14, 21, 41–42, 97, 111, 112, 113, 125, 174, 204, 206, 214, 215, 221, 223, 224, 227, 245n57, 256nn22,30; National Coffee Institute (INMECAFE), 9, 167; National Indigenous Congress (CNI), 247n15; National Indigenous Institute (INI), 38; National Institute of Migration (INM), 10, 11, 216; National Institute of Statistics and Geography (INEGI), 13; Nationality Law, 52–53, 241n6; National Security System, 11; naturalization in, 38, 40–41, 44, 45, 47, 51, 52–53, 62–63, 64, 70, 71; neoliberalism in, 8–9, 41, 74, 77, 85–86, 87–89, 100–101, 112, 113, 128, 146, 219, 227; Office of Anthropology, 38; Oportunidades/Prospera, 63; paramilitaries in, 222; PEMEX, 188, 191, 202, 254n13; peso devaluation, 89, 112, 128, 151; Plan Puebla-Panamá (PPP), 11, 145, 223–224; Plan Sur (Southern Plan), 10; privatization in, 146, 202; Programa Frontera Sur (Southern Border Program), 11, 12–13, 26, 137, 216; refugee policies, 39–41; relations with IMF, 88; relations with United States, 8, 10–12, 13–14, 141, 156–57, 215; resource extraction policies, 13; Revolution, 41, 110; San Andrés Accords, 41; Secretary of Finance and Public Credit, 139; taxation in, 246n4; unemployment in, 146–47

Mexico–Guatemala–Belize Border Region Program, 14

Mexico–Guatemala High-Level Border Security Group, 11

Mexico–Northern Triangle Free Trade Agreement, 11, 140

Meyer, Maureen, 255n32

migrant smuggling, 78, 130, 149, 156, 167; attitudes of border residents regarding, 121, 125, 163, 212–14, 219–20, 221; fees, 214; as illicit, 15, 35, 119, 121, 212, 221; Mexican policies regarding, 26, 211, 212, 213–15; relationship to drug smuggling, 154, 213–14, 218–19, 221, 225, 226

migration, 8, 15, 20, 28, 30, 38, 211; of Central American children, 216–17; Mexico's policies regarding, 26, 137, 211, 212, 213, 215–17; refugees from Guatemala, 10, 27, 39–41, 44, 46–47, 61, 70, 239n45; remittances from migrants, 165, 179, 228; securitization and illegalization of, 211–19, 226; to United States, 5–6, 7, 9, 10, 11, 12, 49, 50, 52, 61, 67, 77, 80, 103, 165–66, 173, 178, 179, 194, 212–15, 216–18, 228, 231–32, 260n128; U.S. policies regarding, 5–6, 10, 11, 12, 69, 214, 216–18, 231–32, 260n128

Millar, Kathleen: on recyclers in Rio de Janeiro, 184

Minsa, 87

mobile highway inspection points, 12–13

Montejo, Victor, 240n1

Morales, Isidro, 257n43

Morales, María, 242n44

Movimiento el Campo no Aguanta Más (MCAM), 244n18

MS-18, 213

Muehlmann, Shaylih, 183, 186–87

NAFTA. See North American Free Trade Agreement

Nash, June, 234n19, 247nn15,23; on CONASUPO, 88

National Action Party (PAN), 128, 129

National Indigenous Congress (CNI), 247n15

Naylor, R. T., 251n99

negociantes, 16, 78

neoliberalism, 233n13, 244n18; defined, 234n20; in Guatemala, 8, 9–10, 219, 227, 257n54; impact of, 8–10, 18–20, 74, 77, 85–86, 87–89, 100–101, 103, 112, 132, 135, 136, 140–41, 146, 184, 186, 209, 210, 219, 227, 229, 231, 257n54; in Mexico, 8–9, 41, 74, 77, 85–86, 87–89, 100–101, 112, 113, 128, 146, 219, 227; relationship to informal economy, 5, 8–10; as securitized, 5, 19–20, 137, 157–58, 218, 219, 224, 227–28, 259n95; in United States, 219; and violence, 227, 231

Nestlé, 137

Nevins, Joseph, 12

Nixon, Richard: War on Drugs, 220

Nordstrom, Carolyn, 132, 154, 157, 172; on border inspections, 155, 156

North American Free Trade Agreement
   (NAFTA): and corn, 74–75, 85, 87–88,
   90–91, 92; impact of, 8–9, 11, 12, 74–75,
   85, 87–89, 90–91, 92, 139, 141, 147, 155,
   183, 217, 245n39; relationship to border
   security, 12, 141; and transnational
   corporations, 139; and Zapatista
   rebellion, 41, 112–13
North Carolina, 5–6, 30, 165, 166, 232
Nueva Vida, 2, 118; corn smuggling in,
   48, 49, 50–51, 78, 83, 101–2; economic
   conditions, 181; as *finca*, 47; nationality
   in, 50–51; politics in, 48; relationship
   with Santa Rosa, 196, 197; returned
   refugees in, 40, 46–48, 49, 117, 226;
   tollbooth (*cadena*) at, 28; tolls levied by,
   28, 104
Nuijten, Monique, 128

Oaxaca, 41
OCEZ, 114, 247n23
official border crossings, 2, 59, 87, 90, 109,
   110, 127, 130, 148–49, 155–56, 157,
   160; Ciudad Carmen, 144; Ciudad
   Cuauhtémoc, 91, 116, 134, 136, 140,
   141–42, 151; Ciudad Hidalgo, 15, 133–34,
   137; La Mesilla, 1, 32, 57, 58, 133, 134–35,
   151, 178; Talisman, 142; Tecún Umán, 15
oil prices, 8, 190, 254n4
Ong, Aiwha, 141
Organization for Economic Co-Operation
   and Development (OECD), 9
Otero, Gerardo, 244n18

Paley, Dawn, 215, 248n35; *Drug War
   Capitalism*, 221
Pan-American Highway, 1, 27, 45–46, 58–59
patronage or patron–client relations, 34,
   77, 109, 112, 128, 143, 163, 171, 176–77,
   185, 209, 214–15, 230, 246n5. *See also*
   clientelism.
Paz y Paz, Claudia, 208, 237n120
PEMEX, 188, 191, 202, 254n13
Peña Nieto, Enrique, 11, 13, 128–29, 137, 202,
   216
Penglase, Ben, 246n61
Pérez Molina, Otto, 48, 100, 157, 221, 226
phone cards, 57
Pickard, Miguel, 249n32
Plan of the Alliance for Prosperity in the
   Northern Triangle of Central America,
   216, 217–18, 257n58

Plan Puebla-Panamá (PPP), 11, 145, 223–24.
   See also Mesoamerican Integration and
   Development Project.
Plan Sur (Southern Plan), 10
Plante, Michael D., 254n4
Playas de Catazajá, 137
politicians, local and regional, 34, 35, 45,
   93–94, 95–96, 99, 101, 111, 118, 124, 125,
   150–51, 157, 170–71, 185, 203, 210, 229
Popol Vuh, 84
Portes, Alejandro, 15–16, 97
Portillo, Alfonso, 224, 259n101
Postero, Nancy, 333n13
Prensa, La, 203
Prensa Libre, 207
PRI. *See* Institutional Revolutionary Party
Programa Frontera Sur (Southern Border
   Program), 11, 12–13, 26, 137, 216
prostitution, 28
Puerto Chiapas, 137
Puerto Madero, 137

Reagan, Ronald, 240n71
Reeves, Benjamin, 237n120
Reeves, Madeleine, 54, 73, 127, 241n20
regionalismos, 55
Renard, Marie-Christine, 167, 172
Ribeiro, Gustavo Lins, 259n122
Ríos Montt, Efraín, 43
Rosas, Gilberto, 184, 235n49
Rousseau, Cecile, 242n44
Ruiz, Samuel, 247n15
Ruiz Ferro, Julio César, 93, 96
Rus, Jan, 112, 113, 114, 115, 247n19
Russ, Roberto, 89–90

Sabet, Daniel, 135, 256n22
Sabines Guerrero, Juan, 250n56
Salinas de Gortari, Carlos, 8, 87–88, 89, 112,
   147–48
Saltillo, 216
San Cristóbal de las Casas, 2, 27, 32, 91, 114,
   115
San Ildefonso Ixtahuacán, 46, 49
San Marcos department, 86
San Sebastián Bachajón, 223
Santa Rosa, 2, 29, 37, 50, 56, 65, 116–17, 129,
   165, 178, 212; Central Americans in,
   213; conflict with El Nance, 190, 193–97,
   199–202, 204, 205; corn smuggling in,
   80–81, 87, 90–91, 100–101; as *ejido*, 45,
   105, 109–10, 126, 193, 196, 200; gasoline

smuggling in, 188, 189–90, 192, 193–201, 204, 205; nationality in, 67–69, 78; relationship with Nueva Vida, 196, 197; subsistence corn farming in, 45; tollbooth (*cadena*) at, 28, 104, 193, 195, 201; tolls levied by, 28, 104–5, 108–9, 124, 126, 188, 193

Scott, James C., 247n29

Security and Prosperity Partnership, 249n32

September 11 attacks, 10, 11

sex trade, 44

Sinaloa cartel, 164, 206, 207, 208, 213, 252n10, 255n38

Smart, Alan, 209

Smith, Hannah, 255n32, 257n43

Snyder, Richard, 206, 255n27

state agents: attitudes of customs agents, 26, 35, 133, 134, 141–49, 150, 151, 154–56, 157, 158, 250n57; bribery of, 115–16, 119–20, 124, 125, 138, 141, 150, 161, 168, 170, 171, 175, 190, 191, 192, 193, 197, 198, 204, 205, 206, 210, 214, 216, 225, 229, 230, 251n99, 255n27; expelled by border residents, 7, 93, 103, 109, 111–12, 114, 116, 143, 230

Stephen, Lynn, 250n57

structural adjustment terms, 8, 88, 147

sugar smuggling, 48, 166, 167–68, 179–81, 213, 221; as business, 162, 163; capital requirements, 101, 164, 168; vs. corn smuggling, 168; prices of sugar, 180–81; relationship to drug smuggling, 182–83

Superintendencia de Administración Tributaria (SAT), 24, 91, 99, 156, 157, 237n140, 245n45

Talisman, 142

Tapachula, 2, 91, 142, 175, 213

Taussig, Michael, 222, 245n59

tax revenues, 130, 131, 132, 137–38, 150, 151, 153, 156

Tecate, 28

Tecún Umán, 15, 123, 134, 140, 212, 213, 245n46

terrorism, 225; September 11th attacks, 10, 11

Thomas, Kedron, 132, 210

Tierra Blanca, 78

Tijuana, 28

Tlateloco massacre, 112, 222

tollbooths (*cadenas*), 28, 107, 110, 119, 123–26, 127, 129, 189–90, 195, 207, 223, 230; El Girasol tollbooth, 111, 118; El Nance tollbooth, 105, 109, 116, 121; La Maravilla lack of tolls, 62; Nueva Vida tollbooth, 196; Santa Rosa tollbooth, 104–5, 108, 188–89, 193, 195, 199, 201; tolls levied at, 7, 28, 34, 61, 62, 75, 83, 104–9, 110, 111, 118, 120, 121, 124, 125–26, 181, 188, 193, 207, 227

tortilla prices, 80, 243n7

tourism, 131, 133–35, 150

tourist agencies, 28

trade agreements: attitudes of border residents regarding, 77, 103, 137–39, 145; CAFTA, 11, 91, 92, 139–40, 217; regarding coffee, 167–68; impact of, 8–9, 11, 12, 18, 25, 74–75, 85, 86, 87, 87–89, 90–91, 92, 137–39, 139, 140–41, 147, 154, 155, 158, 160, 162, 183, 186, 217–18, 227, 245n39, 249n35, 250n41; Mexico–Northern Triangle Free Trade Agreement, 11, 140; relationship to border security, 4–5, 12, 18, 26, 130, 141, 158, 186; regarding sugar, 167–68; transnational corporations benefited by, 130, 139–40, 158, 217–18. *See also* North American Free Trade Agreement

transnational corporations, 157, 257n54; as benefiting from border security, 158, 210, 215, 219, 224, 227; as benefiting from extralegal practices, 159, 202, 210, 229; as benefiting from trade agreements, 130, 139–40, 158, 217–18; and coffee, 167, 172. *See also* neoliberalism

truckers, 172–75, 176–77, 194, 203, 252n5, 254n8; associations of, 76, 165, 174, 253n32; in coffee smuggling, 168–69; in corn smuggling, 7, 16, 22, 26, 34, 75, 76, 78–79, 84, 166; and drug smuggling, 182–83; earnings, 80, 174, 182; as *fleteros*, 16, 163, 167, 174–75, 180–81

Trump, Donald, 232

Tuxtla Gutiérrez, 2, 63, 73, 93, 152, 176, 195, 197, 207, 253n26

Ubico, Jorge, 42

Unión de Maiceros (Union of Corn Producers), 89–90

United Fruit Company, 43

United Nations, 19; Refugee Convention (1951), 39; UNHRC, 47, 240n85

United States: border security policies, 4, 10, 11–12, 13–14, 216, 220, 231, 235n49; Bureau of International Narcotics and Law Enforcement Affairs (INL), 14;

United States (*continued*)
   CIA, 42–43, 240n71; Department of
   Defense, 14; Department of Homeland
   Security, 11; Department of Justice, 11;
   drug demand in, 219; drug policies,
   216, 220–21, 224, 257n43; Immigration
   and Customs Enforcement (ICE),
   232; Immigration and Naturalization
   Services (INS), 11; immigration policies,
   5–6, 10, 11, 12, 69, 214, 216–18, 231–32,
   260n128; lack of gun control in, 219;
   migration to, 5–6, 7, 9, 10, 11, 12, 49,
   50, 52, 61, 67, 77, 80, 103, 165–66, 173,
   178, 179, 194, 212–15, 216–18, 228,
   231–32, 260n128; and NAFTA, 8, 11;
   neoliberalism in, 219; relations with
   Guatemala, 11, 42–43, 224, 240n71;
   relations with Mexico, 8, 10–12, 13–14,
   141, 156–57, 215; September 11th attacks,
   10, 11
Universidad Autónoma de Chiapas
   (UNACH), 156
Ureste, Manu, 216

Van Schendel, Willem, 16–17, 98
Vega, Carlos Alba, 259n122, 260n123; on
   globalization from below, 228
Velasco, Juan Carlos, 27, 28, 29, 35, 92,
   245n46
Videgaray, Luis, 136
Vigil, Diego, 115
Vila, Pablo, 250n57
Villafuerte Solís, Daniel, 100
Villatoro Cano, Eduardo "El Guayo,"
   207
violence, 175, 184, 213, 228, 230; in
   Guatemala, 19, 207–8, 224–25; in
   Mexico, 211, 215, 221, 222–23; and

neoliberalism, 227, 231; relationship to
   aggressive policing, 14, 18, 26, 189, 209,
   211, 215, 218, 219, 221; relationship to
   drug smuggling, 14, 26, 120, 204, 206–8,
   219, 221, 222–23, 226, 258n66, 259n107;
   relationship to migrant smuggling, 211,
   219; violent pluralism, 189

Washington Office on Latin America
   (WOLA), 13
Watanabe, John, 246n62
weapons smuggling. *See* arms smuggling
Wise, Timothy, 89, 245nn35,39
women, 16, 32–33, 84, 105, 162, 166, 178, 201
World Bank, 8, 19, 89, 148
World Trade Organization, 88–89, 245n45,
   249nn20,35

Ybarra, Megan, 224
Yucatán: Campeche, 40; Quintana Roo, 40

Zapata, Emiliano, 41
Zapatista Army of National Liberation
   (EZLN or Zapatistas), 96, 112–15, 117,
   223, 234n19, 244n18, 245n49, 248n40;
   attitudes of border residents regarding,
   114, 115, 126, 142–43; and NAFTA, 41,
   112–13; rebellion of 1994, 41–42, 113–14,
   142–43, 207, 244n18
Zedillo, Ernesto, 41, 139
Zelaya, Manuel, 257n54
Zetas, 127, 206–7, 208, 213, 216, 219, 224, 225,
   252n10, 255n38; criminal tax collected
   by, 127, 207; and Gulf cartel, 207, 222,
   248n35
Zilberg, Elana, 18; on boomerang effects,
   260n128
Zucarmex, 180, 253n36

CPSIA information can be obtained
at www.ICGtesting.com
Printed in the USA
LVHW112206050919
630139LV00002B/377/P

9 781503 603981